50
True Tales
of Terror

Edited by
JOHN CANNING

BELL PUBLISHING COMPANY · NEW YORK

Contents

		Page
EDITOR'S NOTE		8
The Doomed Conspirator	*John Burke*	11
Masada: The Zealots' Last Stand	*Anthony Burton*	20
The Gytrash of Goathland	*Michael and Mollie Hardwick*	28
The Entertainment of Genghis Khan	*Ian Fellowes-Gordon*	38
The Synagogue of Satan	*John Burke*	47
"Go Back, King James!"	*Michael and Mollie Hardwick*	56
The Heart Offerers	*John Burke*	66
Bloody Sunday	*Frank Usher*	75
"I'll Cut Thee into Collops"	*Michael and Mollie Hardwick*	86
The People Eaters	*C. E. Maine*	99
The Campden Wonder	*Michael and Mollie Hardwick*	107
The Approach of Henry Morgan	*Anthony Burton*	119
The Massacre at Glencoe	*Clare Smythe*	128
The Salem Witches	*Anthony Burton*	140
The Black Hole of Calcutta	*Frank Usher*	150

CONTENTS

		Page
Two Views of the Scaffold	*John Burke*	160
Haiti: The Slave Uprising	*Anthony Burton*	169
The Ruthless Pursuit	*John Burke*	178
Thuggee	*Anthony Burton*	187
The Widows of Pudupettah	*Ian Fellowes-Gordon*	196
Ordeal by Fire and Water	*Michael and Mollie Hardwick*	206
A Swim with the Sharks	*Michael and Mollie Hardwick*	216
The Resurrectionists	*Anthony Burton*	225
The Secret of Sophie Dawes	*Michael and Mollie Hardwick*	234
Tapu	*John Burke*	245
Terror in the Outback	*Ian Fellowes-Gordon*	254
The Grease that Caused a Mutiny	*C. E. Maine*	264
Terror in the Court of King Thibaw	*Ian Fellowes-Gordon*	274
The First Ascent of the Matterhorn	*Anthony Burton*	284
The Defence of Rorke's Drift	*Clare Smythe*	293
The White Death	*Charles Chilton*	302
Krakatoa	*C. E. Maine*	314
San Francisco Shake-Up	*C. E. Maine*	322

CONTENTS

		Page
Dusseldorf's Reign of Terror	*Frank Usher*	333
Dinner in Valparaiso	*Ian Fellowes-Gordon*	342
The Cellars of Death	*Michael and Mollie Hardwick*	350
The Killers in the Signal-Box	*John Burke*	367
Desert Flight	*Anthony Burton*	375
Invasion from Mars	*C. E. Maine*	383
The Day the Germans Hanged Me	*Ronald Seth*	391
The Warsaw Ghetto	*Clare Smythe*	404
The Final Solution to Oradour	*C. E. Maine*	414
Hiroshima—Death and Rebirth	*C. E. Maine*	423
The Test-Parachutist	*Doddy Hay*	433
The Macfarlane Incident	*Doddy Hay*	443
The Terror at Dead Man's Hill	*Frank Usher*	452
Murder without Motive	*C. E. Maine*	462
The Moors Murder Horror	*C. E. Maine*	471
Dance of Death	*Clare Smythe*	483
Frenzy in Bangla Desh	*Ian Fellowes-Gordon*	490
NOTES ON AUTHORS		499
INDEX		501

Editor's Note

WE LIVE in a terrifying world. I suppose the world has always been a place of fear for those who have lived in it (excepting, perhaps, the saints), a battlefield in which one is eternally waging war against innumerable hostile forces.

We are part of a nature which though the benevolent and beautiful matrix of the race can yet transform itself at times into ugly and shattering forces of destruction. Earthquakes, floods, typhoons, droughts, famine and disease have scourged men throughout time.

And yet, despite this duality, nature has always been impersonal. She exempted no king, no conqueror, no ruling caste from her stringencies. Not so with man. As he emerges from the neolithic shadows into the light of recorded history, he stands revealed as the most vicious as well as the most sublime creature yet to appear on the planet. He has brought a subtlety, a refinement, and a discrimination to cruelty unknown to nature; a depth of degradation in proportion to his enormous powers for good.

Man is the most terrifying thing to have happened to men. Nine-tenths of his suffering has been at his own hands. But even this awful fact has had a positive aspect; for it has created a tension within him that has been a powerful drive in the creation of civilization and its values. Not an exclusive drive, but one of the most compelling.

I have gathered together in this book fifty true tales of terror. A proportion of them are natural disasters, but inevitably the greater part reflect man's inhumanity to man. They are chronologically arranged, and I have endeavoured whenever possible to keep the dialogue between persons to what has been historically authenticated, though here and there where no record exists I have allowed reconstructions within the overall framework of fact.

I recognize that this book presents our world in a terrible aspect. And yet I think it is worth so doing for three reasons. Firstly, because the stories are of absorbing interest. Secondly, because even these accounts cannot altogether obscure the sublimity of the human spirit. And thirdly, because I hope it may lessen the load of apprehension and fear we all carry around with us. By experiencing these emotions vicariously, in small doses, we tend to get rid of them—a sort of homoeopathy of the mind. Aristotle remarked that the performance of a tragedy, through arousing pity and fear, accomplished the purgation of such emotions. And what is true for the stage is, I believe, at least equally so for the printed page.

JOHN CANNING

The Doomed Conspirator

The sovereign emperor was dead; and only three men knew
it. The tyrant who had craved immortality was shown to be
mortal like the rest. Who would his successor be?

Wary and mistrustful of one another, the three debated
the matter.

The emperor Ch'in Shih Huang Ti had accomplished
much for his country, but in doing so had made his name
hated. Tens of thousands of lives had been ruthlessly sacri-
ficed in the building of the Great Wall to keep out the
barbarians. On the suggestion of Li Ssu, his grand councillor, he had exterminated all intellectuals who preached the
philosophies and disciplines of the past, so that nothing
should stand in the way of his plans for modernizing
the land that was coming to be known as China. For
hundreds of years afterwards he would be spoken of as
the emperor who "burned the books and buried the
scholars".

He dealt out death with a liberal hand but dreaded it
himself. He built more than two hundred palaces within
easy reach of the capital, Hsien-yang, and only his
immediate entourage knew where he was spending any
given night. The palaces were linked by secret passages so
that he could flee from one to another when fear of assassination nagged at his mind.

Now he could flee no longer. In the year 210 B.C. death

had claimed the First Divine Ruler while on a tour of his dominions. He was a thousand miles from home.

Feeling his end to be near, he had written a letter naming his heir. This letter he trustingly handed to his favourite son, Hu Hai, who had been accompanying him. But the name in the letter was not that of Hu Hai.

The young man brought the letter to the two advisers who had also been travelling with the emperor: Li Ssu, the grand councillor, and the eunuch Chao Kao, who was Hu Hai's tutor.

It named the oldest son as successor.

Fu Su, the first-born, had been banished to a military detachment on the Great Wall because he had dared to criticize his father's persecution of the intellectuals. But at the last moment the emperor had realized that only a strong, honest man such as this could hold the country together. Hu Hai might be his favourite but he was a weakling and a libertine.

"When your brother Fu Su comes into his own," said the eunuch after reading the letter, "you will have nothing. What do you propose to do?"

"If it is what my father wishes," said Hu Hai, "then what *is* there to do?"

Silently Chao Kao consulted the grand councillor. They discussed the matter together, in a courteously roundabout way.

Only the three of them knew, so far, of the emperor's death and of his choice of successor. Rebellions were simmering all over the land. Once word of the death was out, they could boil over. Fu Su was far away in the north, and by the time he was summoned and established on the throne, it might be too late.

Li Ssu was a great believer in legality. He was made uneasy by the eunuch's hints, though he saw much truth in some of them. The emperor had chosen his heir: that was immutable.

But was it?

Chao Kao was subtle. When Fu Su did return to the capital, he slyly asked, would he not be liable to bring influential friends with him? He was unlikely to retain Li Ssu as his grand councillor—Li Ssu, whose advice to the late emperor had resulted in those very measures which had driven Fu Su into exile.

Fear, which Li Ssu had once administered with calm assurance, now turned back to nibble at him.

It was true that he had inspired many of Ch'in Shih Huang Ti's worst excesses. Rising by study and hard work from a background of poverty to one of the highest positions in the land, Li Ssu had enriched himself and many of his relations not merely by following the emperor's wishes but by anticipating them, making himself indispensable, drafting laws which he knew would appeal to his master's temperament. He had indeed instigated the attack on the intellectuals. Fu Su would never look kindly on him. If Fu Su were in power, what future could there possibly be for the ageing grand councillor?

Chao Kao suggested that the two of them would be better served by young Hu Hai.

The grand councillor saw all too well what was in the opportunist eunuch's mind. Already a man of some influence, how much greater would that influence be if the new emperor were to be his own pupil!

Li Ssu wavered. He was afraid of the eunuch; yet equally afraid of what might happen to him under a vengeful Fu Su.

The plan might work. Together he and Chao Kao could run the country as grey eminences behind the throne. The better elements of Ch'in Shih Huang Ti's achievement could be retained, the rest discarded. They could be stern, but just. They could tell Hu Hai what decisions to make, what orders to issue, what gifts to bestow.

But how were they to cope with Fu Su when he came back to the city?

Chao Kao suggested that there was no need for Fu Su to come back at all.

So Li Ssu was committed. He himself penned a letter purporting to come from the emperor, nominating Hu Hai his successor and ordering Fu Su to take his own life. Li Ssu perhaps shivered as he wrote, sensing that he was bringing down a terrible curse upon himself.

The letter was dispatched bearing the imperial seal.

Fu Su's friends declared that the message must be a forgery. They urged him to ignore it and hurry home. But the prince refused.

"When a father orders his son to commit suicide, it would be a defiance of filial duty to await a second command."

He obeyed, and killed himself.

Now the country was told of Ch'in Shih Huang Ti's death, and preparations were made for his burial.

Although he had longed to become immortal, the late emperor had taken the precaution of building for himself a mausoleum as vast as any Egyptian pyramid. Its rooms were filled with treasures, and at its heart was a huge bronze relief map of China with rivers of quicksilver flowing between miniature houses and palaces modelled on those of the outside world.

Now he was laid to rest. His wives and concubines were herded inside so that they might accompany him into the shades. Craftsmen made their final adjustments to delicately constructed mechanisms which would trumpet an alarm and fire arrows into any invader blasphemous enough to desecrate the tomb.

When these skilled artisans turned to leave, there was the thunderous crash of a portcullis and they, too, were sealed in. No one who knew the innermost secrets of the mausoleum would ever be allowed to tell of them.

The young Hu Hai assumed the title of Second Divine Emperor and settled himself on the throne. His first official act was to appoint Chao Kao his palace chamberlain, with the special duty of supplying uninterrupted delights and luxuries. The whole point of being emperor was to be able to lead a life of pleasure.

But his father had left nearly a score of other sons, each of whom could provide the spearhead of a revolt. How could he enjoy himself with such dangers threatening?

Li Ssu was ready with advice. But the new emperor turned instead to Chao Kao. Here was the man who pampered him, and therefore the man he trusted.

Li Ssu wished he could retrace his steps. He ought to have consolidated his position much more securely before entering into this conspiracy.

Chao Kao advised sternness. Hu Hai must send his brothers into exile. If any treason were spoken, not merely the traitor but his entire family must suffer.

Hu Hai granted his faithful friend authority to deal with such matters.

The reign of terror began. Twelve of the new emperor's brothers were arrested on flimsy charges and executed in the market-place of the capital. Ten royal princesses were torn limb from limb with due formality, so that officials, soldiers and the public might see what was in store for anyone who whispered against the young ruler or in any way disturbed his tranquillity.

Li Ssu had once recommended that men should be ruled by a meticulous system of rewards and punishments, with punishments predominating. He had dispensed fear with righteous calm. Now, as he himself began to taste it for the first time, he understood what others must have suffered.

Chao Kao grew more and more domineering. One day he led a stag down the imperial audience chamber before the astonished gaze of other ministers.

"Your Majesty, I bring you the gift of a horse. Is it not a noble specimen?"

Hu Hai stared. "Surely this is a stag?"

Chao Kao consulted the group of functionaries. "Gentlemen, do you or do you not see before you a horse?"

One or two recognized the threat in his voice and nodded meekly. Others said that this was ridiculous. The creature was a stag. What was the palace chamberlain's game?

They soon found out what the game was. Within a week or two all those who had been impertinent enough to contradict Chao Kao had been put to death on one trumped-up charge after another.

Li Ssu saw disaster in store for the country, and trouble in store for himself. But he was still grand councillor. He summoned up his courage and remonstrated with the emperor, asking for more attention to be paid to the problems of the country's farther provinces and less money to be spent on the palace and its pleasures.

The emperor was indignant. Chao Kao was sourly amused. It was plain that he and the grand councillor were no longer allies. How long before they became open enemies?

Did Li Ssu dare?

Perhaps if he were patient long enough there would be a revolt. Hu Hai would be overthrown, and with him the arrogant eunuch. Then the rebels would need the grand councillor's wisdom and would turn to him.

He saw less and less of the emperor. Chao Kao kept Hu Hai contentedly locked away, indulging in every sensual delight which could be provided. Any messages destined for the emperor had first to pass through the palace chamberlain's hands. News from the provinces grew worse, but Hu Hai was shielded from all knowledge of this. There was famine, despair, incipient anarchy. The palace chamberlain showered more sweetmeats on his master.

Li Ssu sought an interview with the emperor.

Chao Kao silkily promised that as soon as the emperor had a free moment his old comrade would be informed.

The day came when Chao Kao notified Li Ssu that the emperor was prepared to receive him. Li Ssu hurried to the palace, only to be given a message that the emperor could not be disturbed.

Again he tried; and again was sent away.

Then he learned through one of his few remaining friends in the palace that Chao Kao was deliberately choosing times when the emperor was enjoying himself with women and feasting.

"When I have time during which it is meet that the grand councillor should report to me," complained Hu Hai, "he does not show his face. But as soon as I am privately occupied, then he comes demanding to discuss State affairs with me."

Chao Kao agreed that the grand councillor had been growing insolent of late. He was too haughty for his own good or the good of the country. It was even rumoured that he was in contact with brigands who had recently harried an outer province. Why else should he have been so anxious to hush up that little episode concerning his son?

When Li Ssu heard by roundabout ways of this charge against him, he knew that his days were numbered. Because the charge had a poisonous grain of truth in it.

Thanks to the grand councillor's influence, one of his sons had been appointed administrator of a northern province. Unfortunately he had neglected to take enough precautions against barbarian infiltration, and a band of invaders had overrun one district and inflicted great damage. An inspector was sent to investigate, but issued no official report: Li Ssu, worried about his son's status, had paid him well to keep his mouth shut.

Chao Kao had discovered the details.

Li Ssu, feeling a remorseless fate about to close on him, staked all on a wild outpouring of letters to the emperor. Friends smuggled them in for him. He accused Chao Kao of lusting for power and doing grave injury to the revered name of the emperor. He quoted chapter and verse. But the emperor had no wish to read chapter and verse. He had other interests.

Li Ssu's letters grew more agitated. After dispatching an especially virulent one, he realized that he had gone too far. The emperor was bound to confide in Chao Kao.

The emperor did.

It took only ten minutes of specious argument for Chao Kao to provoke the emperor into the fateful decision: Chao Kao could do whatever he chose about Li Ssu.

Chao Kao did not hesitate. His men dragged the grand councillor from his house into the street, and threw him into prison.

There Li Ssu lay and repented his past errors.

He had delivered his country into the hands of a megalomaniac. Ministers who might have averted disaster had been slaughtered one after the other. Grandiose buildings had been erected, money had been squandered on the whims of a weakling—not a son of heaven, but a tool of the devil.

Li Ssu was hurried to trial and accused of conspiring with his son against the life of the emperor. He was charged also with allying himself with barbarians who planned the downfall of the country.

The prosecution was eloquent and convincing. It was handled by Chao Kao himself.

To make sure that the prisoner told the truth with the minimum of delay, Chao Kao decreed early in the proceedings that he should be flogged with a thousand strokes.

The seventy-year-old grand councillor endured less than a hundred before breaking down under the intolerable pain. He confessed. Shivering with the throb of his wounds, he signed an admission that he had been engaged in treasonable activities.

He was flung back into a prison cell to await the verdict.

As the agony ebbed away into numbness, he made a last attempt to speak out. He wrote another letter, outlining

for the emperor's benefit all the good things he had achieved
and tried to achieve

He might have guessed who would read this recantation.
Not the emperor, but Chao Kao.

It was a pattern that was to be repeated down the
centuries. Victim and persecutor alike would recognize the
horrors of the twentieth century without difficulty. Forced
confession, recantation . . . and then final humiliation.

Chao Kao decided there was no point in troubling his
lord and master with Li Ssu's grovelling pleas. He ordered
a continued flogging so that there should be no doubt in
Li Ssu's mind as to who was master. And there were other
more refined punishments, prepared with aesthetic skill by
specialists in the art.

Li Ssu prayed for the end.

It was not to be a quick one. Chao Kao wished, as tyrants
before and after him have wished, to make a public exhibition of his one-time friend.

Li Ssu, once grand councillor to the emperor of China
and now a racked old man, was led out with his son into the
market-place. Many times he had watched the butchery of
scholars, soldiers and dissident officials on this very spot.
Now it was his own turn.

Slowly, before the eyes of the crowd and the imperious
palace chamberlain, within sound of the emperor's hysterical giggles and the gloating shrieks of his womenfolk,
Li Ssu was sawn in two.

When he and his son were dead, and while the blood was
still caked upon the market-place, all their relations as far
as second and third cousins were hunted out and destroyed.

After the death of Li Ssu, rebellion broke out just as he
had for so long been predicting. One conspirator was
hideously dead; and vengeance awaited the other. Chao Kao
believed that he could appease destiny with one mad
gesture. As trouble blazed up on every side, he murdered
the emperor whom he and Li Ssu had placed on the throne,
and fervently declared that the rightful ruler could be none
other than the son of Fu Su, that forgotten heir who had
been cheated into taking his own life.

Chao Kao's nominee accepted the task. His uncle's first
act as emperor had been to elevate Chao Kao to the position

of palace chamberlain. The young man's first act was to order his execution.

The palace chamberlain had hardly been killed before a rival group of rebels stormed the palace, slew the new emperor, and razed to the ground that flamboyant building which had caused so much misery and aroused so many warring passions.

One cannot help envisaging the reunion of all those enemies and conspirators in the shades: the dead emperor whose last wishes had been flouted, face to face with his successors who had come to such bloody ends—his suicidal son, his murdering and murdered younger son, the treacherous eunuch, the grandson who so fleetingly tasted power before being deprived of it . . . and the doomed, misguided grand councillor with his sadly divided mind and gruesomely divided body.

Masada: The Zealots' Last Stand

In A.D. 72 the Roman Empire stretched from Britain in the north across most of Europe and encircled the whole of the Mediterranean. From time to time there was trouble among some of the subjects of the outlying provinces, but the Romans had the strength, the power and the discipline to deal with rebellions.

One such uprising had occurred six years before, when the Jews in Judaea had revolted against their Roman overlords. But the rebellion had been efficiently crushed, the city of Jerusalem had fallen to the Roman siege, and the Temple had been destroyed. The event had been properly celebrated: triumphal arches had been dedicated in Rome and a special medal had been struck, showing a Roman soldier looking down on a Jewish slave.

In theory, Judaea was now at peace, the last of the rebellion was over. But this was only the theory; in practice, there still remained one determined group of rebels inside Judaea who defied the might of Rome. These were the Zealots—a particularly strict religious sect. A thousand of them—men, women and children—were together in a desert stronghold by the Dead Sea, which they used as a base for raids against the Romans. The name of the stronghold was Masada.

Masada completely dominated the region of the desert where it stood. The natural rock itself rose in sheer cliffs for thirteen hundred feet to a plateau measuring two thousand feet from north to south and six hundred and fifty feet from east to west. The only real path up to the summit twisted perilously along the cliff face. It was known as the Snake, and had so many bends and turns that the traveller had to walk a total distance of three and a half miles in order to reach the summit.

The huge rock was fortress enough in itself, but it had been made apparently impregnable by King Herod the Great a hundred years earlier. He had surrounded the summit with a great defensive wall eighteen feet high and twelve feet wide, and at strategic places he had erected seventy-five-foot high towers, all joined together by passages inside the walls themselves. Behind this protective barrier he had built storehouses for food and armaments, living quarters and even a swimming pool. For such a barren spot, Masada was a place of comparative luxury. Water supplies were assured by a series of great cisterns carved out of the rock and fed by aqueducts. Food could be grown on the summit, where the soil was comparatively rich, and extra supplies could be kept in the storehouses. Finally Herod had built himself a luxurious palace on the top of Masada —not that he wanted to live in the desert, but he was an unpopular ruler and Masada was a possible retreat should his countrymen turn against him.

This then was the fortress occupied by the last group of Jewish resisters. It was built to withstand siege, for years if need be. The Zealots themselves had captured it in a surprise attack on the Roman garrison there at the very outset of the war in A.D. 66. They had held the position ever since, and had split up the great apartments of Herod's palace to make smaller units for the families who had come to live on the top of the rock. Well supplied and leaving the heights only to make forays against the Romans, they were confident they could hold out indefinitely, whatever the Romans attempted to do.

This last outpost of resistance was an intolerable insult to Roman prestige, and made a mockery of the arches and medals commemorating the end of the war which refused to finish. In A.D. 72, the Roman Governor Flavius Silva determined to put an end to the Zealots. He marched towards Masada at the head of a formidable army. The main force consisted of the Tenth Legion with all its auxiliary troops in support. The supplies—food, water and building materials—were carried by hundreds of Jewish prisoners of war.

From the top of Masada, the great column of men could be clearly seen approaching the rock. The Zealots began work, strengthening their already formidable defences. Flavius Silva began his preparations for a long siege.

Silva built a great retaining wall, stretching for over two miles right round the base of the rock. Eight camps were also set up around Masada, encircling the Zealots. Silva wanted to make quite certain that no one escaped, possibly to start up resistance again in some other part of the province. All this activity could be clearly seen by the men on the summit, and they knew that while the Romans remained in their camps there was no way out. But time, it seemed, was on their side; there was a limit to the length of time that the Romans could remain out there in the desert with no water supply immediately at hand. In the summer months, conditions must strongly favour the Jews. Silva was aware of the situation as well, and now began his plans for taking Masada in the shortest possible time.

The obvious problem facing Silva was how to get his men up to the summit so that they could tackle the actual fortifications. To attempt to lead his army up the steep, winding Snake path would have been suicidal. The Zealots would have had no difficulty in dealing with such an attack. They had a vast store of great stone balls stored on the summit which could be rolled down to crush any attackers. So the track was impossible, and would not in any case have been wide enough to allow the great siege engines to be brought into place. As there was no natural path to the summit open to Silva, the Roman commander decided to build his own.

At the western end of Masada, Silva began the construction of a great ramp of earth which was to rise from the base of the rock almost to the summit. This vast earthwork, when it was finished, was over two hundred yards long; and the base, too, stretched two hundred yards across at its widest point. At the top of the ramp a seventy-five-foot wide platform was constructed to support the siege engines.

During the actual construction of the ramp, the Romans began the first active stage of the attack. Huge catapults, capable of throwing stones right into the centre of the fortress, were dragged into position at the base of the cliffs. As soon as these started to operate they caused considerable damage to the buildings and also killed and wounded many of the defenders on the summit. Even so, it remains a mystery today why the Zealots allowed the work on the ramp to continue. The most probable explanation is that the Romans used the prisoners of war for the actual construction work, and the Zealots were unwilling to attack their unfortunate fellow countrymen. Whatever the reason, the ramp and the platform were completed and Silva could, at last, begin the real attack on the fortress.

Early in A.D. 73 Silva was ready to launch his forces. The great machines of war were dragged up the ramp and into position. The main siege tower was constructed on the platform at the top of the ramp. The tower was ninety feet high and covered with overlapping iron plates. From inside, the Roman archers could fire directly at the Zealots and small catapults and slings could be used to keep up a steady bombardment. The main piece of equipment to be used in the attack was a giant battering-ram, which also had positions for archers and catapults in its superstructure.

Against this array of armour, the defenders had very little with which to offer real opposition. They had the great stones that they could roll down on the attackers, but once the towers were completed and in position, the defenders could do little more than try to protect themselves from the showers of arrows and heavy missiles.

When the preliminary bombardment was over, Silva ordered his men to begin working with the battering-ram against the stone walls. Time and again the ram shuddered into the stonework until the masonry began to crack and crumble. By nightfall a whole section of wall had been breached and the way into Masada was open. But the defenders were not yet beaten. As Silva led his men away to their camps to rest and prepare for the final assault on the following day the Zealots set to work to fill the gap in the wall. There was no time to prepare new stonework, and besides they had already seen how these defences had fallen to the battering-ram. Instead they hauled huge baulks of timber into place in the breach, and packed them round with earth to fill in the spaces and to hold the wood firmly in position.

The Roman commander had not thought it possible for the defenders to repair the breach in the wall overnight, and when he came to resume the attack the next morning was forced to call again for the battering-ram. But this time the ram had no effect on the wall. The pliant timber, instead of cracking under the pounding, gave with the blows and the force was dissipated and absorbed. Silva had to decide on a change of tactics, and withdrew the battering-ram from the walls. If the wood would not crack and break, it would burn. Silva ordered his men to take flaming torches and hurl them against the timber. Soon small flames began to sprout from the wooden barricades, and within minutes huge fires were leaping skywards.

For a time, however, it seemed as if Silva's ruse would work against him. The mountain wind caught the searing flames and blew them back at the Romans; there was a period of panic among the Roman soldiers, as they worked furiously to save themselves and their equipment from the flames. But in the mountainous district round Masada the unpredictable wind can shift in a few moments, and this is what now happened. The wind direction changed from north to south—the flames were carried away from the attackers and the barricade began to crumble and fall in the fire.

The way was once again open for the Romans. The gods had intervened to assure their victory. They looked forward to the next day when the last remnants of resistance would be overcome.

Inside the fortress, the defenders also saw the sudden reversal of the wind as an omen, but in their case it was a sign that God had turned his back on them and thrown them to their enemies. The men gathered together to listen to their leader, Eleazar ben Yair. The last great, heroic but tragic, event in the history of Masada was about to begin.

Under the shadow of the great rock, the Romans kept watch, ready to deal with any last desperate attempt by the Zealots to break the noose that surrounded them. But Eleazar had no such intention. He had decided that the turning of the wind was the final sign that God had rejected His chosen people. The Jews had sinned and He had punished them already by allowing the Romans to destroy the city of Jerusalem and the Holy Temple. Now Eleazar believed that it was the will of God that the whole Jewish race should be exterminated.

However, he was not prepared to submit to the Romans. The Zealots had been among the first to rise in rebellion, and now they were the last to continue the struggle. Eleazar knew the terrible retribution that would be exacted by the Romans. They had shown no mercy when Jerusalem had fallen, and for the Zealots the end would be harder still. The very best they could hope for was a life-time of slavery for every man, woman and child. The wall was broken down, God had turned his face away from them, and the end of the struggle was certain.

In this situation of total despair, Eleazar offered a desperate solution. He addressed his followers, explaining to them the fate that would befall themselves and their families should they be taken by the Romans. He reminded them of the vows they had taken and of the years of struggle that lay behind them. At last he came to his proposal: that they should not allow themselves to be taken, they should never permit themselves to be forced into the position of standing helplessly by while their wives were raped, while their children begged them for help they were unable to give. They were still free men and their families were free—now was the time to die as free men. Eleazar then put forward the crux of his terrible proposal: as an act of spiritual atonement they should themselves destroy Masada and every human being that lived there.

It is not surprising that even among that courageous company there were some who shrank from the idea, not of killing themselves but of deliberately slaughtering their own wives and children. But Eleazar was filled with an overwhelming sense of divine purpose, and he began again to speak to the assembled men. He told again the stories of the Romans' treatment of the Jews, and gradually he fired them with enthusiasm for his idea. They would never give the conquerors the satisfaction of defeating them in battle; they would die by their own free choice exercised as free men. The Zealots cut short Eleazar's oratory—they were convinced.

Each man set off for his own home. Their eyes streaming with tears, they said a last farewell to wives and children, then drew their swords and killed them. Not one man shrank from what they had all agreed. When wives, small sons and daughters were all dead they took their few possessions, piled them up together and set fire to them. Then they lay down on the floor beside the bodies of their families, and in their turn waited for death to come.

Before the slaughter had begun, the men had drawn lots among themselves and ten of their number now had the job of killing their comrades. The ten went round from home to home and the Zealots soon joined their families in death. When all was finished, the last ten again met together and solemnly drew lots.

In this way the last man was chosen. The other nine lay down on the ground and bared their throats. The chosen man drew his sword and slit the throats of the nine. Their blood gushed out and they lay still. The sole survivor was alone on the great plateau of Masada—alone among the magnificent buildings, now scarred and damaged by the Roman bombardment, alone in the night with only the bodies of nine hundred of the people who for six years had been his friends and companions.

But he had not yet finished his work. Slowly he made his way from building to building, from room to room, and carefully he inspected the bodies of the fallen as he went on his lonely and tragic way. He had been given the final responsibility of ensuring that Eleazar's plan was properly carried out. So he examined each body as he went for any sign of life—the bodies of old friends, of women he had talked to in his spare time, of children who had played games with his own children. After he had killed the last nine, he looked at nine hundred and fifty bodies. And where he thought he saw any spark of life, he extinguished that spark.

Eventually the man was satisfied that he alone remained alive among the carnage on the summit of Masada. He then took a torch and began systematically to set fire to the palace and the other buildings of the fortress. Only the food stores were left untouched, for it had been Eleazar's wish that the enemies should know that it was not hunger that had driven the Zealots to their last desperate action, but that they had taken the choice of their own free will. With Masada aflame around him, he felt able to join the others. Drawing his sword, he placed it with the hilt on the ground and the point upwards and threw himself upon it, forcing his body down on to the blade. He too fell to the dust.

The following morning, 15 April, A.D. 73, the Romans armed themselves and marched up the ramp towards the summit. Gangways were thrown across from the platform to the walls and the men poured across into the fortress. There they stopped, confused and puzzled. All night they had been preparing for the fight, but the enemy seemingly had vanished. Everywhere on the top of Masada was silence. Nothing moved but the smoke that drifted upwards from the smouldering ruins. The men shouted, and the sound echoed out and away into the surrounding hills.

Then a tiny group appeared: two women, leading five terrified children. When the slaughter had begun, they had hidden in one of the conduits that led into the water cisterns. All night they had remained concealed, mute witnesses of Masada's ghastly death throes. Now they had come out into the open, and they told the Romans of what had happened. At first the latter were incredulous, but investigation by scouts soon confirmed the story. So the legion marched into the fortress of Masada, not as triumphant conquerors happy in their victory, but solemnly and quietly. They stopped and stared at the rows upon rows of corpses, and silently paid tribute.

So Masada was taken by the Romans. The Jewish uprising had at last been ended. The story of the last stand and the terrible self-sacrifice of the Zealots has come to us from the writings of the historian, Josephus. Recent excavations have confirmed the details of the story; the rock of Masada still stands with the ruins of Herod's temple and the remains of the Roman camp. It is a lasting tribute to nine hundred and sixty human beings who showed that the love of freedom could be greater than the love of life.

The Gytrash of Goathland

"A horse was coming; the windings of the lane yet hid it but it approached. I was just leaving the stile; yet, as the path was narrow, I sat still to let it go by. In those days I was young and all sorts of fancies bright and dark tenanted my mind: the memories of nursery stories were there amongst other rubbish; and when they recurred, maturing youth added to them a vigour and vividness beyond what childhood could give. As this horse approached, and as I watched for it to appear through the dusk, I remembered certain of Bessie's tales, wherein figured a North-of-England spirit, called a 'Gytrash'; which, in the form of horse, mule, or large dog haunted solitary ways, and sometimes came upon belated travellers, as this horse was now coming upon me.

"It was very near but not yet in sight; when, in addition to the tramp, tramp, I heard a rush under the hedge, and close down by the hazel stems glided a great dog, whose black and white colour made him a distinct object against the trees. It was exactly one mask of Bessie's Gytrash—a lion-like creature with long hair and a huge head: it passed me, however, quickly enough, not staying to look up, with strange pretercanine eyes, in my face, as I half expected it would. The horse followed—a tall steed, and on its back a rider. The man, the human being, broke the spell at once. Nothing ever rode the Gytrash: it was always alone; and goblins, to my notions, though they might tenant the dumb carcasses of beasts, could scarce covet shelter in the common-place human form. No Gytrash was this—only a traveller taking the short cut to Millcote."

The girl was Jane Eyre, the traveller Mr Rochester, the animal his Newfoundland dog, Pilot. Had it been the Gytrash indeed, that goblin creature of Yorkshire legend, Jane's fate might have been very different from the romantic story we know. For it was said—at least in the wild region of Eskdale—that whoever was overtaken by those padding footsteps before they could reach their home would sicken and die the next day. What the sickness was, none could say. The symptoms were not those of the plague, which the people knew well. The victim would suddenly develop a fever, swollen glands and ankles, would become weak, sluggish and sleepy; then, the fever subsiding, he would fall into a coma and slip away from life. More often than not the victim would be a young girl, just such another as Jane Eyre.

The story began so long ago that one might marvel at its remaining in the minds of Victorians. Some say one thing, some another, but it seems most likely that the events which led to the dread hauntings happened some time during the ninth century, when Saxon England suffered under her cruel conquerors, the Danes. For many years they ruled her, with fire and sword, throwing down the Christian altars and suppressing the culture which had come to the land through the Romans, and later through the great leaders and teachers, Caedmon and Bede.

Amongst the most brutal of Danish overlords was one they called Julian of Goathland, who ruled the Vale of the Mirk Esk from what is now the town of Pickering to the village of Grosmont. Perhaps his name was not Julian, for it is a Roman name, not that of a Dane. It may be that his own was unpronounceable to those he ruled, and they called him instead after one of the Roman conquerors who had long since gone. But to this day a place among the moors near the village of Goathland is called Julian Park, for it was here, they say, that he built his castle: and so began the tale.

It was a good place for a fortress, with Malyon Spout hard by to provide ever-running water, plentiful wood for fires, and wild life for eating. Here, he thought, he might live in safety from his enemies; and they were many, for, as King Alfred's *Anglo-Saxon Chronicle* tells us, "By God's mercy, the invader had not utterly broken down the English nation". It should be the strongest castle in Northumbria, that kingdom which stretched from coast to coast and northwards to the border of Scotland. So he vowed to Thor, next mightiest of the gods to his father Odin, wielder of the great hammer Mjolnir, wearer of the Belt of Prowess which gave him threefold strength, and of the mighty iron gauntlets with which Mjolnir must be gripped before he could strike fire from the mountains. Another oath he took by the Ravens of Odin, the black birds Hugin and Munin, who perched upon his shoulders at night to whisper in his ears all the doings of men.

To appease the gods, and to ensure the security of such a building as Julian's Castle, one thing must be done: a living object must be built in within its walls, a sacrifice of blood. Nobody in those days thought this cruel. A cat or a dog would serve, more often than not: their small mummified remains are still discovered within the walls of ancient buildings. And so, when the stone walls had risen above a man's height, the master of the masons came to the castle's lord and asked what creature he should immure.

Julian turned from the fire which smoked in his living-hall, a pot of ale in his hand. He was a big, fair, ruddy man, like many of his race, small-eyed and loose-mouthed. His long hair hung to his shoulders, his bushy beard swept his jerkin. Between a rough frieze kilt and the leather thongs that bound his calves his legs bore the still-red scars of sword-cuts.

"What creature, churl?" he repeated. "What creature but a woman?"

The mason gaped. His lord was not a man given to joking, but it seemed that this must be some pleasantry. He essayed a timid smile; it would not be safe to laugh openly unless he were quite sure a jest was intended. His master's response was to seize a heavy branch of kindling and strike him over the head with the smouldering end. The man reeled back and fell to his knees, stammering a plea for mercy.

"Why do you grin, knave? Did you not hear me aright?"

The mason had been brought up in the Christian faith.

He was shocked to the soul by his master's speech. But he knew that it was as much as his life was worth to argue or disobey; and not only his own life, but the lives of his wife, children, and any other relatives on whom Julian could take revenge. He thought quickly. Women were precious to that small moorland community, mothers and rearers of children, helpmeets of men. Few among them could be spared: none, whose working and bearing years were not yet over. He searched his memory for even one female who might be expendable, and who might not suffer as cruelly as another for his master's barbarous whim.

"Lord—there is old Elfrida, that dwells in the hut by the beck. She is so old that her neighbours have to care for her, out of their charity, and gone in her wits, they say. If only this will appease the gods, she might serve——"

Julian laughed uproariously. "Fool! What should Odin and Thor do with an old crone? It is maiden blood they ask, and the fairest maiden that may be found. Go, fetch me Gytha of the Mill."

The mason's face whitened. "Gytha, lord? But she is— she is her father's only child—and all praise her beauty and goodness——"

"The fitter sacrifice, then! Besides, she flouted me t'other day when I met with her on the moor. Fetch her, I say!"

"Sire, sire, kill me if you will, but I cannot! How could I take her from her father? Gurth would slay me with his own hands sooner than let her go."

Julian aimed a kick at the man. "Out of my sight, milk-faced ninny, and back to your tools. My men-at-arms will do my errand, if you are not man enough for it." And he raised his voice in a summoning roar.

"She was at her spinning-wheel when they took her", says the *Chronicle*. Before the door of the mill-house she sat, in the Spring sunshine, singing as she worked, a lovely girl of fourteen whose golden plaits, thick as ropes, hung to her waist and shone bright against her blue gown. When she saw the men-at-arms approaching a flicker of fear crossed her face. Then she smiled, for smiles came easily to her, and she thought that the coming of the soldiers meant no more than a raid on her father's stores, for Julian took what he would of his folk's goods without a by your leave, and it was a wise householder who let them go without resistance

Two of the men advanced and pulled her roughly to her feet. She looked from one to the other, startled. "What do you want with me?" she cried. "It is my father you must ask——"

"We ask him nothing and we want nothing of him," replied one of the men. "It is you, maid, that our lord seeks."

Struggling in their grasp, she called "Father! Father!" And Gurth of the Mill came running at his daughter's voice; and seeing her between the men, rushed forward to free her, with a roar of anger. But a merciless blow on the side of his head felled him, as an ox is felled, and he dropped at his shrieking daughter's feet. The man who had struck him kicked aside his inert body and snatched up the girl in his arms. Together he and his comrade strode through the little crowd of frightened villagers who had gathered, and made for Julian's headquarters. And, says the *Chronicle*, "they brought her before her lord with the spindle still in her hand".

It seemed that she could not understand when they told her what was to be done to her. She had feared rape, the fate of other girls and women who had attracted their lord's passing fancy. But the terrible death that was planned for her was beyond imagination, beyond belief. When she could speak for trembling, she pleaded at Julian's feet; begged for mercy at any price. She would be a slave in his house —anything, if he would only spare her. Behind her, held between two soldiers, her father struggled, his face still bloody from the blow, weeping, swearing, and pleading for his daughter's life.

Julian stood listening, saying nothing, so that Gurth paused in his ravings, thinking that perhaps they might have roused some pity in the iron man before him. Then said Julian:

"Why do you speak to me in your barbarous Saxon tongue? Take him away, teach him some honest Danish."

Grinning, the henchmen dragged the miller to the door, outside which a crowd of Gurth's neighbours huddled. Julian raised his voice.

"And when you have taught him, tell him this—that he himself shall build his daughter into my walls!"

The miller halted between his captors, and a terrible cry came from him.

"I will not do it!"

"Then we shall find a way to make you, by Thor's beard. And you, you Saxon rabble, you shall be made to know what obedience means!" Snatching up a many-thonged whip, he strode among the gathered folk and lashed them until they gave up their prayers and threats, and ran for safety. By the fire in his hall, Gytha lay unconscious, one of her loosened braids singeing among the ashes.

By a mercy that cannot have proceeded from the cruel gods of Valhalla she did not come again to her full senses, but lay for days and nights in a coma of shock, staring and speechless. And when, within a week, the walls of Julian's keep had risen high enough, they carried her from the pallet in her prison-hut to the place where she was to remain for ever, and brought her father to her. She could not have known him, even in her right mind, for his hair had become white and his face was the face of an old man. They had tortured him with burning stakes until his spirit was broken and his body only strong enough to lift one small stone upon another.

Julian exclaimed with disgust when he saw the miller's ruined state. "Fools, you have robbed him of his strength and me of my jest! Do the work yourselves, but make him help you as he can."

When only a small aperture remained in the great wall, they lifted Gytha into the recess within, where a rough seat had been constructed.

"Now," said Julian, "put beside her a flask of water and a loaf of bread, for I would not have her die too soon; and give her her spindle and spinning-wheel. It fits not girls to be idle—she may well find time hang heavy on her hands."

The soldiers obeyed him, as the people moaned and wept, and Gurth looked dumbly on his child's entombment. And when only two stones remained to be put into place before she was hidden from the light for ever, Gytha's senses returned and she began to scream.

For four full days, they say, her cries and sobs were heard, and then they ceased, and the castle walls rose above her grave, ever taller.

Even for those dark times, it was a deed to appal men's minds. The echo of it came to Alfred the King, and the priests of the White Christ urged him to take action against the Danish lord. But to do so might have imperilled Alfred's whole kingdom, so strong and so much feared were the Danes. The holy hermit of Eskdaleside had more courage, and went to Julian's castle to preach to him of sin and repentance; but Julian laughed, and set his great hounds on the hermit, who was forced to fly or be torn to pieces. The tyrant was then to go scatheless, muttered the people; and Goathland and all the Vale of Esk went in great fear.

A year passed by. The Spring came again, and the anniversary of the entombment of Gytha. On his bed in the solar Julian lay, planning new fortifications for his castle. He was pleased with its building, secure in the strength which it afforded him. A distant cry roused him from his thoughts: the wail of a woman, it sounded to his ears. Such cries were not uncommon. Only when it came again, and nearer, he stirred, and cursed, and the village girl who lay by his side muttered in her sleep. Nearer and nearer the cries came. Where and when had he heard them before? A memory came to him of a day whose events had not troubled his mind for a year, and with the memory came a twist of fear. He opened his mouth to call the guards who slept about him, but no sound came from it. A dream, he told himself; the familiar dream in which one can neither speak nor move. And as he lay, trusting to waken soon, there appeared in the doorway of the solar a misty figure, uttering the wails which had grown louder and louder in the last few moments.

The figure approached, with silent feet, and stood at the foot of his bed. The moon shone palely, but he knew that it was Gytha, in her blue gown, her hair loose and her eyes wild as he had last seen her, and the spindle in her transparent hand.

Slowly she stretched out her hand until the spindle was over his feet. Still he tried to call out, but no sound came, nor did the sleeping guards move to help him. Back and forth, back and forth, the wraith moved the spindle, and with each movement Julian felt a sensation as though a giant spider were weaving steely threads around his feet and ankles. Cold and numb they grew, and "upon him there came a great horror", says the *Chronicle*. When her weaving was finished, the ghost turned from him and glided away, her wails fading as she descended the twisting stone stairs, downwards to her tomb.

Julian awoke next morning still heavy from what he thought a dream. But when he tried to stand, his feet would not obey him. He could walk only with a clumsy shuffle, like an old man.

It was a passing thing, the effect of some cramp which had come upon him while he slept, he thought. But day followed day and he grew no better. When a year had passed, and the anniversary night came round again, he did not sleep; it was in no dream that he heard the phantom voice of Gytha as she wailed her way towards him from the keep where her bones whitened. Again she stood at the foot of his bed, spindle in hand, and wove it now across and across his knees. When daylight came he was paralysed from the knees downwards, suffering not only numbness but sharp pain. Lying helpless on his bed, he cursed the gods who had led him to sacrifice Gytha. "You have betrayed me, O Thor and Odin!" he cried. "I followed your commands and gave you the blood you sought, and now see what I suffer! I will break down your altars and build to other gods than you!"

Hearing of Julian's vow, the hermit of Eskdaleside came once again to the castle. This time he found its lord ready to listen to him; even to pray to the White Christ, and to raise a church in his honour. This was done, and Goathland Church stands on the spot to this day.

Whether repentance came too late, or whether Julian's conversion was effected through fear and not true belief, it is not known; but still on the same night of April the spirit of Gytha visited him and wove her threads higher and higher, until his body was wholly paralysed, and pain racked him night and day. One such night, when a storm raged across the moor, his pains ended and his soul was taken from him; and what became of that soul has passed into the legend.

It was long ago, few could write or read, memories fade. But the tale has come down many centuries that on the night when the castle's lord lay dead a villager of Goathland was battling through the wind and rain when he saw leaping over the low wall of the new churchyard a thing having the likeness of a great black animal, with fire-burning eyes, and rushed past him into the blackness. He could not tell his family, when at last he got home, whether it was dog, horse or goat; only that its feet made no noise but a padding sound like the bare soles of a human being. It was no wonder that his description was no closer, for he could barely speak for terror. Within a few hours he died, not of cold and exposure, but of some disease which had never been seen in Goathland before.

He was the first to die of those who met with "Padfoot", or the Gytrash, as they called the black thing. None with whom it caught up ever escaped, young girls being its favourite victims. It was said, too, that the spirit of Spinning Gytha still haunted the castle which was now falling into ruins. And so the dale was still ruled by fear, though its tyrant was dead: dead, at least, in body, for they swore that his soul was housed within the Gytrash.

The hermit was sent for. With bell, book and candle, he came, and said the Christian rite of exorcism over the churchyard from which the Gytrash seemed to come, and the wall in which Gytha was buried. His prayers and incantations were ineffectual. In despair, the villagers sought help of the Spaewife of Fylingdales, a white witch of great power and knowledge.

At first she would not listen to them, for they had treated her harshly in the past. Then she yielded, and for a week she pondered on a spell that should set the district free. When they returned, she told them: "I will give you but three words—work on them for yourselves, and read me right, or the Gytrash shall roam for ever and the Spinning Maid never be quiet. This is my spell—tane to tither, tane to tither!"

Now "tane to tither" means, in our speech, "the one to the other", and it came at last to one of the brighter brains among the folk of Goathland that the witch meant that they should set the two wraiths to do battle.

"Because the Gytrash lives on new corpses, we must prepare the bait for him," said one of the village elders. We must dig a pit on the moor, and seem as if to hold a funeral there, so that he may be decoyed into the grave, and Spinning Gytha may seal him in with her spindle."

The Spaewife confirmed that they had interpreted her spell rightly. "Lay a trail of honey from her tomb to the pit," said she, "sprinkle salt and corn upon it, and bury in the pit a Cornsheaf Child dressed in grave-clothes." This they did, carrying the sacred Mell Baby which is made out of a sheaf of corn when the harvest is done. Just before midnight they laid it in the pit they had chosen (many had been dug before they could find ground soft enough) and retreated, to watch the spirits' encounter.

Just at the twelfth hour the dreadful padding footsteps were heard, and the eyes shone red in the darkness, as the thing approached, looked about it, and plunged into the pit in search of the newly-dead flesh it thought it had seen carried there. As it did so, along the honey-trail from the castle came the glimmering shade of Gytha, spindle-in-hand. By the side of the mock grave she stood, weaving, weaving, but wailing no more, as though she knew her spirit was at last to be free. Then from the bottom of the pit came a dreadful cry; the earth fell in and buried the Gytrash utterly from sight, and in a few moments it was as though no grave had ever been dug. That is why, to this day, the other Killing Pits, or Kiln Pits, are still to be seen by Goathland, but only a spot on which grass will not grow remains of Padfoot's prison.

When the ground was once more flat, and the howl of the Gytrash had died away, Gytha smiled, and raised her arms towards Heaven, the spindle dropping from her hand; and never was she, nor the creature which had been her murderer, seen in Goathland again.

The Entertainment of Genghis Khan

It all began, they will tell you, many, many years ago, when the Grey Wolf lay with the Tawny Doe, and they, the Mongol people of Central Asia, were offspring of this unlikely alliance. They very soon multiplied, without further help from the beasts, and swarmed over a vast and indefinite area of country, some 1,700 miles in width from west to east, and 1,000 from north to south.

To be more accurate, the area is contained roughly between 84 and 124 degrees East Longitude, and between 38 and 53 degrees North Latitude. Within that sizeable chunk of Asia the temperature varies, each year, between an incredibly cold minus 45 degrees Fahrenheit and the heat of 101 degrees plus. The terrain changes from dense forest in the north, to steppes further south, right down to the arid emptiness of desert—the Gobi Desert in the extreme south.

This land of the Mongols is now in two very distinct halves. The so-called "Inner Mongolia"—nearer to the coast of Asia—has become a part of China. "Outer Mongolia", far from the coast and deep inside Asia, is still an independent state, at least in name. It is the independent People's Republic of the Soviet Union.

It is in fact an eager socialist state, becoming modernized and sovietized, and its inhabitants are, as ever, a proud people. They are as proud as they were in their great day, when they and half the world were ruled by Genghis Khan.

He was born, not Genghis Khan, but Temuchin, and even that was the accidental result of the chief, his father, having on that day defeated a rival of the name. It seemed fitting for Yesugei to commemorate his victory over Temuchin by passing the name on to his own new-born son. This was a common practice in the twelfth century, though it seems odd to us now.

The year was 1167, and Yesugei was proud of his infant son. The boy grew up like his father, a tough, bow-legged little horseman, wearing body armour of boiled leather and rejoicing in the challenge of open air, blistering heat, unbelievable cold. Like other Mongols, he was seldom far from his horse; for, to this Mongol, the horse was not only his vehicle, but his wealth, and for much of the time his home. The Mongols did not cultivate the soil (and few of them do to this day) but rejoiced in a wealth of horses and sheep and cattle. They seldom camped for long in one place, but picked up their felt tents, their *yurts,* and rode away with their flocks and their herds to another part of that world they were so certain they owned.

Temuchin was only thirteen when his father died. And by this time the Mongols already did own a large part of Asia, having galloped into its farthest regions to hack and burn all who resisted. By the time Temuchin had reached manhood, he had been in the forefront of much fighting, taken part in much conquest. In 1206 when his horde of Mongols had vanquished, killed or made reluctant allies of almost all the tribes in Central Asia, he was elected "Genghis Khan"—the King of Kings.

It was a period, over most of the world, of extreme cruelty, and Genghis Khan was perhaps the cruellest of all, though he had rivals for that honour. In the course of spreading his Mongolian empire east and west, he sacked towns and cities —most notoriously Bokhara, Samarkand and Merv, where he put all the inhabitants to death, piling their heads in enormous mounds by the ruined city walls. The policy was tactically sound, for often his terrified enemies fled long before the arrival of the dreaded Genghis, rather than fight a battle and be butchered. By the time of his death in 1227, when he was sixty, the empire of Genghis stretched from the Yellow Sea of China to the River Dnieper.

The monument to this wholesale murderer might well be those mounds of whitened skulls, traces of which remain to this day. But in fact Genghis Khan has a tomb, for all to see, at the Chinese town of Huhehot, in a part of his once great empire.

It was the custom of the day for a warrior worthy of his shield to capture a bride in battle, having killed off most of her male relatives. The custom was cheerfully accepted on all sides, and a girl obtained in this way foreswore all former allegiance the moment she was flung across the back of her new owner's pony. On arrival at his *yurt* she would start to cook and care for him as if there had never been another.

So it was that Genghis obtained his own, his fair Yisugen. She had not been the property of another man, she was a virgin, with an equally handsome older sister Yisui; and when she explained all these facts to Genghis, who had just butchered most of her other relatives, he was faced with an urgent and unavoidable problem of etiquette. He wished to make Yisugen his wife, and he would do so: he only wanted one wife, at present; but etiquette demanded that he marry the older sister as well.

Yisugen was well pleased that her new and forceful lover would marry Yisui: not to have done so would have been unthinkable. As for herself, she was delighted to be his wife, and at the rough ceremony and later in the great man's *yurt* she made this plain. She felt no jealousy against Yisui who would share him. Yisui would be summoned to the *yurt* in good time, and that would be very right and proper.

But the next day Yisugen was surprised and distressed to see her older sister moping and miserable. "What is it?" she asked. "Are you not proud like me to be a bride of the King of Kings, ruler of all the world?"

Yisui looked at her, and dropped her eyes. She said nothing.

The next few days and nights were spent in preparing a bridal banquet. For this, hundreds of sheep would be slaughtered, roasted and placed before the guests, to be devoured all night and into the next day, with potent fermented milk, and other delicacies. The two young wives of

Genghis took part in the preparations. Yet still Yisui seemed downcast.

The preparations went on, and during the afternoon of the appointed day guests began to arrive, hundreds of them. Some were from the conquered tribes—this was always the custom of Genghis—but most were from his own, all-powerful, horde.

There were serving men and women too, not all of them familiar. The men were stripped to the waist, roasting sheep, deer, even scrawny cattle, over huge open fires under the darkening sky. When these were ready they would be hacked into pieces and placed on captured gold and silver salvers before the guests.

Yisugen's work was over as was her sister's. She squatted comfortably, Mongol fashion, while the first great haunches of meat were placed before the guests. She noted with pleasure that her older sister now seemed smiling and happy.

The open-air banquet occupied a very large area of barren steppe, with guests stretching away out of sight, and hundreds of fires dotted in every direction. Genghis squatted at the place of honour, his two wives near him among the more important guests. He looked at them both, and he was radiant with pride and happiness and fermented milk.

But suddenly as Yisugen was picking up half a leg of lamb in her right hand (etiquette forebade the use of the left) she found herself observing the start of a tragedy. To her horror, she saw Yisui staring with love and delight at a man who stood beside her.

But he was only a servant. And yet there was no doubt that he too was looking, almost beseechingly, into the eyes of her sister Yisui.

The man half turned and Yisugen nearly fainted with fright.

He was a young man of their tribe, hers and Yisui's, and she remembered now that he had paid court to Yisui, had openly admired and desired her. But that now seemed in another life; their tribe had been defeated, its women annexed by the victors. If Genghis discovered this man, the consequences would be horrifying.

How had he come? Had he been invited as guest, and then decided to join the servants instead, in order to get closer to Yisui? Was he mad? Was Yisui mad?

The man left, with a long backward glance at Yisui, and the older girl became downcast again, almost as if a cloud had drifted across her features. And Yisugen saw, with a stab of fear, that this was quite plain to their husband. He was watching his wives through narrowed eyes, even though devouring a large piece of meat whilst entertaining a sycophantic group of guests. These were giggling nervously, congratulating him, grovelling.

The meal went on, and Yisugen remembered that the young man's name had been Aktari. As she did, he returned, the naked upper half of his body gleaming in the firelight as he bent to place a large golden bowl before Genghis.

Yisui looked suddenly up at him, and in full view of all the guests stared at Aktari with an expression of rapture. And Aktari stared back, seemed about to embrace her.

There was a sudden silence, broken only by the gentle whine of the evening breeze. Then Genghis spoke. "Yisui," he said.

It was some time before she looked at him. "Yes?"

Genghis pointed up at the man between them. "This—this creature," he said, "is he known to you, Yisui?"

The girl said nothing.

"This sweating servant, is he friend of yours, friend of the bride of the King of Kings?"

Still she said nothing.

"Seize him!" roared Genghis. A dozen sycophants struggled to their feet and did so. "Bring him to me."

The young man made no resistance. Half smiling, he was brought to the king.

"You are," said Genghis, "a man of the Shira tribe which I have vanquished, the people from whom my two wives come. Is that so?"

The man, his brown, half-naked body gleaming in the firelight and the moonlight and the oily gleam of butter lamps, nodded.

"And you admire my bride, my Yisui?"

"That is so."

"You have known her, in your country?"

The man said nothing.

"Speak! Have you known my bride Yisui?"

Suddenly it was Yisui herself who was shouting: "No—he

has not known me! But I have seen him, loved him! I love him still!"

Slowly, Genghis Khan dropped the bone he had been gnawing, got to his feet, and the two men were face to face. Then, almost without movement of the hand, there was a flash of steel and the King of Kings had severed the head of his rival.

There was a gasp of horror as it landed at Yisui's feet and bright red blood gushed over the guests, dyeing crimson the roasted meat. The face was smiling as it came to rest, smiling and staring up at the stars.

"Take it away," said Genghis, and men came from the shadows to remove the smiling head, the twitching body. The king sat down again as if nothing had happened, picked up his blood-soaked bit of meat, and started to chew. His two wives sat facing him, white with fear and horror, staring at the crimson earth in front of them. What punishment would be meted out to Yisui?

It came soon, and Yisugen was glad to know that her brave older sister would not be put to death. She saw what was in her husband's mind, watched now as he wrenched off a piece of mutton, dipped it slowly and carefully into a pool of the dead man's blood.

He beckoned a servant and the man came over, took the meat away on a salver, walked round the guests and re-appeared at Yisui's side.

She was staring in horror at her husband and now, with a courteous little wave of the hand, he made it clear what she was expected to do.

Yisui paused, then closed her eyes and took the meat from the serving man. In one convulsive move, she swallowed it.

When she opened her eyes, Genghis was staring at her, through her, lost in thought. Then he looked about among his guests, and his brow wrinkled.

A little later one of these guests got to his feet, perhaps to deal with a call of nature, perhaps to lie down and sleep for an hour. He could hardly be leaving the great banquet so soon without permission.

"Stop him!" roared Genghis Khan. Men rushed to obey, and the guest found himself held tight.

"No one leaves, for whatever reason, until I give the order. No one as much as walks away from this meal. For

I have decided on a great entertainment, in which some of our guests will take part." He turned to the Mongol nearest to him, spoke softly for some time, and the man got up and went off.

The banquet went on, far into the night, with the King of Kings leading the festivities. Many guests now wished to leave, if only for a short time, but this was not possible and Genghis was enjoying his hold over them. The moon went slowly down in the west and a pale dawn appeared.

Suddenly the great Khan shouted an order and men seized half a dozen men of the Shira tribe of Tartars, Yisui's and Yisugen's tribe, men who had been graciously bidden to the conqueror's banquet. Within seconds these had been bound with leather thongs.

The King of Kings now led his guests away from the meal, a little way across the flat plain, to where a big fire had been lit and six great copper cauldrons were standing. The party stumbled uncertainly towards the place as the dawn rose slowly, the sun still below the horizon but the sky a pale blue.

They reached the spot and the great Khan gave another order. The six men were dragged roughly over to the fire; each was placed beside a gleaming copper cauldron, and there held firmly by a pair of Mongols.

The King of Kings made an expansive gesture and everyone except the six prisoners and their guards sat down on the ground. The bandy-legged little king made another regal gesture with a thick brown arm. "Our entertainment will begin."

Three of the prisoners were now lifted and put into cauldrons, from which only their heads and shoulders protruded. There was a gasp of mingled joy and apprehension, then laughter at the comical figure the three men cut, their frightened faces sticking out of the copper vessels.

Servants came with beakers, dozens of them, and began pouring water into the cauldrons. Beaker after beaker was emptied over the men's heads, to gurgle down inside the vessel and slowly fill it to overflowing.

But this was an exciting, well-managed entertainment, after all! The second trio of guests would have the pleasure of seeing the first three boiled alive, and the hundreds of delighted Mongols would have the added interest of seeing their reactions to the spectacle.

Each of the three copper cauldrons was now manhandled a few feet, to the edge of the large fire, and the embers from this were raked out to surround it, while more fuel was thrown on. The sun had come up by now, and the cauldrons gleamed in its low, horizontal beam, flinging almost human shadows across the plain. The fires were adjusted to give less smoke, to let the audience see better, and now the entertainment had really begun.

Within a few minutes all three men were in obvious distress. One had begun a strange, high-pitched wailing, like a forest animal. When a second joined him, at a slightly lower pitch, Genghis began to roar with laughter and his guests joined eagerly in.

The third began to scream, to shout for mercy, and laughter swept across the plain. Genghis allowed this to go on for perhaps a minute, then shouted an order. The fires were damped down, the ashes raked away from the cauldrons, to delay the process: it would be a pity to end such a fine entertainment too soon. With their cauldrons hot but not yet boiling, these entertainers would give much pleasure for some time.

But one of the three men, the oldest, had fainted away, had simply sunk down into his cauldron, out of sight, leaving his two companions to continue the protest at the top of their lungs.

More orders were given and now the three remaining prisoners, who had added considerably to the entertainment by their woe-begone expressions, were lifted into the three remaining cauldrons and water splashed over them. The cauldrons then were manhandled right into the fire, and at the same time the fire around the earlier ones was banked up again; the time had come for the climax of the entertainment.

The huge audience sat back gratefully to watch. Yisui and Yisugen, forced to sit with them, remained with their eyes closed. From time to time Yisugen put hands up over her ears to drown out some of the screaming, but Yisui, though her eyes were firmly closed, seemed to have accustomed herself to the noise. Her hands remained clenched in her lap.

Then suddenly she leapt to her feet and ran wildly away. The audience turned to watch, but the great Khan merely glanced in the direction of his fleeing wife, shrugged shoulders and turned again to his entertainment.

By now there was a highly diverting cacophony coming from the cauldrons. The two survivors of the first trio were screaming at the top of their lungs in what was soon to be their death agony, and which Genghis had decided not to delay a second time. The second batch were wailing in different keys, and one of them, a very young man, younger even than the beheaded Aktari and not unlike him in appearance, was shouting as well, almost barking like a dog, and this Genghis found hilarious. Several times he clapped his hands like a child, with delight.

Then the sound of the first prisoners' screaming dwindled and stopped. All three of their cauldrons were boiling merrily and silently, with great clouds of steam rising from them. Two of the men had vanished, sunk down into their watery coffins, but the third was somehow propped up, dead, with his tongue sticking comically from an open mouth.

Someone pointed this out and there was more hilarity.

Yisugen could stand it no longer and, with rather more dignity than Yisui, made her way away from the ghastly scene, but the sound followed. After a while, curiosity compelled her to look back; at least this was better than having to view the entertainment from the front row, have one's reactions studied by the other guests.

This second batch of prisoners was not lasting so well as the first. Perhaps it was because their ordeal had not been so cruelly lengthened, perhaps they were just weaker men. From this distance, unobserved, Yisugen began to watch the entertainment with interest and even a little admiration for her strong husband who made such a spectacle possible. After all her sister had been most unwise, most indiscreet, and no doubt it was better that she learn her lesson at this early stage in married life. And that man, Aktari, he had deserved his punishment. What a blow that had been from her strong ferocious husband, who had the speed and the strength of a leopard! She knew now that she loved her husband very much. She was glad that from now on her sister would be the less loved of the two.

She watched the six steaming cauldrons in the distance. Then she saw the squat, bow-legged figure of the King of Kings rise to its feet and clap hands above its head. The breeze brought his words to her. "Go! Go!" he was shouting. "The entertainment is over."

The Synagogue of Satan

The siege was at an end. For nine months they had held off their attackers. Recently there had been a constant pounding from the giant siege-engine, hurling stones into the huts below the walls and into the walls and even over the walls into the constricted space where they lived. Night and day, watchful and ready to repel any direct assault, they had prayed; and survived. Now at last it was over.

Corba de Perella, the wife of the castle's *seigneur*, looked out across the valley from the battlements. On the far slope soldiers were constructing a huge wooden enclosure. Working parties brought faggots from the surrounding hills. The terms of an armistice had been agreed, and this was all part of it.

"They make their intentions very clear," she whispered.

Her husband put his hand on her arm. "Apart from that, we got the best terms we could."

She smiled at him. He had behaved gallantly throughout and had no cause to reproach himself. There was no shame in the surrender.

She asked: "How long do we have?"

"Fifteen days."

A fifteen-day truce in which to make their peace with this world or the next. They had defended themselves heroically, and it had been agreed that the garrison would be spared

47

the death sentence. Past crimes and rebellions would be forgiven. The fighting men could go free with their families, their arms and their goods, provided they made a formal recantation of the errors that had led them into this battle. The castle itself must be handed over to the administration of the Pope and the King of France. All other persons within its walls would be subjected to purely nominal light penances, provided that they too abjured their heretical beliefs and made confession before the Inquisition.

Those who did not recant would be burnt at the stake.

From the battlements the lady Corba de Perella looked out again at those grim preparations. As wife of the castle's master and joint commander of the garrison, she was free to walk out when the day came. Not for her the horror of death by fire—unless she was mad enough now, at this last minute, to choose it.

At last she said : "I think I shall ask the Bishop for initiation."

Raymond de Perella had not flinched during the grinding siege nor during the whole campaign. Now he went pale.

"You cannot do this."

Steadily she said: "I believe I can."

But how strong was her belief, really? She could have gone to the Bishop that very day and announced her intention. Instead, she waited. Her husband implored her to think, and think again. Once she had committed herself she must have no more to do with him or with other worldly concerns. And since they had so short a time together now, she must postpone the decision even though in her heart of hearts she was sure what it must be.

Sure—quite sure?

During the fifteen days allowed by the besiegers before the formal investiture of the castle, provisions were brought in. The incessant battering against the walls had ceased. They could talk and relax with their families. Talk, and think.

In some ways it was worse now than it had been during those defiant months. It was one thing to resist and hurl back an enemy, quite another simply to sit and envisage the future.

Perhaps the Inquisitors waiting out there were hoping that the lull would give the heretics time to repent. The victors sent in food and polite messages, and spies. They assessed the situation and, as a visible warning of what was to come, broadened the base of the bonfire.

Fifteen days in which to think . . .

The Cathar heresy had spread with alarming speed over the southern regions of France. The Count of Toulouse cautiously encouraged the heretics because, like himself, they wanted to prevent the encroachments of the King of France. For some time he had been aware that the Pope had been playing him off against the king. Politics counted for more than piety. Devising his own political game, the count fed the rebellious Cathars with hopes and promises. He rarely came out into the open, and if there was a danger of anything going wrong he was prepared to wash his hands of all responsibility for these heretical supporters. He even undertook, from time to time, to wipe out such blasphemers in the name of the Church; but then surreptitiously assured their leaders that it was better for him to put up a pretence of dealing with them than to leave them to the tender mercies of the Inquisition.

The Cathars, or Albigensians, made a practice of piety and virtue in an age which had little time for either. They condemned the corruption of the Church of Rome and preached against the wickedness of a dissolute hierarchy. At times the Pope might almost have been thought their ally. Addressing his own clergy in the very area where Catharism was strongest, he thundered: "Blind, mute dogs who cannot bark! Simoniacs who sell justice, absolve the rich and condemn the poor! Accumulators of benefices who leave the priesthood and ecclesiastical dignity in the hands of unworthy priests and illiterate children!" But whatever the threat from his corrupt underlings, it was nothing when compared to the menace of the heretics. Declaring in 1208 the first Crusade against fellow Christians, he anathematized them as "worse than the Saracens themselves".

The basis of Cathar belief was that in the whole of Creation there were two equal and opposite principles: God, who had created a purely spiritual and eternal universe; and Satan, the Jehovah of the Old Testament, who had constructed the utterly evil material universe. Man was a fallen angel, imprisoned in a fleshly strait-jacket. His only chance of salvation was in the abandoning of all physical desires and in aspiring to an austere spirituality.

There were two kinds of Cathar, the "Perfects" and the "Believers". Believers were allowed to continue with their ordinary lives, producing families and eating and drinking in the normal way; but it was their duty to succour the Perfects and listen to their teachings, and, in due course, to train themselves for ordination as Perfects if they were considered worthy.

The discipline of a Perfect was so strict that Believers were never urged to seek elevation until they were on their deathbed or until it was obvious that they might soon die in battle or at the hands of persecutors. This was not a sly evasion of responsibility, but rather a sign of Cathar tolerance towards human frailty. They knew how difficult it was to lead an ascetic life, and because the spiritual consequences of weakness and backsliding were so terrible they did not want any of their brothers in the spirit to be tempted beyond their endurance.

The most famous section of the Believers was the group known as Troubadours, the founders of lyric poetry in Provence, who wandered in pairs about the land, singing the enigmatic, symbolic songs in which so many of the doctrines of the sect were camouflaged.

Women could not be regarded as the equals of men but they were not debarred from becoming Perfects. They might withdraw from the world to lead a life of prayer and fasting or might remain in the world as guides and teachers of their families. Once they had made their vows, however, they must have no physical contact with their husbands, and all human yearnings must be subordinated to spiritual laws.

In 1237 the Inquisition began an orgy of trials in Toulouse. They were so anxious to demonstrate their resolve to stamp out heresy that they even dug up the bodies of supposed heretics from their graves and paraded the decomposing corpses through the streets on hurdles, while a crier intoned: "Whosoever does the like shall suffer the like".

Old grudges were paid off by malicious informers. It was enough to declare a man a heretic for him to be questioned, tortured, and put to the fire. Members of leading families who had reason to fear false testimony went into hiding.

Those who truly adhered to the Cathar faith but felt that they preferred to spread the faith rather than have it charred to a cinder sought refuge far away.

As the campaign against them intensified, the Believers converged on the one place where they knew they would be protected. The Church of Rome might dub it "the Synagogue of Satan", but to the Cathars it was the last impregnable sanctuary.

The castle of Montségur clung to a 3,500-foot mountain peak in the northern Pyrenees, surrounded by deep valleys and the higher, towering crests of its neighbours. The citadel itself was surrounded by huts where meditative Perfects lived, and could be reached only from its western flank. Even here the path was steep and tortuous. It could not be taken by surprise. It could not be taken by frontal assault.

Raymond de Perella had hardly expected, when he allied himself with the Cathars, that his castle would become a shrine rather than a fortress. If he had any regrets, he did not show them, even when his third daughter chose the dangerous path of a Perfect. His other two daughters were married to young officers, one of whom de Perella promoted to joint commander of the garrison.

The community was swelled by many distinguished refugees. Bertrand Marty, Bishop of Toulouse, himself came to celebrate the simple rites of their religion and to give constant spiritual advice to his flock.

They worried about their friends and supporters outside. Word came that Brother Arnaud, an Inquisitor, was working his way through the countryside with six fellow Dominicans in search of heretics. The Count of Toulouse sent word to Montségur that, although he himself could not act openly against the Inquisition at this stage, he would very much like these tormentors put to death.

Knights and men-at-arms set out from the castle on an errand which was greatly to their taste. They reached the town of Avignonet at nightfall and were guided by willing helpers to the house where the monks slept. The door was battered down and the Inquisitors were killed and mangled with axes, maces and daggers.

There was such jubilation throughout the region that the Count of Toulouse summoned up the courage to declare an open rebellion against the King of France.

The rebellion failed.

As the might of France and the might of Rome once more squeezed in on the count's domains, defeated soldiers and fleeing Cathars flocked towards the already crowded pinnacle of Montségur.

The time had come to choke this defiance once and for all. The Seneschal of Carcassonne and the Archbishop of Narbonne assembled an army to lay siege to the fortress which by now had become the ultimate symbol of heresy. In May, 1243, they pitched camp at the foot of the mountain. The inhabitants must be starved into surrender.

It was not as easy as the besiegers had anticipated. Gifts from Believers and the continued intake of stores into the castle had given it ample reserves. It survived through the dry summer until the rains came. Thirst would not win a victory. To make matters worse, supporters who knew the district continued to filter into the castle and bring more supplies.

Impatient, the commanders conscripted Basque guides to show them a way up to a spur closer to the fortress, and succeeded in establishing a siege-engine which would hurl stones against the walls. But the walls stood firm.

Gradually the net round the mountain was tightened. No further supplies got through. Inevitably there was a growing weariness. Nobody was going to come to the aid of the garrison: there would be no relieving army to raise the siege. By any worldly reckoning the Cathar cause was lost.

The worldly reckoning was not the one which mattered most. If, for the sake of the soldiers and their families who were not committed to the full rigour of Cathar doctrine, the Perfects agreed that resistance should end, it was in the assurance that their own spiritual future was beyond the reach of the enemy. They were above fear.

On 1 March, 1244, Raymond de Perella and his son-in-law negotiated for surrender.

Fifteen days. They drained away too swiftly.

The Perfects shared out what little property they had among those who were going to live. The gifts were tokens rather than wealth: having lived so austerely, the Perfects could offer little but personal mementoes.

Bishop Bertrand Marty gave oil, salt, pepper, wax and a

fragment of green cloth to the *seigneur*'s son-in-law, Pierre-Roger de Mirepoix. The young man's wife was presented by her grandmother with all her remaining belongings: she was old, she was going to enter a better world with no encumbrances. Other Perfects made gifts of their shoes and clothes, of anything which remained to them.

There were no decisions to recant. Indeed, there was just the opposite. Seventeen members of the garrison who could easily have walked out as free men and women now decided to take the dread step of becoming Perfects, thus announcing their own death sentence.

Corba de Perella said nothing. She noticed how her daughters and their husbands glanced at her from time to time, and knew that her husband must have spoken to them. After his first instinctive revulsion, he had nobly refrained from pleading with her or asking any further questions.

This was what made it so agonizing for her. He would not argue, would not try to sway her. The decision must be hers and hers alone. In the face of such patience, could she bring herself to leave him?

Tomorrow she would speak to the Bishop.

Tomorrow, and still another tomorrow.

Twelve days. Eleven, ten, nine, eight . . .

She tried to imagine what it would be like to be lapped in flame. Would she be holy, then: would she have the courage not to scream, not to recant in that awful moment when it would be too late?

The lady Corba reached her decision only on the evening before the truce period ended.

She kissed her husband for the last time, and went to see her married daughters. It was clear that they had been expecting her.

"We have known it would be like this," said Pierre-Roger de Mirepoix. "We have never had any doubts that this was how you would choose."

Corba declared herself to the Bishop. Three times he asked her if she was sure that she wished to take this step, and three times she firmly said yes.

"You are strong enough," he asked gently, "to endure what they will inflict on your earthly body? Strong enough not to fail and blaspheme in your death throes?"

"With God's help."

"Such a lapse means eternal damnation," he warned.

"This I know."

The *Consolamentum*, the initiation ceremony, was grave and simple. Corba de Perella promised that from now on she would eat no meat, eggs, cheese, oil or fish. She would touch no man, would kill no fellow human being, and would never reveal any of the mysteries of the faith.

The Bishop then read in his deep, measured voice the Prologue to the Gospel of St John. When he had finished he once more asked if she was sure in her belief and ready for acceptance.

"I have the will," said Corba. "Pray God give me the strength."

The Bishop came closer. She knelt before him. He kissed her on the brow. A terrible fire seemed to burn through her veins. It was done: she was changed, she had received the only sacrament which a Cathar could honour—the kiss of peace which was the baptism of the Holy Ghost.

There was no turning back now.

As she rose to her feet, the Bishop presented her with a small woven cord. This she must always wear round her body. It was a sacred emblem—and, in the eyes of any Inquisitor, an irrefutable mark of heresy.

Corba de Perella spent her last night on earth not with her husband but in prayer. In the morning, the gates of the castle were thrown open and the defenders left it for the last time.

Soldiers and their families plodded down the precipitous path with packs on their backs and bundles under their arms. The besiegers respectfully saluted the knights who had put up such a gallant defence.

A group of dark-habited men with dark, stern faces waited at one side. As the Perfects came out, keeping together to show themselves stalwart in faith and making no pretence of not being what they were, soldiers moved into position and shepherded them towards the Inquisitors.

"Will you recant and abjure your sin? Will you, each and every one, confess your grievous fault?"

There was silence.

The Inquisitors went slowly along the ranks and asked each man and woman individually to speak and thus be spared. Gently at first, then more and more insistently, they urged recantation.

Nobody wavered.

Suddenly there was an end to gentleness. At a signal from an Inquisitor, soldiers hurled themselves in among the Cathars. The Bishop was fettered and kicked down the slope like an animal on its way to the abattoir. Others were driven behind him to an accompaniment of shouts and curses—driven across the valley towards that huge pyre which had been fifteen days in the making.

The palisade was enough to hold two hundred men and women. Its builders had evidently known how many victims to expect. They had not bothered to erect individual stakes inside the enclosure. Faggots had been heaped over the grass and rock, topped with straw and pitch to make sure they would ignite.

Some of the older folk stumbled and fell on the way. They were dragged along by their captors and simply hurled on to the mound.

When all the heretics were packed in, the gate into the palisade was closed. The Inquisitors and their attendant monks began to chant psalms.

Soldiers with flaming brands set fire to each corner of the palisade. When they were sure that the victims were completely ringed by fire, they moved back from the rolling smoke.

Corba de Perella tried to grope her way towards her mother, but it was impossible to move without treading on the half-conscious older people who had collapsed on the deadly kindling. Smoke and flame roared in upon them.

For hours the fire burned and crackled. Those who were still moving their belongings out of the castle could smell the roasting, blistering flesh as the sickly smoke curved and swirled up the slopes of the valley. After nightfall, when there was no semblance of a human shape left in the heart of that furnace, the embers still made a glowing, bubbling carpet that dwarfed the flickering campfires of the soldiers on the hillside.

When at last the embers died, the Cathar cause died with them.

"Go Back, King James!"

The east wind off the Firth of Forth bit keenly into his
cheeks and he urged his horse to a trot through the sodden
sand. Its harness jingled a wild tune to the grumbling
accompaniment of breakers and the hiss of flung spume.
The newly-risen moon seemed buffeted by the clouds which
raced across it, from time to time extinguishing it and leaving the party of horsemen without any glimmer of light to
guide them along the beach.

For all his poetic leanings, the thoughts of James I, King
of Scotland, were less upon the romance of a wild nightfall
than on the promise of food, drink and a log blaze at the
end of a weary journey. It was a journey that should have
been ended before sundown. Progress from Edinburgh had
been slower than expected and there was still some little way
to go to the place from where boats would ferry the party
across the Firth to where they would lodge for the night
before pressing on again towards Perth and a welcome
season of Christmas festivities at the Dominican monastery
of Blackfriars.

The moon disappeared yet again, and James felt his horse
check, hesitating as it picked its way unseeing amongst the
rocks around which the edge of the surf surged and receded.
Suddenly, as quickly as it had vanished, the moon shone
forth again with icy intensity. The king's horse reared
and halted, nearly unseating him. A wild, dark figure stood,

arms upraised, on a low rock directly in the path of the cavalcade.

As the horses of his followers, brought to a sudden halt by his own, plunged and neighed behind him, James peered hard at the spectre-like form in front. It wore a long robe, flapping in the wind which whipped its long hair, silvery in the moonlight, about its neck and ears. In one of its hands it held what seemed to be a shepherd's crook.

James nudged his horse into a few reluctant paces forward. Now he was able to see that this was no apparition, but an old woman, her face deeply lined, her eyes intense as they caught and held his.

"What want you, woman?"

There was no answer. Slowly, the upraised arms were lowered from their commanding gesture. James heard the rustle and jingle as his party's horses edged up to his, and the anxious voice of his queen, Joan, asking, "Who is she? What does she want?"

The king repeated his question more sharply. Instead of answering it, the old woman demanded, "Which is the king?"

"Why ask you?" a courtier demanded, spurring his horse between the stranger and the king.

The shepherd's crook was banged down hard on the rock. "Which is the king? I speak to the king alone."

James called, "I am the king. Come here, old woman."

Slowly, stiff-limbed, the woman came down from the rock and moved to James's stirrup, peering up as if anxiously into his face, the lines in her face etched deeper as she struggled to recognize him. At length she nodded.

"Aye. 'Tis he."

"Well, then?"

A skinny arm was upraised, and a bony forefinger pointed in the direction from which the party had ridden.

"Go back, King James!"

There was a merry laugh from some of the courtiers at this show of presumption. The king did not laugh, but bent from his saddle, searching the old face.

"Why should I go back, old woman?"

"Because, once cross that water, and never shall you return again alive."

The pointing hand now reached for the horse's bridle and jerked it, as if to turn the animal. The horse tossed its head and snorted. James tugged the ends of his cloak more snugly about him and dug his heels sharply into the horse's flanks. With a slither of hooves and a jingle of harness bells the animal started forward across the rocks, and the others followed, one or two of the riders making quips at the ragged figure as they passed it. Only Queen Joan did not smile. As she rode by her eyes searched the woman's, seeking to judge whether sane sincerity or madness animated them. There was no telling; but as the party wended its way along the beach a receding cry followed it: "Go back, King James! Go back!"

Warnings of approaching doom were nothing new to James I of Scotland. Only recently he had been told that with the dawning of the new year of 1437 there would follow the death of a king in Scotland—and there was no candidate other than he. One thing was certain: if he were to die, it would need no supernatural agency to bring it about. He had enemies enough on earth and in the country whose ordinary folk had welcomed him back from exile in England thirteen years earlier, along with his "high-born English lady" queen, the daughter of John Beaufort, Earl of Somerset. For the arrival of a king intent on restoring justice and order to a lawless land had not at all suited the wild nobles who had taken the running of the country into their own hands, regardless of any man's interests save their own. "There was no law in Scotland, but the great man oppressed the poor man, and the whole kingdom was one den of thieves", a chronicler had noted sadly. But then the king had returned, declaring: "If God but grant me life there shall be no part of my realm where the key shall not keep the castle, and the bracken bush the cow, even though I should lead the life of a dog to accomplish it."

He had done more than utter fine words. With a ruthlessness startling even in the fifteenth century he had proceeded to bring the nobles to heel. In the first months of his reign he had arrested Sir Walter Stewart and Malcolm Fleming, son and brother-in-law of Robert of Albany who had been virtual ruler of Scotland in James's absence and had made no move to ransom him from his captivity in England. Both these men had been executed, together with the second

Duke of Albany and his son and many others. Hundreds of common criminals who had terrorized innocent communities by theft, murder and rape were also liquidated. They were harsh measures, but well meant. James was determined to bring his country under parliamentary rule and in thirteen years he had gone a long way towards achieving his ends. But his methods, and especially his seemingly overdone persecution of the Albany family, had earned him the deep hatred of many still-powerful men, who, feigning allegiance to him and sympathy with his aims, were only waiting for their opportunity to strike back.

As well as the motive of revenge there was a more positive reason for some men to wish the king off the face of the earth. Six years earlier, in 1430, the queen had given birth to a son, James. For Walter Stewart, Earl of Atholl, this implied a future King James II and the end of his own hopes of kingship over Scotland. For some time a conspiracy had been growing, involving Atholl and others and led by Sir Robert Graham, who had been imprisoned by James and then banished.

This, then, as the king and his party rode towards the ferry on that bitter night, seemed the likeliest source of any actual threat to his life; but that a seemingly crazy old woman, met on a lonely seashore, should have any prophetic inkling of danger was too ludicrous to damp the spirits of these men and women on their way towards a period of feasting and merrymaking that would extend over several weeks.

So Christmas passed, and the time of New Year, and the celebrations continued unabated. Night after night, under the monastery roof where the entire court was assembled, the wine flowed, the great dishes of food were hurried out in the flickering rushlight, and the soft sound of harp and voice hung on the air. Of all those who performed for the company, none outdid King James himself. His years of exile had not been wasted. Henry V of England had treated him kindly while keeping him captive at Windsor, ensuring that he was taught all the artistic accomplishments necessary to a gentleman, and James had quickly proved himself a natural poet and gifted musician. Not what might be termed a romantic figure—he was rather short and stout, though well built and good looking—he could nevertheless melt the hearts of a gathering with a rendering of his own delicate poem "The King's Quair", widely believed to have been composed for Queen Joan.

Yet, as he plucked at the harp and sang his lines during those evenings of festivity James knew too well that there were hearts amongst his audience that he would never melt. In the flickering light he could catch the gleam of eyes belonging to his bitterest enemies—men like the Earl of Atholl and Sir Robert Stewart. That they were present at all was a matter of courtesy: James had made an example of such men, had stripped them of much influence as a demonstration to other nobles who had taken the law into their own hands; but they retained their place at court, and watched James, and waited . . .

It was the night of 20 February, 1437. The celebrations were at last coming to their close. Soon King James would lead his court back to Edinburgh. For the last time he drew the harp to him and began to play and sing—and then paused, frowning, at a commotion near the door. An apologetic usher bowed his way forward.

"Pardon, my Liege. It is the old woman."

"Old woman?"

"The one who stopped you at the ferry, my Liege. She says she must speak with you."

"She can wait until tomorrow."

"But, my Liege, she insists there must be no delay."

"Impertinence! Send her packing."

The usher retreated, bowing. James caught his queen's eyes, saw the anxiety in them; but he shrugged and pulled the harp towards him again. Instead of beginning to play, though, he waited until the usher returned.

"Well?"

The man answered hesitantly. "We turned her away, my Liege, but at first she would not go. Then, when we threatened her, she wrung her hands and went . . . but she cried out again and again . . ."

"What did she cry?"

" 'Woe! Woe! I shall see his face no more.' "

There was a deathly silence in the big hall and a sudden chill, as though a ghost had passed through. King James pushed the harp away and called loudly for the final cup that would end the festivity. All drank, and then the assembly broke up and went off in ones and twos to the sleeping chambers.

The king and queen remained in the hall while the ladies of the bedchamber prepared their bed, curtained off in an alcove. Joan moved close to her husband and took his hand, seeking assurance; but he had none to give. For two months he had lived in half-expectation of some attempt against him. Very soon he would return to the comparative safety of Edinburgh. If anything was going to be tried it must surely come at any instant—and how coincidental was it that the old woman had returned just now to try to repeat her warning?

As they sat uneasily in the firelight, the king and queen suddenly heard, thinly from outside, the almost despairing cry, "Go back! Go back, King James!" And at that instant one of the serving women, glancing out of a window, cried out in alarm. James leapt to his feet, hearing as he did so the growl of many men's voices from outside the walls. Hastening to the window, he was able instantly to sum up what was happening. A swarm of torch-bearing men was surging into the courtyard below. He could see they were Highlanders, and that there was naked steel in their hands. James spun round to his queen.

"It is Sir Robert Graham—he is come at last!"

He turned to the women.

"Lock all the doors!"

They hurried to obey—but to their horror they found that every key was missing, every keyhole stuffed with material to prevent its use.

"The bolts, then!"

But the bolts had been removed. Even the bars were missing. Methodical treachery from within had made sure that the prearranged attack should not fail. Unarmed, unable to shut his attackers out, prevented by thick iron bars at the windows from even a desperate leap into the moat a long way below, James seemingly could only wait to be cut down. He knew no shred of mercy would be forthcoming.

Already the shouts were ringing clearly up the stone stairway. James took his beautiful queen in his arms for what he knew must be the last time—and was surprised to find himself being pulled sharply away from her and another woman's voice hissing urgently, "Take these. Wrench up the floorboards."

James stared at the long, heavy fire-tongs that the serving woman, Catherine Douglas, was thrusting towards him.

"The monastery vaults are below here. You can hide there. Quickly!"

Without more delay the king attacked the stout floorboards at the spot Catherine Douglas was indicating. The endeavour seemed a hopeless one. The voices outside were closer and feet were clattering on the stairs. But there came a new sound—the clash of steel on steel. The faithful pages were holding their post. Inevitably, they would be overcome, but the precious delay might just enable James to wrench open that entrance to the vaults.

With a groan and a screech the board gave: a rush of cold air confirmed that the woman had been right. With a hasty kiss for his queen, James slipped into the gap and dropped out of sight. Catherine Douglas turned without hesitation to the queen: "Try to replace the boards while we hold the door."

Queen Joan obeyed, while the serving women put their shoulders to the vast oak refectory table, hoping to make it a solid barricade for the door. It would not budge an inch. And now there came a dying cry and a roar of triumph; the last of the guards had fallen. Feet surged towards the room. Voices called for the king to prepare to meet his end.

Catherine Douglas glanced round. The queen was working desperately on the floorboards, trying to cover the hole. She would never succeed. The women might put their shoulders to the door but they would be hurled aside instantly by the rush of the burly men outside.

Then Catherine Douglas saw one last chance of gaining a few vital seconds' delay. She placed her arm through the sockets which should have held the door bolt.

The voices and clamour surged right up to the door now. There was a shove: the door trembled, but the bolt of living flesh and bone held. There was a pause, a rush of feet, and then a great crash of shoulders against the outside of the door. With a pistol-like crack Catherine Douglas's arm snapped, the muscles tore, and she fell unconscious as the doors burst open and the Highlanders rushed shouting over her prostrate body. But the brave deed had achieved its purpose: the floorboard was back in place, rushes scattered innocently over it, and the queen standing serenely in the middle of the room.

In the darkness of the vault, James could only wait and listen to the men rushing to every part of the room, thrusting aside the women as they searched every corner and stabbed their swords and dirks into dark places where the king might be hiding. He clenched his fists with impotent fury as he heard one man's voice demand, "Where is the king?" He could imagine the brute standing there, gripping Joan by the shoulder, his dirk at her throat. But James heard no reply; only an angry growl from a voice he recognized as Sir Robert Graham's as he sent the man about his business, telling him it was the king alone they were seeking.

It brought James some relief. Reluctant as he was to leave the queen exposed to his pursuers, he felt certain they would not harm her, while the two of them would have had no chance of escaping together. However he was to get away it would be at risk to life and limb. She was better where she was, as had just been proved.

To his sudden joy King James heard Graham order his men to search the rest of the monastery—every room, corridor and stairway of it. The entrance to the hiding place had gone undetected. They must have presumed that he had fled from the hall as they approached and was now concealed elsewhere. He heard the rush of their feet, and their curses, as they left the hall to the sobbing women.

In the silent dark, James thought desperately what to do next, and cursed a coincidence that might spell his doom. Only a few days earlier he had given orders for a gap in the wall of this vault, leading to the tennis court, to be filled in because whenever he played he had kept losing balls through it into the vault. The work had been done, and now he was sealed off from every way of exit save by the broken floorboard into the hall above.

Now James made a fatal error. Thinking his pursuers were safely occupied elsewhere he called to the queen to have him helped out of his hiding place. It was not easily done. A rope of sheets was lowered to him, but it was beyond the women's combined strength to haul him up. Catherine Douglas's help might have achieved it, for she was the biggest and strongest of them; but she lay barely conscious, in agony from her shattered arm.

Again and again the desperate women tried to raise the king and failed. They tied the sheets to the heavy table leg— but it stood too far from the hole and the makeshift rope proved too short to reach into the vault. During one attempt Elizabeth Douglas, Catherine's sister, was pulled off her balance and crashed headlong into the vault, to lie injured and immovable on the stone floor beside the helpless king.

Suddenly James heard a clatter of men's feet and saw the women hastily thrust back the floorboard, shutting off all light again. The pursuers had returned—and moments later he saw the dread sight of the board being wrenched back and torch-lit faces peering triumphantly down into his.

There was a pause, while swords hacked away more of the flooring and the ring of grinning faces enlarged. James knew that only a miracle could save him now: a miracle or the ringing of the monastery bell that would alarm his followers and the townspeople and bring them running in the nick of time.

But the bell did not ring. No miracle occurred.

With a cry Sir John Hall swung his legs into the gap and leaped down into the vault, quickly springing to his feet, dagger at the ready, to face the king. He was too slow. Poet and scholar though he was, King James had studied the martial arts, too. He was an excellent sportsman and wrestler, and before Sir John Hall could regain his balance he found himself jerked off his feet and flung to the ground, with the king's foot pinning his chest.

The next man down was Sir Thomas Hall. His feet had barely reached the vault floor before the king seized him by the neck and pitched him on top of his brother. There was a roar of fury from the watchers above as James swiftly knelt on the two men, his hands impossibly occupied trying to grip them by the throats and at the same time to wrest away their dirks. It was more than anyone could have done. He sustained cut after cut on his hands and arms without getting a grip on either knife—and now it was too late. Looking up, he saw that Sir Robert Graham had dropped softly into the vault and was standing over him with drawn sword.

Still kneeling on his opponents, James said calmly, "My

time is come. Sir Robert Graham, for thine own soul's sake, grant time for a priest to shrive my soul."

Graham answered, "James, my sword is all the shrift thou shalt have this night, and that a short one."

And he ran the king right through the body.

As James fell, clutching the blade, the other two struggled to their feet and began hacking furiously at him with their dirks. As they did so, the great bell of Blackfriars began to sound, too late to save King James I of Scotland.

He did not go unavenged. Flying to the safety of Edinburgh Castle, Joan, now the Queen Mother of James II, sent troops to track down every one of the conspirators. When she had them, she put them to death with the most fearful tortures that could be devised; but that is a tale of terror into which we prefer not to go.

The Heart Offerers

They had hacked their way through sweltering jungle and shivered across bleak mountain ridges. Coming upon a massive wall stretching away as far as the eye could see, they had marched through its one opening without knowing if they would ever live to return this way. They passed sinister pyramid temples, reeking of death and piled high with bones. But the captain-general did not falter and did not allow his men to falter. He was driven on by two passionate convictions: that these bloodthirsty heathen must be converted to Christianity, and that all their gold must be acquired for his homeland, Spain.

There was no doubt that the treasure was there, waiting for them. Messengers who came to parley brought beautifully worked gold as presents. Each side sized the other up. Slyly they sounded each other out.

The Spaniards numbered 400, augmented by 400 native auxiliaries and 1,000 porters acquired en route. They had fifteen horses and ten cannon, things unknown in this new world that was really such an old, savage world. Ahead of them lay a fabled city of some 300,000 inhabitants. Yet the leader was undaunted.

"To Mexico!" had been his cry when they left the coast, repeated incessantly as he urged his men on: "To Mexico!"

And now here, at last, they were.

On 8 November, 1519, Hernando Cortes set foot on the

main causeway leading to the city called Tenochtitlan, or
Mexico. Beside him was the woman they had christened
Doña Marina.

Of them all, Marina was the one with most reason to fear
what was in store. She knew more than any of these invaders
could know. Shielding her eyes against the brightness of that
city floating on its burnished lagoon, and watching the
magnificent procession that was streaming out to meet them,
she knew how easily they might all be killed . . and how
hideous the killing would be.

Marina was of noble birth but had been sold into slavery
from her Aztec tribe. With her gift for languages, she had
already learnt from earlier explorers along the coast the
tongue of these white Conquistadors. Cortes and his men
had relied on her from the start; and now Cortes loved her,
and she was his mistress.

The procession drew closer. Marina had never dreamed
that the day would come when she must translate the
words of this ruler whose name was mentioned only
in whispers, this man with absolute power over life and
death.

His dress was rich with gold and emeralds, resplendent
with feathers. Servants bore gilded mats, garlands of flowers
and flasks of perfume. The gap closed.

Montezuma and Cortes were face to face.

Montezuma descended from his litter. Marina saw that
the sandals on his feet were soled with gold and the straps
ornamented with precious stones.

He said: "You are welcome."

It was a simple enough phrase to translate. Cortes's reply
was equally banal:

"Tell the emperor I wish him very good health."

The two men bowed and exchanged a few more cour-
tesies, while their companions eyed one another as though
deciding where to strike if the formalities suddenly dissolved into violence.

But Montezuma hospitably ordered two of his nephews
to escort the Spaniards to quarters within the city. The sun
blazed down on their entry, and there was a rich smell of
spices and incense. Seeping through it, Marina recognized
another smell that was never entirely absent from any Aztec
settlement, whatever its size. She glanced at one great shape

against the harsh sky, and looked away. A colossal pyramid, a great flight of steps, and at the top the huge temple . . .

They moved out of the glare into cool shadow. They were to be accommodated in what had been the palace of Montezuma's father.

"You and your brothers," said Montezuma to Cortes, "are in your own house. Now you may rest."

That night Marina lay awake long after her lover had fallen asleep. It was incredible that they should have been allowed to get this far; incredible that they should be granted a royal palace to themselves; and even more incredible, surely, that they should ever be allowed out again?

Cortes wasted no time. In spite of Marina's trepidation, he asked next day for an immediate audience with the emperor, and launched into a plea for the establishment of the true faith in this land. Marina had difficulty in expressing the concepts of Christianity to the stony-faced Aztec. When she had finished, Montezuma nodded tolerantly and said:

"But we have been content to worship our own gods here through the ages, and know them to be good. Possibly yours are good also, but I see little point in your telling us any more about them."

Cortes prepared to argue, but Marina intervened. "My dear lord, do not be too hasty. You have done your duty for today—let it rest awhile."

Montezuma signalled that new gifts should be brought for Cortes and the three or four officers in attendance on him. He must have seen the greed in their eyes as they received these further examples of the goldsmith's art.

"I am sure," he hastened to say, "that on your way here you have heard many false rumours of my wealth. Jealous chieftains tend to exaggerate such things. I trust you will not be misled?"

Cortes looked at the hem of the cloak which had been draped round his shoulders, and remained silent.

"I am flesh and blood like yourself," Montezuma went on. "The dwelling-places of my city are simple stone and wood. I am a poor man like others—a humble servant of the gods."

Cortes asked the question which Marina had been dreading. "What gods?"

The imperial litter was sent for. The two leaders were escorted to the huge teocalli, the holy pyramid which loomed over the rooftops of the city. Its terraces were linked by one hundred and forty steps. Two chieftains flanked Montezuma and helped him to the top, but Cortes refused all assistance. With Marina at his side he climbed to the door of the sanctuary, and entered.

Cortes had never shown a flicker of fear or even of uncertainty on the arduous journey from the coast. Now, for the first time, he flinched.

In the gloom of the interior, the glazed eyes of gem-encrusted idols stared balefully down on the sacrifice that had just been offered. Five Indians lay stretched out with their breasts torn open. Five hearts, still palpitating, lay in a sizzling brazier. Blood was coagulating on the walls and floor, and the priests' hair was matted with it. The stench of burnt and putrefying flesh was overpowering.

Cortes turned furiously on Montezuma. "These idols of yours—these are not gods, these are devils!"

In fear and trembling, Marina croaked the translation.

"We will erect a cross on top of this abominable place," Cortes raged on, "and dedicate a chapel to Our Lady. Then you will see how puny your idols are."

Montezuma's rage equalled that of Cortes. "If I had known you would utter such insults I would never have shown you my bountiful gods."

Cortes was dismissed from the temple. Thankfully he and Marina escaped into the open air, down the dizzying steps.

Cortes warned his officers that there might now be trouble. They must be perpetually on the alert. But he had no intention of moderating his demands. He had a mission, and it should be accomplished.

To the astonishment of the Spanish captains, Montezuma agreed that a chapel should be erected. Not on the territory of his own gods, though: the Spaniards must choose another site.

While they were looking for the right place, they speculated and wondered. Against 300,000, how could they hope to survive unless the emperor was willing that they should survive? And why should he be willing, when the captain-general had derided his religion and cast acquisitive eyes on his treasures?

Only Marina understood. She tried to explain to Cortes, but although he seemed to grasp the general trend of what she was saying, its real meaning eluded him: it was too utterly alien.

Montezuma was not merely emperor: he was the high priest of the god Huitzilopochtli. But this god had once had a brother, the man-god Quetzalcoatl, the Plumed Serpent, who had founded the Aztec Empire. One of his last recorded utterances before disappearing from the world had been a solemn promise to return one day—to return by the eastern sea in the form of a white and bearded man.

And now here was such a white and bearded man, attended by others of his kind and by miraculous thundering cannon and strange four-legged creatures.

Marina might lie awake under a stifling cloud of fear, waiting for the Aztec anger to ravage the presumptuous handful of invaders. But was not Montezuma also, perhaps, lying awake, praying for guidance from his god? It was not hard for her, reared in the Aztec traditions, to guess at the conflict raging in his mind. If Quetzalcoatl reappeared he would take precedence over Huitzilopochtli. Montezuma, emperor and high priest, would be cast aside. He would lose everything. Yet without direct, unequivocal commands from Huitzilopochtli, he dared not risk the blasphemy of attacking this man who might be Quetzalcoatl. Was the newcomer truly a god; or was he not?

So an uneasy lull settled on Mexico. For how long?

While seeking the site for the Virgin's chapel, the Spaniards stumbled on a strong-room holding the imperial treasure, a huge accumulation of gold and precious stones. Oppressed by the hot and sullen hostility of the city, the soldiers began to murmur. They wanted to divide the loot and start for home. Although they had none of Marina's insight into the superstitions of the Aztec mind, they suspected that it would take only one little shift of mood for the emperor to fall savagely on them.

To placate his men, Cortes agreed that the treasure should be shared out. At the same time his captains put a suggestion to him. Why not take Montezuma into their own custody—have him in his father's palace where they could keep an eye on him, and use him as a hostage if need be?

Cortes brushed such an idea angrily aside. "We have been generously treated here. What possible justification is there for such a step?"

Fate, which had played so many tricks on both sides, chose this moment to play another one. News came that natives had attacked the small coastal garrison which Cortes had left before setting off inland. There was evidence of Montezuma's complicity, even of his having sent direct orders for the assault.

Cortes hesitated no longer. With a few men he stamped into the imperial palace. Marina translated his demands and watched as incredulity flooded the emperor's face.

"Before the eyes of my people?" he protested. "Do you not understand the humiliation? That my priests should see this happen . . . my captains . . ."

Cortes was implacable. The emperor's litter was brought, and before the astonished gaze of his people he was carried towards his father's palace. At every step Marina waited for the outcry. Montezuma had only to summon up his courage and raise one hand. He had only to speak.

But he was silent. And a greater silence now fell on the city. Everyone crouched indoors as though waiting, thought Marina, for a celestial storm so vast that it would obliterate the whole of mankind.

Not content with this annexation of the emperor and high priest, Cortes decreed an end to human sacrifice and ordered the removal of the statues from the teocalli. Down toppled the god Huitzilopochtli. And still no vengeance blazed down from the skies.

The Spaniards whitewashed the reeking walls and set up an altar to the Virgin on the sacrificial stone itself.

The suffocating, smouldering silence continued.

Cortes's first setback came not from the Aztecs but from his fellow-countrymen. Spanish rivals from across the sea were planning to dislodge him. Marina was baffled by the complexities of these antagonisms between men who claimed to serve the same ideals. All she gathered—as mistily and uncertainly as Cortes had gathered impressions from her of the mysteries of Aztec religion—was that eighteen vessels and some nine hundred soldiers had landed with the intention of overthrowing him.

Cortes took a mere seventy men and set off for the coast

to deal with the threat, leaving a faithful officer, Alvarado, in charge of the city of Mexico itself.

Within three weeks he had overcome his enemies and returned triumphantly with 1,300 picked Spanish fighters whom he had converted to his cause. Nobody came out from Mexico this time laden with gifts; but nobody came out to oppose him, either.

It was not until he was within the city walls that he realized he had walked into a trap.

The bridges on the causeways were cut. Barricades were raised. The Aztecs fell on the Spaniards with everything they could lay hands on—clubs, daggers, obsidian spears, stones, and the sheer weight of their bodies.

In Cortes's absence, Alvarado had clashed with the populace. On a religious feast day they had dragged out the deposed statue of Huitzilopochtli and set it up in the main square. News was brought to Alvarado that a human sacrifice was to be offered up. The Spaniards fell without warning on the crowd and cut many of them to pieces. They were still masters of the situation, but not for long: sullen resentment turned, as Marina had always known it would, to active hostility. Marina's nightmares were about to come true.

Penned more and more closely together, the Spaniards had no room for manœuvre. Their horses and cannon were useless. Slowly and inexorably they were driven into a huddle. At one stage, most grotesque irony of all, they had to seek refuge up the steps of the grisly teocalli itself. But to stay there would be folly. They could hurl back any assault—but they would inevitably starve.

There was only one hope. Montezuma must be brought out and ordered to speak to his people. He must put an end to the fighting.

Montezuma, still a prisoner in his father's palace, heard out the translation of Cortes's instructions, then lifted his head and said:

"I think there is nothing I can do to end this strife. It is reported to me that my people have already chosen another lord and have sworn that none of you shall leave this city alive."

Marina waited for Cortes's decision. He was a long time reaching it. She knew that he longed to stay and convert these barbarians, to establish a permanent hold on the country and the people in the name of his king and his country. But his men could not hold out forever. They wanted to take their booty and get away. Later, with stronger forces, he could return.

The clamour of the horde outside grew deafening.

Cortes said: "Tell the great lord that if his people will grant us safe conduct, we will leave these lands."

He omitted to add anything about coming back, and Marina allowed no hint of this into her translation.

Montezuma agreed now to speak. He was escorted to the battlements and looked down on the yelling crowds. As he raised his arms the shouts died away to a murmuring groundswell.

"My people, I entreat you to end this warfare. If you will cease to molest our friends, they will leave Mexico. This they have promised me."

One of his own captains stepped forward from the throng.

"O lord," he said. "Our great lord, we are truly desolated by the misery that has fallen upon you. But we must tell you that we have chosen one of your kinsmen as our new lord. And it is ordained that the battle must go on until death has settled all problems. We pray for you . . . and we beg your forgiveness."

As though this were a signal, there was a volley of sharp stone darts. The Spanish soldiers, straining to catch Marina's translation of what the Aztec had been saying, had allowed their guard to slacken, and one stone drove viciously into Montezuma's temple. He fell.

Marina watched as he was carried away. She watched beside Cortes as the wound was dressed, and as the emperor, crying out in anguish, tore the dressings away.

"Let me die!"

Two hours later, he died.

"The people must be told," said Cortes bitterly, "that only our respect for this great prince has prevented us from destroying not only their gods but their whole city. Since he is dead, we have no further obligations. Either they work peacefully with us, or we fight them to the death."

It could only have been a fanatical bravado that prompted him to have the emperor's corpse carried out and exhibited to the people. At the sight of the dead emperor—dead though he might be at their own hands—the Mexicans fell with new fury on the Spaniards.

For two days Cortes and his men held them at bay. But when, at dusk, rain began to fall and there was a lull in the fighting, both the priest and the astrologer forecast that this was an auspicious moment for flight.

Silently, in rain and darkness, the Conquistadors filled their pockets and pouches with treasure. They stuffed their horses' saddle-bags with gold. Then they set out warily towards the causeway.

The alarm was given, and the Aztecs raged out once more. Those Spaniards who had been greediest for gold suffered worst. Weighted down, they were driven off the causeway into the water and sank immediately.

Marina was torn from Cortes's side. She blundered on through the rain until another of the womenfolk dragged her to safety.

Not many reached the shore. Of the men Cortes had brought with him, and those he had acquired on his sortie to the coast, there remained only some 440 men, plus a few scared natives. Most of his best men and most of the cherished gold had disappeared into the lake.

The Spaniards marched away. There was a pursuit, but it was not as intensive as might have been expected. Marina knew why, but refused to let herself think of it. If the others also had thoughts of their comrades who had not escaped from the causeway, they did not speak of them.

What had held most of the Aztecs back was not merely the desire to reclaim their sunken gold from the water. The richest loot was that of living human beings who could be dragged back into the city—human beings whose living hearts could renew the briefly abolished tradition of sacrifice to the hungry gods at the top of those monstrous, reeking pyramids.

Bloody Sunday

They called it the blood-red wedding, for it led to the most terrible and bloody massacre in the history of France.

The bride, Marguerite de Valois, nineteen-year-old sister of King Charles IX, was the reigning beauty at the Court of the Louvre, and was gowned in glittering splendour. The groom, King Henry of Navarre, also nineteen, was dark-haired with eyes that gleamed with humour and vivacity. But despite the pomp and magnificence which surrounded the young couple of destiny, the atmosphere in the great Cathedral of Notre Dame was heavy with foreboding.

The man at the side of Marguerite de Valois was no choice of hers. Not that she, as a princess of the blood, expected to choose her own husband. But she had been bitterly opposed to Navarre. He was a Protestant for one thing, and as a Catholic that grossly offended her. She disliked him personally for other reasons. He was vulgar and provincial, dressed without distinction or elegance, and he smelled of sweat like any common countryman. He had endless affairs with females of no birth or breeding, and had the impertinence to accuse her of being as unchaste as Messalina.

Her mother, Catherine de' Medici, stood at the bride's elbow and the Princess Marguerite strongly felt that dark presence, for she was the only woman in the world she was afraid of. The Queen Mother had ruled France ever since the death of Marguerite's father, Henry II. She had insisted on this marriage with Henry of Navarre in order to bring together the Protestants and Catholics who had been bitterly fighting each other since the doctrines of Luther and Calvin had split the Mother Church.

Behind her stood her favourite brother, the King, whom she loved, and whose intimate relationship with her had been the cause of the displeasure of their terrible mother, who until recently ruled King Charles IX's mind as she did the French nation.

It was the crux of the marriage service. The Archbishop asked her if she would take King Henry of Navarre to be her husband.

Marguerite had just glanced across the nave and met the glittering eye of the Duke of Guise, who had recently ceased to be her lover on account of her forthcoming marriage, and whom she greatly preferred to the man standing at her side.

Her silence to the crucial question caused a profound sensation in the packed cathedral where both Protestants and Catholics crowded the nave, and everyone knew were ready to fly at each other's throats for the slightest reason. It was as if her silence could light the torch of blood and terror which was ready to set Paris aflame.

Suddenly she felt the King's hand upon her head, pushing it forward and downward forcibly, compelling her to bow in token of assent.

She then said, "Yes, I do. I take this man to be my husband." But her voice was so low that very few heard her.

The marital ceremonies continued for two days amid a riot of religious magnificence, which offended the Calvinists, and hectic balls and tournaments, which pleased everyone except the jealous Duke of Guise.

Marguerite quarrelled with her husband on their wedding night. He accused her of being Guise's mistress, and even of committing incest with her brother. She told him she wouldn't consummate the marriage until the court physician had assured her that he had not caught some disease from one of the vulgar country wenches he frequented. Moreover she was a Catholic and disliked being surrounded by his Protestant attendants.

"Well, your brother the King has a Protestant as his most important adviser," replied Navarre, his renowned good-humour failing somewhat before the biting tongue of his sophisticated young wife.

"Ah, Admiral Coligny." Marguerite fell silent. Coligny was the leader of the Protestant faction in France and was trying to gain ascendancy over the King at the expense particularly of Catherine de' Medici. Coligny wanted the King to lead a French army to the relief of the persecuted Protestants in the Low Countries.

Marguerite's loyalties were divided on the subject of Coligny. Her fondness of the King prompted loyalty to his royal wishes. But her lover Guise hated Coligny who had been held responsible for the murder of his father, the second Duke of Guise. Coligny, as a Protestant, aroused little but animosity in the mind of Marguerite, now Queen of Navarre.

The blood-red wedding had taken place on 18 August, 1572. It was an unnatural marriage designed to bring harmony. It brought instead hatred and slaughter. The Protestants had congregated in Paris in their thousands for the wedding, despite numerous warnings that a long-planned slaughter would take place. Marguerite was well aware of the gathering clouds. There had been massacres of Protestants before, but she had no idea on this occasion exactly where the danger lay—that in fact it was so perilously close to her. She knew that she was being kept deliberately ignorant of what was going on. Her nurse, Juliette, who had an ear for palace secrets, was her most valuable informant.

It was from Juliette that Marguerite heard about the attempt on Admiral Coligny's life on 22 August. It was a hot day, and her husband, in an attempt to heal the breach between them, had been extolling the cool breezes and lush valleys of mountainous Navarre. On hearing the news, Henry of Navarre had quickly left the palace to restrain the anger of his Protestant supporters, eager for revenge.

"The admiral had just left the King," Juliette said, "and was walking past the house of Canon Willemar when Maurevert, a partisan of the Guises, lurking behind a curtain, opened up with an arquebus. Just then the admiral bent down to adjust his shoe. One ball took off his thumb. Another lodged in his arm. His Majesty was greatly angered, and has ordered a very strict inquiry into the affair. Some

Protestants are fleeing Paris. Others are calling loudly for vengeance."

Marguerite was greatly disturbed. She felt dangerously exposed, in the middle of the arena, with a Protestant husband, herself a Catholic in love with the Duke of Guise, a man who had sworn to take the admiral's life, in vengeance for the murder of his own father.

"What of the admiral?" she asked.

"He will make a good recovery, madame. They say he did not even flinch when the surgeon cut off the remains of his mangled thumb with a pair of scissors, though it must have given him terrible pain."

"Has Maurevert been taken?" asked Marguerite.

Juliette shook her head. "They say he is under the protection of my lord of Guise. They do say, madame," continued Juliette in a low voice, mentioning the matter almost apologetically, well knowing her mistress's relationship with Guise, "that certain retainers of my lord of Guise have been stretched on the rack by His Majesty's investigators, and have confessed complicity in the attempt on the admiral's life."

Marguerite was well aware that Guise had a hand in the attempted murder. She knew also that her brother the King was afraid of the power of the Guises, as was her mother Catherine de' Medici.

It was a situation so threatening that Marguerite greatly feared for her own life, placed as she was in the middle of this deadly game of power between the Guises, Coligny and the royal house.

It was whispered to her that stifling afternoon, when the windows of the Louvre had to be closed against the fetid odours of the Seine, that Catherine de' Medici herself was deeply involved in the plot against Coligny, and that one of her Italian servants, with shoulders broken and dislocated on the strappado, had confessed as much.

Whether this was so or not, it had obviously not come to the King's ears, for Queen Marguerite of Navarre, with other members of King Charles IX's Court, was summoned to the throne-room. The young King, weak-minded, unstable, in many senses a pathetic figure, was trying in vain to assert his royal authority. The scene was dominated by Catherine de' Medici. She undoubtedly had a hand in the plot against Coligny; but she was as devious as ever and was loudly deploring the dastardly attempt on the admiral's life.

"Let you and your whole court, sire," she said to her son, "go and pay homage to the victim of this foul deed."

Charles IX showed himself to be still under his mother's influence by ordering the court to follow him to Coligny's house.

And so, preceded by trumpeters and precursors, the King and his courtiers processed to the house of the admiral. It was not far away, which was as well, considering the temperature was in the nineties and the putrid air of ill-drained Paris quivered with stench, heat and hatred. In Paris that afternoon the threat of terror could be felt by all, from the painted popinjays of the king's court to the stinking beggars and cut-throats who haunted the caves of the Seine.

Marguerite walked close to her elder sister Claude, the Duchess of Lorraine, who was telling her that terrible things were afoot, and that Marguerite's marriage had put her in a cleft stick—suspected by the Protestants because she was a Catholic, and by the Catholics because she had married a Protestant.

"But I married Navarre at the King's command," said Marguerite. "Surely my brother must protect me."

Claude shrugged. "Wherein lies our brother's real power?" she asked.

Their mother stopped their conversation just then and made them walk apart. Catherine de' Medici stage-managed the whole thing, and Marguerite was one of the few she permitted in the bedroom of the wounded Coligny, where the King swore a great oath that the attempt on his life would be avenged in a manner so dreadful that it would remain for ever in the memory of man.

After the courtly pantomime in the house of the wounded Coligny, Marguerite returned to the apartments she shared with her husband, who was still in the city endeavouring to restrain the vengeful ardour of his Protestant supporters.

The Palace of the Louvre was full of both Catholics and Protestants, as Paris was just then. Marguerite de Valois, Queen of Navarre, the King's sister, the daughter of the all-powerful Catherine de' Medici, suddenly found herself cold-shouldered by all. Even the most insignificant courtier found it embarrassing to talk to her. She was well aware of the reason. Her marriage had put her incommunicado.

The whole court was in a state of commotion. The Protestants were in despair at the wounding of the admiral and what it might lead to. The Guise faction kept themselves to themselves, whispering in corners, obviously afraid lest the King might carry out his threat to punish the authors of the crime.

Marguerite knew that her brother's court was a hot-bed of plotting and conspiracy. It always had been. Tonight, on the eve of the Feast of Saint Bartholomew, the atmosphere was quite intolerable. It was as well that no one spoke to her, for she had no desire to be dragged into the dark conspiracies which were afoot.

She was obliged to go to the *coucher* of her mother, and she went and sat next to her sister Claude, who obviously knew what was being planned and looked disconsolate. But she had no opportunity to say anything to Marguerite, for their mother said sternly:

"It is time for you to retire, Marguerite."

Marguerite stood up and curtsied to her mother.

"Good night, madame."

Claude suddenly seized her sister's arm and burst into tears, exclaiming: "Mon Dieu, sister, do not go!"

Marguerite was then quite filled with terror.

Catherine de' Medici turned angrily to Claude.

"You will say nothing to Marguerite," she exclaimed.

"But, madame, you cannot send Marguerite to sacrifice like that," said Claude imploringly. "If they discovered anything they might avenge themselves upon her."

"Madame, I beg you, tell me what there is to know," beseeched Marguerite.

Her mother ignored her. She was speaking in angry undertones to Claude, finally saying: "If it so pleases God, she will come to no harm. But she must go from here, for fear they suspect something." She then sternly ordered Marguerite to go to her bed.

Marguerite had no option but to obey, and she and her sister parted in floods of tears.

Devoured by fear, Marguerite returned to her apartments. In the Navarre bed-chamber was the sound of many anxious voices. She retired to her closet and began to pray desperately to God to take her under his protection from the terrible but unknown dangers of this night.

"His Majesty, your husband, is already in bed," whispered Juliette, "and requests that you go to bed also, madame."

"Oh, Juliette, what does this night hold for us?" asked Marguerite fearfully.

"By our Lady, I wish I could say. I only know that Her Majesty the Queen Mother had an awful audience with the King, who later rushed out of the council chamber crying: 'Kill them all! Kill them all!' But I do not know who is to be killed, madame. And they said that His Majesty looked quite deranged, not himself at all."

"My poor brother," whispered Marguerite, half to herself. "He does not understand. What have they persuaded him to do?" She looked at the crucifix lit by a single flickering candle. "I must pray for him too." She closed her eyes and crossed herself.

Then Juliette helped her into her robe and she went into the royal bed-chamber of Navarre, carefully concealing the fears she felt, for royal bed-chambers were not private places. Marguerite found the bed surrounded by thirty or forty of her husband's Huguenot followers, men she did not yet know, for she had been married only a few days.

Throughout the night these Protestant noblemen and her husband discussed the attempt on Coligny's life, and resolved that in the morning they would ask the King of France for justice against Guise, and if he refused they would seek justice themselves.

And so the night passed with Marguerite in the recesses of the curtains, alone and ignored, praying and counting her beads, unable to get a moment's sleep.

As Sunday dawned the tocsin in Saint-Germain l'Auxerrois began to ring. No one knew what it meant. A few minutes later there was a knock on the outer door and a voice said that His Majesty of France wished to see the King of Navarre immediately. Henry of Navarre went, escorted by his armed gentlemen.

Later Juliette came with news that all her husband's gentlemen had been disarmed, and God only knew what had happened to them.

"But what of my husband, Juliette?"

"He went into the King's chamber, madame, and Her Majesty the Queen Mother was there with the King, who said to him: 'Mass, death or the Bastille!' It is said that your husband, His Majesty of Navarre, agreed to abjure his religion, which was not worth more than his life to him."

"That at least is good news," said Marguerite. "We must pray for him."

Against the dread sound of the tocsin, Marguerite could hear the tramp of heavy feet going through the palace corridors. She told Juliette to bar the door, and then fell asleep out of sheer exhaustion, and the terrible cries she heard in the distant regions of the palace she thought were in her dreams, until there was a thunderous battering on the door and a man cried: "Navarre! Navarre!" Thinking it was her mistress's husband, Juliette opened the door.

A man burst in covered in blood, pursued by four archers. The wounded man threw himself on the bed and grasped the young queen's body in his bloodstained hands to protect himself. She screamed with terror and threw herself on the floor between the bed and the wall, and he came after her still holding her body.

Petrified and outraged at such a thing being done to her, Marguerite screamed for help. She had no idea who the man was and whether he was there to insult or attack her. As for the rough soldiers who had burst into her apartment, she did not expect them to be anything but brutes ready to kill her. After what her sister had said the previous night she thought that only the worst could happen. The archers were trying to get at the wounded man, and for all she knew they were aiming at her too.

At the open doorway, Juliette was yelling for help. The palace was in uproar as the murder squads rounded up the Protestant lords. Some were killed in their beds. Others in rooms and galleries. Many were thrust into the courtyard where the soldiers dispatched them with their pikes.

Eventually de Nançay, captain of the King's guard, came to the Navarre apartments. Marguerite knew him well. Many of these young officers of the guard had fallen for her languorous eyes and inviting beauty, and with one at least she had had a secret affair. Marguerite never passed herself off as a saint.

She practically fell into de Nancay's arms, beseeching his

protection, her flimsy garments covered with the blood of the wounded man.

Angrily Captain de Nançay ordered the archers to go, and berated them for their indiscretion.

"In the name of God, what is happening?" demanded Marguerite.

"His Majesty, your brother, has ordered the execution of certain Huguenots who were conspiring to seize power."

"And is the palace a suitable place for execution?" demanded Marguerite. The captain shrugged, indicating it was a question he could not answer. "And what of my husband, the King of Navarre?"

"He is perfectly safe and is in the King's apartment. He was not involved in the plot. It was your mother, Her Majesty the Queen, who appraised His Majesty of the Huguenot plot . . . As for Admiral Coligny, he was killed at midnight by the followers of my lord of Guise."

Marguerite said nothing. These were not matters to discuss with the Captain of the Guard. She demanded that the life of the man who had burst into her apartment be spared. He was now kneeling at her feet, his face twisted with pain, kissing the tip of her garment which he held in his bloodstained fingers.

De Nançay looked at the wounded man with indifference. "You had better hide him here, madame. Meanwhile I will escort you to the room of your sister, the Duchess of Lorraine. It is better you should not be here just now."

Marguerite changed her bloodstained chemise, and as Juliette threw a *manteau de nuit* over her she told the nurse to see that the wounded man was put to bed in her closet and his wounds dressed.

Captain de Nançay escorted her to her sister's apartment. The palace was like a scene from the Inferno. The corridors and galleries were littered with bodies of the Protestant lords and their servants. Marguerite encountered dying men, their throats freshly cut, arms outstretched imploringly. The place was a welter of blood. She was half fainting with horror. The captain had to support her as they went.

As they entered the ante-room of her sister's apartment, all the doors of which were open, running footsteps clattered down the corridor towards them.

A man in his nightshirt, pursued by armed soldiers,

almost ran into them. He was stopped in his tracks, three steps from Marguerite, by a halberd thrown by one of the soldiers, the point of which crashed into his back and pierced right through his body. He fell with a groan at her feet. Marguerite swooned into the arms of Captain de Nançay who carried her into the apartment of the Duchess of Lorraine, while outside in the corridor the soldiers brutally dispatched the wounded man.

While Marguerite was recovering in her sister's room, two members of her husband's suite—de Moissens, the first gentleman, and Armagnac, the first valet-de-chambre—came to her and begged her to intercede for their lives. They knew that Henry of Navarre was not able to do much for them, but she was the King's favourite sister.

Marguerite went to see the King. Her mother was there also. Averting her eyes so that they would not see the reproach in them, she went down on her knees to them and begged for the lives of de Moissens and Armagnac.

After some dispute her request was granted. Her mother told her harshly that the Protestant party was directly threatening the monarchy, that Coligny's house was an arsenal of weapons and that he was plotting to seize power and turn her brother Charles off the throne.

"And is all this bloodshed the only way?" asked Marguerite.

There was a wild look in her brother's eyes. It was one she had seen before, but never imagined that it was anything other than a look of weakness and frustration.

"I told Her Majesty, your mother, last night," he said, "that if the admiral must be killed, then all must be killed. I will not have one Huguenot left to reproach me."

Catherine de' Medici swept to the door, followed by her lady-in-waiting and secretary.

"You have what you wish, Marguerite. Be content. Your husband is safe and you are safe. No royal blood will be shed."

She left, and Marguerite was alone with her brother.

"Charles," she said in a low voice, "what has become of you this night?"

"You do not understand," he told her. "And would it not be proper for you to be more fittingly attired in the presence of your King?"

He turned to the balcony which overlooked the Seine. The sun was sending its first hot gleams across the city, and Marguerite could hear a strange, unfamiliar roaring. On the balcony an arquebus was set up. The loader cried:

"Sire, here come more Huguenots."

Marguerite followed her brother on to the balcony. Bodies, many of them alive and struggling in the current, were floating past in the river. Charles got busy with the arquebus, finishing off those who were not dead.

All around was a nightmare scene of carnage. Protestants were being dragged out of houses, thrown out of windows and hacked to death in the streets. The murder squads wore white armbands and crosses on their hats. All the Protestants' houses had been previously located. None was spared.

Marguerite heard the chant: "To arms! Kill ! Kill! Glory to God and the King!"

Marguerite stood there for a few moments in utter horror.

"Ah!" cried the King suddenly. "I got that one. See the way she threw up her arms!"

"Well hit, sire!" exclaimed the loader.

"My brother! My poor brother!" whispered Marguerite, reeling back into the room.

The nightmare that had started at dawn on Sunday went on for days. Marguerite locked herself in her room and would see no one. When at last it was over, her brother was no longer capable of ruling and his mind was rapidly disintegrating. That suited Catherine de' Medici, now completely back in the seat of power.

One night Marguerite was summoned to the King's bedchamber very late. He was in bed, his eyes staring wildly, his gentlemen making hopeless gestures.

"These fools say they cannot hear it," cried Charles IX. "Those shrieks and groans. Those screams. They are deaf if they cannot hear them."

"I am not deaf, Charles," said Marguerite softly. "I hear them."

"You see!" the King shouted at his attendants. "She hears them. I told you she would." He turned to her pathetically. "I am not mad. You *do* hear them don't you, Margot?" It was years since he had used that name for her.

She looked at him sadly. "Yes, sire. I often hear those shrieks and groans, and I hear them again tonight."

"I'll Cut Thee into Collops"

Astonishing, how the most violent deeds may leave behind no impression upon the places where they happened. To visit the village of Calverley, in the West Riding of Yorkshire, you would think that nothing had occurred there but the humdrum affairs of a spot that was remote until modern Bradford grew up four miles from it, a mere century and a half or so since. It stands high above the River Aire, looking across the valley. Children play round a bronze angel of Peace, bearing a wreath; young mothers push prams to the shops. A pleasant, orderly place, better situated than many, with no sinister air about it.

Yet there occurred in Calverley, over 360 years ago (what a drop is that in the ocean of Time!), a tragic crime whose echoes lasted almost until the bustle and bright lights of the twentieth century silenced them: some say they are not silenced yet. Little remains of the scene of that crime now. In the north wall of the ancient church are two stones carved with crosses, and there are other memorials in the churchyard. A part-medieval building which has lost its character and dignity is pointed out to interested visitors. They are surprised to find it fallen so low, but perhaps the old place itself is glad to have shed its memories. For once it was Calverley Hall.

Young Walter Calverley lived there when the first Queen Elizabeth was in her autumn years, and her people flocked to see the plays of Shakespeare. His home was the Great House of the district. It had been built in the days of the Wars of the Roses; it was rich with carved oak, fine panelling, lancet windows, its ceilings dripped with the plaster ornamentations dear to Tudor builders. For the Calverleys were rich squires. Old Squire Calverley, Walter's father, had been a Roman Catholic like his ancestors. But when Elizabeth came to the throne he made outward signs of conforming to Protestantism. Perhaps he did not greatly care which church he attended. He had a reputation for leading a wild, reckless life, and it was even whispered that from his mother's family some seed of madness had descended to him. His wife was a gentle creature, who had learnt to detach herself from the violence her husband and his companions brought home with them. Her younger son inherited her nature. He had gone early to Cambridge, where in 1604 he was studying Divinity.

Walter had also studied at Cambridge, twenty years earlier; or rather had attended the University, for his studies seem to have been minimal. His mother heard bad reports of him oftener than good ones. It seemed that he was growing like his father, and she sighed, for one scapegrace was enough in the family. There were gambling debts, rumours of a duel fought and a man killed. There were, particularly, stories of Walter and women. In those days men of humble birth seldom took revenge upon noblemen who had seduced their daughters and wives, or Walter's life might have been in danger, for his fancy lay in the direction of waiting-maids, college servants and such low-born girls.

"It's time he married," said his father. "And time he came home. I'll not have my substance wasted by such a roistering good-for-nothing." His lady glanced up from her embroidery, but refrained from any comment about pots calling kettles black. After all, her husband was quieter these days in his old age. She, too, would be glad to see Walter home and settled down, with her grandchildren about him and a pleasant daughter-in-law to gossip with in the long, lonely days.

And so in the summer Walter returned from Cambridge. He had neither degree nor honours to show for his years there, only pouched eyes, empty pockets, and a taste for drinking.

"A pretty sight, to be an heir of mine!" sneered old

Calverley. "Better wed swiftly and get money from thy wife, for I'll give thee none of mine!"

His mother gazed ruefully at Walter's dissipated, bearded face, shabby clothes, and careless bearing. He did not, even to her loving eyes, look a likely candidate for the hand of a local heiress. Then, as now, Yorkshiremen had a well-deserved name for liking value for money; it would be an unworldly father who gave his daughter away to such a suitor as Walter, even with Calverley Hall and its estates as his inheritance. But needs must, she reflected, and began to draw up a list of those young ladies in the Riding whose fathers might be persuaded that Walter's vices were merely the wildness of youth. And yet not even that held, for he would soon reach his thirtieth year: old to reform, old, even, to marry.

Less than a week after his return, Walter burst unceremoniously into the Great Parlour where his parents sat at dinner.

"Lay aside your thinking-cap, madam, for I've found me a bride!"

His mother clapped her hands together, and even his father's reproof was arrested in mid-oath.

"Hast been courting for thyself, then, Wat? Her name, her name!"

Walter poured himself a glass of wine and downed it. "'Tis Alice, Farmer Royd's lass."

Squire Calverley rose from the table with a roar. "A farmer's wench! Art out of thy senses?"

His son poured another glass, and refilled his father's. "Drink her health, sir, for her and her only will I marry!"

The scenes that followed would have discouraged any but the most ardent lover. Old Calverley bellowed and raved, his wife wept, the servants cowered. The temper of the son leapt to match that of the father until the Hall was a bear-pit of snarling and blows. But still Walter continued in his determination to marry the pretty Alice, who had nothing in her disfavour but the lack of lands and blue blood.

When the tussle had continued for more than a fortnight old Calverley sent one morning for his son. He sat at the table where he and the steward worked out every week the household accounts. For once his face was grimly composed. There was a paper in his hand.

"I've had just now a letter from thy guardian. The messenger has come swiftly from Kent, for I wrote My Lord there was haste."

Walter was silent. His father held out the letter.

"My Lord writes that he gives you his grandchild Philippa Brooke in marriage. Sit down and indite to him your joyful thanks."

"I will not do it!" Walter shouted, his face scarlet with rage. "I'll marry Alice Royd and none other. Let Cobham put his girl on the streets of Rochester, for I'll none of her!"

His rage was in vain. Lord Cobham, his godfather and guardian, was a powerful noble, the friend of Raleigh, brother-in-law of Sir Robert Cecil. His money and his influence were too great to be ignored, even by wild Walter; he would see that his ward suffered in pocket and person, it might be, if his commands were disobeyed.

And so Walter and Philippa were married. She was another such as his mother, gentle and yielding, yet a good housewife and a learned lady. Strange to say, Walter's surly manners and ravaged face seemed to have no ill effect on her. She was a religious young woman, willing to believe good of all men; and, besides, was not in her first youth, so that there was gratitude in her heart towards Walter for giving her the key to that great desire of women, married life and the joys and dignities it brought.

Soon after their marriage old Calverley died. His health had been worsened by his conflict with Walter, and by the shock of discovering that Walter had seduced Alice Royd, in anticipation of marrying her, and that her father's rage against the Calverleys was so great that they went in fear of their lives outside the Hall.

To the surprise of the village, Walter Calverley and his bride left the Hall after his father's death, deputing the care of his estates to his mother and her bailiff. They removed to London, where they lived in a house provided for them by Lord Cobham; perhaps the suggestion came from Cobham in the first place, so that he might keep an eye on his troublesome ward.

In spite of its ominous beginning, the marriage at first seemed a reasonably happy one. If it were not, Philippa Calverley did not allow it to show. Those who knew the couple noted that she followed her husband about with eyes devoted as a spaniel's, and that any lecherous approaches made to her by his wild friends were icily received. Two sons were born to the pair, their arrival apparently giving pleasure to Walter, who made a heartily affectionate if somewhat incalculable father, frightening the babies on occasions by his noisily drunken ways and over-rough sports with them.

In Yorkshire, his mother thanked Heaven for her son's seeming reformation; marriage had, it seemed, done for him what she had hoped and wished. Her joy was sharply arrested when Oliver, her bailiff, brought to her one morning a letter which had come by the London carrier. It told her that a large slice of the Calverley lands was now mortgaged to a squire living in Essex, and that this was by the wish of her son.

" 'Tis as I feared," she said to Oliver. "As we are, so shall we be. There is no changing the nature of a man. I must know all Walter's state and behaviour; Oliver, you shall go to London for me."

"I, madam?"

"You have travelled, and your wit is sharp. Go to Lord Cobham at his house in Kent, tell him you are my messenger, and pray him from me to find you lodgings near to my son's. Mark what he does and what he spends—who his companions are—how looks my daughter-in-law and my dear grandchildren. Spare me nothing."

Oliver's discoveries were not pleasant hearing. Walter Calverley was up to his eyes in gaming debts. Every night he gambled, holding noisy gatherings to suppress which the Watch had been several times called out by angry neighbours. He was drinking to excess—was sometimes drunk for two or three days together. Somewhere in Westminster he visited a woman of ill reputation. His wife was pitied by all, yet never complained of him by one word or look, nor did he seem to lack affection for his two boys, who would run to meet him when he staggered home from some drunken gaming bout as eagerly as though he were the most delightful father in the world. His wife was again pregnant. The worst news was that Lord Cobham was no longer in a position to step in and discipline Walter, or place him where he would be forced to reform: he had been arrested for complicity in the plot to put Arabella Stuart on the throne of

England, where James I now sat, and with him to the Tower had gone the great Raleigh.

Whether the bad news struck her to the heart, or some sudden illness attacked her, we do not know; but Walter Calverley's mother died before he came home in that winter of 1603, with his wife and sons.

The new baby, also a boy and christened Henry, was born at Calverley Hall. Walter did not greet it as he had done the elder ones, but muttered to his exhausted wife something about bringing another beggar into the world, and stumped out. Philippa, lying with her baby beside her, heard him stumble down the stairs, call for his horse in the courtyard, and ride away; and she turned her face into her pillow and wept.

It seemed to be from that moment that the character of Walter Calverley changed. Wild and debauched he had been, but now it was whispered that a devil had taken possession of him, so sullen and evil-tempered he became.

> As much unlike
> Himself at first, as if some vexed spirit
> Had got his form upon him.

So says the distressed Philippa, in the play which was written a year or two later, when all England had heard of Walter Calverley. Thus the playwright (who some said to be William Shakespeare) reported the conversation between husband and wife, when Philippa at last determined to plead with Walter.

PHILIPPA: Good sir, by all our vows I do beseech you,
Show me the true cause of your discontent!
WALTER: Money! money! money! and thou must supply me.
PHILIPPA: Alas,
I am the least cause of your discontent,
Yet what is mine, either in rings or jewels,
Use to your own desire; but I beseech you,
As you're a gentleman by many bloods,
Though I myself be out of your respect,
Think on the state of these three lovely boys
You have been father to.
WALTER: Pooh! bastards, bastards, bastards,
Begot in tricks, begot in tricks!
PHILIPPA: Heaven knows how those words wrong me, but I may
Endure these griefs among a thousand more.

> Oh, call to mind your lands already mortgaged,
> Yourself wound into debts, your hopeful brother
> At the University in bonds for you
> Like to be seized on. And——
> WALTER: Have done, thou harlot,
> Whom, though for fashion's sake I married,
> I never could abide. Think'st thou thy words
> Shall kill my pleasures? Fall off to thy friends,
> Thou and thy bastards beg: I will not bate
> A whit in humour!

Weeping and clinging to him, Philippa protested her innocence; she had never for a moment turned her eyes towards another man, had always loved him fondly. She would give him all—the last of her jewels, the dress off her back. When he had torn himself from her clutches and rushed away, half-mad with rage, she sat down and wrote a pitiful letter to one of her Brooke relations who still had influence at Court, despite Lord Cobham's imprisonment, begging him to find some employment for Walter which might redeem his fortunes and their happiness.

Her uncle, somewhat surprisingly, replied with the offer of a small but valuable place at Court, on condition that Walter did not disgrace him there. Joyfully she ran to tell her husband, who, instead of showing gratitude, threw her down with filthy words and accusations of trying to imprison him. She ran from him, sobbing: "Will nothing please you? Will nothing please you?"

That day there came to Calverley Hall a gentleman of Cambridge. His errand was to point out to Walter that his young, brilliant brother, who had unwisely stood surety for Walter's debts, was in a desperate situation. He had been arrested and was now in prison, his studies at a halt, his hopes of the Church receding. And this, warned the scholar, would come home to Walter in the form of retribution if he did not amend his ways.

"And take this from the virtuous affection I bear your brother, never look for prosperous hour, good thought, quiet sleeps, contented walks, nor anything that makes man perfect, till you redeem him."

Surprisingly, Walter took this quietly, even with signs of sorrow and repentance. The scholar's words, he said, had brought him to his senses.

"Sam, bring me a bowl of wine," he called to his body-servant. When it came, he invited the scholar to drink with him to his brother's health: "I pledge you, sir, to the kind man in prison," replied his guest, then, at Walter's invitation, went to take a stroll in the grounds, remarking, as he went, that he had come on a lucky day, for it was 23 April, the feast-day of England's patron-saint.

A few minutes later Walter's eldest son, now a child of about six, appeared in the parlour, whipping his spinning-top before him. He found his father standing in the middle of the small room, his legs apart, his chin sunk on his chest. And, says the old play, he looked laughingly up at Walter and said:

"What, ail you, father? Are you not well? I can't whip my top while you stand so—you take up all the room with your wide legs."

Walter glared down at the boy with a terrible face, the face of a fiend, at which the child broke into merry laughter. He had seen his father pull faces before.

"Pooh, you can't make me afeared with this! I fear no vizards, nor bugbears."

Roughly Walter dragged him up from the floor and shook him to and fro. The child's expression changed to one of fear.

"Oh, what will you do, father? I am your 'white boy'." (So Walter liked to call him.)

"Thou shalt be my *red* boy!" cried the maddened man, and, drawing his dagger, stabbed the screaming child in many places, and threw him dying to the floor.

"Bleed, bleed, rather than beg!" he shouted, and dragging the small blood-spattered body, rushed headlong from the room.

In the nursery the dead boy's younger brother was taking a day-time nap, watched by his nurse, Nan, who sat by his cot, working at her mending, and humming quietly, as the four-year-old liked her to do before he went to sleep. Suddenly the door burst open, and a wild figure she hardly recognized as her master's burst into the room.

"Harlot, give me that boy!" he cried, pouncing on the cot. When she shrieked and struggled with him, and called for help, he yelled at her, "What, are you gossiping, prating? I'll break your clamour and your neck!" and, dragging her to the door, threw her down the steep stairs outside. There was a scream and a thud; then silence.

Within a moment Philippa rushed into the nursery from her bedroom nearby. The sight she saw froze her with horror. Her husband stood by the cot, his face a mask of savagery, holding in his arms the wailing newly-wakened child, and pointing a dagger at its throat. She dashed forward, almost tripping over the corpse of her elder son, which had been hidden by the cot's hangings. Uttering shriek after shriek she clutched at her husband's arm in a desperate attempt to save the living child. "Your own boy, your own sweet boy!" she screamed. Walter sneered at her.

"There are too many beggars!" he snarled, and with one vicious stab ended the life of his second son, and turned his dagger on the mother who clung wildly to him, weeping and pleading. "Have at your heart!"

Philippa fell at his feet, across the body of her son, striking her head violently in her fall. He kicked her aside and ran down the stairs, passing without a look the broken-necked body of Nan. Within a moment he was in the courtyard, pursued by Oliver, who had heard the dreadful cries and feared that his master had committed deeds to match them. Snatching at his master's boot, as he mounted his horse, Oliver found himself kicked with demoniac force to the ground.

"Stay, sir, stay!" he cried. "Where do you go?"

"Why, to my brat at nurse, my sucking beggar! Fates, I'll not leave you one to trample on!" And Calverley was gone, riding like the madman he was, towards the village of Norton where the baby, Henry, was in the charge of a wet-nurse, for Philippa had been too ill to feed him after his birth.

Oliver, dazed and bruised, dragged himself up. His face was bleeding where Calverley's spur had cut it. But, thinking nothing of his own injuries, he limped quickly to the nursery from which such terrible sounds had come, and at the sight he saw he wept.

Kneeling by Philippa, and raising her head, he found that she at least was not dead, but only stunned. The strong steel corset which was fashionable in that year of 1604 had prevented the dagger from entering her body. Oliver carried her from the room, so that when she returned to consciousness she would not see her dead sons. Laying her on her bed, he went as quickly as he could for help; and within as little time as it took to summon his fellow-servants and saddle horses, the chase after Walter Calverley had begun. Leading it was the scholar from Cambridge, who had returned to the house in time to hear the cries of the murdered younger child.

Calverley galloped on the road to Norton as though the devil and not his bloody spurs lent his horse wings; and as he went he sang and shouted and cursed. More than a mile behind him his pursuers began to give up hope for the baby. They could not warn the nurse to hide it—she would be killed, and the child with her, unless some miracle intervened.

On a flat stretch only a qarter of a mile or so from the village, the miracle happened. Calverley's horse stumbled and threw him. Then, flinging up its head, it galloped away from the rider who had flayed its sides so cruelly, and soon was lost from sight. Calverley lay groaning and cursing; he had injured his leg in the fall and could not rise. Soon the sound of hooves reached him. The pursuers were almost upon him. With triumphant shouts they reached the spot where he lay, and the Cambridge scholar was the first to dismount and stand by his side. To his accusations Calverley returned only coarse taunts; and, as they bound him and dragged him to a horse, cried out loudly that his only regret was that he had missed one of his victims.

They could get no admission of repentance from him when he was brought before the justices. He would only reiterate that he was sorry "that one is left unkilled", and when asked by the justice if he could explain his monstrous cruelty, replied: "In a word, sir, I have consumed all, played away long acres, and I thought it the charitablest of deeds I could do to cozen beggary and knock my house o' the head."

Whatever lunacy had possessed him, they say that when Philippa visited him in prison, showing no reproach but only an angel-like pity towards him, his senses were suddenly restored and he wept bitterly and begged her forgiveness saying that he now longed only for death, and eternal punishment.

At his trial in York he refused to plead, and "stood mute", as the law books say of one who, being arraigned for a crime, either makes no answer or answers foreign to the purpose, thus refusing tacitly to throw himself upon his country for trial. There was a grim reason. Had he stood trial and been found guilty, as he certainly would have been, his estates, such as they were, would have been forfeited to the Crown and his wife and surviving child left penniless. By "standing mute" he condemned himself to a terrible end, the *peine forte et dure*, or pressing to death.

They took him to the prison-yard, and bound him, and piled flat heavy stones upon his body, calling upon him all the time to plead and save himself. But he would not, for all his agony. Only he cried out to his servant Sam, who stood by in tears, to "lay on a pound more of weight, lay on!" that the torture might be soon ended. Breaking from the group of bystanders, the old man ran to his master's side and flung himself on the pile of stones that hid him from sight. It was enough: Walter Calverley's moans suddenly ceased. But the gaolers seized Sam, and took him away, and hanged him for interrupting the process of the law.

Walter Calverley's flattened body was buried near the spot where he had died, at St Mary's, Castlegate, York. Legends say that Philippa secretly substituted another body, or an empty coffin, and had her husband's remains brought back to Calverley, to lie with sixteen earlier generations of his family in the churchyard. If this was so, it may explain why the murderer's spirit would not leave the place where his body had lived. Stories of his hauntings mounted. Many said they had seen him at night on a headless horse, leading a troup of ghostly followers, who delighted to ride down and trample any wayfarer they met. At last the Vicar of Calverley stepped in, offering to exorcize the "Bogie". In the room where the younger child had been murdered he held a service with bell, book and candle, ordering Walter Calverley not to appear again "as long as hollies grew green in Calverley Wood".

Still, to this day, the hollies grow green, but the spirit of the madman did not (perhaps could not) obey the clergyman's command. About 1812, over two centuries after the mass crime, the Reverend Richard Burdsall, a Wesleyan minister, was entertained at the Hall during one of his preaching tours. It was a cold January night. "About twelve o'clock", he records, "I was conducted up one pair of stairs into a large room which was surrounded by an oaken wainscot after the ancient plan . . . after my usual devotions I laid down to rest. I had not been asleep long before I thought something crept up to my breast, pressing me much. I was greatly agitated, and struggled hard to awake . . . the bed seemed to swing as if it had been slung in slings, and I was thrown out on the floor."

Mr Burdsall crawled back to bed, prayed, and lay there for about fifteen minutes. Then he was a second time thrown out; and a third, asking God as he felt himself once more dragged out from the bedclothes, "Lord, am I in my right senses?" At last, about one o'clock, the troublings ceased. But he sat up all night, afraid to lie down again in that terrible room.

About 1872 a bell in Calverley Church tower suddenly began to toll. It was the hour of one, the time at which Mr Burdsall had been freed from his tormenting. The bell went on tolling until the villagers, one by one, awoke and ran into the street, "struck dumb with terror and cold". The church keys were missing. "Toll, toll, toll! still went out the mysterious sounds in the night winds. At last came the keys; but just as they rattled at the keyhole the noises stopped, and all was silent as death."

A Bradford man was reminded by this incident of his own youthful days in Calverley, when he had joined a group of other lads in a joking attempt to raise the ghost of the "Wicked Squire". After school hours they met in the dusk near the church. Putting down their caps on the ground in a pyramidal form (with some unconscious memories of the magic pentagon, perhaps) they formed a circle, holding hands, and marched round singing:

Old Calverley, old Calverley, I have thee by the ears,
I'll cut thee into collops, unless thee appears.

As they marched, they scattered on the ground bread-crumbs mixed with pins, and others of their schoolmates went round to each of the church doors, whistling through the keyholes and repeating the same doggerel. What happened then is hard to discover. But it seems that Something appeared: some figure so terrifying that the boys ran for their lives, leaving their caps where they lay.

Poor Walter Calverley, most unhappy of ghosts, whose

inherited seeds of madness turned him into a mass murderer. Perhaps he rests now, near by the place where the bronze angel holds out her wreath, and young mothers wheel their babies. Yet, in Calverley, the tradition of his "walk" still lingers. The childhood of at least one inhabitant of what remains of Calverley Hall was shadowed by fears of what Old Walter would do, if she stayed out after dark. Within, the old ceiling beams look down on the spot where Calverley met with the scholar from Cambridge, and the stairs are firm down which he rushed to his last ride. All looks innocent enough, in the bright Autumn sunshine; but Shakespeare, who may or may not have made Walter Calverley's tragedy into a play, wrote truly enough that "the evil that men do lives after them".

The People Eaters

From time to time in the course of human history natural depravity plumbs new depths—and not only during wars. The Sawney Beane case in the early seventeenth century concerned a family that lived in a cave and chose murder, cannibalism and incest as its way of life. For twenty-five years this family, rejecting all accepted standards of human behaviour and morality, carried on a vicious guerilla war against humanity. Even a medieval world accustomed to torture and violence was horrified.

Because over the years a large family was ultimately involved, most of whom had been born and raised in fantastic conditions under which they accepted such an existence as normal, taking their standards from the criminal behaviour of their parents, the case raises some interesting legal and moral issues. Retribution when it finally came was quick and merciless, but for many of the forty-eight Beanes who were duly put to death it may have been unjust.

The story itself is simple enough, though scarcely credible, and has been well authenticated. Sawney Beane was a Scot, born within a few miles of Edinburgh in the reign of James VI of Scotland, who was also James I of England. His father worked on the land, and Sawney was no doubt brought up to follow the same hard-working but honourable career. But Sawney soon discovered that honest work of any kind was not his natural métier. At a very early age he began to exhibit what would today be regarded as delinquent traits. He was lazy, cunning and vicious, and resentful of authority of any kind.

As soon as he was old enough to look after himself he decided to leave home and live on his wits. They were to serve him very well for many years. He took with him a young woman of an equally irresponsible and evil disposition, and they went to set up "home" together on the Scottish coast by Galloway.

Home turned out to be a cave in a cliff by the sea, with a strip of yellow sand as a forecourt when the tide was out. It was a gigantic cave, penetrating more than a mile into the solid rock of the rather wild hinterland, with many tortuous windings and side passages. A short way from the entrance of the cave all was in complete darkness. Twice a day at high tide several hundred yards of the cave's entrance passage were flooded, which formed a deterrent to intruders. In this dark damp hole they decided to make their home. It seemed unlikely that they would ever be discovered.

In practice, the cave proved to be a lair rather than a home, and from this lair Sawney Beane launched a reign of terror which was to last for a quarter of a century. It was Sawney's plan to live on the proceeds of robbery, and it proved to be a simple enough matter to ambush travellers on the lonely narrow roads connecting nearby villages. In order to ensure that he could never be identified and tracked down, Sawney made a point of murdering his victims.

His principal requirement was money with which he could buy food at the village shops and markets, but he also stole jewellery, watches, clothing and any other articles of practical or potential value. He was shrewd enough not to attempt to sell valuables which might be recognized; these were simply stock-piled in the cave as unrealizable assets.

Although the stock-pile grew, the money gained from robbery and murder was not sufficient to maintain even the Sawney Beane's modest standard of living. People in that wild part of Scotland were not in the habit of carrying a great deal of money on their persons. Sawney's problem, as a committed troglodyte, was how to obtain enough food when money was in short supply and any attempt to sell stolen valuables taken from murdered victims might send him to the gallows. He chose the simple answer. Why waste the bodies of the people he had killed? Why not eat them?

This he and his wife proceeded to do. After an ambush on a nearby coastal road he dragged the body back to the cave. There, deep in the Scottish bedrock, in the pallid light of a tallow candle, he and his wife disembowelled and dismembered his victim. The limbs and edible flesh were dried, salted and pickled, and hung on improvised hooks around the walls of the cave to start a larder of human meat on which they were to survive, indeed thrive, for more than two decades. The bones were stacked in another part of the cave system.

Naturally, these abductions created intense alarm in the area. The succession of murders had been terrifying enough, but the complete disappearance of people travelling alone along the country roads was demoralizing. Although determined efforts were made to find the bodies of the victims and their killer, Sawney was never discovered. The cave was too deep and complex for facile exploration. Nobody suspected that the unseen marauder of Galloway could possibly live in a cave which twice a day was flooded with water. And nobody imagined for a moment that the missing people were, in fact, being eaten.

The Sawney way of life settled down into a pattern. His wife began to produce children, who were brought up in the cave. The family were by no means confined to the cave. Now that the food problem had been satisfactorily solved, the money stolen from victims could be used to buy other essentials. From time to time they were able to venture cautiously and discreetly into nearby towns and villages on shopping expeditions. At no time did they arouse suspicion. In themselves they were unremarkable people, as is the case with most murderers, and they were never challenged or identified.

On the desolate foreshore in front of the cave the children of the Beane family no doubt saw the light of day, and played and exercised and built up their strength while father or mother kept a look-out for intruders—perhaps as potential fodder for the larder.

The killing and cannibalism became habit. It was survival, it was normal, it was a job. Under these incredible conditions Sawney and his wife produced a family of fourteen children, and as they grew up the children in turn, by incest, produced a second generation of eighteen grandsons and fourteen granddaughters. In such a manner must the earliest cavemen have existed and reproduced their kind, though even they did not eat each other.

It is astonishing that with so many children and, eventually, adolescents milling around in and close to the cave somebody did not observe this strange phenomenon and investigate. The chances are that they did, from time to time—that they investigated too closely and were murdered and eaten. The Sawney children were no doubt brought up to regard other humans as food.

The young Sawneys received no education, except in the arts of primitive speech, murder and cannibal cuisine. They developed as a self-contained expanding colony of beasts of prey, with their communal appetite growing ever bigger and more insatiable. As the children became adults they were encouraged to join in the kidnappings and killings. The Sawney gang swelled its ranks to a formidable size. Murder and abduction became refined by years of skill and experience into a science, if not an art.

Despite the alarming increase in the number of Sawney mouths which had to be fed, the family were seldom short of human flesh in the larder. Sometimes, having too much food in store, they were obliged to discard portions of it as putrefaction set in despite the salting and pickling. Thus it happened that from time to time at remote distances from the cave, in open country or washed up on the beach, curiously preserved but decaying human remains would be discovered. Since these grisly objects consisted of severed limbs and lumps of dried flesh, they were never identified, nor was it possible to estimate when death had taken place, but it soon became obvious to authority that they were connected with the long list of missing people. And authority, at first disbelieving, began to realize with gathering horror the true nature of what was happening. Murder and dismemberment were one thing, but the salting and pickling of human flesh implied something far more sinister.

The efforts made to trace the missing persons and hunt down their killers resulted in some unfortunate arrests and executions of innocent people whose only crime was that they had been the last to see the victim before his, or her, disappearance. The Sawney family, secure in their cave, remained unsuspected and undiscovered.

Years went by. The family grew older and bigger and more hungry. The programme of abduction and murder was organized on a more ambitious scale. It was simply a matter of supply and demand—the logistics of a troglodyte operation. Sometimes as many as six men and women would be ambushed and killed at a time by a dozen or more Sawneys. Their bodies were always dragged back to the cave to be prepared by the women for the larder.

It seems strange that nobody ever escaped to provide the slightest clue to the identity or domicile of his attackers, but the Sawneys conducted their ambushes like a military operation, with "guards" concealed by the road at either side of the main centre of attack to cut down any quarry that had the temerity to run for it. This "three-pronged" operation proved effective; there were no survivors. And although mass searches were carried out to locate the perpetrators of these massacres, nobody ever thought of searching the deep cave. It was passed by on many occasions.

Such a situation could not continue indefinitely, however. Inevitably there had to be a mistake—just one clumsy mistake that would deliver the Sawney Beane family to the wrath and vengeance of outraged society. The mistake, when it happened, was simple enough—the surprising thing was that it had not happened many years earlier. For the first time in twenty-five years the Sawneys, through bad judgement and bad timing, allowed themselves to be outnumbered, though even that was not the end of the matter. Retribution when it finally came was in the grand manner, with the king himself taking part in the end game—the pursuit and annihilation of the Sawney Beane tribe.

It happened in this way. One night a pack of the Sawney Beanes attacked a man and his wife who were returning on horseback from a nearby fair. They seized the woman first, and while they were still struggling to dismount the man had her stripped and disembowelled, ready to be dragged off to the cave. The husband, driven berserk by the swift atrocity and realizing that he was hopelessly outnumbered by utterly ruthless fiends, fought desperately to escape. In the vicious engagement some of the Sawneys were trampled underfoot.

But he, too, would have been taken and murdered had not a group of other riders, some twenty or more, also returning from the fair, arrived unexpected on the scene. For the first time the Sawney Beanes found themselves at a disadvantage, and discovered that courage was not their most prominent virtue. After a brief and violent skirmish they abandoned the fight and scurried like rats back to their cave, leaving the mutilated body of the woman behind. At last the authorities had found a living survivor, a dead victim, and a score of witnesses. The incident was to be the Sawneys' first and last serious error of tactics and policy.

The man, the only one on record known to have escaped from a Sawney ambush, was taken to the Chief Magistrate of Glasgow to describe his harrowing experience. This evidence was the break-through for which the magistrate had been waiting for a long time. The long catalogue of missing people and pickled human remains seemed to be reaching its final page and denouement; a gang of men and youths were involved, and had been involved for years, and they had to be tracked down. They obviously lived locally, in the Galloway area, and past discoveries suggested that they were cannibals. The disembowelled woman proved the point, if proof were needed.

The matter was so serious that the Chief Magistrate communicated directly with King James VI, and the king apparently took an equally serious view, for he went in person to Galloway with a small army of four hundred armed men and a host of tracker dogs. The Sawney Beanes were in trouble.

The king, with his officers and retinue, and the assistance of local volunteers, set out systematically on one of the biggest manhunts in history. They explored the entire Galloway countryside and coast—and discovered nothing. When patrolling the shore they would have walked past the partly waterlogged cave itself had not the dogs, scenting the faint odour of death and decay, started baying and howling, and trying to splash their way into the dark interior.

This seemed to be it. The pursuers took no chances. They knew they were dealing with vicious, ruthless men who had been in the murder business for a long time. With flaming torches to provide a flickering light, and swords at the ready, they advanced cautiously but methodically along the narrow twisting passages of the cave. In due course they reached the charnel house at the end of the mile-deep cave that was the home and operational base of the Sawney Beane cannibals.

A dreadful sight greeted their eyes. Along the damp walls of the cave human limbs and cuts of bodies, male and female, were hung in rows like carcasses of meat in a butcher's cold room. Elsewhere they found bundles of clothing and piles of valuables, including watches, rings and jewellery. In an adjoining cavern there was a heap of bones collected over some twenty-five years.

The entire Sawney Beane family, all forty-eight of them, were in residence; they were lying low, knowing that an army four hundred strong was on their tail. There was a fight, but for the Sawneys there was literally no escape. The exit from the cave was blocked with armed men who meant business. They were trapped and duly arrested. With the king himself still in attendance they were marched to Edinburgh—but not for trial. Cannibals such as the Sawneys did not merit the civilized amenities of judge and jury. The prisoners numbered twenty-seven men and twenty-one women of which all but two, the original parents, had been conceived and brought up as cave-dwellers, raised from childhood on human flesh, and taught that robbery and murder were the normal way of life. For this wretched incestuous horde of cannibals there was to be no mercy, and no pretence of justice—if ever any one of them merited justice.

The Sawney Beanes of both sexes were condemned to death in an arbitrary fashion because their crimes over a generation of years were adjudged to be so infamous and offensive as to preclude the normal process of law, evidence and jurisdiction. They were outcasts of society and had no rights, even the youngest and most innocent of them.

All were executed on the following day, in accordance with the conventions and procedures of the age. The men were dismembered, just as they had dismembered their victims. Their arms and legs were cut off while they were still alive and conscious, and they were left to bleed to death, watched by their women. And then the women themselves were burned like witches in great fires.

At no time did any one of them express remorse or repentance. But, on the other hand, it must be remembered that the children and grandchildren of Sawney Beane and his wife had been brought up to accept the cave-dwelling cannibalistic life as normal. They had known no other life, and in a very real sense they had been well and truly "brainwashed", in modern terminology. They were isolated from society, and their moral and ethical standards were those of Sawney Beane himself. He was the father figure and mentor in a small, tightly integrated community. They were trained to regard murder and cannibalism as right and normal, and they saw no wrong in it.

It poses the question as to how much of morality is the product of environment and training, and how much is (or should be) due to some instinctive but indefinable inner voice of, perhaps, conscience. Did the younger Sawney Beanes know that what they were doing was wrong?

Whether they knew or not, they paid the supreme penalty just the same.

The Campden Wonder

Ask us which is the most beautiful little town in Britain,
and we shall answer without a pause: Chipping Campden.
Challenge us to name the most harmonious street of any we
have seen in the world, and we shall declare that the single
street which constitutes Chipping Campden is that one.
Press us to say which place, of all places we know, transmits
most vibrations from the centuries of its past—and you can,
by now, guess what our reply is going to be.

Our work and life does not take us much into the Cots-
wolds—worse luck; but we seem to find ourselves in dear
Chipping about once a year, for a day or two. We have been
there at most seasons. Summer, of course, or warm spring or
autumn, are the times when the twin rows of ancient houses
appear at their most enchanting: when the light plays on
their stonework and brings out those yellows and purples
which no other stone seems to possess; and the warmth seems
to be seeping into the very marrow of the buildings, a store
of snugness against bleaker times.

But it is in winter that we ourselves feel shivers of the past
at Chipping Campden. After dark we venture from our hotel
and walk the length of that fine street, meeting never a soul
and oblivious to the occasional motor vehicle that hisses past
on the damp road. A strong Cotswold wind is in our faces
and leaves whirl about our feet as we pass the open-ended
Market Hall and one after another of those large and small

houses of the fourteenth, fifteenth and sixteenth centuries which blend so well together that they might have been built simultaneously to comprise a town plan of unsurpassed inspiration. Curtains are drawn in the little leaded windows; but here and there a chink shows through, yellow as lamplight, rather than electricity; and just occasionally there is an uncovered window, and only the glow of firelight, and a passing glimpse of a small, low-ceilinged room with dark oil paintings and heavy old oak.

We cross the road and climb the few stone steps to the walled terrace which passes in front of the almshouses given in the seventeenth century by Baptist Hicks, first Viscount Campden, the wealthy mercer who carried the name of his little wool town to the part of London he owned, Campden Hill. The church is in front of us now; a tall, square tower, ghostly white in the moon, with four weather vanes swinging in the wind which is tossing the trees below. And to our right, even more spectral in this timeless moment, are the strange remains, twin gazebos, of a once magnificent house built by Hicks but destroyed not long after his death by the local royalist garrison commander to prevent it falling into the hands of Cromwell's men.

It is as we stand beneath that church tower, with the trees restless around us and the moon lighting those pale remains like a setting for some intensely atmospheric stage play, that our thoughts invariably turn to that seventeenth day of August in the Year of Our Lord 1660 when people came tumbling out of those very houses we have just passed to search for a murdered man; and then again later to see John Perry being hustled before the Justice of the Peace to account for his curious movements of the night before, when he had started out from this very place to seek his master, who had not come home: an examination that prefaced a time of terror for two people and first revealed a mystery that has never been solved—"being one of the most remarkable Occurrences which hath happened in the Memory of Man".

Edward Harrison, son of William Harrison, Steward to the Lady Viscountess Campden, deposes: "Upon Thursday, the sixteenth day of August, 1660, my Father, being seventy years of age, walked from Campden to Charringworth, about two miles, to receive my Lady's rent; and, not returning so early as formerly, my Mother, between Eight and Nine of the Clock, sent her servant, John Perry, to meet my Father on the Way from Charringworth. But neither my Father nor John Perry returning that Night, the next morning early I went towards Charringworth to enquire after my Father. On the Way I met Perry coming thence, and, being informed by him that my Father was not there, we went together to Ebrington, between Charringworth and Campden, where we were told by one Daniel that my Father had called at his House the Evening before, in his return from Charringworth, but stayed not. We then went to Paxford, about Half a Mile thence, where, hearing nothing of my Father, we returned towards Campden.

"On the way, hearing a man speak of a Hat, Collar and Comb having been taken up in the Highway between Ebrington and Campden by a poor woman working in the fields, we sought her out. She showed us the items, and we knew them at once to be my Father's. The Hat and Comb were hacked and cut and the Collar Bloody. The Woman then brought us to the Place where she found them, near unto a great Furz-brake, and there we searched for my Father, supposing he had been murthered; but nothing could we find."

The news of this, spreading like fire through little Campden, had brought its whole population—men, women and children—hurrying into the streets and down the Ebrington road to search for William Harrison's body. They found nothing. Mrs Harrison, apparently not altogether happy with her servant's manner and the account he gave her of his efforts to find his master the previous night, approached the Justice of the Peace and asked him to conduct an official examination of the man's account.

John Perry, servant to William Harrison, Steward to the Lady Viscountess Campden, deposes: "My Mistress sending me to meet my Master betwen Eight and Nine of the Clock in the Evening, I went towards Charringworth a short distance and there met William Reed, of Campden. I acquainted him of my Errand, and told him that, it growing dark, I was afraid to go forwards and would therefore return and fetch my Young Master's Horse and return with him. William Reed walked with me as far as my Master's gate, where he parted with me and I stayed still. Then John Pearce came by and I went with him about a Bow's Shot into the Fields, and then returned with him to my Master's gate again. Then I went into my Master's Hen-roost, where I lay about an Hour, but slept not; and when the Clock struck Twelve, arising I lost my Way, and so lay the rest of the Night under a Hedge.

"At daybreak this Morning I went to Charringworth where I enquired for my Master of Edward Plaisterer, who told me he had been with him the Afternoon before and had given him three and twenty Pounds. I then went to William Curtis, of the same Town, who told me he had heard my Master was at his House yesterday, but, not being at Home, did not see him. So I returned homewards, and on the way met my Master's Son, with whom I went to Ebrington and Paxford as he hath related."

The men Perry had mentioned were examined in turn and confirmed his account. The Justice of the Peace turned to Perry:

"John Perry, how account you that, being afraid to go to Charringworth at Nine of the Clock, you yet became so bold as to go thither at Twelve?"

"Because at Nine of the Clock it was dark, but at Twelve the Moon shone."

This, too, was corroborated.

"And why, returning twice Home after your Mistress had sent you to meet your Master, went you not into the House to ask whether your Master were come home unbeknown to you?"

"I knew my Master was not come Home because there was a Light in his Chamber-window which is never there so late when he is at Home."

Perry's story was plausible, yet odd. The Justice, evidently reluctant to leave so unpredictable a man at large, ordered him to be remanded while a further search was made for the missing William Harrison. Perry spent a week in custody, part of it in an inn, the rest in prison, before being called before the same magistrate. He told the same tale and was remanded again. But a day or two later he was back before the Justice, who this time had some further questions to ask him.

"John Perry, it hath been said that during your Restraint you have told some who pressed you to confess what you know concerning your Master that a Tinker killed him; and to others you have said that a Gentleman's Servant of this Neighbourhood robbed and murthered him; and to others again you have told that he was murthered and hid in a bean-rick. And you have also said that, were you to be carried before me again, you would discover unto me that which you would tell no one else. John Perry, how say you, then?"

"Sir, my Master was murthered—but not by me."

"If you know him to have been murthered, then you must know by whom."

"I do, Sir."

"Then you will tell me now."

"Sir, my Master was murthered by—my Mother and Brother."

There was a moment's silence. Then the Justice leaned towards the prisoner and addressed him gravely.

"John Perry, you would do well to consider what you have said. It may yet be proven that you yourself were guilty of your Master's Death, as hath been suspected, and if that be so, you should not draw more innocent Blood upon your Head; for what you now charge against your Mother and Brother may cost them their Lives."

Perry swallowed hard. "Sir, what I have charged is the Truth. I would swear it still if I were about to die at this moment."

Pale but firm in what he said, he went on to tell what had happened.

"Ever since I came into my Master's Service my Mother and Brother have been going on at me to help them to Money, telling me how poor they were and that it was in my Power to relieve them."

"In what way?"

"By giving them Notice when my Master went to receive my Lady's Rents, for they would then waylay and rob him."

"And is this what occurred?"

"Yes, Sir. Upon the Thursday Morning when my Master was gone to Charringworth I was in the Town upon an Errand and met my Brother. I told him whither my Master was going, and, if he waylaid him, he might have his Money. That Evening, when my Mistress sent me to meet my Master, I met my Brother before my Master's Gate and we went together to the Churchyard, and round the Church, and so on to the Way leading to Charringworth till we were come to a gate, about a Bow's Shot from the Church, that leads into my Lady's Grounds. There I told my Brother that a man was just gone before us into the Grounds whom I thought to be my Master, though it was too dark to discern any Man so as to know him. I told my Brother that if he followed him he might have his Money, which accordingly he did. Following my Brother into the Field, I came upon my Master lying on the Ground, my Brother kneeling on him, and my Mother standing by."

"Was your Master dead?"

"No, Sir. Just as I came to them he cried out, 'Ah, Rogues, will you kill me?' At this I told my Brother I hoped he would not kill my Master; whereupon my Brother answered, 'Peace, peace, you are a fool!'—and strangled him."

Watching Perry intently, the Justice commanded, "Continue."

"Sir, having strangled my Master my Brother took a Bag of Money out of his Pocket and threw it into my Mother's Lap. Then my Brother and I carried my Master's dead Body into the Garden adjoining to that place and consulted what to do with it. My Mother and Brother bade me go and hearken whether any one was stirring while they would throw the body into the great cesspit behind the garden. I did so, and they carried my Master's body away; and if it be not found in the cesspit, then I know not where it is, for I did not return to them again, but went towards the Town and met William Reed and John Pearce, and walked with them a little as I have related, and then, as I have related, lay down in my Master's Hen-roost until Twelve of the Clock."

"What did you do then?"

"I had brought with me my Master's Hat, Collar and Comb. I gave them three or four Cuts with my Knife, then took them into the Highway and threw them where they were after found."

"What did you intend by doing so?"

"I did it that it might be believed my Master had been robbed and murthered."

"John Perry, is this your true account?"

"Yes, Sir."

John Perry was remanded in custody again. Orders went out for the arrest of his mother and brother, Joan and

Richard Perry, and for an immediate search in the great cess-pit. But when this disgusting task was done it revealed no trace of the body of William Harrison; nor did a search of the fish-ponds, ditches and other such places of Campden, and the ruins of Campden House. The following day, Joan and Richard Perry stood white-faced before the Justice of the Peace and heard him detail the charges laid against them by John Perry.

And this is where the Campden Wonder ceases to be a tale of mystery and becomes one of terror: for both Joan and Richard Perry knew, and the Justice of the Peace thought he knew, that John Perry's tale was a pack of lies from beginning to end. That John Perry had murdered William Harrison, no one doubted much; but why should he have concocted a story that would take his mother and brother to the gallows with him? Yet he had done, and he was sticking to it.

"Villain!" cried Joan Perry to her son, when she had heard the story. "Thou knowest this to be lies!"

John Perry smiled an icy smile back at her, and slowly shook his head. Desperately, Richard Perry appealed to his brother to tell the Justice he had invented the whole thing. Again the head was silently shaken. Aghast, mother and son appealed to the magistrate, who once more put the question to John Perry:

"Do you still say that all you have said is true?"

"Every word."

There was nothing for it but to remand them all. They were escorted back to prison, John Perry in the lead and his brother quite some distance behind. Feeling a sneeze coming on, Richard Perry pulled out his handkerchief, and as he did so something fluttered to the ground. A guard picked it up. It was a piece of white tape with a slip-knot in one end. When the guard showed it to Richard he shrugged and said it was a head-band of his wife's; but instead of giving it back, the guard thoughtfully took it to John Perry, and, without saying how he had come by it, showed it to him. John Perry at once shook his head sadly and said, "It is the string my brother used to strangle my master. I know it to my sorrow".

Every effort to arrive at the truth of this strange situation seemed doomed to failure. Further questioning by Justices elicited nothing fresh. The Minister of Religion tried his hand, and failed, too. Joan and Richard Perry continued vehemently to protest their innocence and to beg John to tell the truth, that they were wholly innocent of the murder. Their entreaties and tears could not budge him. He insisted that they knew full well they were guilty. He even added to their burden by deposing that it had been his mother and brother who had carried out a robbery at the same William Harrison's some time earlier and stolen a sum of money, a crime which had never been solved. Again they denied it. And when the leaves were beginning to yellow at Campden that September, and Gloucester Assizes began, the three Perrys were charged with this robbery as well as the murder. For some reason other than that they were all telling the truth, they pleaded Guilty to the robbery. Perhaps they did not wish to try the Court's patience by defending themselves; and in any case they knew they could seek pardon under the new Act of Oblivion, introduced by Charles II's Parliament to cover certain offences committed under the Commonwealth. They were duly pardoned, and it seemed that whatever diabolical revenge John Perry was seeking against his mother and brother, even at the cost of his own life, was going to misfire, for the Judge refused to try the murder charge because no body had yet been found.

Nevertheless, the Perrys remained in gaol—John claimed that his mother and brother were trying to poison him in prison, and said he dared not eat or drink with them—and when another Assizes came round, in the Spring, and William Harrison's body had still not turned up, a less scrupulous Judge tried the case. Again, Joan and Richard Perry protested their innocence; but this time, instead of repeating his implacable accusations against them, John Perry stated that his previous confession had been made in the grip of madness, and that he had not known what he was saying. The Jury were unconvinced. Having heard the evidence again they found all three Guilty.

The Perrys were hanged together on Broadway Hill, overlooking Chipping Campden. Joan Perry was executed first. She was widely believed to be a witch—a woman she was reputed to have bewitched some years before, who had been bedridden ever since, is said to have risen from her bed quite well again after Joan's hanging—and the authorities believed that by putting her to death first her influence over her sons would be ended and they would be free to clear up the mystery. No such thing happened. Richard, pausing on the gallows ladder, besought John for the last time to tell the truth, even if only to satisfy the world and clear his own conscience. But with death only moments away, John, "with a dogged and surly Carriage, told the People he was not obliged to confess to them; yet, immediately before his Death, said he knew nothing of his Master's Death, nor what was become of him, but they might hereafter possibly hear."

John Perry was left hanging in chains. Richard and their mother were buried beneath his dangling feet. Three days later, a woman who claimed to understand something about witches hired a man to open the grave, so that she might search Joan's body. She got a closer acquaintance with the corpse than she had bargained for. When the grave was open the woman approached it on horseback. The horse, frightened by the sight of the staring corpse, reared; the woman's head struck the swinging feet of John; she lost her balance and fell into the grave.

Now, this has been a terrible enough chronicle. The spectacle of a man deliberately bringing his mother and brother to the gallows for a crime of which he knew them to be innocent is ghastly to behold. And he *did* know, and we know, that his story of Richard's strangling William Harrison in the field that night, and of the body being taken to the cesspit, was all fabrication—for William Harrison did not die until more than twelve years after the hanging of the three Perrys for his murder.

Two years after the mass hanging the people of Campden once again came all together out of their houses to gossip excitedly in the street. Their topic was the return "from the dead" of William Harrison. With the weather-faded bones of John Perry still hanging from the gallows, the man he and his family had not killed sat down in his house again and penned his account of the Campden Wonder.

"On a Thursday in the Afternoon, in the Time of Harvest, I went to Charringworth, to demand rents due to my Lady Campden. I expected a considerable Sum, but received only Three-and-twenty Pounds. In my Return Home, in the narrow Passage amongst Ebrington Furzes, there met me one Horseman . . ."

Suspicious of the horseman's demeanour, Harrison said,

he had struck the horse on the nose, at which the man had attacked him with a sword. Another man had come at him from behind and together they had overpowered him.

"They did not take my Money, but mounted me behind one of them, drew my Arms about his Middle, and fastened my Wrists together with something that had a Spring-lock, as I conceived by hearing it give a Snap as they put it on; then they threw a great Cloke over me, and carried me away."

They had ridden until nightfall and spent the dark hours in a hay-rick. In the morning they had stuffed a large sum of money into his pockets, heaved him back on to the horse, and journeyed on. After three days' riding, by which time Harrison was more dead than alive from his wounds and "being sorely bruised with the Carriage of the Money", they reached Deal, on the Kent coast. There they met a man, and Harrison heard the sum of seven pounds mentioned. He was then carried aboard a ship. After some weeks at sea he and other prisoners were transferred to a Turkish vessel and taken to that country, where they were thrown into a prison.

"And then came to us eight Men to view us; they called us, and examined us of our Trades and Callings. I, after two or three Demands, said I had some Skill in Physick. It was my Chance to be chosen by a grave Physician of Eighty-seven Years of Age, who lived near to Smyrna, who had formerly been in England, and knew Crowland in Lincolnshire, which he preferred before all other Places in England. He employed me to keep his Still-house, and gave me a silver Bowl, double gilt, to drink in."

After a year and three-quarters of this slavery, Harrison's aged master had fallen ill and called him to him, to declare that he was about to die and tell him to do the best he could for himself. Clutching his precious bowl, Harrison made haste to the nearest port, where he found a German ship bound for Portugal. Its crew had been reluctant to take him aboard, for fear of what the Turkish authorities might do if they found out; but the sight of the silver bowl had done the trick. He had been taken to Portugal and there put ashore, moneyless, to shift for himself.

"I knew not what course to take, but, as Providence led me, I went up into the City, and came into a fair Street; and, being weary, I turned my Back to a Wall, and leaned upon my Staff; over against me were four Gentlemen discoursing together; after a While, one of them came to me, and spoke to me in a Language that I understood not. I told him I was an Englishman, and understood not what he spoke; he answered me, in plain English, that he understood me, and was himself born near Wisbeech in Lincolnshire; then I related to him my sad Condition, and he, taking Compassion on me, took me with him, provided for me Lodgings and Diet, and, by his Interest with a Master of a Ship bound for England, procured my Passage and recommended me to the Care of the Master of the Ship, who landed me safe at Dover, from whence I made Shift to get to London, where being furnished with Necessaries, I came into the Country."

It is a story as full of holes as a colander. The whole circumstances of, and motive for, the abduction of this old man are implausible: his picture of himself, handcuffed, with his pockets stuffed with money and a cloak over his head, being ridden tandem on a horse for several days in broad daylight to the seaside, there to be sold for seven pounds, is ludicrous. The circumstances of his slavery and his return leave detail after detail to be explained.

Harrison's account clearly did not satisfy his contemporaries much, though they preferred, out of charity to him, to accept that something of the sort had occurred. The alternative was too awful to contemplate: he must have wished to disappear for a while—either because he had embezzled some of his employer's money, or because he knew too much about certain local persons' activities under the Commonwealth, and wished to keep out of their way until the heat of retribution was off—in which case, he probably got John Perry to help him and to invent his cover story of a murder. Why Perry should have used this to get himself and his mother and brother hanged is a question for psychologists; but in the many studies, factual and fictional, of the Campden Wonder that have appeared there has been no shortage of suggestion that Perry did, indeed, take them all to the gallows out of some twisted fixation that was yet not quite insanity.

The Campden Wonder provoked one more death: that of William Harrison's wife, "a snotty covetuous presbyterian", as she was described. She fell into a deep melancholy during his absence and hanged herself after his return. Perhaps she knew the truth, or something of it, and the knowledge that she had helped to send three innocent people to the gallows on her husband's behalf proved too much for her mind.

A contemporary comment on the whole affair puts forward the expectation that "Time, the great Discoverer of Truth, shall bring to Light this dark and mysterious Business". It never has, but if you go to Chipping Campden now, and walk forth on a windy night and stand near to where it all happened, with nothing modern in sight and only those buildings around you which stood there when William Harrison disappeared, and the Perrys were hanged, and William Harrison came back again, you might feel, as we have done, that you are on the verge of being shown the answer plain.

The Approach of Henry Morgan

It was in the Year of Our Lord 1671 that the terrible events occurred. I, Anselmo Ortega, can remember so clearly the day that the news first reached us in Panama. It spread like wildfire through the city, no one talked of anything else: the English buccaneer, Henry Morgan, had captured our great stronghold of San Lorenzo on the Caribbean coast and planned to lead his cut-throats to attack our own city.

There was not one among us who did not know the reputation of these animals, who had not heard of the murder, pillage and rape that had befallen other noble Spanish settlements. It is not surprising that we were fearful for our homes, our kin and our lives.

We had thought San Lorenzo was impregnable. The forces there had been ready for Morgan's men, but still they had been beaten. Now the authorities had to rely on a new ally—the jungle. No one who has not seen our jungle can know how fine a defence it forms—without a trail a man would soon be lost among the dense trees and foliage, the thickly knotted undergrowth; and even had the way to take been plain, an army would be needed to force a path through that great green wall.

There was only one possible route for Morgan—along the Rio Chagres by boat as far as the settlement of Venta Cruces, then across land by the trail that led here to Panama. This was the way Morgan must come—and our authorities were

determined that he should not find the way an easy one.
They planned to make sure that there were no settlements
left along that trail for him to pillage, no food for his
murderous pack. Some argued that Morgan's band could be
attacked from ambush along the trail, but others said no.
If our troops lost, then their arms and supplies would fall
to the attackers: better to leave it to the jungle—even along
the Venta Cruces–Panama trail, a formidable foe. The plans
were laid, and we waited for the reports to reach us.

We waited for the news we dreaded, and the news duly
came. Morgan had set off with over a thousand men on 18
January. But the news was not at first bad. The jungle was
already coming to our aid. The Rio Chagres was low, and
there was not sufficient depth of water to float Morgan's
longer boats. The jungle comes right down to the banks of
the river, so there was no way for them to march. They were
forced back to their canoes, shipping the men in relays.
Their progress would be slow.

Hope began to spread again. Without food, perhaps the
buccaneers would starve, or fall with disease, or at least be
too weak to stand against an army. But it was a faint hope
that we felt. It was such a short time ago that everyone had
been saying that Morgan could never get past San Lorenzo;
yet San Lorenzo had fallen. While we waited for more news,
plans were being made to save what we could from our city
should the worst happen. It seemed impossible that our
beautiful city could be destroyed, and even thinking of such
an eventuality lessened the slight hope to which so many of
us tried to cling.

The news that reached us however was still encouraging.
The pirates were making slow progress, and the policy of
destroying all possible food supplies in their path was proving a success. The messengers who brought the news
reported that arguments and fights were already breaking
out amongst the hungry men, and the noise they made as
they came along was enough to scare off every wild animal
for many, many miles around. There would be no food for
these vile men.

So the days passed, and the news seemed good. One report
told how, on the fourth day, these pirates had fought over
a few old leather bags left behind at one of our guard posts
on the river. Men laughed as they heard how the renegades

had scrabbled on the muddy river bank just for a piece of leather to boil up for food. It cheered us to think of our enemies in such a plight, but our laughter had a bitter edge. These men might be hungry, they might fight among themselves, but still they came on. Each day saw them a little closer to our city. There were few who were ready to promise they would never arrive. There were many of us who prayed and lit candles in the cathedral.

The governor had already wisely made plans to save our city's treasure from the ravaging mob. A galleon stood out in the bay, and we began to load her holds with gold plate and treasure from every part of Panama. The nuns of the city, too, were sent aboard. Whatever else might happen in the days to come, we were determined that the holy sisters should never be subjected to the bestial will of the criminals who were marching towards us.

As we worked at the defences of our city, we listened to every rumour that spread, and waited for each new report. Each day the news was the same: Morgan and his men still have no food, but still they come forward. It was clear that they would soon reach Venta Cruces The order was given for the settlement to be destroyed. The poor people of Venta Cruces took what few possessions they could and set off for Panama. What they could not carry they destroyed. All that was left of this once-proud settlement were a few thin, stray dogs that roamed among the burning houses. Each of us, I am sure, felt the same way—better to destroy everything that we possessed than give help to that accursed band of thieves. But even so it was a sad thing to see the scattered groups of settlers with their pitiful little bundles being led into our city. No one spoke, but the thought was ever present in all our minds. How long before they reach us? How long?

Still as the reports came in, hope continued to flicker. Morgan had reached Venta Cruces, but his men were weak and sick. Surely even if they arrived here in Panama they would not be able to stand against our army? Everyone spoke of our victory over the buccaneers, but more to raise their own spirits than with real belief.

Other rumours were spreading. The buccaneers had witches among them who gave them magic potions to enable them to endure the hardships of the journey. Some even claimed that the Evil One himself walked among them with a troop of demons. Although I never believed the stories, I found my nights were filled with wakefulness, and the few hours' sleep with disturbing dreams.

The day after we heard that Morgan had reached Venta Cruces, two more reports came into the city. The first brought great hope and delight to everyone. Some of our loyal Indians had set an ambush for the English. They had waited, with their bows and arrows at the ready, beside the trail. As the English made their way through the jungle paths, the hail of arrows had dropped on them and many of the pirates had fallen, dead or injured. The Indians had then escaped, but a few brave but foolish men had stayed to fight. They had fallen to the musket-balls of Morgan's men. Of course, we were sorry for those men, but we were happy that at least the first blow had been struck against the invaders.

The second report that came that day turned our happiness to horror. It hardly seemed possible that it could be true. One of the Indians had stayed behind in hiding in the jungle. He had watched the aftermath of the fight from his cover in the trees, unable to move for fear of discovery. He had seen the buccaneers take the bodies of the fallen Indians and strip them of their few articles of clothing. Then they had built fires, and the clearing had reeked with the stench of burning flesh and hair as the half-starved men cooked and ate the human bodies. We had all heard of the dreadful deeds perpetrated by the buccaneers, but this surpassed even our most nightmarish imaginings. I remember to this day my feelings first of disbelief that even these most barbarous of Europeans could perform such acts, and then of a conviction which brought a terrible, numbing horror. These creatures that could feed on human flesh must in very fact be demons.

It is hardly surprising that many wished to flee the city, but where was there for them to fly? There were no ships in the harbour to take them—the last galleon had gone—and the only trail led straight into the arms of these inhuman creatures. I, Anselmo Ortega, am not ashamed to admit that I too felt terror and mounting panic. They were now so near, and it seemed as if there were no power on earth that would stop them.

After a while, the panic died away and a strange calm came

over the city. Now we knew the worst—the pirates would come to Panama, and only by the strength of our arms could we save the city and its people from destruction. Already we had taken steps to save the treasure of the city—but the greatest treasure of all still remained. At the centre of our city stood its greatest building—the cathedral built to the glory of God and to give thanks for the providence that had led us to this place. Inside the church was a great cross of solid gold and behind it a screen of the same precious metal. It was unthinkable that such holy and precious things should fall into the hands of the barbarians. But they were too massive to be moved to safety, and no man could say what place would be safe. We decided on a plan. The beautiful, shining metal was entirely covered by paint until not a glint of gold was to be seen. Then we left the cross and the altar screen standing in the cathedral, hoping that Morgan would pass them over as worthless. We prayed that our Lord would protect the sanctity of His Holy Image.

That night it rained, and as I lay in the shelter of my home I thought of the men out in the open so near to our city. I prayed for the blinding rain to go on and on until fever and starvation would drive these men from our doors. I fell asleep with the sound of rain drumming over my head. I awoke to silence. The rain had stopped—the issue would be decided in battle. It was almost a relief after the days of waiting, of reports and wild rumours, to know that the terror would at last be met out in the open. Before we had had the hope that somehow the jungle would save us; now we knew that that hope would not be realized. I took my musket and joined the other men in the city to await the orders for defence.

As we were gathered in the square, we heard a commotion outside the walls. For one moment I thought the buccaneers were upon us, that we had become victims of a sudden attack. But the voices were Spanish voices. The gates were opened and a terrified group of men rushed in to gain the protection of the wall. I recognized some of them as herdsmen from the countryside round the town.

An officer stepped towards them, his face taut with strain. He asked the leading herdsman where the cattle were. The silence that followed the question was answer enough. I felt bitterness and deep shame that these cowards should live amongst us. They had heard that the buccaneers were almost upon them, and, despite the oft-repeated instructions of the garrison commander, had fled leaving their herds behind.

All the careful planning of the city's officers had been wasted. For weeks they had organized the withdrawal of all sources of food from the path of the invaders. True, they had still arrived at Panama, but they had come weak and half-starved. Now all that was changed. In my mind, I could see them gorging themselves on the fresh meat, their strength returning with every mouthful they took. The sacrifice of the settlement at Venta Cruces had been for nothing. We should have to fight men ready for battle.

Our horsemen set out from the city, splendid in their gleaming armour. The moment for the battle was near. We followed on foot, marching out across the pasture-land outside the walls. It would be false now to say that we did not feel a chill fear at what we were to meet. My friend, Luis Gomez, was convinced that we would be meeting demons, and continually made the sign of the cross as we heard the trumpets of the horsemen far ahead of us. As we marched the sounds of the trumpets became louder, and we knew that they must have stopped. The enemy was close by.

We joined our cavalry at dusk, and found them facing the buccaneers. The Englishmen we could see making camp. Even at a distance of some hundreds of yards we could see that they were filthy, their clothes torn to rags by the march through the jungle; and in the flickering light of their camp-fires they seemed to us not very different from the demons we all of us now more than half-believed they were.

I settled down for the night with the other soldiers, but there was no sleep—only the thought of what the morning would bring. Across the clearing we could still see—and smell—the pirates feeding on the meat left by the cowardly herdsmen. I talked with my friend, Luis Gomez, and tried to give him some of the confidence I did not myself have. Before dawn we were preparing for the battle.

Our horsemen were the first into the fight, and we cheered them on their way, as much to give ourselves boldness as to encourage them. But our cheers were in vain. The horses stumbled as their legs sank into the swampy ground, and the muskets of the buccaneers had easy targets. The cavalry was forced to retreat. But we had other plans prepared. As the horsemen were slowly forced back to our lines some of our Indian slaves drove a herd of wild bulls at the English force. They were a terrifying sight as they rumbled forwards, their huge horns splayed wide and gleaming in the sun. But the buccaneers stayed where they were, and at the sound of their guns the bulls scattered. I felt my face grow cold and damp with fear. I am no coward, but I doubted if I could have stayed still in the face of that wild charge. What chance had we of beating these fierce men in battle?

Now the cavalry was scattering under the musket fire. Not far away from me a foot-soldier threw down his weapons and, screaming that they were demons indeed, started to run back towards the city. Soon the cry was taken up by others, and men everywhere were running for their lives. Luis was struck down dead beside me.

I stood at my place as long as I dared; but now I could see the wild, exalted faces of the Englishmen advancing upon us. There was no chance of standing to fight. My heart ached with shame as I, too, turned and ran back to the city walls. Behind me I could hear the cries of my less fortunate comrades who had been caught by the pirates.

Back at the city we made our last stand. We had cannon loaded with scraps of metal, pieces of iron, broken swords, indeed anything we could find. The blast from these pieces swept through the advancing English, but now it was certain that nothing would stop them. They had come so far, and now they were aware only of the scent of gold in their nostrils. Their attacks kept coming, and soon fires had broken out in the city. Resistance collapsed, as we fought to save our homes from the blaze. By nightfall we were at the mercy of Morgan and his men.

I will not tell of the scenes of murder and rapine I was forced to witness. They were too terrible and painful for me to describe. Even sadder to me was the sight of some of our womenfolk—happily, only a few—who submitted willingly to the beasts who had conquered us. Everywhere the mob could be seen searching homes for loot, raking through the smouldering ashes for any pieces of gold they might find there, and cutting down any man who was brave enough or foolish enough to stand in their way. I pray that I shall never be forced to witness such sights again.

I was taken, with other men, to one of the few buildings that had been left standing after the fire. None of us dared even to consider what our fate would be. Each of us held in our hearts one secret that we had vowed to keep from our enemies—the secret of the golden treasure that still stood untouched among the ruins of the cathedral.

It was the following day that I was taken for questioning by Morgan's men. Only one question interested them— where could they find gold?

Tempers were high, and though I could not understand their language, I guessed that they were furious at the small amount of treasure they had been able to find. I was pushed forward into a ring of pirates and forced to kneel in the dirt at their feet. Many of them were drunk; and, though I tried to remain calm, I confess to you, my friends, I felt there was litle chance of my remaining alive. One of them, who spoke Spanish, began questioning me about the city's treasure. I told them of the ship that had taken the gold plate away. There seemed no harm in this, for the treasure was by now well beyond their reach. But the answer only infuriated my questioner, who called me a liar and began shouting at me in English.

I could not answer, for I could not understand. But my silence only made the buccaneers angrier still, and soon I found myself on the ground while blows and kicks fell all over my body. When I thought that I would at last lose consciousness, the kicking stopped and I was dragged back to a kneeling position. My questioner then drew his sword and again demanded to know where the treasure was hidden.

Now, my friends, I am not a coward, nor am I a brave man. I felt at that moment that I was to die, and I was afraid. I knew that I could save my life by telling them of the gold cross and the gold altar screen, but the fear of God can be greater than the fear of men—even these men. I told them again that there was no treasure, it had all been sent over the sea. For a second only, I caught the flash of sunlight on the blade of the sword as it swept down towards me. I shut my eyes, and my head seemed to explode with pain. I fell to the ground, but I was still alive. I could feel warm blood pouring down my face, and through the pain I could hear the noise of the men gathered round me. They were laughing. I opened my eyes, and saw my questioner standing above me. In his hand was a piece of flesh, still dripping blood. He had cut off my ear.

To roars of laughter, I was dragged back to rejoin my comrades. A few days later we were herded together and forced to join the buccaneers as they marched away from the ruins of Panama. During the march some of us escaped into the jungle, and others were bought back from the English renegades by relatives and friends. The horror was over. Morgan and his men returned the way they came.

I, Anselmo Ortega, have not told this story to bring glory to myself. There is no glory in losing a battle, but I am proud that I never revealed the secret of the cathedral, and prouder still that my comrades too kept faith, in spite of the torture and mutilation. Today we are building a new Panama to the west of the old town that was destroyed. But the ruins of the cathedral still stand and the golden cross and altar screen remain where they were on that day in January, 1671, when Morgan led his men into Panama.

The Massacre at Glencoe

Winter in the Highlands of Scotland can be vicious and cruel, and so it was in the pre-dawn hours of 13 February, 1692. Even so, the snow, ice and freezing temperature were no more treacherous than the soldiers of the Earl of Argyll's Regiment who deliberately set out, in what is probably the only act of planned genocide in British history, to murder the entire MacDonald clan of Glencoe who, for two weeks past, had been their hospitable hosts.

That the massacre failed to achieve its horrific target of total annihilation was due in no small measure to the severe weather at the time—a blizzard driven down the narrow Glencoe gorge by a relentless gale—illuminating, perhaps, Shakespeare's words:

> Blow, blow, thou winter wind,
> Thou art not so unkind
> As man's ingratitude . . .

Nevertheless, thirty-eight men, women and children were slain, and of the three hundred or so MacDonalds who managed to escape into the icy wilderness dozens more were to die from exposure and starvation during the ensuing days.

Glencoe has been described as "one of the sweetest glens of the Highlands". Running east to west along the northern border of Argyll, it is a deep valley eight miles long, curving northwards like a bow at its western end and flanked by formidable mountains rising to over three thousand feet. The only natural entrances to this elongated fortress are at either end—marsh-ridden Rannoch Moor in the east and Loch Levenside in the west. To the north a tortuous trail winds over the jagged escarpment known as Aonach Eagach; this is the Devil's Staircase, and it descends not into Glencoe valley but into Rannoch at the eastern entrance. To the south, a pass through less precipitous mountains, where cattle can be grazed on the lower slopes, also terminates in Rannoch Moor.

Through the glen runs the river Coe, fed by hundreds of tributaries and swelling here and there into pools and small lochs. At the centre of the curve of the bow, north of the river, is a massive dominating outcrop known as Signal Rock.

In this wild, rugged valley lived the equally wild and rugged MacDonalds of Glencoe, the smallest arm of the Clan MacDonald. They could compete with any in their arrogant pride, and could trace their ancestry back to the Lord of the Isles (the self-proclaimed title of the son of Angus Og of Islay, who had fought with Robert Bruce at Bannockburn). The five small townships strung along the Coe valley sustained some four hundred MacDonalds who owed fealty to tall, burly Alasdair MacIain, who had inherited the fiery red hair of his family.

Born in the 1630s, Alasdair had followed the tradition of the sons of Highland chiefs by spending several years in Paris to acquire some gloss of culture and civilization. He returned to Glencoe when his father died in 1650, and duly married a kinswoman. She bore him two sons—John and Alasdair the younger. The latter, as he matured, proved to be spirited and hot tempered; he was ever willing to join in any wild venture, particularly raids upon neighbouring Campbell territory—and yet he married a Campbell. She was Sarah, the great-granddaughter of one of the Campbells of Breadalbane who had suffered most sorely from MacDonald attacks and ravages.

The MacDonalds, it should be recognized, were by temperament men of violence, cattle thieves and plunderers; and the Campbells, whose territory lay only twenty miles to the south-east, were their main target for greedy aggression.

During these raids, many men were killed on both sides, but generally it was the Campbells who came off worst. On one occasion Alasdair MacIain was captured by the Campbells and jailed on a charge of having murdered some of his own clansmen—but he escaped and never paid the penalty for his crime. After that alarming incident he seems to have behaved with more circumspection, but nevertheless the MacDonalds had already become so notorious because of their violent forays that they had earned the nickname of "Gallow's Herd".

In addition, the MacDonalds were among the more recalcitrant of the Highland Jacobite clans still effectively in active revolt against the Protestant regime of William and Mary, who were now firmly established as rulers of England and Scotland. In support of their Stuart king, James II, in exile in Paris, the rebel Jacobites continued to stir up unrest and harry the patrols of King William's army whenever the opportunity arose. The Protestant Campbells, on the other hand, had raised a regiment in support of King William; thus the feud between the MacDonalds and the Campbells had political as well as personal motivations.

To resolve the guerilla warfare, King William built forts in the Highlands to maintain law and order. Then, in August, 1691, he made an offer of amnesty and pardon to all rebels who would take an oath of allegiance to the Crown —but it was also an ultimatum, for they had to do so before 1 January, 1692, or face the consequences.

The MacDonalds were unimpressed by either the gesture or the implied threat. John Hill, commander of the newly built Fort William about ten miles north of Glencoe was, although an experienced soldier and a dedicated Protestant, a kindly and reasonable man who believed in persuasion rather than force, and he resisted the orders of his superiors to use arms against the rebels. Had he been allowed to pursue his policy for a few extra months it is conceivable that he might have succeeded in gaining the allegiance of the rebels without bloodshed, but other factors were at work.

Hill waited anxiously for news that the local chieftains had, on behalf of their clans, travelled to Inverary to take the oath before the Sheriff of Argyllshire, in accordance with the king's edict. But the response was slow, and as the end of the year drew near Sir John Dalrymple, Master of Stair and Secretary of State for Scotland, saw an opportunity to teach the rebel clans a lesson they would never forget—and at the same time wipe out the marauding and murdering MacDonalds.

Aided and abetted by the Earl of Breadalbane, nephew of Campbell of Glenlyon and chief of the Glenorchy Campbells, he hatched a plot which was to "extirpate that sept of thieves", the MacDonalds. Motivations differed: while the Master of Stair was working obsessively for the union of the Scottish and English Parliaments, the Earl of Breadalbane's intention was to make Glenorchy the most important house of the Clan Campbell and then revenge himself for the long catalogue of MacDonald wrongs. But to both men the MacDonald clan was expendable.

The unexpected happened. As late as December, 1691, old Alasdair MacIain, chief of the MacDonalds of Glencoe, was finally persuaded to take the oath of allegiance, probably influenced by his elder son, John who, unlike his excitable and rumbustious brother Alasdair Og (the younger), was a thoughtful individual with a diplomatic turn of mind. True, he had joined in many marauding attacks upon the Campbells, but his spoils included any books he could lay his hands on. He was married, with a young son, and cared deeply for the welfare of his people.

"It is inevitable," he told his father, "that you will have to accept the oath of allegiance in the end. King James is living in France, a pensioner of Louis XIV. It is unlikely that he will ever again be able to raise the money and support to fight for his throne. For the sake of the people you must submit to King William."

Old Alasdair was stubborn. Had he not already taken an oath of allegiance to James II? Until the messengers who had been sent to France to ask James to release his subjects from their bond of loyalty returned, how could he make such a treasonable decision?

The messengers concerned, two Jacobite officers, had in fact set off for Paris in August, but James II, always an indecisive man, was unable to make up his mind. He finally submitted on 12 December, 1691, and one of the emissaries, hurrying back to Edinburgh with the royal dispensation, arrived exhausted just before Christmas. It was still not the end of the year, but another week elapsed before the news reached the western Highlands.

John Hill at Fort William was delighted—there was time, but only just enough time, to save the clans from the full weight of military retribution. Old Alasdair MacIain could afford no further delay. He alone could take the oath for his own clan, but the thought of having to make it before the Campbell sheriff at Inverary was more than he could stomach.

So late on the evening of 30 December, 1691—just a little more than twenty-four hours before the end of the amnesty, he trotted on horseback up to Fort William, accompanied by his gillies, and demanded to be allowed to swear the oath of allegiance there and then. Hill, for his part, was irritated and apprehensive; he knew that Old MacIain must be well aware that he had, by requirement of law, to report to the Campbell sheriff at Inverary, and at the same time he was anxious about the fate of the old man and his people, for he had no doubt that the Master of Stair, Secretary of State for Scotland, would relish the opportunity to punish the rebellious MacDonalds. And in the severe icy weather he realized only too well that MacIain could not hope to reach Inverary before the official time limit.

He therefore wrote a letter to the sheriff, Campbell of Ardkinglass, urging him to receive MacIain as "a lost sheep" and allow him to take the oath of allegiance, even though he arrive late. With this letter tucked safely into the fine buff coat which he always wore, Old MacIain set off for Inverary—a distance of fifty miles over rough freezing roads and tracks.

Misfortune struck in the form of a patrol of redcoats— part of the advance guard of a force of four hundred men of the Argyll Regiment. Old MacIain and his gillies were promptly arrested and taken to Barcaldine Castle where, despite John Hill's letter to the sheriff, they were imprisoned for twenty-four hours.

Although they were then released, it was 2 January before MacIain and his gillies reached Inverary, only to learn that the sheriff was away at his house in Ardkinglass. By the time he returned it was as late as 5 January. When MacIain presented himself at the Courthouse the sheriff, ignoring John Hill's letter, refused to administer the oath. "You are five days late," he pronounced solemnly, "and the Proclamation of King William gave you five months warning, which was more than enough."

Old MacIain was now genuinely afraid for his people, for at last he accepted the fact which previously he had scorned—that rebel clans which did not take the oath in the time allotted were liable to punishment "to the utmost extremity of the law", and in those days that could only mean death. Tears streamed down his ancient leathery cheeks as, still proudly facing his clan's ancient and traditional enemy, he begged the sheriff to administer the oath, guaranteeing on his personal honour the good behaviour of his kinsmen.

Campbell, well aware of the sacrifice MacIain was making to his fierce and arrogant Highland pride, softened a little. Although he could not promise indemnity under the circumstances, he agreed to send John Hill's letter with his own recommendation for clemency on to Edinburgh. And so, triumphant and yet defeated, Old MacIain went home to Glencoe to advise his people that provided they lived peaceably under King William they had nothing to fear.

His hopes were built on sand. When the sheriff's list of names of those who had taken the oath at Inverary, with both his and Hill's favourable letters of recommendation for MacIain, were submitted to the Edinburgh authority, Alasdair MacIain's name was struck off. There were several Campbells on the Administrative Council, and they had an old score to settle.

The Master of Stair then wrote to Colonel Livingstone, Commander-in-Chief of the Forces in Scotland, ordering him to be ready to ravage the MacDonald clan in Argyllshire. He angrily expressed his regret when he heard a false rumour that Alasdair MacIain had, in fact, taken the oath in time, but his joy was renewed when a few days later he learned the truth. He wrote to Livingstone: "I rejoice. It is a great work of charity to be exact in rooting out that damnable sept."

Plans now went ahead with determination. The master of Stair, with full authorization from the king, issued specific orders to Livingstone and John Hill concerning the extermination of the MacDonalds. Harrying their cattle or burning their homes was not enough, he considered. The "thieving tribe must be rooted out and cut off", and, he added, "let it be secret and sudden".

Livingstone, knowing full well John Hill's reputation for reason and mercy, by-passed him and wrote directly to James Hamilton, his second-in-command, ordering him to raze Glencoe and "do not trouble the government with prisoners".

John Hill, sick and ageing, was horrified by this murderous assignment, but he was not directly implicated. It was Hamilton who implemented the orders, and he chose Campbell of Glenlyon, the bitterest enemy of the MacDonalds, to lead the two companies of troops which were to march upon their victims.

Campbell of Glenlyon might be relied upon to show no mercy. Having plunged his family deeply into debt by his drinking and gambling, he had been brought to ruin and even to near starvation by marauding MacDonalds, and finally reduced to taking a commission in the Argyll regiment. But he could not be relied upon to keep a secret and therefore he was not told the true purpose of his move into Glencoe—merely that he was to wait there for further orders concerning a special duty.

When a mile within the Coe valley, the soldiers encountered a group of waiting Highlanders. Campbell halted his men and sent an officer forward. John MacDonald, at the head of the Highlanders, regarded the officer with deep distrust. Farther back in the valley the MacDonalds were busily hiding their weapons in case the soldiers had come to search for them—they could imagine no other danger, for had their chief not had the sheriff's promise of protection, and also that of John Hill?

"Are you here as friends or enemies?" asked John MacDonald.

"As friends," replied the lieutenant. "On my word of honour as an officer and gentleman I assure you that no harm will befall any MacDonald. But I have here military orders, signed by Colonel Hamilton, requisitioning quarters in Glencoe for two companies of foot. We have newly arrived in Argyll and Fort William is full. In such bitter weather it is impossible for men to sleep in the open."

Reluctantly MacDonald took the orders. An instant later

Robert Campbell stepped forward, holding out his hand and boisterously slapping his old enemy on the back. "It will be good to see my niece Sarah again after so long, and Sandy, her husband. I'm sorry to have to demand your hospitality like this, but in such freezing weather what can one do? We shall be very glad of such room as your people can spare while we wait for orders."

Highland hospitality was as famous then as it is today; John MacDonald had no choice. Of all men Robert Campbell of Glenlyon was the one he was most reluctant to accept within his own house, but he was obliged to put a good face on it. He took the hand of his enemy, and dispatched messengers along the valley to make ready for their unexpected guests. The Campbell soldiers marched into Glencoe.

At Carnoch, in front of the chief's house, the soldiers halted again. Old MacIain himself and his wife came out to greet their unwelcome guests. Campbell requested the customary Highland hospitality. "We shall only be here," he explained, "until we receive orders to march upon Glengarry where a clan chief has not yet taken the oath of allegiance to the king." MacIain politely, but without enthusiasm, made him welcome.

So the Campbells were accepted trustfully, but not without some misgivings, into the homes of their traditional enemies. The troops were dispersed among the five small towns along the glen, billeted two or three to a cottage. On both sides the men were wary, but on their best behaviour. No mention was made of the Campbell booty that enriched this MacDonald valley, and if a Campbell soldier happened to recognize a cow or a cooking-pot that had once been his, he said nothing. Gradually over the next two weeks the soldiers and the MacDonalds relaxed and established friendly relationships.

During the short winter days the MacDonalds would watch with some amusement as the troops paraded and practised their drill, changed their sentries, and carried out their routine duties. In the afternoons all joined together in Highland games, archery and shinty, and at night they drank and gambled and sang.

Robert Campbell had chosen to stay with MacDonald of Inverrigan, a small town a mile or so up the glen. Perhaps there were too many of his own possessions now adorning the chief's house for him to be able to stomach Old MacIain's hospitality, or perhaps it was because he was closer to the home of his niece Sarah and her husband—Old MacIain's younger son, who distrusted him intensely. Nevertheless, with young Alasdair and John, with Mac-Donald of Inverrigan and his family and with his own officers, Campbell of Glenlyon spent every night drinking and gambling, and still his further orders did not arrive.

The delay was caused by John Hill, who found himself unable to sign the final orders authorizing Hamilton to go ahead with the massacre. He had written to the Secretary of State for Scotland in London, begging him to reconsider as the Highlands were now quiet and peaceful, and even MacDonald of Glengarry had finally submitted to the rule of law. But the Master of Stair would not change his mind —he was determined to teach the lesson, even though the lesson had already been learned. Hamilton had his orders; Hill must countersign them. Hill was old, failing and disheartened. In the end, on 10 February, 1692, having delayed matters as long as he reasonably could, he authorized Hamilton to carry out Livingstone's orders.

Hamilton, eager to move into action, immediately instructed Duncanson to march with his men to western and eastern ends of the Glencoe gorge where, at 7 a.m. on the 13th they were—in conjunction with Campbell's infiltrated force—to fall upon the MacDonald's and destroy them. The message was passed on to Robert Campbell.

He wrote: "You are hereby ordered in the name of His Majesty King William to fall upon the rebels and to put all under seventy to the sword. You are to have a special care that the old fox and his sons do upon no account escape. You are to secure all the avenues so that no man escape."

But, he added, the order was to be put into execution at five o'clock precisely in the morning, promising that he (Duncanson) and his men would arrive in Glencoe at that same hour. As Duncanson's own orders had clearly specified 7 a.m. for the start of the operation, it seems only too probable that by introducing the two-hour time delay he was hoping to throw the major responsibility and guilt for the bloody deed upon Campbell and his men—which at least indicates the possibility of an element of conscience in Duncanson's military mind.

On the evening of 12 January John and Alasdair MacDonald junior were at Inverrigan's house playing cards with Robert Campbell, as they had done so often in the past twelve days One of Campbell's lieutenants brought in the order paper. Campbell read it slowly without reaction or expression.

"My orders have arrived at last, gentlemen," he announced. "On behalf of all my men, I wish to thank you most sincerely for your generous hospitality. Your burden will soon be eased. Now, if you will excuse me, there are many things I must attend to."

The party broke up, and the MacDonalds returned to their homes. The weather, which had been bleak enough, was rapidly worsening, with a strong wind rising and driving snow before it. While the MacDonalds built up their fires to make their houses snug against the invading fingers of frost, Campbell's messengers ploughed through the blizzard to deliver orders to the commanders of the various detachments of troops scattered along the valley.

The ordinary foot-soldiers were not warned what was expected of them until the final moment before the massacre began. By then it was too late to debate the ethics or morality of it, or even pause to think—not that the common soldiers of the day were concerned with ethics, morality or even thinking. Nevertheless, in the Highlands hospitality was regarded as almost a sacred thing, and to accept it put the guest under the strictest obligations of honour to the host. The majority of the Campbell soldiers were apparently happy to ignore their obligation for the chance of paying off old scores.

The N.C.O.'s were briefed in advance, however, and it is almost certain that a number of sergeants and corporals warned their hosts and perhaps even assisted them in making their escape in the blizzard before the final murderous onslaught. But on balance it was not through the mercy of the Campbells that so many MacDonalds escaped, but rather through the inefficiency of the military operation coupled with the severe inclemency of the weather.

John MacDonald, after his game of cards with Campbell,

had gone home to bed, but before dawn he and his wife were awakened by shouting voices. Going to the window, he saw soldiers moving about, muskets in hand and holding flaming torches.

"It is nothing," he told his startled wife. "The troops are getting ready to march off. Campbell of Glenlyon had his orders from Fort William this night." Nevertheless, John was secretly alarmed. When his wife had gone to sleep again he dressed and went out into the wind and snow to Inverrigan. There, in MacDonald's house, he found the room full of soldiers, fully dressed and preparing their arms.

"You are early astir," he said to Robert Campbell. "What is afoot?"

Campbell, aware of the suspicion in the other man's voice, shrugged his shoulders nonchalantly. "You don't know what life is like in the army, my friend. You get your orders and they have to be obeyed at once."

As MacDonald still seemed dubious, he added: "You don't believe we mean Glencoe any harm, do you? If such were my orders do you imagine I would not have warned my niece and her husband, whom I love?"

At that MacDonald was reassured. He shook hands with his people's murderer and went back home, not knowing that in another room of the house lay MacDonald of Inverrigan and eight members of his household, bound and gagged, awaiting the prescribed slaughter which was duly carried out on a dunghill behind the house at the appointed hour of five o'clock. Campbell believed in obeying programmed orders to the very second—that way there could be no criticism from higher up.

Iain MacDonald, chief of the clan, was shot while trying to dress. He fell across the bed and his wife threw herself protectively over his body; the soldiers dragged her off, ripped the clothes from her and bit the rings from her fingers with their teeth—but they did not kill her.

John MacDonald was awakened by a servant to find some twenty Campbell soldiers plunging through the snowdrifts towards his house. Frantically he roused his wife and called his household together and, hastily grabbing their plaids, but still wearing night attire, they managed to escape into the freezing inhospitable mountains. There they encountered Alasdair Og (junior) and a few others.

The Campbells drove the people from their houses and mercilessly murdered all they could find—from tiny children to old men of eighty—in the "name of the king". Every house was set on fire—fourteen people, it was said, were burned alive in one cottage. Cattle and sheep were driven off into the snow, and the soldiers looted everything they could lay their hands on.

By the time Duncanson's and Hamilton's reinforcements arrived in the glen the slaughter was over. But of some 400 MacDonalds, only 38 had died—though many more failed to survive the bleak wintry conditions in the mountains. When it was learned that both John and Alasdair Og MacDonald had escaped, Duncanson and Hamilton were furious.

After the soldiers had departed a few of the survivors crept back. John and Alasdair found their mother, tended her bitten fingers and buried their slain father. But they did not stay, for they were afraid that the soldiers might come back. The MacDonalds took to the mountains, living as best they could, and seeking whatever help they could obtain from friends who were prepared to risk vicious and brutal punishment.

There the story of the massacre at Glencoe ends in its dramatic sense, but as in all true history there is inevitably a sequel. The news of the massacre took nearly two weeks to reach London, but no official action or inquiry was begun. In August of that year John MacDonald finally brought the broken remnants of his starving people down from the mountains and took the oath of allegiance to King William; at that point he had little alternative.

Partly because of publicity and pressure from pamphleteers and the embryonic press of the day, an official inquiry under the chairmanship of the Duke of Hamilton, Royal Commissioner to Scotland, was ordered in 1693, but little was achieved. The duke died in the following year.

Two years later the king ordered a commission of inquiry into the massacre. Although the policy of the English government and its delegates was held to be "abominable", nobody was charged or tried or punished. All that happened was that some years later the Master of Stair relinquished his post as Secretary of State for Scotland; but that may have been merely "coincidental".

The Salem Witches

A Spring day in Salem, Massachusetts, in the year sixteen
hundred and ninety-two. The small settlement of wooden
buildings looked out across the grey Atlantic towards the
settlers' old homeland. Inland, the scattered farm-houses
stood isolated among the fields that stretched to the edge of
the forest. The forest marked the boundary: here the wilderness began. For the forest and the Appalachian Mountains
beyond were the home of the Indians, and any day a raiding
party might erupt from the woodland to attack one of the
isolated farms before disappearing back into the dark unknown land.

Normally on a fine Spring day there would be men out
working hard in the fields, the township would be bustling
with activity. For this was a strong, hard-working community where idleness was looked on as a mortal sin. It was a
deeply religious community, too—a community that had
been formed from men and women who had fled from
religious persecution in the old England to seek another way
of life in the New England. But the religion that they
followed in the new world was as harsh and exclusive as any
they had left behind.

The Reverend Samuel Parris, minister of the town's
Congregational Church, could be relied on to keep his congregation on the straight path with visions of hell-fire for
those who strayed even an inch from that narrow way. This

was the community that on a fine Spring day should have been about its lawful business. But in the Spring of 1692 the fields were empty, the streets were deserted. A strange sound echoed round the empty streets—the sound of young girls screaming. The noise came from the court-house, inside which the citizens of Salem were gathered. They were there to see one of their neighbours being tried for witchcraft.

Among the fascinated spectators at this trial sat an elderly couple, Giles and Martha Corey. Giles Corey was one of Salem's "characters". He was one of those men who seem to be not so much accident-prone as suspicion-prone. Whenever some untoward event occurred in Salem—a crop caught fire, a cow was missing—the rumours started and they invariably linked the name of Giles Corey with the incident.

But Giles was a cantankerous man with a well-developed taste for litigation. As soon as the rumours began to fly Giles Corey was there, ready and willing to slap writs on his detractors. Sometimes he won a case, sometimes he lost a case, but whatever the outcome he thoroughly enjoyed himself. So he was taking a special interest in the trial that was in progress—for him the court-room was a home from home. However, there was more to Giles Corey than just his cantankerousness. He had the essential toughness of character that had enabled him to hold out against the difficulties and dangers that beset the first New Englanders. His wife, Martha, who sat next to him, was a very different personality. Where Giles was illiterate and untutored, she was well read and delighted in her books and her learning. She had none of Giles's quick temper, but she did share with him the strength and independence that enabled them both to work together to conquer the land.

Together they now watched and listened as the learned judges from Boston examined the accused who was standing trial for practising witchcraft. It was this that had drawn together the crowd that packed the building. They had come to hear the sensational details of this most sensational of accusations, for witchcraft was a capital crime, and the accused must either prove innocence, or find another on whom the blame for the enchantment could be laid. The people of Salem were set on a spiral of accusations and fear.

Sarah Good, who was then being interrogated, had been charged with bewitching the children of the village.

Evidence had been heard from the Reverend Parris's negro servant, Tituba, who had described how she had seen Sarah Good and another old woman at a sabbat, or witches' meeting. She had told how Mrs Good had appeared as a wolf, and how she had a familiar spirit that came to her in the shape of a little yellow bird. Among her other activities, Sarah Good was supposed to have ridden through the air on a pole and signed her name in the devil's book. When the evidence of the old servant had finished no one questioned it, even though it was given in a prison cell under the threat of the hangman's rope. Tituba had ensured that her own life would be saved.

More evidence was added. Even Sarah Good's four-year-old daughter had been called in to testify against her mother. The little girl agreed at once with the imposing judges that she had indeed seen her mother with the yellow bird on her hand. Now the excited audience were listening to Sarah Good's contemptuous denial of the accusations. No, she said, she had never made a contract with the devil: and no, she had never tried to hurt the children of the village.

Then the children were brought forward and ordered by one of the judges to turn to face Mrs Good. They turned to look at her, and at once they were seized with convulsions. Their small bodies twisted and writhed as though they were being subjected to an unbearable agony. Their screams filled every corner of the court-house.

The Coreys, like the rest of the spectators, were on their feet so as to get a better view of the incredible scene. Old Giles was transfixed. He had been in court often enough, but he had never in his whole life seen anything to compare with this. Like most of his neighbours he had now seen and heard more than enough to convince him that the devil had been walking the streets of Salem and that Sarah Good was one of his disciples. She was a witch.

The judges shared Giles Corey's opinion. They managed at length to get the girls calmed down, and then began the fierce examination of poor, confused Sarah Good. Under their relentless pressure, she finally broke down and named the old bed-ridden woman, Osborne, as the one who had been responsible for tormenting the children.

At the end of that day—as at the end of each day's proceedings as the trial progressed—the crowd streamed out of the court-house to gather together in small groups and discuss the case. On these occasions Giles Corey was always a prominent figure, and his opinion on the more abstruse legal matters was always eagerly sought. He expounded at length, and with a great deal of relish, the fate that would await a convicted witch. He discussed the issues raised by the judges, and explained to those with less practical experience of the courts than himself, exactly what procedures would next be followed. He agreed readily with his neighbours that it came as no surprise to discover that Good and Osborne were both witches. So they talked on into the evening, until gradually the groups began to break up and the farmers turned back to their homesteads. For many, the enjoyment of the new spectacle was to prove short-lived.

As the trial continued, the most pious of Salem's citizens felt it necessary to hold a solemn service of humility to renew their allegiance to God in the face of the tangible evidence of the devil's presence among the community. The children were all there, all those who had been witnesses at the trial. As the service began one of the children, twelve-years-old Abigail Williams, suddenly cried out that she was possessed with a terrible vision. The congregation was silent as the little girl told of another communion service attended by citizens of Salem: a communion where the wine and the bread were as red as blood and where the minister was not a minister of God but of the devil. She saw in her vision her neighbours at a sabbat.

This fresh evidence of blasphemy and sin in the Puritan community set tongues clacking as never before. Respectable married women saw themselves being raped by the devil in person. Hysterical teen-agers imagined themselves participating in wild sexual orgies. But the centre of all the interest was the children. Every day the court-room was crowded, as everyone waited to see which way the accusing finger would point. If Abigail had seen other villagers at the sabbat it surely couldn't be long before more of the guilty were exposed. Old Giles Corey was practically overwhelmed by the excitement of it all, which so far surpassed that of any of his own many cases.

The new accusations were not long in forthcoming. Led by Ann Putnam, the daughter of one of the leading men of

Salem, and Abigail Williams, the children began to name more names, and to describe more of the witches' behaviour. The witches' spirits came to them at night. They bit them, they tried to suffocate them, the poor children were almost strangled to death by the evil spirits. When the names of the witches were revealed, a thrill of horror ran through the audience. These were no bed-ridden old hags. These were respectable citizens, members of the church, apparently devout Christians. The first two women to be named were Rebecca Nurse, the wife of Francis Nurse, a highly respected member of the community, and—Martha Corey.

For the Coreys it seemed as though the whole world had suddenly collapsed. They had been carried along on the wave of excitement, amounting to hysteria, that had engulfed the whole of Salem. Now, suddenly, everything had changed. They were no longer mere spectators avidly watching the scenes that unfolded each day in the court-room. Terrifyingly and with brutal swiftness they had become principal actors in the macabre drama.

But Martha Corey was no simpleton. She was literate and educated, and she felt confident as she faced her accusers that justice would be done.

Old Giles watched her in silent apprehension as the testimonies began. The girls told of their persecution by Martha. They told how she came to them in their rooms in the black of night to torment them. She brought them a book, they said, which she tried to force them to sign. The book was the devil's book in which he recorded the names of all his disciples. When, as good Christian children should, they refused to sign, Martha Corey only tormented them the more. The judges turned to Martha. Why was she treating the children in such a terrible fashion, they asked. Martha angrily denied the charges. To her the stories seemed self-evidently to be nonsense. She looked over to the group of children and, with a mixture of pity and scorn, dismissed them as "distracted creatures".

As though these words were a signal, the girls at once fell into an uncontrollable fit. Their high, screaming voices rang round the room as they huddled together staring frenziedly at Martha. As Martha stared, bewildered, back at them, they pointed shaking fingers at the empty space behind her back. The spectators craned forward to try to see what it was that was terrifying the girls. There was, of course, nothing to be seen. But the girls were now roused to an ecstasy of feeling. Their piercing treble voices rose ever higher. There, they cried, there behind Martha. The space behind her remained as empty as before. The insistent voices screamed on: there he stood, a huge black man, whispering in her ear, urging her to new acts of devilment against the innocent children. The little yellow bird was there again, yelled another child. The yellow bird was flying round and round Martha Corey's head, just as it had flown round Sarah Good.

What was Martha Corey to say? That there was no black man, no yellow bird? That no one could see these things except the children? That in itself was enough to convict her. If only the children could see these things, then surely that was evidence to show that she had bewitched them. Against such evidence there was no defence.

By the end of the day's hearings, the court-room had been the scene of incredible pandemonium. The accusatory outbursts of the children had been repeated when Rebecca Nurse had stood to face her accusers. The girls had been completely out of control. Finally the two bewildered women had been led away to the cells to await the next day when they would have to face more accusations and more witnesses. For now there were plenty of others who were willing to take their share of the excitement of the trial. Some had been carried away by the girls' hysteria. To others the trials seemed to offer a perfect opportunity for the settlement of old scores. It was becoming obvious to many that there was little the accused could do to defend themselves against the witchcraft allegations, and if the accused were found guilty then their goods and property were confiscated. There were some in Salem who saw here a unique opportunity for personal enrichment.

Outside the court-room the usual excited groups were still discussing the new events. But Giles Corey no longer had any stomach for the discussions. He left the chattering groups behind and walked home alone to his farm. As he trudged along the muddy paths, he remembered all those cases in which he had been involved over the years, the legal battles he had fought, the pleasure he had got from the experience. The pleasure had now turned to agony. His wife stood facing a charge for which the penalty was death. He wondered if there was any chance of her escaping the dreadful fate. He wondered, too, how long it would be before yet others were made to face the screaming girls who pointed so surely and with such conviction at the invisible spirits they saw in the court-room.

Over the days and the weeks, the evidence against Martha Corey continued. There were two principal witnesses. The first was the young girl, Ann Putnam. Her story was the now familiar one of night-time visitations, of tormenting and persecution. It is worth noting, however, that Ann Putnam's father was an important local landowner. This gave his daughter's evidence greater weight and authority. It also so happened that he was one of the few men with enough capital to buy up confiscated land, and was therefore one with the most to gain from the conviction of his neighbours.

The second witness was Mother Hobbs. She had been one of the first to be charged with witchcraft. Although when the charges had first been brought she had denied them, she soon changed her testimony and gave the court a full confession of all her secret pacts with Lucifer. A witch who freely confessed her guilt was spared execution, and the more details she provided of her supposed activities, the more lenient the court became. As the evidence of self-confessed witches and young girls continued, so more and more names appeared in the evidence. Giles Corey watched every day as the proceedings against his wife continued. Soon the inevitable happened. Mother Hobbs testified that she had attended a sabbat. Among those she named as having been present were the accused, Martha Corey, and her husband, Giles.

Giles Corey may have been a difficult old man to get along with, but even his detractors granted him two things. He had never in his whole life shown fear, and he knew the law. He had built up his farm and his holdings by the labour of his own hands. He had fought unceasingly the farmer's old enemies of intractable land and bad weather, and he had fought when necessary against the bands of marauding Indians when they came down on the settlements from out of the wilderness. Giles had fought and worked hard for what he owned, and now in his old age he had made his will. All his property was to pass, at his death, to his sons-in-law.

Giles knew that a condemned witch would have all his property confiscated and that his family would be disinherited. He knew, too, from the long days he had spent watching the witch trials, that his chances of evading conviction were negligible.

He brooded and grieved at the thought of his precious land being taken away from him and his family to be handed over to some greedy and unscrupulous member of the Salem community. But Giles was not a man to be defeated by the law if there was any possible way out. He found a loophole. He could only be tried and condemned as a witch if he answered to the indictment. If he refused to plead either "innocent" or "guilty" then, if he died, his family would still be able to claim the heritage that he had willed to them. So the old man resolved that no matter what the court might do to him, they would not persuade him to answer the charges.

By now no one in Salem was safe from accusation, and where the fingers of the young girls of Salem pointed the hangman's noose was soon at work. Many confessed, and so saved their lives, but others refused and held out firm to the end, protesting their innocence of the vileness and obscenity with which they were charged. Martha Corey was among those who stood firm. On a fine September day she was taken from her cell. She joined five other women and two men, and together they were taken to the gallows. There Martha Corey and the other seven were hanged by their necks until they were dead.

So the trials and the slaughter continued. Giles Corey was brought before the court. The sickening rigmarole was enacted yet again. Witnesses who had themselves been accused were only too eager to confess and save their lives, and in their confessions they blurted out the names of neighbours and friends, who in their turn were accused. Mother Hobbs claimed that Giles Corey was part of a conspiracy to bewitch the whole village. Teen-age girls came forward with the most lurid tales of the old man's sexual assaults on them. Throughout all the accusations Giles remained completely silent. Vituperation poured over him, but he would not open his mouth. The old man who was known for his courtroom eloquence said never a word. Frustrated, the judges took their decision. Giles Corey must be made to talk. They ordered that he should be taken back to his cell, and that there he should be pressed with weights.

Giles Corey was taken from the court-house. In his cell his clothes were stripped from him. He was laid down on his back and a flat wooden board was laid on top of his body. The judges asked again if he would answer to the indictment. He made no reply. Then the torment began. The gaolers began loading weights on to the board. As each weight was added the pressure on Giles's body increased; and each time the judges asked if he would plead to the charges. But Giles Corey remained silent. More weights were added, and still more, until at last the old man's brittle bones snapped under the strain. Pressed flat, the final breath was squeezed from his lungs, and for Giles Corey the agony of Salem had ended. During all the agonizing torture he never answered his accusers.

Giles and Martha Corey were only two of the victims of the Salem witch trials. The small group of girls were taken from Salem to other towns and villages in the area, where they continued to collapse in convulsions whenever they were faced by a "witch". But in time the madness began to die away. Too many good men and women were falling victim, and people began to sicken of the whole procedure. The girls' evidence was no longer enough to ensure the automatic conviction of anyone they indicted; and once doubt spread of the girls' honesty the whole fabric began to crumble.

Those who had confessed to witchcraft to save their own necks now began to come forward and admit that they had indicted others only from fear. But it was a slow process. The whole affair had begun in February, 1692, but it was not until the October of the following year that the trials came to an end, and with them the bloodshed. During that period nineteen men and women had been hanged for witchcraft and one man had been crushed to death. Hundreds of others had been put in prison.

Those who suffered had done no wrong. They were not evil men and women. Like Giles and Martha Corey, they were upright, God-fearing, hard-working people who had fled from injustice in the old world to try to find a better life in the new. They could not have known, as they hacked down the forest trees to make their simple homes, as they ploughed and planted the land, as they fought to hold what they had won in a hostile world, that their end would come as it did.

They could never have guessed that they would die a violent death because a group of hysterical young girls had one day pointed their fingers at the empty air and declared it to be full of birds and demons. They could never have imagined that they would be the victims of a terrible madness that would begin to grow one Spring day in Salem, Massachusetts, in the year sixteen hundred and ninety-two.

The Black Hole of Calcutta

Holwell remembered the appalling terror of that night for the rest of his life. As the panicking mass of human beings was pushed and forced into the confined space of the Black Hole prison, he had been among the first to be thrust in. He was assisting two wounded men, and he got them by the windows nearest the door. Neither he, nor any of them had ever been in the Black Hole before. They did not know its dimensions, or they might have turned upon the guard, considering it a lesser evil to be shot and cut to pieces.

The Black Hole prison was well known in Calcutta. It was about eighteen feet square and had two small barred windows. It was no better or no worse a place of incarceration than any other in the eighteenth century—given its normal complement of prisoners.

But on this June night of the year 1756, one hundred and forty-five men and one girl were crushed into that small space. The temperature was in the very humid nineties. As they swept in under the pressure of those behind, Holwell glimpsed the girl, Mary, the young Indian wife of Peter Carey, a seafaring man who had fought in the siege. Holwell knew them both well. Peter was gripping his wife's waist to protect her from the frenzied crush.

Many were exhausted or wounded, and collapsed immediately in the already stifling atmosphere. Those who fell were trampled to death in the first few minutes of that awful night by others pushed and kicked and cudgelled through the entrance by the guards, who squashed the last one tightly through the door, then pulled it to and locked and barred it from the outside.

Some fought desperately in a nightmare of claustrophobia. Others collapsed, squashed and suffocated, unable to breathe, their bodies held upright by the tremendous press of those around them. In an endeavour to escape the crush, a number had got underneath the platform which ran the length of the prison, but immediately found themselves worse off from lack of air, and were struggling vainly to get out.

The first instinct was to make for the two small windows, the only source of air, and that was little enough. In the sultry Bengal June nights the only air that stirs comes from the south and the east. The two windows opened to the west and were overhung by the stone archways of the verandah. Many pushed their fellows aside, trampling on them, trying to get to the windows.

Those near the opposite wall were so crushed together that they were unable to move. Peter Carey and his wife had got on to the platform which ran along this wall and was intended as a bed for prisoners. They were safe here from being crushed and trampled underfoot, although they were half suffocated from lack of air. The men nearest the door were desperately trying to force it; but the door opened inwards, and having only their bare hands they were unable to shift it.

It took a few minutes for Holwell, still clinging hard to the window, to gather his senses.

"Why have they done this to us?" he asked of Lushington, a young writer in the East India Company's service, who stood next to him. "The nabob gave me his assurance on the word of a soldier that no harm would come to us."

"There was an altercation between several of our Dutch mercenaries and the guard," said Lushington. "I heard said that the nabob ordered us to be put in the place of detention used by the Europeans."

"But not in this place! Nearly a hundred and fifty of us!"

"They have no sense of proportion," said Lushington with an attempt at humour, despite the suffocating press.

Holwell felt that some duty devolved upon him. Suraj-ud-Daula, the young, British-hating nabob of Bengal, had attacked the company's settlement at Calcutta on Wednesday, 15 June, 1756. By Saturday his army had conquered and looted Calcutta and were breaking into Fort William where the Europeans made their last stand. On Saturday night the women and children were taken on board the *Dodaldy*, and there was tremendous indignation at the fort when Mary Carey, who had devotedly nursed the wounded, was not allowed on the ship because she was not white.

Holwell had been greatly incensed at this inhumanity, but there was nothing he could do. Disaster followed disaster. In the confusion of defeat, Governor Drake and the garrison commander suddenly deserted their posts, boarded the *Dodaldy* and left the remnants of the beleaguered defenders to their fate. In the helpless fury which raged at Fort William all turned for leadership to Holwell, whose authority derived from the fact that he was chief magistrate and member of the council. Holwell negotiated a surrender. What the nabob was after was the treasure which the East India Company was reputed to hold in its vaults at Calcutta. Holwell's assurance that a man in his position was not likely to know anything about the company's treasure had not really convinced the nabob, whose men were already burning, looting and plundering. The warehouse was in flames and the governor's residence, robbed of its valuables, was set on fire.

The last thing Holwell expected was that they should be treated in this inhuman fashion. But Lushington's explanation made sense. He felt he owed something to his companions in suffering who had made him their leader. He called for silence, which they eventually gave him.

"You have placed your trust in me," he said, "and you have given me ready obedience during the day. Now in this awful night of suffering, I beg you to do everything to save your lives. Your only hope lies in keeping calm and as still as possible. To let loose your passions or your feelings will merely result in your destruction. We *must* survive this night. The morning will bring us air and liberty."

His companions had so much respect for Holwell that his words had an immediate effect, and there was for some time relative quiet, broken only by the cries and groans of the wounded and the dying. Holwell was filled with utter despair. Despite his words, he did not think that any of them could survive unless there was some alteration in their circumstances.

Outside, the Indian guards were still posted, and among them Holwell noticed a jemadar, an Indian army officer, older than the others, who seemed disturbed at the appalling state of affairs in the Black Hole. Holwell called him and offered him 2,000 rupees, a very large sum, if he could find a senior officer and endeavour to get them separated, half in one place and half in another. The man went but returned with the answer that such a thing could only be done by the nabob's order. But he was asleep and no one dare awake him.

This news broke another tide of panic in the jam-packed cell. Everyone was now streaming with perspiration. It flowed off them in a manner which Holwell would have considered inconceivable if he had not experienced it. With their bodies drained of moisture, they soon developed a raging thirst.

In an attempt to get more room and air, they stripped off their clothes. Someone suggested they should sit on their hams; but this only resulted in more of them not rising again, and lying unconscious, even dead on the floor, to be trampled on. By nine o'clock their thirst grew intolerable, and all were finding the greatest difficulty in breathing. Some suffered from heart failure, collapsing with agonizing cardiac pains.

Many shouted insults of the foulest and most provocative nature at the guards in the hope that they would fire upon them and thus end their sufferings. But the guard did not fire, afraid doubtless of the consequences.

Holwell at this point was nearly unconscious, even though he had managed to keep his face between two of the bars and breathe in enough air to satisfy his tortured lungs.

From the gasping, moaning throng behind him now came an almost rhythmic, chanting cry: "Water! Water!" The old jemadar, who had previously taken pity on them, brought skins of water to the bars of the prison. Holwell was greatly alarmed at this, for he immediately foresaw the effect it would have.

His fears were fully realized. The appearance of the water caused not only wild confusion and panic, but resulted in violent struggles and fights. The only means of conveying it into the prison was by means of hats forced through the iron bars. The very sight of it served to inflame their thirst. Until the water appeared Holwell had not suffered much from thirst. He endeavoured to dissuade the jemadar from bringing it, but so great was the tumult from inside the Black Hole that he was unable to speak privately to the man, the only one of their Indian guard who showed them any sympathy.

Although those at the windows managed to bring hats full of water through the bars, those behind them fought so desperately and violently for it that most of it was spilt, many were injured, and some even killed in the struggles. It was, thought Holwell, like sprinkling water on fire; it served only to feed the flames. In vain he tried to control the situation. The very thought of water just increased their sufferings. The cries and ravings of those in the remoter parts of the dungeon, who had not a hope of obtaining a single drop, were heart-breaking.

The fearful tumult inside the Black Hole, as the victims fought for the water like wild animals, attracted the attention of the less humane guards. Here were the mighty British fighting each other for a drink of water! This was entertainment without compare for the humble Indians, to whom the white man had been the lord of creation. They came rushing with more water in order to prolong the spectacle, and held torches at the bars to see the fun better.

In agony and despair, his face through the bars, Holwell endured the cruel derision of the guards for nearly two hours. By the time the Indians had tired of the callous sport, many more inside the dungeon had died, the weaker being trampled to death by the stronger. Others had completely lost their senses. Holwell himself was nearly crushed to death against the window from the press behind and was quite unable to move. His two wounded companions at the window died under the pressure. Their bodies were pushed aside and others took their place.

Holwell, thinking himself near to death, finally struggled away from the window, around which the youngest and strongest had forced themselves in order better to breathe in the vapid air of the steaming Bengal night. In the flickering flames of the still-burning governor's residence the sight in the Black Hole was hideous beyond belief. He had to walk on a carpet of bodies, some already beginning to putrefy; the stench made him reel. The crush was still overwhelming. By the inmost wall, where the temperature was hottest and the air foullest, stood a phalanx of the living and the dead. Those who had died were kept upright by those who still lived, the dead arms and heads flailing and nodding grotesquely with the struggles of the living.

It was still extremely difficult to move, even though Holwell reckoned that at least fifty of their number had died. But just then other members of the guard, seeking more diversion, brought water to the other window in the expectation of seeing more fighting among the prisoners. The half-crazed men, most of them soldiers, rushed towards the window to get the water, and this allowed Holwell to struggle towards the platform at the farther end of the prison. He shivered with horror at the dead beneath his feet, wondering whose bodies he was stumbling over.

On the platform were several people he knew, some of them dead, some dying, some accepting their terrible situation with calm resignation. Among these was the Reverend Gervas Bellamy, the chaplain, Holwell's close friend; he sat still, his lips continually moving in prayer. Next to him lay his son, Lieutenant John Bellamy, quite dead, holding tightly to his father's hand.

Close by was Mary Carey sitting with an air of imperturbable patience which Holwell would remember for the rest of his life. Next to her was Peter, gasping in the fetid air, every now and then weakly scooping the sweat from his bare chest with which to wet his parched tongue and lips. The torches of the jeering guards shone on the mob fighting for water by the window. They shone too on Mary's lovely young face as she turned and looked at Holwell. It was streaming wet, like everyone else's. Her dark eyes glistened in the torch beams. She hardly moved a muscle and, it seemed, hardly breathed either.

There was no space on the platform, only bodies. Holwell felt he had come there to die also, and he slumped down on top of the corpses, commending his soul to heaven. He believed he was at the end of his sufferings. It was about eleven o'clock.

But death did not come. Instead a raging thirst, an

increased difficulty in breathing in the foul, poisoned air, the stench of which grew worse every minute. Then suddenly piercing pains in his chest and palpitations of his pulse warned him of an approaching heart attack. As the pain once more smote his chest, he made the decision not to submit tamely to death like this. Many of his friends, gentlemen of the East India Company, had collapsed on the floor to have their faces trampled on by any common soldier. He stood up, deciding to resume the terrible fight for life. He glanced at Mary, whose motionless resignation looked as though it was to be her salvation. But Peter was in a bad way, gasping and panting. He could never emulate his wife's eastern tranquillity.

Seeing a lane open momentarily in the seething mass of humanity, Holwell made a way quickly towards the second window where water was still being handed in by the jeering guards. He believed that the air at the window would give him relief from the excruciating pain in his chest, and he was right. But his thirst remained intolerable. He cried aloud for water.

Those at the window, who had thought he had died, recognized him as their leader and immediately gave him water. But he did not drink much, for it did not assuage his thirst. After that he sucked the perspiration from his shirt sleeves.

By half-past eleven Holwell had got his face through the bars of the window, with an intolerable crush of bodies around him each struggling to gulp in the heavy air of the sultry Indian night.

Many of those alive were now in a state of delirium. They no longer fought for the water, discovering like Holwell that it gave them little or no relief. It was lack of air which caused their greatest suffering. Those too weak to fight their way to the window and dislodge those already there slumped down one by one on to the corpse-strewn floor, wishing only to die. Others tried to stay upright and avoid joining the unfortunates on the floor. But the appalling stench and lack of oxygen further weakened them, and eventually they too plunged down to die.

A Dutch soldier climbed on top of Holwell to get his face near the top of the window. He supported himself half on Holwell and half on the man next to him, and remained there for two and a half hours. There was nothing Holwell, himself considerably weakened, could do to dislodge him. The burden became almost unsupportable. His legs were giving way and he knew he could not remain standing for much longer. He noticed that Peter Carey was now behind him, unable any further to tolerate the conditions on the platform. He was panting and gasping for air.

"Take my place, Carey," Holwell said.

But no sooner did Holwell move than the Dutchman slipped down in front of him and took the place. Neither he nor Carey had the strength to dislodge him.

"Thank you for the thought, sir," muttered Carey. "I'll go back to Mary."

"I'll come with you," Holwell said.

Together they forced their way from the window to the platform. Nearer the windows there was a little more room, and a little more sanity than in the serried, crazed ranks towards the far wall.

Carey went straight into the arms of his wife; he died within a few minutes. Holwell fell back on the bodies lying on the platform. Next to him the chaplain, now dead, was still hand-in-hand with his son, and Holwell did not wish to die in better company.

Not far away Leech was dead, but he was caught pressed in the throng, a standing corpse; his head lolled like a rag doll, sadly grotesque, in the awful, frenzied movements of that doomed mass of ill-used humanity. Tears streamed down Holwell's face when he thought of Leech, for whom he had done many good turns in the past, and to repay which Leech had come back from freedom especially to rescue him after the fall of the fort. But Holwell could not desert those who had placed their trust in him, and Leech had stayed on at his own choice.

Choked and in utter despair, Holwell felt a great stupor coming over him. This was the second time he had come there to die. His senses reeled. He loosened the sash at his waist and lost consciousness. But though all sensibility fled, he knew somewhere deep down in his mind that this was not death. After a fathomless time, a sudden feeling of fresh air on his face brought him back to life and the realization that he was being supported by two others in front of the window.

He realized, too, that this third journey to the window had been made more easily than his other fraught passages. With dawn's first light the reason was clear; the majority of his companions had now succumbed, forming in death a thick carpet of horrifyingly tumbled limbs.

Daylight was now coming in wild extravagance across the sky, and between him and the blackened ruins of the governor's residence, he saw one of the nabob's officers. This man told Holwell that when the nabob heard what had happened, he had sent urgently to find out if he, Holwell, was alive. Orders were instantly given for the door to be opened and the prisoners released.

But corpses were piled up against the door which opened inwards and so the task had to be performed by the weakened, retching survivors within the Black Hole. It took twenty awful minutes. Still gasping and endeavouring to recover himself by the window, Holwell could hardly bring himself to look at the terrible and grisly scene which the light of day fully revealed. Of the 146 who had been packed into the dungeon, 23 survived the night. Among the living was Mary Carey. As the door was finally opened, she, with Holwell, was among the first to be hustled out, staggering and gasping as they gulped in lungs full of the fresh air of heaven. It was six o'clock. They had been in the Black Hole for ten hours.

But for Holwell the terror was not yet ended. He was hurried straight off to the nabob. They carried him as he was unable to walk, one of the officers telling him as they went that he had better say where the East India Company's treasure was buried, otherwise he would be shot to pieces from the mouth of a cannon. But Holwell knew nothing of the treasure, or even if it existed. Aware of this, the nabob spared his life.

He and three other survivors were shackled in irons and made to march up-river in the noonday heat to the nabob's capital. Some weeks later they gained their liberty.

The rest of the survivors were freed, with the exception of Mary Carey, who was far too young and lovely to escape. She was taken into the nabob's harem. The dead were carted out of the Black Hole and dumped in a ditch like the carcases of rotting cattle and covered with earth.

POSTSCRIPT: The nabob's victory was short-lived. Clive took swift revenge, destroyed his army and deposed him. A year later he was dead. It was evident that when he ordered the prisoners to the Black Hole, he had no idea of its dimensions. Holwell was later made Governor of Bengal. He died in 1798 at Pinner, Middlesex, at the age of eighty-seven. As for Mary Carey, no one knows how she fared in the nabob's harem, but she was not there for long. She returned to Calcutta and later married an English officer named Weston, by whom she had three children. When Weston died, she significantly changed her name back to Carey. She died in 1801 at the age of sixty. She was thus on the night of the Black Hole a mere sixteen years old.

Two Views of the Scaffold

Her brother was a king, and heading towards madness. The husband into whose arms she had gladly fled was also a king. He was also, as she discovered too late, mad.

Christian VII was just seventeen years of age when he ascended the throne of Denmark in 1766. He had been brought up by a sadistic tutor against whose brutal discipline he rebelled at every opportunity. His sensitive nature was warped into petulance; his yearning for love became a greedy search for sensation. Pride became defiance, of a kind which led him impulsively into any degradation he was offered. By the time he became king he was already sick and dissipated, despised by all the men who were now to become his supposedly dutiful ministers.

A good marriage was essential. Perhaps it would help to stabilize him. His father, a libertine like himself, had been kept under reasonable control by the English princess he had married and whom he had loved in spite of his other follies. A match was arranged between Christian and another English princess, his cousin Caroline Matilda, sister of George III. They were married in the year of Christian's accession, when she was fifteen.

At first she was contented enough, even happy. The young man was handsome and could exert considerable charm when he wished. In addition, he was flatteringly eager to seek her advice.

He certainly needed advice. He was no match for the intriguers and political strategists who tussled for power within the privy council. By the end of a year the king had almost given up the attempt to assert his royal authority. The chief marshal, Moltke, and the foreign minister, Bernstorff, played games whose rules he could not grasp. To make matters worse, another member of the council was his former tutor, Reventlow.

"They won't listen to me," he complained to his wife after a gruelling day in conference. "And Reventlow bullies me as though I were still a child. It's not fair!"

"If they won't do what you want," said Caroline Matilda, "why don't you get rid of them?"

He dismissed Moltke and Reventlow. But the confusion was such that in a short time they had to be reinstated.

Now Christian turned on Caroline and blamed her for the bad advice she had given him. What he really wanted in a wife was someone to blame whenever things went wrong.

They quarrelled; were reconciled; drifted apart again. A son and a daughter marked happy moments; the king's peevish disappearances in search of other amusement marked the bad ones. His favourite haunt was Hirschholm, a huge palace north of Copenhagen with parkland and deeply wooded groves surrounding it. Here he chased his mistresses down paths and along corridors, raged and stormed, sobbed and rejoiced, and returned when the fancy took him to dabble unavailingly with the mysteries of government.

The dowager queen, Juliane Marie, his father's second wife, watched and disapproved.

Caroline Matilda knew that Juliane Marie disliked her and would welcome any turn of events that gave her a chance to take over the virtual running of the country. Caroline could almost hear the envious whispers, the derision, the insidious threats.

Plans had been made for Christian to tour Hanover, France and England in 1768, but his ministers were afraid that his behaviour while abroad would discredit Denmark. It was decided that a personal physician must be appointed to watch over the king. Caroline was shocked, yet had to agree that she herself had proved inadequate and that he needed a stronger guardian.

Juliane Marie was also shocked. If any influence was to be wielded, she preferred it to be hers. She was overruled by the councillors, but it was clear that, whatever doctor was chosen, she would automatically disapprove and make his life difficult.

The doctor was Johann Friedrich Struensee from Altona. He was a free-thinker, a man of liberal views in politics and private affairs, and a shrewd psychologist. Women found him irresistible—with the exception, that is, of the dour Juliane Marie, who declared that he was a social climber and that no good would come of his appointment.

Christian's tour went off unexpectedly well. He impressed his hosts with his intelligence and modesty, and returned to Copenhagen glowing with self-satisfaction.

Struensee wasted no time. The precarious balance of the king's mind depended, obviously, on his personal relationships and particularly on his relationship with his wife. Gently the doctor talked to him of his duties to the beautiful girl he had married. Gently he talked also to the beautiful girl. Caroline Matilda listened to his persuasive voice and allowed herself to believe for a while that Christian was truly royal and truly her husband and truly an ideal lover. If, in his arms, she had any misgivings, she could always think of Doctor Struensee and hear the echo of his hypnotic tones.

Grudgingly the dowager queen admitted that the German doctor had worked a minor miracle. Beneath the surface, she went on seething ominously away and waiting for things to go wrong.

Struensee was not content to be merely the king's physician. Because of his power over the young man and the young man's consort, he gained the free run of the court and could not refrain from dabbling in politics. He began to pull strings, to make his royal puppets dance. In defiance of all accepted procedure he was appointed chief minister of the cabinet. Assessing his rivals, he engineered the dismissal of the loyal Bernstorff. Knowing that the nobility regarded him as an upstart, he in return despised them for being out of touch with the real needs of the country and the people. He instituted reforms, coaxed the king into reorganizing the entire national administration, and even took measures to curb the powers of the church.

"I must ask what Doctor Struensee has to say about it," was the king's answer to any query put to him.

The dowager queen was heard to growl: "This upstart shows signs of turning into another Ulfeldt."

Still not well versed in Danish history, Caroline asked her husband who this Ulfeldt had been. He took great relish in telling her the grisly story.

In the seventeenth century the king's favourite daughter, Leonora Christine, had married a dashing young courtier, Corfits Ulfeldt. The young man had begun to play the game of court politics, but reached too far, made mistakes, and made too many enemies. They conspired to have him and his wife arrested.

By guile and daring, the couple escaped, and for a time ranged Europe to gain support from kings and princes who had once won favours from them. Leonora Christine herself tried to reclaim money which Charles II of England had been glad to borrow from Ulfeldt, but which he was not so eager to pay back. Charles slyly delivered her back into the hands of her Danish enemies, and she was finally imprisoned in the Blue Tower in Copenhagen for twenty years.

Still Ulfeldt remained at large. In their anger his enemies, among them the vicious Danish queen, contrived a malevolent joke. Not only did they take pleasure in demolishing Leonora Christine's beloved palace and recounting to her every detail of its destruction, but one night they sent workmen to erect a scaffold beneath the window of her prison. Who was to be executed: did she dare to hazard a guess?

In the early morning a woman attendant came screaming into the room. "Lady, they are bringing your husband!" The princess fainted but was callously revived and forced to stand at the window overlooking the scaffold. She had to watch as Corfits Ulfeldt was brought out.

But it was not the living Ulfeldt; not her husband. An effigy had been made of him, so lifelike that when placed in the adjoining room it had convinced Leonora's attendant. Now she watched the hideous symbolism of his execution— the effigy was being hanged, drawn and quartered, and the head being then stuck on a pole and carried away for display on the town hall.

This was the reward of overweening ambition.

Was that how people were beginning to look on Doctor Struensee?

It was not how Christian thought of him. And not how Caroline thought of him. She listened to him as devotedly as ever—so devotedly that she found herself in his bed, and for the first time since reaching Denmark was utterly, unquestioningly happy.

There were few in the court who did not soon guess what was going on. The king himself suspected, though he never put it into words. In some perverse way he was drawn closer to Caroline Matilda. Spasmodically jealous and frequently brutal, he was nevertheless fired to a new interest in her by the knowledge that his physician found her desirable. His casual liaisons continued but no longer satisfied him as they had once done. He alternately swore eternal fidelity to his wife, and cursed her; and in either mood enjoyed his sensations to the full.

If Juliane Marie wished to assert her influence over Christian she would have to catch him in one of the moods when he was prepared to be recklessly angry with Caroline.

However splendid Struensee's liberal reforms might be, there were many who hated them. Influential land-owners and merchants saw him as a potential wrecker. The nobles resented him. The army was against him. Count Rantzau-Ascheberg, once a friend of Struensee but now a disappointed and vindictive enemy, began to plan a military coup. Juliane Marie was a ready collaborator.

On the evening of 16 January, 1772, a magnificent fancy-dress ball was held in the court theatre. A shifting rainbow of sparkling costumes pulsated across the spacious stage. Music flowed like wine, the wine bubbled like music.

In her tiny, luxurious boudoir in the wings of the theatre, where they had so often met behind drawn curtains, Caroline drew Struensee close to her.

"There is something wrong." She had been trembling all evening. "I feel that something terrible is going to happen."

Struensee laughed. She had often felt a breathless fear at the risks they ran, knowing how easily Christian could turn vindictive and knowing how eagerly his step-mother watched for her opportunity. But Struensee was always so comforting, always so skilled at making her feel safe.

"Nothing more terrible than usual," he said, kissing her reassuringly.

" They hate you. Can't you feel it?"

"Many of them have always hated me. It doesn't frighten me."

Outside somebody began to call her name with drunken insistence. It was her husband.

"I must go."

She went out. Juliane Marie was watching. From another corner of the stage Count Rantzau-Ascheberg also watched as, after a decent interval, Struensee emerged from the boudoir.

Christian had drunk too much and was in a bad temper. He wanted to know where she had been hiding and how she could dare to make a fool of him in public. "And stop looking round for that damned doctor while the king is talking to you."

The dancing continued. But some did not dance. The dowager queen spent most of the evening chatting to a group of army officers. When they smiled, there was a sinister promise in the smiles.

It was long past midnight when Caroline Matilda at last went to bed. She tossed and turned for a while, then fell into an exhausted sleep.

She was awoken by a thundering on her door. Her maid, white and trembling, came in with two armed guards. A tight-lipped officer followed them in.

"You will dress, madam, and accompany us."

She looked from face to face and read the worst. Abruptly she dodged between the guards and fled down the corridor towards the rooms where Struensee lived. She was still some feet away when the door opened and Struensee was dragged unceremoniously out. Caroline tried to reach him, but the guards caught up with her and held her back.

She was rushed away in a carriage with her little daughter. They rumbled on through the bitter dawn, up the coast of Zealand past the rolling parkland where Christian enjoyed his lascivious sports, and on to the bleak fortress of Kronborg in Elsinore.

The little Louise Augusta whimpered incessantly. She could not understand why they should have left the comforts of Copenhagen. Nor could she understand why, in the days that followed, she was confined to these freezing turret rooms, not allowed to play beyond the guards at the ends of the corridor below—and why was her mother weeping, why did Pastor Lehzen come to them with such anguish in his face?

From the pastor Caroline learned enough to construct a blurred, frightening picture of what had happened after that *danse macabre* in the Court Theatre.

In the company of her fellow conspirators, the dowager queen Juliane Marie had shaken the king into befuddled wakefulness and thrust an order under his nose.

"You must sign this."

"Sign . . .? What . . . at this hour?"

"They have been plotting your overthrow. Struensee is preparing to commit treason, and your own wife is his mistress and accomplice. They must be stopped—*now*."

Christian groped for understanding and tried to argue. But he could not make himself heard through the solemn reading of the order which decreed the immediate arrest of the queen, Struensee, and one of Struensee's closest associates. Through the haze he remembered that he had been angry with Caroline—and he had had good reason, hadn't he? He could believe anything of her. Anything. Besides, he would get no sleep, no respite, until he signed.

Christian signed.

Caroline Matilda demanded to see him. The demand was refused. She had forfeited all right to his company. All she could do now was confess her guilt.

"But I am guilty of nothing."

"You have conspired to dethrone the king. You have been guilty of an immoral relationship with one of the king's ministers, and were aware that the said minister had in any case committed an act of *lèse-majesté* in procuring his appointment."

"No," said the queen resolutely.

She intended to remain resolute and not to say anything which could harm the one man in this country who had made life tolerable and then blissful for her. She denied both her guilt and his and settled down to work at her embroidery, filling the hours with its intricacies so that she might not think and despair.

Her resolve did not falter until Pastor Lehzen sadly

brought her the impossible news that Struensee had confessed all. He and the queen were guilty of the charges brought against them.

From nobody but the pastor would Caroline have accepted the truth of this report. Had they tortured Struensee, threatened or cajoled, made false promises? There was no way of telling. All she could do now was bow her head and admit her own guilt—but only a personal guilt, never under any circumstances treason.

What would happen to Struensee? And what would her own fate be?

There were certain gruesome parallels between her plight and that of the wretched Leonora Christine. Over and over again she thought of that dreadful history. But there was one important difference: Ulfeldt's enemies had never captured him; Struensee's enemies had him securely in Copenhagen.

The malicious Juliane Marie must have something in store. Caroline waited fearfully, hardly daring to speculate about the humiliations which were doubtless being prepared for her.

Early one morning she was driven back to the city. She was taken out on a balcony above a great open space. Juliane Marie and Count Rantzau-Ascheberg were watching her, just as they had watched on the night of that fancy-dress ball. Their smiles were different now—savage and exultant.

Crowds flocked into the square. It was all just as she had imagined it must have been for Leonora Christine . . . complete with the scaffold at the centre.

Caroline's knees went weak. She was about to collapse; wanted to collapse and see no more, hear no more; but Juliane Marie insisted that she should be supported and kept facing the scaffold.

Soldiers marched into the square and formed up below the steps.

To the sombre tap of a drum, Struensee was brought out. This was no effigy. It was Struensee himself.

The charge and the sentence were read hurriedly, as though to gloss over their absurdities. Struensee was denounced for having failed to learn the Danish language and constitution, and for wantonly misleading the king. Under the king's law, his added offence of having "done injury to the king or queen" warranted the death penalty.

Struensee made no reply and offered no plea for mercy. He mounted the scaffold, proud to the last

The executioner's assistant seized Struensee's right wrist and held it across the block. The executioner's axe rose and fell, and the assistant stepped back holding the hand which had touched Caroline, caressed her, communicated to her the only real tenderness she had ever known. Then Struensee was forced to his knees. His head was thrust down upon the block. Again the axe rose, hesitated for a moment, then slashed down. The assistant grabbed Struensee's head by the hairs and held it aloft, dripping. The crowd howled with delight.

What was left of Johann Friedrich Struensee was then strapped to a wheel and broken upon it.

Caroline Matilda was taken back to her turret prison in Elsinore.

In a trance she continued to work at her embroidery. She played with little Louise Augusta, and talked—or, rather, listened numbly—to Pastor Lehzen. She waited for the official verdict on her own behaviour; and for the sentence.

It was the gentle pastor who at last brought her the news that there would be no verdict and no sentence. A British warship had arrived off Elsinore. Deranged as he might be, her brother could not ignore the clamour of his people. They did not believe the garbled tales they heard from Denmark, and demanded that their beautiful princess should be subjected to no further persecution.

Caroline Matilda was freed. It was not until the last moment that she realized the authorities were not going to let Louise Augusta accompany her. The child was literally torn from her arms, and Pastor Lehzen had to help the British officers force her aboard.

Lehzen was presented with the tragically exquisite embroidery which had occupied her during the imprisonment. Through his family it came into the hands of Queen Victoria and eventually into those of Queen Elizabeth II.

But Caroline Matilda did not return to England. For her its memories were little happier than those of Denmark. She was taken instead to Hanover and died three years later of a broken heart, known to her friends and sympathizers then and ever after as the queen of tears.

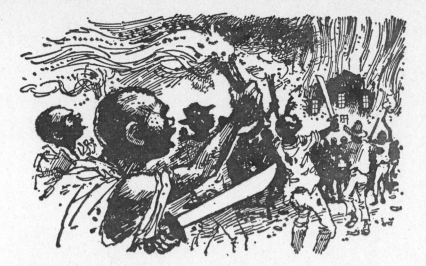

Haiti: The Slave Uprising

The island of Saint-Domingue lies some fifty miles east of
Cuba. Today, the eastern part of the island is known as
Haiti, and the western end is the Dominican Republic; but
in the eighteenth century it was one of the richest of France's
overseas possessions. Life for the *colons* was good—idle,
luxurious and elegant. But it was a way of life based on
repression, cruelty and slavery, and it could only be maintained for as long as the half-million black slaves remained
subservient to their forty thousand white masters.

The plantation owners were aware of the danger inherent
in their position; but in their luxurious mansions they were
unable to consider any threat as serious, and they had only
one answer to any faint stirrings of discontent—punishment.

Cruelty grew out of slavery as naturally and as inevitably
as a plant grows from a seed. When a human being has been
bought and sold, then he loses his humanity in the eyes of
his owner. He becomes an object, a mere possession for the
owner to deal with as he wishes; and just as the slave forfeits
his dignity, so the master loses his compassion.

Terrible stories have come down to us of the treatment
of slaves in Saint-Domingue. We hear of one master who
wanted to show off the new pistol he had just acquired from
Europe. He demonstrated its accuracy by shooting a slave.
But, although the Europeans acted with impunity, there was
always present the shadow of fear that one day the slaves

would rise up and turn on their masters. So the masters tried to repress the slaves by punishing any infringement of the rules with savage cruelty. The most common form of punishment was a lashing with the bull-hide whip. The victim— man or woman—was staked out flat on the ground and whipped until the bones showed through the bloody, mutilated flesh.

Even this was not sufficient for some of the more sadistic plantation-managers. They would rub salt into the gaping wounds, and some devised their own punishments. One manager discouraged his slaves from running away by cutting one leg off a slave who tried to escape. Not all the plantation-managers shared his wanton cruelty; some, by the standards of the time, were kindly men. But even the kindest were still slave-owners—they still traded in human beings. The society of Saint-Domingue stank with corruption. It was inevitable that, sooner or later, the Europeans would push the half-million negroes too far, and that when that happened the slaves would take a terrible vengeance.

The black slaves who were brought to Saint-Domingue came from many different parts of Africa, and they brought with them a mixture of religious beliefs. These African religions were welded together to form a new cult which had its own special flavour, effected as it was by the experience of slavery. This cult was known as Voodoo. It had its own priests and priestesses, who had dark, magical powers; for they could bring the dead back to life as Zombies. It was a religion of fear and sacrifice and total obedience. But it was more than just a religion. Spreading to all the plantation slaves it became a secret society, uniting all the negroes of the island. It was a ready-made instrument for revolt.

One of the *papaloi*, or high-priests of Voodoo, was a slave called Buckman. He was a *commandeur*, a kind of slave foreman, but his privileged position in no way lessened his hatred of his white owners. He determined to use his position of power in the Voodoo priesthood to lead a mass uprising of the slaves. The summer of 1791 saw a good deal of unrest on the plantations and the owners resorted to the usual tools of repression—the whip and the gallows. There was a temporary halt to the disturbances, and the *colons* relaxed again, reverting to their normal life of luxury and ease. But the feelings of resentment had not been killed;

instead the brutal repression had turned smouldering resentment into burning hatred. Buckman felt the time had come for the uprising which would end white domination of the island for all time.

In August of that year Buckman began holding secret meetings with the plantation slaves, to secure their help and bind them to him by the powerful bonds of the Voodoo rites. The first of many meetings was held in the woods near one of the large plantations. The black, tropical night shook with the ominous rolling of thunder, and the faces of the slaves were briefly lit by the flashing lightning as they made their way to the meeting place.

The men gathered in a circle in a clearing in the woods. Slowly and softly the drummers began their rhythmic, hypnotic beating. The crowd remained motionless as Buckman stepped forward into the circle. The beating of the drums began to quicken and grow louder, and Buckman started to move around the circle. In his hand he held a small bowl, from which blue and white flames licked upwards into the still air. As the drumming became more and more frenzied, his movements took on the character of a reeling, grotesque dance. He stumbled round and round the circle, his limbs jerking spasmodically. His eyes rolled upwards until the pupils disappeared up under the lids and only the whites were visible, giving his face the appearance of a mask. His lips drew back from his teeth and he began to shout in a strange high-pitched voice. He had now entered a complete trance state, and he spoke with the voices of spirits and demons.

As the audience swayed, participating in the dancer's trance, Buckman stopped before the statue of the snake-god Damballah and hurled the small vessel at the front of the statue. The flaming mass burst out on to the ground, and Buckman fell into the middle of the burning fire, rolling over and over the flames, still crying out in the voice of the gods.

The drummers now worked themselves into a frenzy of noise, the throbbing drums rivalling the thunder that still rolled overhead. Buckman, his body arched high over the ground, raised his voice to scream above the drumming, ordering the men gathered round the clearing to kill the white demons, to burn their houses, to put their families to death. The crowd shouted their ecstatic acceptance of the order which the Voodoo gods had given through the mouth of their priest.

Buckman collapsed back on to the ground, and the lesser priests, the *mamaloi*, dragged him away. Still the incessant drumming went on. Others took up the strange, ecstatic dancing, and as they touched their neighbours so they passed on the trance-state as though it were a contagious disease. Soon the clearing was alive with the tortured dancing and the rhythmically rocking bodies of the watchers. One young man took his cane-cutting knife and began to whirl round and round the circle, the sharp blade twisting and shining in the firelight. Then suddenly he buried the blade deep into his arm. There was no cry of pain, no change of expression on his face, as he danced on, the knife still embedded in his flesh. The trance was complete.

The rhythm of the drums changed to a slower beat. The dancers, their bodies gleaming with sweat, subsided to the ground, to be pulled away by the *mamaloi*. Buckman returned. Behind him came the *mamaloi*, dragging a black boar. The beast's head was pulled back exposing its throat. One of the *mamaloi* drew the ceremonial knife, and with one slash cut the animal's throat. The blood poured on to the ground, and spattered the priests. Buckman took the still twitching body of the boar and held the gaping wound up to his mouth, drinking the warm blood. He then swung the carcase round to the other men, so that they too could drink the life-blood of the sacrificial animal. When all had drunk, the lifeless creature was laid at the foot of Damballah's statue.

Buckman turned to his followers. His lips gleaming red from the fresh blood, he told them they were now bound in a solemn oath to follow him. No word must be spoken of the secret ceremony of that night, and when Buckman gave the word they were to rise against their masters to kill until no white man was left alive on the whole island. The gods had given them this great mission to perform; the men had sealed the bargain by participating in the blood sacrifice to Damballah. They were now under the protection of the gods of Voodoo, and they could not fail. Fighting by their sides would be the Zombies, the indestructible living dead.

Solemnly, the oath was taken. The drumming ceased, and silently the men slipped away to their wretched huts on the plantation. The dark woods were empty. The night was silent, except for the cries of the wild animals and the distant rumble of the thunder as the storm passed away over the island.

During the following weeks, the scene was repeated at many different plantations, until Buckman was satisfied that he/had sufficient support to give the signal for the uprising to begin. He had hundreds of followers, bound to him by an oath that they dare not break even had they wanted to do so. Buckman settled on 22 August as the day when he and the other slaves would take their vengeance.

For the white masters of the plantations, life went on as usual. The stirrings of trouble in the earlier part of the summer had been satisfactorily suppressed, and the usual round of feasting and drunkenness could continue. The house servants still waited at table, cleaned the house, looked after all the needs of the *colons*. A careful observer would have noticed something different about the servants, a subtle change of mood. They were still subservient, but they had about them an air of watchfulness and waiting. The observer would have had his suspicions roused. But the *colons* were not observant—they were victims of that special blindness that came from an inability to see the black slaves as people. The negro was an object to be bought and sold, a piece of flesh that could be made to perform certain tasks that would add to his owner's comfort and prosperity. He was not a person with ordinary human feelings, so there was no point in watching him. You don't watch a lump of stone to see what it's going to do next. So when the blow fell, the Europeans were completely unprepared. The years of savage brutality were about to be repaid with a matching viciousness. The insensate stones were about to come to life.

Buckman was *commandeur* on the Turpin plantation. One of his jobs each day was to call the field-workers together and herd them to work with cracks of the bull-hide whip. On the night of 22 August, Buckman called the Turpin workers together, not to go into the fields to harvest the crops, but to kill, to rape, to burn, to pillage, to destroy the white man and everything he had made. They answered the call of the man who was to be general of their army and who was a high-priest of the Voodoo gods. They remembered the oath, sealed by the blood of the sacrificial boar.

No records remain of what the men, women and children on the Turpin plantation thought or how they acted on that night. No one was left alive to write the record. But the scene was to be repeated in many places that night. The field-workers moved out from their rough barracks on the plantation, their path lit by the flare from many torches. As they moved forward they began to fire the crops and the out-buildings. Slowly the fire spread, until the Europeans in the big house at last became aware that this night was not to be a night like other nights. They called for their servants to run and find out what was happening, but there were no servants left in the house to answer the calls. They had slipped away into the night.

For the first time the planters were alone. There was no one to fetch and carry, no one to run messages, no one to do anything for them. Perhaps, at first, they believed that this was another minor disturbance that could easily be quelled; the ring-leaders would be hanged and life would return to normal. But as the flames got nearer, the reality must have been plain. Behind the glare of the flaring torches came a great army of black men. In their ranks, the drummers beat out the insistent rhythm of the Voodoo ceremony; the prayers to the Voodoo gods were called out above the sinister beating. Some of the army that marched relentlessly on the big house were already in a state of ecstatic frenzy, others walked as though in their trance they had joined the Zombies themselves.

As realization dawned on the Europeans, they rushed for weapons to defend themselves. Doors were barricaded, shutters thrown up against windows. The chanting mass of men were near to the house when the defenders opened fire. Firing at point-blank range it was inevitable that some of the slaves would be hit, but as the wounded fell they were left where they lay and the rest moved inexorably forwards. Now they were near enough for their faces to be clearly seen in the light from the flaming torches. If the owners had been unable to distinguish any new emotion in the faces of their slaves before, they had no trouble now. The men who had once been mutely acquiescent were transformed, their faces were twisted with ugly hatred as they yelled their threats of vengeance.

The handful of white men desperately fired at the

advancing black wave that threatened to engulf them, but they were too late to turn the tide. Soon the house was surrounded, and Buckman gave the order to set it on fire. The wooden verandah where the owners had sat, watching the workers in the distant fields, was soon ablaze. The fire spread to doors and window-frames, and within minutes the whole house was alive with flames. Inside, the defenders choked in the billowing black smoke and tried to back away from the dreadful heat. Screaming children clung to their mothers' skirts, while the despairing men tried to beat out the flames. But the fire was too much for them. They had only two choices open to them: stay where they were and burn and suffocate to death, or try to fight their way out through the chanting mob outside. They chose to try and escape, for the heat inside had become, literally, unbearable.

With drawn swords, the men led the dash through the flaming front doorway out into the open air. They tried to blink away the tears caused by the acrid smoke, to look for a possible way of escape. But everywhere they looked they could see nothing but the hate-filled faces of their former slaves. Some of the women fell sobbing to their knees, begging mercy from the negroes to whom they had never shown any mercy themselves. The men slashed around with their swords, but were soon overwhelmed.

The Europeans were caught and held. The fight was over, their only hope lay in the better feelings of their captors. It was no hope at all—whatever better feelings the slaves had possessed had been flogged and beaten out of them by the creatures who now stood terrified before them. They had come to take their revenge—and the revenge they took was terrible.

While the men were firmly held, the victors began on the women. The helpless females were thrown from man to man; their fine, expensive clothing was ripped from their bodies. Round and round they staggered as they were punched, torn and kicked, until they fell to the ground exhausted. Then, under the eyes of their menfolk, they were raped. At last, an end came to the torture and misery. The slaves drew their knives and fell on their victims, hacking and cutting until the ground was awash with streams of bright, red blood, and the last *colon* had died. No one was spared, not even the children. At last the killing was over and the fury abated. A grim and grisly banner was constructed to serve as an emblem for the slaves: the mutilated body of a small child was strapped to a pole and lifted high over the head of the exultant crowd.

The burning of the Turpin plantation had been a signal. All around the countryside was lit by flames, as one by one the great houses were put to the torch. Smoke billowed out across the fields, and the night air was filled with noises—the chanting of the slaves and the screams and cries of their victims. If the dark gods of Voodoo required a blood sacrifice then that night they were sated. In a few hours the hatred born of years of humiliation and torture was released, and the evil that flowed in the island was terrible. As the word spread through the countryside, and more plantations were fired, the Europeans fled in panic from their homes, stumbling through the black night to try to reach the safety of the port of Cap-François. A few who had not shared in the general bestiality of their fellow countrymen were helped to safety by their slaves. Some reached safety by their own efforts. Many met only a horrible death.

The news of the atrocities reached the fleeing French and spread even greater panic amongst them. They heard of men being nailed alive to gates before being hacked into pieces, of men being sawn in half, of women and young girls being ravished. So those that could raced for the city, while the stragglers played a deadly game of hide-and-seek with the bands of slaves that roved the blazing countryside hunting for fresh victims.

By dawn the first wave of violence was spent. The Europeans had drawn back into their besieged city and were busy assembling and ordering their forces to deal with the revolt. Women and children were embarked on to the ships in the harbour for greater safety. It was a dark dawn that day. The sun was almost obliterated by the clouds of black smoke that rose from the burning land, the smouldering remains of the mansions. Buckman and his slave army gathered round Cap-François. They too were exhausted by the long night of murder.

The uprising of 22 August, 1791, achieved very little of itself. Soon the *colons* were hitting back in force, exacting, in their turn, their own brutal revenge. But it was a beginning, the beginning of a movement that would lead eventually to the establishment of an independent, black kingdom of Haiti.

Yet that one terrible night of violence and fear had done two things: it had lanced a great blister of hatred that had grown for year after year, and it had shown the negro that his white overlord was not invincible. In itself that was not enough, for the slaves had acted instinctively, driven on by their hatred and by the passions roused in them by the Voodoo priests. There was nothing heroic about the night. The *colons* had acted viciously and inhumanely; the slaves in their turn had done the same. The very fact of slavery had spread its poison equally between the slave-master and the slave. The night of 22 August, 1791, saw a victory only for the spirit of evil.

The Ruthless Pursuit

His name was Jonathan Strong. It had not always been so, but after a few weeks of having it bellowed at him he learned to answer to it. He even became proud of it. They called him Strong because that was what he was. Even a slave had to have something to be proud of. Besides, it was safer to grin and look obedient and dutifully display his strength than to show sadness. If you grew mournful and slack, they said these were the first signs that you were planning to run away; and there was only one cure for that:

"Whipping the devil out of them—that's the best measure against absconding."

Ever since Sir John Hawkins broke the sixteenth-century Portuguese slave monopoly and began to do business shipping Africans to the Spanish colonies, England had done well at the trade. When her own colonies expanded and labour was needed for the sugar plantations and estates of the West Indies, she was already expert in collection and transportation.

In the early days, raiding parties gathered their supplies from the African coast. Then the natives grew wary, kept regular watch, and withdrew into the bush at the first sign of sail on the horizon. Some traders ventured inland in pursuit, but soon found it simpler and safer to deal with exploiters prepared to barter their own people for cloth, beads and, above all, firearms and alcohol.

The man now called Jonathan Strong had been a handsome, vigorous youth whose tribe lived safely in the interior. Safely, that is, until war broke out with a neighbouring tribe. After fierce fighting, Jonathan was captured and taken to the enemy village.

He was not put to death. The local chief had better use for his captives than that. Jonathan was sold off, along with some of the chief's own subjects who had committed minor crimes, to the next slave dealer who passed.

The caravan set off towards the coast.

Resting at a water-hole, Jonathan broke away and fled, running with the insane energy of fear; but that same fear made him breathless, and his pursuers soon overtook him. He was beaten, and then his neck was locked into a slave-stick—a long pole with a crook at the end which rasped and tormented his neck and throat until he longed for death.

He did not die. But others did. Their bodies were left to rot and add to the pattern of bones marking the much-trodden route.

The ship waiting for them had been specially fitted out for the trade. Its hold was divided by shelves rather than decks, each allowing no more than three feet of head-room. Jonathan was handcuffed to another man, and the two of them were thrust on to the lower shelf. They were pressed close together as other couples were stacked into place.

In one of the most profitable years for the slavers, who packed their ships as tightly as possible with valuable cargo, as many as one hundred thousand slaves crossed the Atlantic.

The voyage known as the Middle Passage was the worst of the regular runs. Hostile winds or demoralizing calm could delay arrival for several weeks. Then food and water, at the best of times not lavished too generously on the slaves, grew even scarcer. Heat and filth made the air between the decks unbreathable. Men sickened and died. Some went mad.

One day, when they had been lying becalmed for longer than Jonathan could remember, and it seemed that he would never see the outside world again or discover what lay beyond the sea, feet stamped along the gangways and orders were shouted. The black prisoners were taken up on deck in groups.

"Dance!"

The word meant nothing to them. But when the sweating, shouting white men demonstrated, they began obediently to caper up and down.

"I want you lot healthy when we get there."

Their feeble legs could produce only a pitiful travesty of the jubilant dances they had known back in their own, lost country.

In spite of the captain's efforts to keep his stock in saleable condition, disease struck and spread rapidly.

Again men were ordered up on deck. This time only the sick were chosen. It was not a compassionate move. Those who remained below heard, faintly, a long succession of splashes—more than a hundred of them. The captain was clearing his ship of illness by tossing the afflicted overboard. His insurance policy contained a clause which made the insurance company liable for the cost of any items of cargo jettisoned to save the rest.

When one such case was brought to court in London, the Solicitor-General declared that, so far from there being any question of a murder charge against the owners, there was not even the slightest imputation of cruelty. The Chief Justice himself added that "the case of the slaves was the same as if horses had been thrown overboard".

But those who died and those who survived knew nothing of such fine legal points. The dead sank below the surface of the ocean; the living and the half-living lay on their scorching shelves, waiting for the journey to end.

They reached Barbados at last, and staggered or crept on to dry land. Many found it impossible to stand upright.

The captain carried out a quick inspection. Where shoulders had been rubbed raw against woodwork, or skin had been opened up by storm damage or the descent of a whip, everything possible was done to conceal the wounds. Then the slaves were put up for sale in the market. The owners and overseers came from the plantations and strolled around the merchandise, prodding and pinching, sneering at some of the stooping wretches whose backs could not be straightened even by the touch of the lash.

"Not a very good parcel this time . . . poor condition."

Shrewdly estimating the prices he was likely to get, the captain assembled the less prepossessing specimens, the sick and the ailing women, into a separate group. They could be sold off cheap in the accepted category of "refuse".

Jonathan fetched a good price, and joined the gang on a sugar plantation.

He was at work every morning while it was still dark. So were his masters.

"We eat breakfast every day," one of them wrote at the time, "and have everybody at work before day dawns. I am never caught in bed after daylight, nor is anybody else on the place; and we go in the fields till it's so dark we can't see to work. That's how we do it, every day the same."

Every day the same. They were, really, all slaves of the plantation.

You were allowed to sing, if singing made you work faster. If the song grew mournful and the tempo slackened, the whip would soon make you cheerful and active again.

Some slaves who yearned for a respite tried to injure themselves. One man on Jonathan's gang had the ability to wrench his left shoulder out of joint when he craved a rest from labour. Another, who had fallen foul of his overseer, cut off his own right hand in a gesture of defiance. A woman who did not wish to be sold to another land-owner, away from a male slave she had dared to grow fond of, cut off her fingers so that no price would be offered for her.

For most, who did not reach a stage of such desperation, the pace was steady and numbing. The rhythm of work became so hypnotic that the mere idea of being sold off to another owner was frightening because it meant a disruption of the mindless routine.

Sales were nevertheless frequent. Speculators would sell up their estates and get out on a whim. They would get out even more quickly if faced with serious losses. One bad year could mean the failure of a plantation.

Jonathan's owner lived in England and paid a manager to supervise his property. When the manager ran into trouble, the absentee landlord decided to cut his losses. Long before the estate itself was disposed of, the slaves were auctioned off: better to sell them than feed them. Jonathan was bought by a lawyer, David Lisle. A sadist who liked his servants to cower when he approached, Lisle admired Jonathan's physique and at the same time longed to humiliate him. He flogged this new vassal without mercy, often until Jonathan could hardly walk.

Lisle was derisive when a missionary showed up, anxious to baptize the slaves on the island and to preach brotherhood, trust and co-operation among all men.

"Never trust a negro. Never. The only way to keep a black honest is not to trust him."

When Lisle returned to London he took Jonathan with him. It was fashionable to show off one's negroes in the home country, and many planters retiring, or settling down while a manager ran their distant estates, brought such picked slaves with them until there were more than fourteen thousand in England.

Lisle maintained his violent ways. If business went badly or anyone crossed him in any way, he sought out Jonathan and flogged him or beat him about the head with a pistol butt. Jonathan's life was what it had been for so long: he had run from enemies in the bush, tried to escape from slavers, bowed beneath the lash in the fields and hidden from punishment until dragged out by his tormentors; and now when he recognized the storm signals in Lisle's face he would flee into a corner and shiver there until his master came and worked off his spleen. Always the same remorseless pattern—flight, capture, punishment and pain.

Lisle's treatment reduced the once-sturdy slave to a quivering, half-blind wreck. One day in 1765 Lisle decided there was no further work or sport left in the wretched creature, and turned him out of doors.

After wandering for some time in a daze, Jonathan was directed to a surgery in Mincing Lane where penniless patients could get free medical treatment. Waiting in the dejected queue, he was aware that a white man was studying him with pity and horror. The same man came into the surgery as the doctor began his examination, and the two of them gently questioned Jonathan.

William and Granville Sharp were brothers, two of fourteen children. William, a gifted and inventive young man, had become a surgeon. The shyer Granville, after one or two business disappointments, settled for a safe if unexciting job as a civil servant.

Distressed by Jonathan's condition, the brothers managed to have him admitted to St Bartholomew's Hospital. It took four months to set him right again. Jonathan could not believe that people were prepared to lavish so much care and kindness on him, not merely to mend his body but to restore his confidence. He dreaded the day when he must walk out of the hospital. In here he was safe. Outside, he would surely have to run again—to run, and inevitably be captured.

When he was discharged he found the Sharps waiting for him. They looked after him until they were sure he was fit for work, then found him a job as a chemist's errand boy.

Some people treated him well, others rudely. The weather was sometimes so cold that he felt he would die. But the chemist was a decent man, patient with him until he got to know the job thoroughly. Jonathan ate well. He began to feel happy. The hunted feeling faded.

Then one day fear struck at him across the street. Waiting to cross and return to the shop, he saw two men watching him. The face of one was all too familiar.

David Lisle seemed to be asking his companion a question. The man nodded, as though agreeing to a deal.

Jonathan wanted to run as he had run so many times before. But could he find safety in the maze of streets and alleys he had learned to know so well on his errands?

As he wavered, a passing coach obscured the two men. Instead of turning away, Jonathan dashed across the road and bolted into the chemist's shop, where he hid trembling in a back room until he was sure they were not coming for him.

That night as he left the shop two burly men seized him and manhandled him down the nearest alley. This time there was no neck yoke or chain, but their hands were just as brutal. In a matter of minutes he was hustled up to a door which he recognized. He had passed it often enough on his rounds. It was the entrance to the prison in Poultry.

Seeing his discarded slave restored to such fine condition, Lisle had decided to reclaim him. He had no further personal use for Jonathan, but offered him to his friend, James Kerr, for thirty pounds. Kerr accepted.

And Kerr was taking no chances. He wanted Jonathan kept in a safe place until transport could be arranged for the West Indies. Money changed hands. The gaoler was given his instructions. Jonathan was thrown into a cell, and the key turned in the lock.

He had foolishly come to think of himself almost as a free

man. Now he was to be shipped across the sea again, kicked about again, made a beast of burden again.

When Kerr had gone, Jonathan tried to reason with the gaoler. He made little impression. The man saw him as Kerr and Lisle saw him—little more than an animal, and a tricky, dangerous one at that.

Locked in the cell, Jonathan had nightmares of again being locked to another man, between those stifling, lurching decks. Then there would be the drudgery, the shacks that were themselves no better than prisons . . .

He again tried pleading with the gaoler. There had been a terrible mistake. He had a good job with a chemist, and had influential friends. Somebody would be in great trouble when it was discovered that he had been kidnapped. He spoke so convincingly about these friends that the gaoler became uneasy. He dared not risk Kerr's fury by setting Jonathan free; but he agreed to send a message to Granville Sharp.

Granville came hurrying to the rescue in the company of another brother, James, who was an influential City merchant. They had no power to free a man who, for however improbable a reason, had been delivered into the keeping of the prison; but they impressed on the gaoler that he must under no circumstances surrender his prisoner without a proper warrant. They then went to see James's old friend, the lord mayor.

The mayor agreed to summon before him anyone who tried to take possession of Jonathan Strong.

Jonathan waited and trembled. Sure enough, Kerr, having made his arrangements for Jonathan's dispatch to Jamaica, came with the ship's captain to collect his slave. Apprehensive but firm, the gaoler refused to surrender him, and told them what he had been instructed to say.

Kerr's attorney and the captain took the bill of sale which had been prepared between Lisle and Kerr to the lord mayor and demanded that Jonathan be handed over.

The lord mayor refused. In the first place, the planter had flouted the law. No man in England could be summarily thrown into prison by a private individual when no charge had been laid against him. Jonathan Strong was guilty of no crime within this realm. It was the mayor's duty, which he proposed to fulfil here and now, to release Jonathan Strong.

Still not really believing that the cloud had lifted, Jonathan walked dazedly out of the court into the street.

At once his arm was seized. The captain, swearing, pounced on him and began to drag him away.

"Cheat your way out of prison, hey? But you won't talk your way off my ship!"

Granville Sharp ran towards them and attempted to grab the captain. He was prevented by a lawyer who had been following the case with interest and now shouted that Sharp mustn't indulge in violence himself.

"A case of assault!" he cried. "Charge him with assault if he doesn't let go!"

Jonathan struggled to free himself. In the heat of the tussle, the shouted exchange of words was meaningless. Then, as though Sharp's swift threat—"Let go, sir, or I shall indeed bring such a charge"—were some magical incantation, the grip slackened and Jonathan was free.

For how long?

Kerr was in a rage. So was the choleric Lisle. They had made a deal together: it was unthinkable that it should be flouted by outsiders. A slave legally purchased in the normal way of business was property; and in England and its burgeoning colonies, property was sacred. Together Lisle and Kerr brought an action for damages of £200 against Granville Sharp.

To his dismay, Sharp found that his legal advisers counselled a quick settlement. There was no doubt about the validity of the sale, or of Kerr's ownership of the slave. Sharp insisted that slavery was not legal within England, and that no man could own and dispose of another in such a way. He was assured that, though this might theoretically be so, in practice it was considered unwise to interfere with the everyday practices of good English businessmen. The Chief Justice himself had come out firmly against vague idealists who wanted to release blacks from bondage and allow them to wander about at will. What would those fourteen thousand already in England do if turned loose, without a master to feed them and keep them usefully employed?

"I cannot believe," Sharp proclaimed, "that the law of England is so injurious to natural rights as so many great lawyers are pleased, for political reasons, to assert."

It was not a remark calculated to endear him to the profession. Nobody would conduct his defence. That being so, he decided to conduct his own, which was, in essence, also the defence of Jonathan Strong and Jonathan's rights.

It took two years of intensive study—two years during which the hunted, haunted Jonathan had to wait for a verdict that might send him on that terrible journey once more.

Sharp had copies made of his final manuscript and sent them to distinguished lawyers. Still none of them wished to represent him, yet the copies he had circulated did their work: he stirred up so much controversy that the advisers of Lisle and Kerr began to dread the eventual confrontation. Lisle and Kerr themselves, fearing that a judgement against them might have widespread effects on slave-owners' rights not only in England itself but eventually in the colonies, and weary in any case of the law's delays and evasions, decided not to continue the action. They were heavily fined for dropping it.

Sharp triumphantly brought out the fruits of his legal studies in print, under the title of *The Injustice and dangerous Tendency of tolerating Slavery in England*, and even had the bravado to declare that under certain statutes he could, if he wished, take action against Lisle and Kerr for their unscrupulous behaviour.

Jonathan Strong was a free man . . . so long as he remained in England.

"And this," vowed Sharp, "is only the beginning."

Hitherto as blind to the evils of slavery as were most of his fellow countrymen, he proposed to devote himself to the abolition of such servitude in his own land. And later, it must somehow be possible to bring an end to the whole foul trade across the Atlantic. The Chief Justice might be against him, absentee landlords and retired profiteers might be against him, public opinion might still be too lazy to be effective; but he would give them no rest.

Devoted as he was to the man who had worked such wonders for him, it is doubtful if Jonathan Strong believed that such sweeping changes would ever be possible. He had been one of the few lucky ones. He had been pursued through a protracted nightmare and was now out in the good daylight. Granville Sharp was lost, he was sure, in a daydream. It would never come true.

Thuggee

A statue of Kali looked down on her worshippers, her chosen people. The hideous face of the goddess was black, with bulging eyes, fang-like teeth and a monstrously huge tongue that hung down on to her naked chest. Snakes coiled around her shoulders, and the snake-belt round her waist was hung with human skulls.

According to legend Kali had once engaged in a fight with Rukt Bij-dana, a gigantic demon. Every time Kali struck the demon with her sword, the blood that spurted from the creature's body fell to the ground and there gave birth to new demons. Exhausted by her efforts, Kali made two men from her own sweat. She gave the men her handkerchief and ordered them to strangle the demons so that no more blood would be spilled. The men did as they were commanded, and when they had finished they offered to return the handkerchief to Kali. The goddess told them to keep it, and to pass it down to their descendants with the order to kill all who were not her chosen people. The men went away to follow the goddess's orders.

Kali herself ate the bodies of the victims, but one day one of her disciples saw her in the act and from that time on they had to dispose of the bodies themselves. They were rewarded with three gifts from Kali: the hem of her garment to use as a strangling noose, or *rumal*; one of her ribs to use as a knife for dismembering the bodies; and one of her own teeth as a pickaxe for digging the graves. These objects became the sacred tools of the men who sat at the goddess's feet, the men who for centuries had terrorized all India—the thugs.

A priest had already selected that day and that hour for the thugs to set out on their mission of murder, and now they were gathered in a jungle-surrounded bungalow to see if the omens were favourable for the journey. The year was 1800.

The priest held in his left hand a brass jug filled with water, and in his right a white handkerchief with three coins, some turmeric, and a pickaxe—the most sacred object of the thug. Then he led the fifty men who made up the band into the clearing and, still holding the sacred objects in his hands, turned to face in the direction in which they intended to travel. Now he prayed to Kali that she would give a sign that she would bless the journey, and the thugs fervently joined in the prayer.

They waited for the omen—if it was bad then they would have to return to their houses, if good then they were free to go out to murder and plunder. Somewhere in a tree a small white owl gave its distinctive, chirping call—the omen was good. Kali would take them by the hand and lead them to their victims. The assassins settled down to wait for night when they could leave on their expedition.

No one knew how many hundreds of thousands of travellers were murdered by these men, but those who had travelled across India knew only too well that their lives were always in danger. Worst of all, they never knew whether the men they met on the way were harmless travellers like themselves, or whether at some moment they would whip the *rumals* round their throats. There was no mark to distinguish the followers of Kali—anyone and everyone was suspect.

So those who had to travel were very careful about choosing their companions, and the farther they were from their homes the more care they took. It was well known that the thugs preferred victims who were far away from friends and relations who might begin asking questions. It was just such a party of travellers who warily kept their eyes open for signs of sinister strangers as they moved with their merchandise towards Nizapur in western India.

The party consisted of two merchants and four servants.

On the night that the band of dacoits began their journey in search of rich victims, they were resting in a village only ten miles away. The elder of the two merchants, Dhunraj Lal, had impressed on his younger brother, Dhurum, the need to keep clear of strangers and to avoid talking too much about their plans. In the morning, as they were saddling their horses and preparing for the day's travel, they saw a second party of half a dozen men approaching them along the dusty village street. The new arrivals stopped by the merchants, and one of the men in the party stepped forward and asked Dhurum Lal which way they were heading. Before he could answer his elder brother came forward and told the questioner that they were still planning their route for the day. He, in his turn, then asked the newcomers where they were going.

Dhunraj Lal's question seemed to confuse the second party. They began talking together in whispers. The spokesman stepped forward again and told Dhunraj that they too had no fixed plan for the day and suggested that the two parties travel together so as to provide mutual protection against robbers and dacoits. Dhunraj Lal was becoming increasingly suspicious but Dhurum persuaded him that the advantages of travelling in a larger party outweighed the risk represented by the newcomers. Besides, they would constantly be on their guard against any possible treachery. Dhunraj Lal reluctantly agreed and told the six men that his party proposed to take the road to Nizapur. The two parties then joined forces, and all twelve set off on the road.

The journey was a silent one. Dhunraj Lal was far from convinced that he had made a wise choice, and more than once he caught sight of the strangers passing whispered messages to each other. Even his younger brother was becoming suspicious, and kept glancing over his shoulder to make sure that none of the strangers approached near enough for a quick attack.

As the miles passed, the feeling of tension among the merchants and their servants increased. In silence they rode on anxiously for several hours. Whenever one of the strangers drew close to one of the Lal brothers, the merchant would spur his horse forward again until there was a safe distance between them.

As evening drew near and Dhunraj Lal was beginning to

worry about the prospect of making camp with the strangers, a third party appeared ahead of them on the road. The two Lal brothers rode forward to exchange greetings with the new travellers. They appeared to be merchants like themselves. The leader was a tall, middle-aged, well-dressed man, and at his side rode a strikingly handsome boy who could have been no more than sixteen years old. Half a dozen servants walked at their side.

The two parties approached each other cautiously at first, but after a while Dhunraj Lal began to feel relief that he had at last found someone who could give him welcome support should his suspicions prove well founded. He told the stranger how the second party had joined with theirs, but thought it wiser at first not to mention his suspicions. The stranger looked across to the six men, grouped together in a silent bunch. He inspected them closely, then beckoned to the Lal brothers to ride a little way off, so that they could talk without being overheard.

When they were out of earshot, the tall stranger began asking more questions about the six men. Dhunraj Lal, satisfied that the stranger had a good reason for his questions, told him of his suspicions. The tall stranger nodded in agreement, then told the Lal brothers that the same men had tried to join his party only a few days ago, but by chance he had caught a glimpse of a strip of yellow and white cloth hidden under the tunic of one of the men. He knew that the *rumal* of the thugs was often a cloth of these colours, so he had sent the men packing. The news he had now heard from the Lals confirmed his own views. There could be no doubt that they had a party of thugs among them.

Anxiously, the men discussed what to do, and the tall stranger argued forcibly that they should insist on the six leaving them at once. The Lals agreed, and called their own servants to them.

The thugs were too deep in their own whispered conversation to take any notice of what the merchants were doing. On a signal from Dhunraj Lal, the men drew their weapons and advanced on them. Their leader at first tried to protest his innocence, but soon realized that he was making no impression on the determined merchants. He gave a sign to his men and they turned, ran to their horses and galloped off into the twilight. The Lals watched the receding horsemen with relief. When they were satisfied that their recent companions had disappeared from sight, they thanked the tall stranger for his help and suggested that they make camp together for the night.

The two parties settled down round the camp fire. The stranger proposed that they set guards all night so as to be quite certain that the thugs made no attempt to creep up on them while they slept. The Lals agreed at once, and that night they slept more easily than they had ever expected to a few hours ago.

The next morning they woke to a fine, bright day. The guards reported that there had been no sign of the six other men, but the two groups decided to travel together the next day as an added protection. So together they set out—a happier party than the one that had taken to the road the previous day.

The tall stranger, who had explained that his name was Roshun and that he too was a merchant, turned out to be an excellent companion for the journey. It seemed that he had travelled all over the country, and had many stories of the exciting places he had visited, and also a fund of anecdotes about some of the people he had met on his journeys. He had a rich sense of humour, and soon the Lals had completely forgotten their recent travelling companions as they rode on, laughing, towards Nizapur.

As evening approached, the party halted and set up camp amidst a small grove of trees a short distance from the roadway. Roshun insisted that the Lals be his guests for the evening. They were now near Nizapur, which was Roshun's own home, so it was his duty to play the part of host. The Lals gladly accepted, and they settled down round the camp fire with Roshun and his young companion. Before the meal started, Roshun insisted that guards be again posted. The Lals thought that the precautions were no longer needed, but agreed that it was better to be absolutely certain when it came to dealing with the thugs. They set their own servants and Roshun's to keep watch, while two of Roshun's men stayed in camp to prepare and serve the evening meal.

The travellers settled down happily to enjoy their meal. Roshun kept up a steady stream of anecdotes and stories, and the sky was dark before they had finished eating. The meal over, they drew in closer to the camp fire and Roshun's young friend took out his *sitar* and began to play. He was an accomplished musician, and the Lal brothers sat engrossed as tune after tune came from his fingers. After a while he began to sing some of the beautiful old songs of the district, his young voice soft and smooth as the night air.

Roshun listened in silence to the music, then gave a signal to his servants to clear away the remains of the meal. The two men moved swiftly and silently so as not to disturb the calm that had fallen over the camp as everyone listened to the songs. Soon they were finished and stood back respectfully to wait for any further orders. Roshun began to hum quietly, adding his own deep voice as an accompaniment to the high soft notes of the boy. The song died away into the still night.

For a moment all was silence, then Dhurum Lal broke the quiet with his excited, quick speech as he praised the meal, and the singer and his music. Roshun and the boy smiled their thanks and the older man asked his friend to sing another song. The boy began, but instead of the sad, wistful air he had just given them, he began a bouncing, hearty song, well known all over that part of India. Roshun rose to his feet, and again joined his voice to the boy's, indicating to the Lals that they should join in as well.

The four voices were soon joined together in the cheerful little song. Roshun stepped quietly back to stand just behind the Lals. One of the servants joined him. Still singing heartily, Roshun reached inside his tunic and drew out a strip of folded yellow cloth. At one end the material was knotted around a rupee. He grasped the other end of the cloth with his right hand, and allowed the weighted end to hang free. He moved to stand directly behind the elder of the two Lal brothers; the servant silently took up his position behind the other, a similar cloth in his own hand. The young man with the *sitar* played on, until he reached the end and climax of the song. As the crescendo was reached, the two Lals threw back their heads to bay out the last triumphant notes to the moon and the night sky; and in so doing their throats lay open and exposed.

At a sign from Roshun, two twisted lengths of yellow cloth were flung out and around the necks of the singers. The knotted ends thudded back into waiting left hands and the *rumals* were drawn tight around the victims' throats.

Roshun and his fellow assassin at the same time placed their knees in the victims' backs, forcing the two merchants face downward into the ground. Then the two murderers were kneeling on the backs of the brothers, their strangling cords firmly round the necks, cutting off all sound. Within seconds the feeble struggles ended, and two more victims of thuggee lay dead. Only the sound of the *sitar*, still being plucked by the smiling boy, disturbed the stillness of the night. Then that too stopped and the night was silent again.

When the sound of the singing had stopped, the merchants' four servants on guard had felt a moment of alarm as they gazed out into the darkness. But it was no more than a moment. The last song had been a signal to Roshun's supposed servants. As it started they crept into position, and when the voices had stopped so suddenly, four yellow cloths had swung out and around the servants' throats. A few moments, then their bodies were dragged back to the camp fire to lie beside those of their masters.

Under Roshun's direction, the thugs systematically searched the bodies and the possessions of the murdered men. Everything of value was taken and put to one side, and then the bodies were stripped of the rest of their clothing which was thrown into the fire. They took from their concealed packings the pickaxes and began to dig one small, shallow grave at the side of the camp site.

When the grave was ready, the corpses were carried over. The men drew their knives and began the systematic mutilation of the bodies. Great gashes were cut into the torsos, and the limbs were disjointed so that the bodies could be folded up like old rag dolls to fit more conveniently into the mass grave. The faces were disfigured so that, if the bodies were accidently uncovered, recognition would be impossible. Finally a deep gash was made between the ribs of each of the victims so that the gases released from the decomposing bodies would not bloat them and lift the soil over the grave. When these grisly rituals were complete, the soil was shovelled back, and no mark of the murders remained.

As the murderers completed the burial of their victims, six horsemen appeared riding towards them. Roshun went forward to greet them. These were the party who had first aroused Dhumraj Lal's suspicions, and had successfully prepared the way for Roshun and his men to commit the murders. The two parties now congratulated each other on the success of their carefully laid plan, and then prepared themselves for the final rites of the thuggee act of ritual murder: the consecration or *tuponee*.

Roshun led the way to a quiet, secluded space away from the camp site, where a carpet was laid on the ground. In the centre of the carpet he placed, as an offering to Kali, a small heap of *goor*, a kind of coarse yellow sugar, the holy pickaxe, and a silver coin. Roshun then himself sat on the edge of the carpet facing towards the west, with two leading thugs on either side of him. The rest of the party surrounded the carpet.

When everyone was in place, Roshun dug a small hole in the ground and, placing a little *goor* in it, offered up a prayer to Kali. The others repeated the prayer, and Roshun then sprinkled water on the pickaxe and on the sugar in the hole. He put a little sugar in the hands of each of the stranglers and gave the sign that was the signal to kill. At that point each of the thugs placed the *goor* in his mouth and ate it. This was the high point of the thuggee ritual. They all believed that once they had eaten the consecrated *goor* they were for ever set in the way of thuggee. No matter how many murders they committed, they would never feel even the slightest twinge of guilt or pity for the victim, and no matter what else they might do, whatever jobs they might take, they were first and always thugs. With the eating of the *goor* the ritual was over—the act of murder had been consecrated and dedicated to the blood-thirsty goddess Kali. The men returned to the camp fire.

Back at the camp, the party settled down to enjoy what remained of the night. The *sitar* was brought out again, songs were sung, and the air was filled with noise and laughter. It was a happy scene, as happy as the one that had taken place a few hours before at the same spot. Only now six of those who had taken part in the earlier feast lay dead, buried beneath the spot where the devotees of Kali were now so happily enjoying themselves.

Not one of them gave a moment's thought to the new grave beneath their feet. The goddess Kali had ordered them to strangle and to rob, and they had done as she commanded. Their victims had been pre-ordained to play their part in the ritual, so what cause was there for grief? They had carried out an act of thuggee in the way laid down by the laws of the religion, and in the manner in which it had been practised for countless generations. Basking in the sultry favours of Kali, they were not to know that within half a century this immemorial barbarity would be all but extinct—due to vigorous action by the British.

The Widows of Pudupettah

In the year 1817 there were 706 recorded cases of *suttee* in Bengal. There is no accurate record of the number in other Indian states and probably the real total in Bengal was in excess of the recorded figure.

At that period, a century and a half ago, when the practice was common in India, and shocking to the rest of the world, the word *suttee* brought a shudder to Europeans. This despite the fact that in northern Europe and elsewhere a similar practice had been indulged in, centuries before, to provide the deceased with female slaves and concubines in the hereafter. Today the word is less familiar.

It means, prosaically, "a virtuous woman", in the ancient Sanskrit language, but the implication is considerably more than that. For the virtuous woman, when her husband died, was expected to join him on his journey to the next world by cremating herself in this one, on his funeral pyre.

Probably the greatest foreign observer and analyst of things Indian was a French missionary, the Abbé Dubois, who lived in the sub-continent during the closing years of the eighteenth century and the first years of the nineteenth. No one since then has succeeded in so distilling the essence of Indian thought and behaviour. Much of that thought and behaviour is still unchanged.

But *suttee* has ended. There is no man living who has ever witnessed such a thing, and we have only the writings of

Dubois (and one or two, less eloquent, others) to tell us what happened. Dubois was a reluctant witness at many instances of *suttee*, and his writings are standard reference.

He preferred not to name names, and those playing rôles in the dreadful drama are usually dismissed as "a rich man", "a king", "a brahmin", and so on. But by filling in the gaps from other sources and, here and there, using our imagination, we can easily produce a detailed and horrifying history.

One true chapter in that history is the story of Indira and Jameela and their husband Pandatu.

The two ladies, Indira and Jameela, were happily married to the same husband—not entirely a common circumstance —and both of them genuinely grieved when he died. The younger, prettier, one, Jameela, had an additional cause for grief, even for feelings of guilt. For Pandatu, who had been weakening for months from an obscure malady, had been warned by his physicians that he must abstain from love, must not sleep with either of his wives.

But at last Pandatu had succumbed to temptation, the temptation of Jameela's young body. And a few weeks later, after a steady weakening of pulse and strength, he died. Jameela had done her best to save him. In the original recounting of the sad tale, "the passion which he felt for the younger of his wives, who was extremely beautiful, overcame all fear of death; and in spite of the fact that for several days she continued to represent to him the dire results that must follow his incontinency, he yielded at last to the violence of his love; and immediately the great sickness and weakness fell upon him".

It was several weeks before Pandatu died. And then, when the sad event had taken place, it became necessary to decide which of the two wives should follow him to the pyre, the middle-aged Indira or the young Jameela. And it was that rarest of occasions when both ladies quite genuinely wished to do so, without threats, or blackmail, from other members of the family. They had loved Pandatu, they both wished to join him in the life hereafter with as much dispatch as possible. Both wished to prove, in this dramatic way, how much they loved him.

As was the custom when a rich and influential man like Pandatu died, a body of brahmin priests gathered to consider the matter in his house. They interviewed the ladies and listened intently as Indira spoke, while they nodded their heads in that sidelong Oriental gesture which signifies agreement. Indira was eloquent, and sincere. She was, she pointed out, the first wife, and much senior to the second; she should be given preference in all things. Her preference now was to be immolated with her husband, and she demanded that right.

Furthermore, she pointed out, Jameela had two children by Pandatu, both of them young. These would require their mother's personal care and attention.

But Jameela had swift answer to this. Were not all children of Pandatu the common property of his wives? Did Indira not regard herself as their mother, even though they were not the fruit of her womb? Why—Jameela even regarded Indira's three grown-up sons by Pandatu as her own, even though two of these were older than herself.

The brahmins nodded.

Jameela shook her little fist at them. "And—shame be on me—it was *I*, *I* alone, who was directly responsible for my beloved husband's death. It was I whom he bedded, not Indira—against all the physicians' orders. It is I who must die with him."

The brahmins retired to consider the matter. A little later they came back to say Jameela's case was proved; as the younger wife, and direct cause of her husband's death, the duty, the privilege, of accompanying him was hers alone. The two widows thanked the jury; the older congratulated the younger on the great honour which had befallen her.

The ceremony was to take place in three days' time, and the news spread swiftly over that part of Bengal. Thousands of people who had known Pandatu—and many others who had not—began to flock in to his village of Pudupettah. Meanwhile, men began excavating a pit some four feet deep and fifteen feet square, on the outskirts of the village. Others brought quantities of sandalwood, and jars of the clarified butter, *ghee*. A flat pile of the wood was made, inside the pit, reaching almost to the level of the surrounding dusty earth. Above this flat pile, upon which the dead man's body would be placed, beside that of his consort—the men erected a scaffolding, a flimsy roof supported on four props, one at each corner. On top of this roof they piled a pyramid of still more sandalwood.

The jars of *ghee* were placed at each corner of the erection, next to the four props, and preparation was complete.

Meanwhile the proud young widow, Jameela, was besieged with messages of encouragement, envy, goodwill. These came from her many relatives, all of whom would be expected to derive blessing through her, reflected, glory, and a more comfortable berth in the life hereafter. Now that she had agreed, even demanded, to go through with the ceremony, she had no alternative but to do so. She could have disgraced herself and her family in the first place by not volunteering, or by refusing when it was suggested her; now that her decision was made, it could not be revoked. If the spirit failed, she would be carried bodily to the pyre and flung on to it.

This of course would mar the ceremony. To avoid any such occurrence, any such embarrassment, a steady stream of brahmin priests called on her, almost every hour of the day, to encourage and congratulate her.

But at this time, something else befell Jameela.

She noticed it two days before the funeral, and it straightway set her to wondering, for it might have an effect on the ceremony. She pondered it, wondered if she could be mistaken, counted again on all her fingers and realized, with experience of the past in mind, that there was no question of a mistake.

She was on the horns of a very real dilemma. Should she admit the existence of this new circumstance, and deny herself and her husband the honour and satisfaction of a journey together into the after-land? Or should she die with her secret intact?

She decided to die with the secret.

Then, on the morning of the ceremony, she confided in her serving maid. The girl had been with her two years, and she replied calmly that she was well aware of the circumstance. Had she not looked after her lady, Jameela, month after month, for two proud and happy years? No woman keeps a secret from her serving maid.

"Very well," said Jameela, "but I pray you to keep the secret between us. No one else must know."

That morning there was a great hubbub of excitement through Pudupettah. The population had more than doubled itself from the previous day; there were smartly turned out soldiers, with swords and spears and musical instruments. The people of the village and others from farther afield were out in their finest raiment, and two fine palanquins had been brought to the door of Pandatu's house and laid on the ground outside. Two men carefully dusted them, again and again, in an endless ritual as more dust swirled up around them.

Jameela's serving maid and several other women, including Indira, now dressed her in her most beautiful, gold-edged, *sari*, and began literally loading her with jewels, so that when they led her to the palanquin she had difficulty in walking at all, under the great weight of gold and silver and precious stones.

But was that the only reason? She felt a strange new sickness and wondered which of several causes could be at the root of it. And though she was proud of what was going to happen to her this day, she could feel herself tremble a bit, could feel a strange, unpleasant, chill about her lips and her forehead.

She was helped into her gaily caparisoned vehicle, and the four men lifted it up to join the long procession which was starting. Immediately in front of her was the even finer palanquin of her late husband, open like hers on all sides, under its little roof, and she saw him sitting boldly upright, cross-legged and for all the world as if he were alive and giving orders to his servants, telling the procession when to move off. His back was towards her, but she knew that his mouth would have been ceremonially filled with *betel*, his eyes closed with golden coins.

There was a wail of music, and it had started. At the front of the procession was a small body of armed soldiers; after them came more, playing instruments, trumpets and drums; and immediately preceding her, Pandatu's handsome palanquin.

Happy, excited crowds of men and women and children pushed up to her conveyance on either side. Some reached boldly in to touch the hem of her *sari* and thereby obtain blessing. Some, already treating her as a goddess, asked advice, and for the first few minutes, despite her feeling of weakness, it pleased her to prattle a little nonsense at them: why, of course this woman would have many fine sons; this young girl would some day marry a rich and handsome man who would cherish her—and so on.

But soon the feeling of weakness overwhelmed her again, and for the first time a sense of something like dread welled up over her, like a sudden tide in the Hooghly River. She felt cold, though the day was blistering hot and getting hotter.

She turned to meet the eyes of the other, older, widow, and Indira smiled. Was there perhaps a hint of compassion in the glance; or was it envy?

Or, perhaps, relief?

Near to Indira in the procession, as the drums banged and trumpets played, was Jameela's own serving maid, the only person sharing her secret. The girl turned, smiled; but now Jameela was too weak, too unwell—and too frightened —to return the smile. The girl stared at her for some little while, as she stumbled along in the crowd, and her smile turned slowly to a frown.

The pyre in its pit had been erected some distance beyond the far end of the village, and the procession had to make its way for a mile to get there. The sun rose higher in the sky, the dust swirled, the music wailed and thumped and now it did so in rhythm with the frantic beating of Jameela's heart. She now knew herself, knew she was frightened, desperately frightened. She saw the serving maid look pityingly at her, and suddenly start to move towards her through the crowd.

The girl reached the side of the palanquin. "Jameela," she whispered—or was she shouting, in this dreadful din? —"you must tell them!"

Jameela could only stare at her.

"You must. And if you will not, I will tell them myself, Jameela. It would be a sin not to, Jameela. And you know that, Jameela, do you not?"

Jameela nodded.

The girl broke away and started moving towards the front of the procession, where a small group of brahmins was marching between two sets of soldiers. Jameela watched in admiration as the little figure bumped others out of its way, got to the edge of the procession and started running.

The older woman came up close. "You are all right, Jameela? You are feeling proud and happy?"

Indira was smiling kindly, but Jameela could only look back at her in dumb horror.

Now, as the procession wheeled away to the right, she could make out, with a dreadful sinking of the heart, the funeral pyre with its group of attendants by the jars of *ghee*; its other, armed, men ready to deal with a last-minute change of mind, a foolish attempt at rescue. The four men by the *ghee* jars held flaming torches over their heads, as if they were trying to see their way down some long passage. Yet the sun was directly overhead.

Jameela closed her eyes. Somewhere in the distance she could hear Indira talking to her, but the words were mumbled and indistinct, and, like the music, they were drowned in the beating of her own heart.

She must have fainted away, for she woke suddenly to find men grasping at her elbows from either side of the palanquin, which had been lowered to the ground.

With a gasp, she saw the pyre a few yards off, by the small pool in which she would be expected to perform a last ablution.

She let the men help her out, while Indira stood at her side. The older woman's smile seemed one of unashamed triumph now, and Jameela noted it without emotion. The soldiers had stopped their playing, were standing on three sides of the pyre. They seemed to be guarding it, guarding the guardians of the ceremony. These stood at each corner of the sandalwood erection, holding their dreadful torches.

But when she descended from her palanquin, it was to find that her legs would not support her. Gasping, she sank to the ground, to be roughly jerked up again by men on either side, and to be literally carried along, the toes of her bare feet scratching the dusty earth.

She got to the muddy pool where by tradition she would immerse herself before taking off jewels, giving them to the mourners. The pool seemed to ooze in front of her like *ghee*, not water; she wondered if she were already dead.

Suddenly there was a shout, almost a scream, and the men, springing to attention, let her fall heavily to the ground at the edge of the little pool. "Lift that woman up!" screamed the same man's voice, and she was dragged to her feet again.

She was face to face with the chief of the brahmins who had interviewed her those few days ago, which now seemed a decade. Beside him was her serving maid. Another, fat, man was standing with them, and he now spoke, breathlessly, for it was a very hot day and the march had been long. "It—it is *true*, then, what this maid says of you?"

She looked at the girl, who nodded her head. "Yes," said Jameela. "It is true."

"It was a wicked thing, to conceal the truth, Jameela."

"I only wished to honour my husband."

"You would not have honoured him. You would have disgraced him, as well as yourself. Come here."

She walked the few steps to the fat man, while people stared at her in silence. The man leaned forward, still breathing heavily, and began removing her jewellery. There were mounds of it, and the removal took minutes, while he pulled and pushed, and puffed and unpinned, handing the pieces over to another man.

At last it was done. "Go," he said. "Go and lose yourself in the crowd." He turned away from her: "And now, good Indira, the honour, the joy, will be yours. I congratulate you, Indira."

Hardly knowing what was happening, conscious that a great weight had been lifted from her soul, greater by far than the weight of jewels which had been taken from her body, she saw Indira, tight-lipped, expressionless, having those same jewels clumsily pinned on her own *sari*.

Jameela caught the older woman's eye, but she made no sign.

By the time Jameela had got away, into the crowd—which was difficult because they kept backing away like cattle, making room for her, so that for some time there was no crowd in which to lose herself—the older woman had completed her hasty ablution and was being divested of the jewels she had so recently put on.

These gone, she was led three times round the pyre. The first time she did it proudly, head in the air. On the second circuit, her feet stumbled; and by the third she was tottering, almost senseless with fright, supported by men on either side of her.

They then held her firm, her *sari* soaked and muddy from the ablution ceremony, her long, greying, hair in disarray, to watch as her husband was put carefully in position on the pyre. He was still seated, his mouth still full of *betel*; and from where Jameela was watching, he faced her, less than forty feet away.

Men made little adjustments, moved sticks of sandalwood this way and the next, tilted the rigid, squatting, body a little this way and the other, before withdrawing.

And now it was the turn of Indira. They led her, dragged her in a state of collapse, to the edge of the pyre. For a moment she seemed to resist, to fight back, but she was no match for half a dozen men and soon she was lying beside the seated body of her husband.

It seemed wrong to Jameela, quite apart from the horror of it, that Indira should be lying, wet and dishevelled, beside her man, while he sat proudly above her, the pair of them shielded from the brilliant sun by the pyramid of sandalwood poised on top, like a roof.

But she had little time to consider this; there was a shout, a scream, the four torch-bearers emptied *ghee* over the sandalwood and lowered their torches.

With a sound like Chinese gunpowder exploding, the flames roared up into the sky, and as they did, the four men, still acting as one, pulled out the props which supported the great pyramid of sandalwood, and it crashed down on the pyre.

Jameela dropped her head in her hands.

Three days ago, she had sincerely demanded that she be allowed to suffer this fate. But *had* she been sincere? Was she not just trying to show the world how fine and virtuous a woman she was?

The men had been merciful, dropping that pyramid of sandalwood so soon, for its weight would almost certainly have crushed the poor widow to death even before the flames had reached her. It was good to know that men, who ordained all these things, in a world of men and women, could be kind.

The crowd stood watching, chattering excitedly, until the flames began to shrink. People started to drift away. There would be no point in standing here, for the ashes would be too hot for at least another day, too hot for any relics to be salvaged from the fire.

She was turning to go, when her little serving maid came up. "Are you glad of what I did, Jameela? Or are you angry?"

Jameela looked at her in silence and the girl dropped her

eyes. Then she looked up again, boldly, and went on. "It is written, Jameela, my lady, that no wife may commit *suttee* if she is with child. So it would have been very wicked, would it not? And that is why I told them, Jameela. You understand?"

"Yes," said Jameela.

"And," the girl went on, "you are too young, too beautiful, to die. As for old Indira, it was her time anyway, was it not? You are not angry with me, Jameela?"

"No," said Jameela. "I am not angry." They started to walk away together from the smoke and heat.

"I hope you will have a boy," said the girl. "Pandatu would have wanted a boy. I hope it will be a boy."

"Thank you," said Jameela. "I, *too,* hope it will be a boy. For Pandatu." But she was not thinking of her husband's wish in the matter. Jameela was looking ahead, twenty, thirty or more years, to when a daughter—if, unhappily, she had one—would be faced with a day like today.

"I *know* it will be a boy," she said. "It *must* be a boy."

Ordeal by Fire and Water

The practice of naming a house after some place proudly or nostalgically associated with its owner's heyday is only rivalled in prevalence by that more curious one of torturing two Christian names into one—*Willthel, Marjbert, Normary*—designed, one might almost suspect, to make passers-by wince. Children have been known to suffer similarly at the font, though spirited clergymen have intervened to save many from this excruciating fate.

Although we suspect it doesn't happen so much these days, there have been times of public emotion, usually associated with war, that have produced a spate of christenings by such names as Mafeking, Ladysmith, Anzac and, no doubt, Alamein. A man whose Christian names were Sherlock Holmes died not long ago, having presumably acquired them at the height of the Holmes fever in the 'nineties. Such practice is hardest on women: it blatantly dates them.

In 1825 a boy baby was given the name Cambria: not a displeasing one, though it sounds better suited to a girl. Some owners of unconventional names get rid of theirs when they reach a discretionary age. This one did not: he bore it until he died, perhaps, partly, from thanksgiving. He might never have had a name at all, nor any life beyond his mother's womb, in which, all unknowing, he embarked in mid-February of that year aboard the East Indiaman *Kent* in the Downs.

The *Kent* was a fine new ship of 2,530 tons, under charter as a trooper to carry soldiers and their families to the Far Eastern stations of Bengal and China. When she raised anchor on 19 February, 1825, she had in her 641 people: a crew of 148, several hundred soldiers, some with their wives and children, and private passengers, adults and children. Any sea voyage at that time implied some discomforts, even privations, and certainly danger; but the *Kent*'s passage held every promise of safety and ease. She was an exceptionally well-found ship, with a good, tough crew and a first-class Master, Capt. Cobb.

A steady north-east breeze drove her smartly down the Channel, the more leisured passengers heedless of the early Spring cold as they stood hour by hour along the starboard rail, picking out landmarks along the coastline they could not expect to see again for a long time.

On the fourth day the watchers saw the last of England dwindle and fade behind them. They were in the Atlantic, the increasing liveliness of the ship's movement reflecting a deterioration in the weather. Capt. Cobb kept up all sail in the moderate gale, which, whatever the more squeamish passengers may have felt about it, made swift progress possible. Then the weather grew dramatically worse. The wind shrieked, the seas rose. Several times the sailors were ordered aloft as the gale increasingly forced Capt. Cobb's hand and made him take in more sail. The sails were reefed. It was not enough, they had to be close-reefed. Then they had to be taken in altogether. By the morning of 1 March the *Kent* lay wallowing helplessly with only the merest rag of canvas —a triple-reefed maintopsail—showing on her otherwise bare poles.

It was a terrible time for all in her. The inexorable violence of the Atlantic threw her from side to side in an endless rolling that destroyed rest, jangled the nerves and made eating almost impossible. It also hurled the unwary and unsteady dangerously about and transformed movable objects into missiles. It even tore strongly secured furnishings from the cleats which held them and smashed them against the ship's reeling sides. This betokened an exceptional quality in her rolling; and there was an ominous threat in it. In the holds, as part of the cargo, lay over a hundred tons of explosives and ammunition, including five hundred barrels of gunpowder and some hundredweights of high-explosive.

There were barrels of a different sort, carrying wines and spirits, and it was one of the latter that an officer of the watch, making a routine inspection shortly before midnight, found had come adrift. It was trundling back and forth in the confined space, threatening to smash. Taking the safety lantern from the two seamen accompanying him, the officer steadied the barrel with one hand and braced the weight of his body against it to keep it still. He ordered the men to look lively and fetch some billets of wood to wedge the barrel firmly.

They had just gone when the *Kent* gave a sudden, violent lurch. Completely off balance, the officer dropped the lantern. He made a spontaneous grab towards it, and in doing so lost his hold on the barrel. It was hurled against something more solid than itself, and smashed. The liquor gushed out, engulfed the still-burning lamp, and went up in a sheet of flame. In only moments the surrounding cargo was ablaze.

The word was quickly transmitted to Capt. Cobb, who hurried below to see for himself. The blaze was fierce, but the immediate site of it chanced to be ringed with water casks which might serve as a fire-break. Hoses were attached to pumps and water from them began to spurt on to the blaze, while a chain of sailors with buckets helped. Sails and hammocks were dowsed with water and flung over the burning area with a great hissing of steam. Yet still the fire burned, and spread.

If all had gone well it would have been over and done with before the passengers even heard of it; perhaps they might never have known. But when day broke it was still burning and wisps of light-blue smoke were seeping up the hatchway for anyone on deck to see. Anxious inquirers were assured that all was under control and the fire would soon be out.

The fire itself gave the lie to this. Before much longer the smoke had become dense and voluminous and was permeating every part of the ship below decks, with a smell of burning pitch. With few exceptions, the passengers and crew now thronged the still-heaving deck, anxious and noisy. Assured that the fire was out of control and spreading towards the site of the explosives, Capt. Cobb made up his mind to desperate measures. He ordered the ports to the lower deck to be removed, and the hatch covers taken off, to let the sea in. It was a gamble in such a sea. Either the fire would be put out swiftly by the inrush of water and all could be made secure again; or the *Kent* would take in so much sea that she would founder.

There was always the other alternative—that she would blow sky-high.

Human tragedy had begun. As soon as the sea was given access it flooded in, giving no time for several sick soldiers to be moved from their berths. They were drowned. So were a woman and several children, struggling to get up on deck. But, for the moment, the march of the flames was checked.

In such a storm, and, with so much water now in her, it became obvious that the *Kent* must founder. The only question was, how long she could stay afloat, and whether, if she did not blow up, she would be seen by any other vessel. It was not like the Channel, where shipping crowded the narrow straits. This was the lonely waste of the Atlantic, with a sea so big that the East Indiaman, now lying even lower in the water, was frequently dwarfed by huge waves which would keep her hidden for much of the time from the view of any ship which might chance to pass near. In any case, she was some degrees off the customary course for this passage: another ship would need to be off-course herself to find her. No sail had been sighted for days.

Terror gained ascendancy over many aboard her—and was by no means confined to those who might have been thought the weakest. Small children, for the most part unaware of the danger, played on. Frail women who had been prostrate with sea-sickness suddenly showed themselves cool and determined, in contrast with some of the men, soldiers among them, who behaved as if paralysed. A passenger, Lt.-Gen. Sir Duncan MacGregor, K.C.B., who later published an account of the disaster which sold widely and was translated into several languages, was detached enough to be able to observe his fellow-sufferers' reactions, and noted that they seemed to be "divided by a broad, but, as it afterwards appeared, not impassable line, on the one side of which were ranged all whose minds were greatly elevated by the excitement above their ordinary standard, and on the other were to be seen the incalculably smaller, but more conspicuous groups, whose powers of acting and thinking became absolutely paralysed, or were driven into delirium, by the unusual character and pressure of the danger".

Among the latter were some old soldiers and sailors who deliberately went to sit in a body on the part of the deck directly over the powder magazine and refused all efforts to shift them, determined that if the *Kent* did blow up they, if no one else, should be killed instantly and not left injured and drowning.

Some others sat about staring straight in front of them, their terror occasionally thawing enough to make them howl and lament before freezing into silence again. A handful prayed wildly; while a few sought that other kind of solace, down below deck where the casks of spirits awaited wasteful destruction. There were even the usual opportunists who roamed about plundering the deserted cabins. They were perhaps the only optimists, expecting to survive to enjoy their booty.

One of the mates sent a man to the foretop to keep watch against the slight chance of a sail. Swung wildly to and fro as the mast dipped at times almost to sea level, the lookout nevertheless kept his eyes peeled and suddenly started waving his hat and shouting above the din, "A sail on the lee-bowl" The words were repeated by hundreds of voices, followed by cheers. Capt. Cobb quickly ordered distress flags broken out and minute guns fired. A few small sails were set and the crippled *Kent* began to make painful way in the direction the lookout indicated.

For much of the time the rearing seas kept the two vessels out of sight of one another. When those aboard the *Kent* could get a glimpse of the other, a much smaller craft, they saw with concern that she gave no sign of changing course or heaving-to. The guns still fired, but she seemed not to hear them. The wallowing *Kent* could clearly not fetch up with her as they were sailing at present, and soon, it seemed, what might be the last hope of rescue would be gone. There was a quarter of an hour's agonizing suspense before, emerging from a deep trough of water, the *Kent* hung poised on a crest for a moment, enough to show the small vessel, crowding all sail, bearing down fast towards her.

She proved to be a British brig, *Cambria*, of 200 tons, on

her way to Vera Cruz with miners from Yorkshire and Cornwall and their stores. She had not heard the *Kent*'s distress guns, but someone had chanced to spot the column of smoke from the burning East Indiaman and the *Cambria*'s master, Capt. Cook, had altered course to investigate.

There was plenty of cheering as the *Cambria* came as near as she dared in such a sea and hove-to; but Capt. Cobb and some others aboard the *Kent* recognized too well that some of their troubles were only about to begin. The brig was less than an eighth the size of the East Indiaman, whose more than six hundred complement, together with those already aboard her, would cram her from stem to stern— always assuming they could be got across to her anyway, in small boats in this wild sea and before the seemingly inevitable explosion.

The *Kent*'s crew began getting out the boats and the military officers conferred.

"In what order are we to move, sir?" a subaltern asked his major.

"In funeral order—juniors first," was the reply.

The commanding officer, Col. Fearon, who was standing near by, added, "And see that any man is cut down who presumes to enter the boats before the means of escape are presented to the women and children."

Officers with drawn swords were posted beside the boats to repel any men who might try to rush them. No rush came. Women and children began entering the boats and the first load started its slow way towards the *Cambria*. It was a long, hard pull, for the *Cambria* dared come no closer. To do so would not only risk her blowing up with the *Kent*, but might get her sunk or crippled by gunfire; for the *Kent*'s guns, already shotted, were beginning to discharge in the heat, putting the *Cambria* virtually under fire.

Now, for many people, especially the women and children, what had been a passive nightmare became an active experience of terror. The first boatload of them were the luckiest: they had been able to seat themselves in the boat before it was lowered from the *Kent*'s side. Even though there had been a moment of dangerous entanglement in the lowering ropes, which a sailor had had to sever with an axe, and even though the passage to the *Cambria* lasted twenty frightful minutes, during which there was constant danger of the little boat's being swamped, the first party at length reached safety. But, returning to the *Kent*, the boat was unable to get snug alongside for more women and children to embark. There was nothing for it but to order the boat under the *Kent*'s stern and to lower its passengers into it by a wildly swaying rope. Women and children were lashed two and two together and dangled in this perilous way over the lurching small boat, the men at the ropes trying to judge the brief moment when they could drop their human burdens into the boat and not into the sea. Many times they judged wrong, and desperately had to haul women and children out of a wave that was half-drowning them, to dangle them once more and try again. It was too much for some of the children: they were dead by the time they could be got into the boat.

It was plain how long it must take to abandon the East Indiaman at this rate, even with several boats going to and fro, and equally plain that the fire, spreading with every hour, must reach the explosives long before it could be achieved. Some passengers began making their own bids for safety, leaping into the sea and trying to swim to the *Cambria*. They had no chance in waves as high as the ships' masts. Those who preferred to wait had to watch them drown. One soldier had three children lashed to him and jumped into the sea. After swimming a few strokes he realized he must sink. A rope was thrown and he was hauled back aboard the East Indiaman; but two of the children were found to be already dead.

The occasion produced the inevitable grim humorist. One of the sailors who had persisted in sitting over the powder magazine, courting a sudden death, grew impatient and cried out in mock exasperation, "Oh, well, if she won't blow up, I suppose I'd better swim for it." He did, and was saved.

There was unconscious humour in a young Irish recruit's solution to a dilemma. When orders were given for every man to find a rope and tie it round his waist, in case he should need to lash himself to a piece of debris and swim for it, the man could find nothing suitable except the cordage on an officer's hammock. Afraid of possible consequences, he went to the lengths of accosting General MacGregor, to ask whether it would be in order to take the cord. The general approved.

The day had been wearing on, and now dusk came with a glorious seascape sunset. Night would bring new perils. The difficulty of getting people into the boats in darkness and ferrying them to the brig was almost unthinkable. But it must go on. The fire raged and the half-scuttled *Kent* settled still deeper. At any time she could blow up or sink, taking several hundred people with her. Many who watched that sun set must have told themselves they would never see it rise again.

The women and children were all gone from the *Kent*, but one woman and twenty children had died. Most of the sailors had been taken off and many soldiers. The prospects for the remainder were not good. In the darkness the small boats tended to lie even further from the *Kent*'s hull, for fear of being dashed against it. It was decided to use the spanker-boom—the spar which protrudes for many feet over a sailing vessel's stern—as a bridge to safety. Men would crawl out along it and then drop by rope into the boats, which were thus enabled to keep well clear of the ship's stern. It was an ordeal, especially in darkness, to crawl the length of the boom and then hang from a wildly jerking rope, drenched repeatedly and half choked, waiting to make a split-second drop into a tiny boat which could barely be seen. Many men achieved it, but some perished. Col. Fearon, when his turn came, was nearly one of the latter. He had to hang on for so long, vainly waiting for his chance, that his grip at last failed and he fell into the sea. Miraculously, the small boat gave a plunge, someone's arm was able to reach out just far enough, and the colonel was virtually dragged to safety by his hair.

Hour by hour it went on, until the flames were bursting from the stern windows. There would be little more chance for the boats to get close enough, and some thirty soldiers were still aboard the *Kent*. A number of these were past caring whether they lived or died: they were below deck, in a drunken oblivion from which they would never awake. The rest were paralysed too—but from fear. Huddled round the inboard end of the spanker-boom, they were simply too terrified of crawling along it to take what was almost certainly their only chance of survival.

Three of their officers cajoled and threatened them. The men would not budge. Reluctantly, the officers allowed themselves to be saved. As the *Kent*'s Master, Capt. Cobb was determined to be the last man to leave his ship. For a long time he harangued the cowering men, while those in the waiting boats shouted their encouragement to them. It was no use, and Capt. Cobb went down the rope into a boat and to the safety of the *Cambria*.

He could not have delayed much longer. The watchers from the *Cambria* saw flames burst out all along the East Indiaman. There was a loud explosion, then others, but she had not blown up yet. The noise was of some of her guns falling through the burning deck and going off inside the ship.

The flames streaked up the masts and rigging. The fluttering distress flags disintegrated into smoke and ash. Then the tall masts toppled, almost together, and fell into the sea with a great steaming hiss.

Not long afterwards the first spark reached the gunpowder. It was enough. With a great roar the magazine's contents exploded together. The *Kent* seemed to disintegrate, pieces of flaming debris being hurled into the night sky like rockets. Remarkably, seventeen of the men who had feared to leave her survived, clinging to spars all night until they were picked up by a Liverpool-bound vessel, the *Caroline*, brought hurrying to the scene by the explosion which had been heard miles away.

Capt. Cook, of the *Cambria*, ordered all sail set for England. There was need for urgency. His small vessel now held over six hundred people, jammed together in every space that could be used. A cabin meant for ten men was made to hold eighty. There was lying-down room for some of the women and children only. There was food for only forty people. The good-hearted miners willingly gave up their provisions and clothes to the survivors, but it was clear that unless England could be reached inside a couple of days there would be more deaths. If, with some English port in sight there should be an unfavourable wind that would prevent the ship from going in for several days, there would be wholesale tragedy. A gale was blowing, but Capt. Cook kept on all sail.

The *Cambria* made Falmouth harbour on the night of 3 March and dropped anchor. An hour later the wind veered to a quarter against which the brig could never have made progress.

When the hatch covers were taken off the holds in which hundreds of men were jammed together, the outrush of their breath could be seen like a cloud of steam. Conditions had been appalling, an extension of the terrifying event that had given rise to them. Few survivors wore more than rags of clothing and many had lost their worldly belongings. But they were safe; luckier than the eighty-one who had died. And they numbered one more than when the *Cambria* had started her dash for home. In one of the packed cabins a baby had been born—the Cambria who began our tale.

A Swim with the Sharks

John Meldrum leaned on the bulwark and stared unseeing
across the glassy Caribbean. The air enveloped him like a
hot blanket. On the deck his bare soles burned. A great
weight seemed to be pressing him, squeezing from his pores
what little sweat remained to be squeezed.

This August day of 1826 had been progressively hard to
bear, even by men acclimatized to the Caribbean such as
John Meldrum and his crewmates of the schooner *Magpie*.
When they had sailed that morning from Port Royal there
had been a light breeze, promising relief from the humidity
that would intensify with the day. But as the sun had
climbed, so had the air become stiller, until now, towards
evening, the *Magpie* lay completely becalmed, her bowsprit
pointing homeward towards Jamaica, but no slightest fleck
of wake under bow or stern.

A shout of laughter from the little knot of men yarning
under the awning forward jerked Meldrum from his reverie.
He thought briefly of joining them, but it was less effort to
stay where he was, pinned down by the heat. Nothing moved
on the sea, and nothing much on the little ship, except her
captain, young Lieutenant Smith, who paced from side to
side impatiently training his telescope in search of the pirate
that he had been ordered to find and take. It seemed to
John Meldrum that his officer was merely wasting energy.
In such a calm it was unlikely that the pirate vessel would be

any more capable of movement than her seeker; and even if
the lieutenant did chance to spot what he was looking for
there was little he could do about it, except order out a boat
and row into action.

Meldrum grinned briefly. He wouldn't put even that past
his high-spirited commander. A regular little tiger, he could
be, tough but fair, and not slow to appreciate a good man.
John Meldrum, the gunner's mate, considered himself such
a man, and so, he had learned to his gratification, did Lieutenant Smith. Only this day he had let it be known that he
was going to put Meldrum's name forward when they
returned to harbour for promotion to gunner.

Well, that would have to be another day. It didn't seem as
if they would see much of Port Royal this night. The heated
air was utterly still, the sea so flat that one might have been
tempted to try walking on it.

When John Meldrum at length heaved himself upright
and walked painfully across the hot planking to join his
mates he found that they had abandoned jesting and brag-
ging for speculation about the aftermath of this calm. One
man told how, following just such a calm in the Pacific, his
ship had within minutes found itself dismasted in a cyclone
and had nearly foundered. The tale was capped by another
sailor, and by another. No good, it was agreed, came of such
calms, and they would be lucky if this one proved any exception. As superstitious as any other sailorman, John Meldrum
agreed and told a tale of his own.

And so the hours passed. Darkness came, forcing the
young officer to shut his telescope with an exasperated snap
and stump off down to fling himself on to his bunk and
brood. The men under the awning fell silent, each retiring
into his own thought. The humidity was total, giving an
impression of greater heat even than when the sun had been
at its height. Only the moon looked cool.

Suddenly, the listless men stirred and began to mutter.
The idle ship had moved. It moved again, and they heard
the unmistakable sound of a breeze rattling the rigging and
flapping the sagging sails. They got to their feet and went to
look out over the moon-brilliant sea. They found the young
mate, Maclean, telescope to his eye, doing the same, and,
following the direction of his gaze, they noticed a small dark
cloud under the moon. As they looked, the cloud seemed to

expand and move in their direction. Shaking his head, the mate hurried below and returned almost at once with Lieutenant Smith. As they reached the deck the *Magpie* began to roll from side to side under the pressure of what had quickly become a strong, steady wind. The man at the wheel brought her head round into it, but the sailors knew before he said it what their captain's command was going to be.

"Take in all sail!"

They scrambled aloft; but even as they did so a colossal fury of wind struck them, trying to tear them from the rigging. Unable to climb another rung, they could only cling on where they were and wait for the vessel's wild motion to ease. It never did; and with a sound at first like an unending sigh, merging into rumble and then a roar, a tidal wave like a solid black wall came leaping across the sea.

Keeping pace with the wave, the menacing black cloud raced across the sky until it extinguished the moon like a slammed shutter. An instant later the solid rampart of sea struck the little *Magpie* with a crash and a force that sent her reeling right over on to her side, a knock-down blow from which there was no slightest chance of recovery. Two of the crew were killed instantly. The rest, after some moments of dazed confusion, found themselves wallowing and gasping in the warm sea.

Treading water and trying to clear his bewildered mind, John Meldrum could hear the shouts of his crewmates. A sudden intense flash of lightning gave him a glimpse of them, scattered near by. He also saw the dark shape of the ship, broken on the water, and realized that he was too close to her for safety. She must sink soon, and might well suck him under with her. Striking out hard, he proceeded to put a comfortable distance between himself and the doomed *Magpie*—and in doing so he encountered a floating oar, and then another. He was able at last to rest securely, his arms hooked over the two.

Incredibly, the sea was once more calm and quiet. The last vestige of cloud whipped away, leaving the bright moon once more in sole command of the heavens. By her light John Meldrum was able to make out one of the ship's boats not far away and heard the firm tone of Lieutenant Smith calling to reassure his men.

As Meldrum saw the boat, so too did the other men. With

a cry, they simultaneously struck out for this one promise of survival. Meldrum was one of the first to get there. He found Lieutenant Smith and two or three others in possession and was grateful to be hauled inboard. A moment later he was back, struggling in the sea: ignoring the officer's warning commands, the other crew members had tried all together to clamber into the little boat from the same side. Inevitably, they had capsized it. It now lay keel upwards, a tenuous hold for the men who clung on desperately.

Smith again asserted his authority, ordering everyone to let go and get the boat turned over. After a moment's hesitation by some he was obeyed and the boat was righted, though brimful of water. Two men had somehow retained their hats all through the disaster, and Smith ordered these to clamber in and start using them to bail, while he and the rest hung on in the sea. It was slow work. The boat was so full of water that as fast as the men dipped in their hats and scooped out a pint or two a similar amount brimmed in. Painfully, they gained ascendancy. By dawn another man had been enabled to clamber aboard and help with the bailing, using his cupped hands, and as it grew light a fourth was ordered to join in.

The spreading light and the bailers' progress brought a dawn of relief for everyone. It was short-lived. One of the men in the water, looking round in the vain hope of being the first to espy a sail, saw instead something which struck terror into him. It did resemble a distant sail; but a second glance revealed it to be something quite different, and too close for anyone's comfort.

"A shark! A shark!"

The man's cry stopped the bailers dead and caused everyone's head to jerk round, eyes staring.

Heaving himself high in the water, Lieutenant Smith followed the man's pointing arm. There was no doubt about it—and as he saw the first fin he saw others, too, slicing through the water in the boat's direction. Urgently, he began to shout an order, but he was unheard. With a wild cry, several of the men tried to heave themselves over the gunwale. The little boat gave a great jerk, catapulting its occupants into the sea and once more overturning. Hours of work had been wasted and now there was no place of refuge for anyone.

Shouts of terror went up. At the top of his voice Smith tried to quell the panic. He seemed to have succeeded when the cries subsided and he was able to make himself heard telling the men to kick their legs about in the water and scare the sharks away—but in reality hysterical panic had given way to the frozen kind, for now the sharks were in amongst them, great gliding shapes flashing through the water, passing to and fro, almost playfully investigating this strange monster that rested its bulky body on the surface and threshed its many legs without their causing it to move.

A man suddenly screamed out that he had been bitten; but he had not—a passing shark, more curious or playful than the rest, had nudged him. A moment later, though, a scream of a different quality went up from another man. Before his mates' horrified gaze he let go his hold of the boat, flung up his arms and vanished under the sea's surface. In his place there welled up a sickening froth of blood.

John Meldrum knew that the time of real dread had come. He had heard often from older sailors that the scent of blood would rouse a pack of sharks to murderous attack on any fleshy thing. Lieutenant Smith knew it, too. There were now a dozen or more fins whipping about the sea, and it could be only seconds before the slaughter began. He urged the men to redouble the threshing movements of their legs, and at the same time to give a good heave and get the boat upright once more. Again he was obeyed; again the boat floated right way up, brimming with water; again two men clambered in and began to bail.

The flailing of legs seemed to be having its effect. The shark pack had moved away a little. Smith shouted encouragement to the men, warning them not to let up, and to the bailers, scooping desperately beneath what was now a burning sun—and then, just as the young officer had finished speaking, a solitary fin scythed in towards him and he felt his left leg taken cleanly off above the knee.

Jamming his mouth shut, he managed to make no sound that would rekindle panic amongst his men. The water was already bloody from the first man's death, and the addition of the lieutenant's blood went unnoticed. But then, mercifully unseen by Smith, the fin came sweeping in again and he suddenly felt his other leg taken.

He could not stifle his groan this time. As the men stared

in horror, realizing what had happened, he let go and, nearly
fainting, began to sink. John Meldrum shot out an arm and
grabbed his shoulder. Another man, at the other side, did
likewise, and with the bailers' help the mangled officer was
heaved into the boat, to lie moaning in the stern-sheets, half-
submerged in water which grew deeper red from his pulsing
blood.

Now the carnage began in earnest. One after another of
the men in the water shrieked, flung up his arms and went
under. Some had their legs taken off; some were bitten completely in two. One or two simply let go and drowned, rather
than await a more terrible end. Yet, from time to time, the
sharks, as though gorged, moved away and Meldrum and his
dwindling comrades knew some respite. The morning
passed, and they still lived. The afternoon began to wane,
and, although fewer, there were still men alive to bail and
others to cling on.

All day, lying in agony under the merciless sun, Lieutenant Smith continued to encourage them. Towards evening
his voice grew weaker, his sentences more laboured. He
knew his end must be near. He called the youngest member
of the crew, a strong boy named Wilson, to move nearer to
him, and said. "You are the youngest and the most likely to
survive. When you reach Jamaica, tell Admiral Halstead
that my men did their duty throughout, and that I hope I
have always done the same. And tell him I asked one last
favour—that he should promote Meldrum to gunner."

He shook hands with as many of the men as he could
reach, and then lay back in the boat to await death. But
Lieutenant Smith did not die of his wounds. A panicky jerk
on the boat's side by some of the men when the cry of
"Shark!" went up again capsized it once more. The brave
young officer was drowned, and again the survivors were
without a refuge.

The mate, Maclean, now took command and ordered the
painful process to begin again. And as the bailing was
resumed the sharks swept in again, and three more men disappeared shrieking. Only Maclean and Meldrum remained
in the sea now, while the boy Wilson and another seaman
bailed. As soon as the level of water in the boat had been
reduced sufficiently, Maclean and Meldrum dragged themselves inboard and began to help with the bailing, while the

sharks passed to and fro, sometimes nudging the boat and threatening to overturn it for what must surely be the last time.

Night fell. The bailing went on. No sail had been sighted all day, no food eaten, no water drunk. There had been only the scorching sun, and the sharks. The combination had been too much, it proved, for Wilson and the other sailor. Both went raving mad in the night, flung themselves overboard and drowned.

Meldrum and Maclean worked on until the boat was as dry as they could get it. Then they dropped into the bottom of it and slept exhaustedly. It was full day when they awoke. The sun was blistering them and they could see the sharks' fins still gliding about the even surface of the sea.

At first the two men talked. Then they grew silent as their tongues swelled with a raging thirst. They could only sweep the empty sea with their gaze, then resume a speechless staring at each other. And as they sat there helplessly, wondering in what order, and in what form, death would take them, each suddenly became aware that the other could, if he chose, kill him with the knife at his belt and save himself by drinking his blood.

It was a fantasy of approaching madness. Neither man thought of doing any such thing; only suspected that the other might be contemplating it. As every hour of relentless sun was endured, so the notion deepened and developed into certainty. Maclean sat in the bow, Meldrum in the stern. Speechless, nearly mindless now, they faced one another and scarcely dared take their eyes off each other's. Both knew, in crazed certainty, that the testing time would come at night. The first man to doze, however momentarily, would become the victim: the other would survive.

Meldrum was suddenly startled out of this paranoiac coma by a hoarse cry. Maclean, wide-eyed, was pointing beyond him, struggling to articulate. Meldrum was about to turn his head when he suddenly caught himself. He had nearly fallen for the fatal trick—pretend there is someone behind your opponent, make him turn his head, then catch him, unguarded. John Meldrum's hand inched down towards the knife at his own belt, his eyes now never flickering away from the mate's.

In another instant Maclean was on his feet—and

Meldrum's knife was out, blade pointing upwards for a defensive thrust against the imminent onslaught. But it never came. The mate was pointing still, his expression genuinely excited, his hoarse voice croaking, "A sail! A brig!"

Hesitating, gripping the knife, John Meldrum cautiously turned his head, then jerked it back suddenly to catch his assailant unawares. The mate had not moved from where he stood. Meldrum turned his head again—and saw the sail.

The near-insanity which might have destroyed them, one way or the other, fell away from both men in the instant. Meldrum did not hear the clatter of his falling knife as his hand shot out to grasp the other's. Tears filled their eyes as they embraced and then turned, side by side, to shout with what little concerted voice they could raise.

As they watched, and shouted, and waved, the brig put on more sail and changed course—away from them. Slowly, John Meldrum stooped to pick up his knife and return it to his belt. It seemed he would need it, after all.

Then a more positive form of madness struck him. He turned to Maclean.

"I'm going to swim to that brig."

Maclean gripped his arm. "Don't be a fool. You'd never reach her. You're too weak. Anyway, remember the sharks."

He pointed. Sure enough, a lazy fin glistened on the surface not a hundred yards away.

John Meldrum freed himself. "It's our only chance. Just ... just take my wife my love if I don't succeed. And if you see a shark coming after me, don't shout. I'd rather not know till it happens."

Without more ado he had leaped over the side and was swimming strongly towards the retreating brig.

As he entered the water Meldrum saw a surge of movement below him and knew that it could mean only one thing. But the splash he had made had evidently scared the shark, for no attack came. He could see more than one fin now; could sense that they were circling him warily; he kept his gaze on the brig, hoping someone would come on to her deserted deck and catch sight of him before one of the monsters took him or he sank exhausted.

He was gaining on the vessel, but his strength was going. At each stroke his arms seemed heavier to lift from the water. He was tempted to stop and lie on the surface and just float until a shark ended it all for him.

And then there was a man, leaning over the brig's side, seemingly looking in Meldrum's direction. The swimmer heaved himself desperately erect, half out of the water, and used the last of his strength for a despairing cry. Then he sank back, almost too feeble to swim another stroke.

But other figures were moving on the vessel now. There was a cluster of them round the first man and the unmistakable outline of a man in the rigging with a telescope trained. Then some of the sails were coming down with a rush and the brig's head was turning.

John Meldrum and Maclean were taken for pirates by the Americans who hauled them aboard their brig and listened unbelievingly to their incredible tale. They took them to Havana where they were put aboard a British warship and returned to Port Royal, where, as the only survivors of a lost ship, they had to undergo the further ordeal of court-martial.

The court witnessed a rare scene. When Maclean had nearly finished giving his evidence, and reached the point of their rescue, the two young men simultaneously burst into tears and embraced. There were few present who did not shed a tear with them, including Admiral Sir Lawrence Halstead himself, who, having heard Maclean testify to his gallant captain's last wish, raised John Meldrum, gunner's mate, to John Meldrum, gunner.

The Resurrectionists

Down the Close and up the Stair,
But and ben wi' Burke and Hare.
Burke's the butcher, Hare's the thief,
Knox the man that buys the beef.

A jewelled ring flashed in the lantern light as the hand moved over to pick up the shining scalpel. Quickly and smoothly the knife bit through the unnaturally white skin and deep into the underlying flesh at the back of the neck. Rows of faces peered down from the tiered wooden benches of the lecture hall to catch each skilful movement of the surgeon's hand. The blade moved on until the vertebrae were clearly exposed, and then Doctor Robert Knox looked up at the students.

"Here, gentlemen, you see the nerve trunk, leaving the spinal chord between the two vertebrae." The knife point moved over the bone to illustrate the words. "The chord itself continues up the spine towards the medulla, which forms part of that organ which will be the subject of tomorrow's lecture; an organ which I fear is all too seldom in evidence in the heads in front of me—the human brain."

The old witticism brought the expected laughter from the students, as they began to gather their books together at the end of the lecture and make for the doors. Doctor Knox laid aside his instruments and carefully washed his hands in a small metal bowl, drying them on a clean, white towel.

Knox was an odd-looking man. Short, bald, with only one eye, he was always impeccably dressed in the height of fashion. With his ringed hands, extravagant lace frills and cuffs he might have seemed somewhat ridiculous, had it not been for the forceful personality which held his students in awe while they listened to his lectures. For Knox was more than a good surgeon. His lectures were not limited to the narrow confines of anatomy, but ranged far and wide through philosophy and the arts.

As one of his assistants helped him into his frock coat, another came in through the side door of the lecture hall and waited quietly until the doctor was ready. When Knox was happy that he was decently dressed again, he beckoned the man over.

"There are two," the attendant searched for the right word, "men to see you sir."

"What do these *men* want?" asked Knox.

The attendant coughed and looked embarrassed.

"Well, sir, I think they have a . . . That is they—"

Knox interrupted brusquely.

"What you mean to say is that there are two body-snatchers waiting to see me and that they have brought the specimen with them. Is that correct?"

The attendant looked even more embarrassed at the doctor's frank statement, and mumbled his agreement.

"Well," said Knox, "let us not keep the wretches waiting."

He marched out of the lecture theatre into a small adjoining room where the two men were waiting. On the floor between them was a large bundle, wrapped in dirty rags. Knox eyed them all with distaste.

"I presume you have a cadaver for me. Well man, don't stand around. Unwrap your parcel, and let's see what sort of condition it's in."

The two men knelt down and began to unwind the rags, revealing the body of an old man. When the corpse was completely uncovered they got up and stood back as Knox came forward for his inspection.

"At least it's fresh," said Knox when he had finished, "which is more than can be said for many that are brought here. Which cemetery did you remove this fellow from, eh? No, on second thoughts it would perhaps be as well if you were to keep that information to yourself."

"We're no grave-robbers, sir," said one of the two men, in a thick Irish brogue. "I keep a lodging house. This fellow died owing me money. It's only right to try and get it back now, isn't it?"

"There's nothing wrong in that now, is there?" put in the other, in an accent as thick as the first's.

Knox looked at the pair with even less pleasure than before. They were big, thick-set men in their late thirties and neither of them was very clean. Knox pulled out his purse.

"Seven pounds ten shillings," he said.

The two men eyed each other greedily.

"Well, sir," began the shorter of the two, his voice taking on an ugly, wheedling tone.

"That is my price," put in Knox firmly.

"We'll take it," replied the tall man.

Knox carefully counted out the money into the tall man's large and grubby hand. When the last coin was in place the big Irishman greedily closed his hand on the bright metal.

"Thank you, sir," he said.

"God bless you, sir," said the other, and the two men turned and scrambled out of the door. Knox watched them go.

"God bless indeed," he said angrily as the door closed. "To think that in the year eighteen twenty-seven a respectable surgeon should be forced to deal with such scum to enable him to continue his work." He turned to his assistant. "Take this body down to the mortuary. I must be getting home."

He turned on his heel and strode, still muttering to himself, back through the empty lecture hall.

Outside, the street was black. The moon was hidden behind the ragged clouds, and the only light was the light that spilled out from the windows of Surgeons' Hall. In the distance, the black bulk of Edinburgh Castle stood out as a deeper black above the jumbled, uneven skyline. The two Irishmen stood in the light of one of the windows, eagerly counting and recounting the money.

"Seven pounds ten shillings," the taller man said. "Seven pounds ten shillings, and just for a bundle of stinking old flesh and bone like that old soldier. He's worth more dead than he ever was alive."

"Seven pounds ten shillings," repeated his companion. "What they want to pay good money like that for a rotten old body?"

"I told you before. Anyway, what do you care as long as you got the money? Come on." And the tall man marched off down the street, the other man following, still questioning.

"No, tell me," he insisted, "why do they want to spend good money on an old dead body?"

The tall man gave in to the repeated questioning. He explained how the only bodies the doctors could have to work on were those of executed criminals. These were far too few to meet the demand, so a new trade had grown up around the medical schools; the grisly trade of the resurrectionists. These men made their living by digging up freshly buried bodies from the graveyard and selling them.

The two men walked through the dark streets of Edinburgh, planning how they would spend their money. Soon they reached the district of Grassmarket, an area of mean streets and mean houses overlaid with the stench of poverty. No one greeted them as they moved over the filthy cobbles, for they were not the kind of men to have many friends. The tall man was William Burke. He had come to Scotland ten years ago to work as a navvy on the Union Canal, but now worked, when he worked at all, as a cobbler. The other man was William Hare. He too had come to Scotland as a navvy, but now he and his wife ran a verminous and tumbledown boarding-house. The body that they had just disposed of so happily was that of one of their lodgers. No, they were certainly not the kind of men to have many friends.

Now they were near the centre of the Grassmarket. The stone walls of the Castle rose high and sheer over the district, frowning down on the squalor that clustered round the bottom of the castle rock. Shouting and singing spread out into the night streets from the taverns dotted throughout the area. Bodies of drunkards too far gone to get home sprawled among the trash of the streets. At streets corners men stood talking or arguing. Here and there fights broke out. And from the darker alleyways came noises that only the very foolish went to investigate. The two men strode through it all, neither noticing nor caring about the scene around them, until they reached Tanner's Close where Hare and his wife had their lodging house.

Inside, in the basement, the two wives were waiting for them. If Burke and Hare were unpleasant characters, their wives were certainly no more attractive. They sat huddled round the smoking fire like two young witches. The firelight flashed from the bottle of cheap gin that was being passed from one to the other as the two men came in. Burke jangled the coins in his hand as he stood in the doorway.

"Seven pound ten shillings. Seven pound ten shillings for old Donald."

At once the two women broke into delighted yells of laughter, joining in the chorus of "seven pounds ten shillings". Now the four began to celebrate their good fortune with relish and enthusiasm. The bottle was passed rapidly from hand to hand, and when that was finished the next was started. The noise of the laughter, the shouting and the clink of glasses crept up the stairs to the derelicts who occupied the tiny rooms of the lodging house. And if those who heard the noise of the celebration knew the cause they kept the knowledge to themselves. Dawn was creeping into the December sky before the four finally slept.

Seven pounds ten shillings represented a good sum of money in 1827, but it couldn't last for ever. Soon the Burkes and the Hares had returned to their normal state of poverty. But now they knew where money could be had: the doctors of Surgeons' Hall would pay well for bodies, nice fresh bodies, not too long in the ground. They discussed it among themselves, the four of them. Burke was ready to go out at once to the graveyard to join the other shadowy figures, scurrying with their spades and dark lanterns among the granite crosses and marble slabs.

But Hare, cunning, vicious Hare, argued against him. The graveyards were being watched, he pointed out. There were too many poor people hoping to make a few pounds from a corpse, and the authorities were starting to tighten up their defences. There was no doubt that a man could make good money, but was it worth the risk of being caught? The argument went back and forth between them; and slowly, at Hare's urging, another plan emerged, a plan for providing the bodies the Edinburgh surgeons needed so badly, a way to get specimens for the generous Doctor Knox.

Abigail Simpson knew nothing of Burke and Hare. She

was an old woman. She herself was not even sure how old, and her appearance was no guide. For the years of poverty and unremitting hard work aged the women of the Grassmarket quickly, so that there was little to distinguish the woman of fifty from the woman of seventy.

Abigail had received little out of life. True enough she had a daughter, and though she talked about the girl she had no more idea of where to find her than she had of where to find the girl's father. Like many of her neighbours she only knew one place where comfort could be found—in the cheap gin of the Grassmarket taverns. It was this need to find comfort, to forget the miseries of everyday life that took her on a cold, January night to a small tavern near Tanner's Close.

At the doorway old Abigail paused to ease her shabby old cloak off her shoulders and to look round the room. It was not easy to see anything. The lanterns on the tables spilled out their tiny pools of light into the darkness. Here and there, faces were picked up by the feeble light so that they appeared to swim as disembodied heads in the gloom. Serving girls moved among the tables, scrunching through the straw that served as a floor covering, and slopping the drinks as they pushed their way around the cramped room. To Abigail, the scene was familiar and pleasant: she was not looking for elegant surroundings, only a temporary oblivion to help drive away the problems of life for a few hours.

She hobbled over to a corner of the room where she found an empty table, and waited for someone to serve her. She had a long wait. The male customers got priority, for the serving girls knew that there was always a chance of making a little extra money from the men. The poor old woman in the corner wasn't going to provide any extra. So Abigail waited. She didn't mind. She was used to this, it was just another small irritation to learn to live with. Eventually she got her tumbler of crude gin and sat sipping it slowly, feeling the warmth of the liquor spread through her body.

Abigail sat clutching her glass, paying no attention to anyone and expecting no one to pay any attention to her. But this night someone was interested in Abigail. Two men had come into the tavern and were standing irresolutely in the middle of the floor. They were whispering to each other, and occasionally sneaking quick looks at the old woman. After a moment they moved over and sat down by Abigail at the next table, the taller of the two shouting out his order for drinks in a harsh, ugly voice. Abigail still paid no attention. She was well used to the raucous crowd that milled around in the Grassmarket taverns. She went on sipping her gin, delighting in the sense of well-being that slowly spread over her.

The two men watched her as they drank their black rum. A full hour went by as Abigail sank further into her own dream world and the two men watched. Then the tall man stood up, lifted his wooden chair and placed it opposite Abigail's. His thin mouth twisted up at the corners in what could have been an attempt at a smile. He began to talk. The words hardly registered with Abigail, but she nodded her head and smiled in return.

The tall man introduced himself as William Burke, and then he brought his friend Hare over and introduced him too. Abigail couldn't honestly say that she welcomed the two men, but it did make a change from sitting alone and unnoticed. As the evening wore on she even began to warm to the two big Irishmen, particularly Hare. He seemed to go out of his way to be pleasant to her, and, almost involuntarily, she found herself telling him about her daughter. He seemed interested. In fact, the more she talked the more interested he seemed to be. She forgot that she hadn't seen her daughter for years and had no idea where she could be found. The friendly man seemed so interested she was sure that one day he would be a marvellous son-in-law who would look after her and keep on supplying her with her glass of gin.

Soon Abigail found herself out in the cold night air again, and the two big men were with her. She wasn't altogether sure what she was doing there, but she was vaguely aware of nice Mr Hare talking about her daughter and what a nice girl she sounded and not like some of the sluts you found these days. She was quite happy to allow herself to be guided across Tanner's Close and into the dark house, then down into the basement.

Once in the basement she paused, blinking in the smoky light. She couldn't remember why she was there but everyone was so friendly. There were two other women there, smiling and chattering. Abigail smiled back, happy with her new friends. For a moment she felt worried. Hadn't Mr Hare been interested in her daughter? And now there was this other woman. But the feeling of disquiet soon passed. It wasn't often that anyone took any notice of poor old Abigail Simpson. At the thought of her neglected life a tear plopped sadly into the glass someone had thrust into her hand. But her new friends were there to comfort her. They crowded round offering her more drink, smiling brightly at her, joking, laughing, cheering her up. She forgot her self-pity and started to laugh until the tears changed from tears of pity to tears of pleasure. Was she getting a little too drunk? Perhaps. But she was with friends. You were allowed to get drunk with friends, weren't you?

She took another gulp of her gin and snickered into the glass. Her friends were all around her. One of them started to sing: a hard, gruff baritone, but a lovely song—"Home, Sweet Home". Abigail joined in the chorus, her old cracked voice faltering and breaking on the high notes. The others laughed, and she joined in. She wasn't sure what the joke was, but it was a nice feeling to laugh. She laughed and laughed, and the more she laughed the more her four new friends laughed, until the whole room was filled with their hilarity.

Suddenly Abigail began to feel tired, and started to pull her old cloak around her, ready to go out into the street and home. But her friends wouldn't hear of such a thing. It was much too late. It was such a cold night. There were so many thieves around in the streets. It wasn't safe. Abigail was glad to agree. She was so tired, and they were so kind. Yes, perhaps just for the one night, since she wasn't feeling so well.

Happily, she let them help her on to the bed. How nice to have such good friends. Would she like a pillow for her head? Yes, that would be nice. The tall Mr Burke brought it for her. He held it up over her head, smiling. The others seemed to be laughing again; and Abigail smiled, glad that everyone was so happy. The laughing grew louder, hysterical, menacing. Somewhere in Abigail's mind a faint twinge of fear jerked. But then the pillow started to come down, closer and closer until it blotted out the light. Too late she opened her mouth to scream, but the soft material covered her face, filling her eyes, her mouth. her nostrils, filling her whole world.

Burke held the pillow down firmly over the old woman's face, until the last movement had died away from her jerking limbs. Slowly he straightened up and stood back from the bed, the beads of sweat glistening on his forehead.

"That's it," he said, and dropped the pillow on the floor.

For a moment the four stood in silence, looking at the pathetic, lifeless body. Then Hare started to laugh again. Not the mad, hysterical laugh that had been the last sound Abigail Simpson had heard, but a low laugh of pure pleasure. Within seconds, the two women had joined in. Only Burke stood silent. Still laughing, Hare moved to the body and began to search it, extracting a few coins from the clothing. When he had satisfied himself that there was nothing else of value, he stood back to allow the two women to strip the body completely. Then they tied it in sacking, ready to be moved. The two women kept watch while Hare fetched his donkey and the bundle was tied in place on the animal's back. When it was quite secure the two men led the donkey away, its hoof-beats echoing hollowly through the dark, night streets.

At Surgeons' Hall, they were taken to see Doctor Knox, who eyed the new specimen with interest. When he was finished he looked quizzically at the two men.

"Another lodger?" he asked.

Burke and Hare made no reply, and Knox continued looking at them for a moment before reaching into his coat for his purse.

"Ten pounds," he said.

Hare nodded eagerly, but Burke remained impassive. The money was counted out and the two men left. Outside in the street Hare jingled the coins.

"Ten pounds," he said. "Ten pounds, and more to come. Lots more."

Burke and Hare slunk off, to be swiftly swallowed up in the dark streets of the city. But the phrases seemed to hang in the air outside Surgeons' Hall.

"More to come. Lots more."

The Secret of Sophie Dawes

Paris, in the winter of 1830. Long years of the tedium, frustration and fear which attend revolution were over. A king was on the throne once more; there was a liberal government, and talk everywhere of universal liberty and artistic endeavour. Frivolity reigned again in high society—and the strange new game of the door bolt and the silk ribbon was all the rage. They were giggling over it in half the salons of Paris; yet its origin had been in terror.

The train of circumstances which brought it about had begun twenty years earlier, in London, in a house in Piccadilly much frequented by wealthy French *emigrés*: a house, not to put too fine a point upon it, of ill repute.

Two men sat drinking and playing cards at a table, gazing idly round at the girls, scarcely listening to the tinkle of the square piano. Their game was desultory, the play of bored men whiling away time. When one of them tossed down an ace he gave only mechanical expression of his pleasure.

"What do you think of that, my dear Artois?"

His companion's response was predictable. "The luck of the Bourbons."

The winner sighed. "Don't speak of luck to me, Artois. Rotting my life away for fifteen years in this waste land. I, Louis Henri Joseph, duc de Bourbon, future Prince de Condé . . ."

With a spark of animation Artois interrupted him.

"You've no more to complain of than I. We've still got our heads on our shoulders—that's worth thanks, any day. We haven't lost our rank or our money—well, not permanently. This place may be different from Paris, but we contrive to enjoy ourselves."

"Enjoy!"

"Yes! You've only yourself to blame, a man of your means, if you choose to live in your nasty back street, and eat in chop-houses, and sit in the cheapest seats in the theatres."

"Economy is a virtue, my dear Artois."

"Coming from the heir to some of the richest estates in France, my dear Bourbon, that simply makes me laugh. Oh, lord, here comes that loathsome Guy."

"Guy is a trusted and loyal retainer," Bourbon protested.

"Trusted old pimp, you mean. I'm off."

Bowing unctuously to the departing Artois, Guy sidled up to his master.

"Monseigneur, there's a girl over there . . . It occurred to me that perhaps . . ."

Bourbon sighed. "I'm sick of them all, Guy. They bore me."

Guy smirked. "This one is different, monseigneur. Not yet twenty. Intelligent. Mature."

"And just about a third of my age."

"I refer, monseigneur, to the servant-girl over there. See!"

Bourbon followed the pointing finger. There was a moment's hesitation, before he ordered, "Bring her to me, Guy."

A moment later she stood before him: a tall, shapely girl, fine-featured and with a flawless English complexion setting off brilliantly blue eyes. Bourbon waved Guy away.

"What is your name, child?"

"Sophie, sir."

"Charming. You're very beautiful, Sophie."

"I'm just a simple girl, sir."

"In *this* place!"

"It's not my choice, sir. I was cruelly used, and came down to serving. It's not what I want."

"What do you want?"

"I long to be educated, sir. I want to learn all I can, and

speak languages, and understand all sorts of things. And then . . ."—she chose her words carefully—". . . I hope I may some day be a credit to some gentleman who will let me serve no one else but him."

The white-haired duke felt his heart pound suddenly. His voice trembled ever so slightly as he said, "You're beautiful *and* intelligent, Sophie. Sit down here beside me."

But she did not move. "I dare not, sir. It isn't allowed . . . not the servants, sir."

The duke recalled his rank and wealth. "Then," he ordered, "take off your apron. The duc de Bourbon invites Miss Sophie to sit and take a glass of wine with him."

Sophie Dawes never served anyone again. Before many years were out she was to have servants of her own—dozens of them. She had been born in 1792, or thereabouts, the daughter of a renowned Isle of Wight fisherman and smuggler, "Dickey" Daw. Unfortunately for his ten children and their mother Daw drank freely of the spirits he smuggled and the entire family found itself in the workhouse. Ten days before the Battle of Trafalgar Sophie was released into the world alone to take work on a farm. Later she is said to have been a milliner's assistant in London, an actress, an officer's consolation, a rich foreigner's toy, a water-carrier's doxy; and, like another of her sex remembered for royal associations, an orange-seller in a theatre. Then, in 1810, she had the fateful meeting with Louis Henri Joseph, duc de Bourbon, a gloomy rake of fifty-two.

It was to be no passing dalliance. Bourbon attended assiduously to her comforts and ambitions. He gave her a fine house in Bloomsbury and £800 a year to spend as she chose. He hired teachers of music, singing, deportment, French, Latin, Greek, and much else. She learnt fast. At length she was able to attempt translations of Plutarch and Xenophon. Within four years she had fulfilled her promise to become a credit to Bourbon; but by then he was back in Paris, his long exile ended; re-possessed of his enormous estates and hoping, for propriety's sake, that he was rid of Sophie for good.

He was not. She hurried to Paris, bombarded him with declarations of affection and loyalty, not unmixed with dewy-eyed reproach. He consented to see her again and again. Then, in 1818, his aged father died. Bourbon inherited the title of Prince de Condé, the last of the line. He also acquired a fortune of millions; the magnificent ancestral chateau of Chantilly; the chateau of Saint-Leu; the Palais-Bourbon in Paris, a house as big as a town; six hundred servants, hundreds of horses, and a devoted peasantry. Avoiding the court of his cousin, Louis XVIII, Condé settled down to the life of a feudal lord, concentrating upon the chase of the stag and the boar, keeping Sophie at a discreet distance.

She embarked upon a more determined chase in which Condé himself was the prey.

She began by suggesting that her service to him could be much more devoted were he to let her live under the same roof, instead of in lodgings near by. He refused firmly. A new respectability was abroad in the land; unlike the bad old days, there could be no question of scandalous talk. Sophie was ready for this. With charming insinuation underlying her words, she proposed that he put it about that she was his natural daughter; and then, for double respectability, marry her off to a member of his household. She even had her prospective husband in mind: Victor Adrien de Feuchères, an officer of the Royal Guard, a brave soldier but a dull dog of so faithful a disposition that he would scarcely dream of suspecting his wife of sharing the prince's bed as well as his own.

As ever, Bourbon was attracted by the piquancy of the situation and agreed. Sophie and de Feuchères were married in London, the groom finding nothing suspicious in her terming herself Madame Sophie Clarck, widow of William Dawes, British India Company agent. He had nervously put one or two questions about her to the prince, to receive only bluff assurances and a welcome appointment as *aide-de-camp*.

The prince's formal recognition of her as his natural daughter invested Sophie with royal blood. The elevation of de Feuchères the following year to baron gave her a title. She also began to lay the foundations of a financial fortune. For four years she worked at it, with growing success; but one thing, respect, eluded her. Villagers resented her airs and stoned her carriage. Servants attended her with bad grace. Then the time came when even de Feuchères could ignore the truth no longer. In a violent quarrel he taxed

Sophie with the truth. She spat back that she was the prince's mistress, and proud of it. With surprising determination, de Feuchères proceeded to horsewhip her, and she was only saved from lasting injury by the prince's intervention.

De Feuchères resigned from the prince's household. This was a blow to Sophie. With no husband to maintain a façade of propriety for her she could not hope to remain. Some time before she had established her mother and sister in Paris, and now she went to live with them. She toyed with the idea of entering a convent; but within a few days Condé begged her to return as his undisguised mistress. In doing so he signed his death warrant.

Sophie returned to Chantilly in triumph. Condé was all too eager to reward her readiness to sacrifice her public virtue and Sophie did not protest when he instructed a lawyer to draw up a will leaving her the estate of Saint-Leu and Boissy. She accepted without demur further gifts which brought her personal fortune to more than a million francs.

She was just over thirty. In fourteen years she had risen from servant in a London brothel to Queen of Chantilly. A contemporary likened her to a stout, fresh-looking cook, who would have disgusted any decent fellow in three days. She was hissed at the theatre one evening. The prince's real illegitimate daughter, Madame de Rully, refused to eat at the same table as her. Sophie demanded the prince turn his daughter out of his household. Protesting feebly, he did.

By one means and another, Sophie gradually gained power, helped by a little clique of her own relatives and sycophants with whom she surrounded herself. But in the one quarter more important to her vanity she found herself firmly rebuffed. While her marriage had remained intact, and with it the fiction of her blood relationship with the Prince de Condé, she had been received a number of times at the court of Louis XVIII. Now the king made it plain that she would no longer be recognized. When she tried to brazen it out by turning up in her court robes an official sent her packing. To her ambition of securing control of Condé's fortune she added the further resolution to gain re-admission to court.

In 1824 Louis XVIII died and was succeeded by his brother, Charles X. The Prince de Condé was now sixty-nine. He suffered from a variety of complaints and was lame from a broken thigh he had sustained in a riding accident. An old campaign wound in the shoulder had left him incapable even of dressing his own hair or tying his cravat. He was not the ideal Romeo to his plump and active Juliet; but so long as he provided the pence, she could—and did—find others to supply the passion.

Since Condé had no heir, Sophie undertook to find one for him who would promise her security in return for her help. She shrewdly chose the son of Louis-Philippe, duc d'Orléans. The duke and duchess had long been her allies and had continued privately to present her in aristocratic society after her exclusion from court. Their motives were not disinterested, as Condé at once recognized. When Sophie put her proposal to him he flew into a rage, declaring that the title of Prince de Condé would never be borne by an Orléans. Determined to get her way, she began the campaign of terror against him which he would escape only by death.

Sometimes quietly menacing, often violent, she preyed on the old man's fear of death and his physical helplessness. What went on behind the closed door of his chamber happened unwitnessed; but every member of the household heard the screech of Sophie's abuse and threats and the feeble prince's cries of fear and pain. There was the crash of shattering crockery, whose fragments were plain to see on the floor afterwards, and more than one glimpse was had of Sophie, as she entered a room, slamming the door violently behind her, almost to catch her master full in the face as he doddered after her.

Almost every day Sophie provoked some quarrel with the prince. Whatever he said she could twist in some way that would give her an excuse to take exception to it. Then she was away, shouting, screaming, gushing tears, sweeping ornaments to the ground, smashing furniture, and finally, shaking or striking the cowering old man, reducing him to an abject heap before she swept from the room, hurling a final volley of abuse over her shoulder and slamming the door with a crash that shook the very walls of the ancient chateau.

Where Sophie left off her minions kept up the persecution in countless small, underhand, but—to her victim—exhausting ways. For all his wealth and rank the Prince de

Condé felt himself hemmed in on all sides by demons dedicated to making his life a misery. They included Sophie's brother James, a former London street porter, whom the prince had, at her instigation, made one of his intimates and created Baron de Flassans; Lambot, the prince's *aide-de-camp*, who was one of her allies and perhaps one of her lovers; her certain lover, the disreputable *Abbé* Briant; and Lecomte, a Parisian hairdresser whom she had made a valet to the prince, who detested him but could not refuse.

The prince protested feebly to his faithful steward, the Baron de Surval, that the prolonged persecution was wearing him out. He could not sleep. He felt his blood heat up alarmingly whenever a quarrel erupted. Yet he was determined not to give in to Sophie's machinations on behalf of the Orléans. Surval offered to reason with her, but the prince, fearing an even worse outburst, forbade it. When he himself ventured to repeat his objections to Sophie she accused him of base ingratitude to one who had selflessly given up her virtue to please him; and then, after the usual self-pitying tears, the shouting and the blows began again.

But Sophie's strongest weapon, ironically, was her pathetic victim's dependence on her. Her trump card, and she knew it, was to threaten to leave him. In vain, Surval begged him to let her go for good. The old man told him wearily: "Anything but that. I'm over seventy. It's gone on too many years now. You don't understand how time and affection can forge chains which I no longer have the strength to break. No, de Surval. Sooner or later, they will get their way."

They got their way. A last effort by Condé's advisers to bribe Sophie out of her intentions with the gift of the domain of Guise, one of the finest and richest of his estates, had no effect. A personal appeal by the prince to d'Orléans was promptly reported to Sophie. The corridors rang with her abuse. The prince capitulated and wrote a new will:

> I institute my great-nephew and godson, Henri-Eugene-Philippe-Louis d'Orléans, duc d'Aumale, my residuary legatee, and appoint him at the time of my decease to inherit all my estates and possessions of whatsoever nature they may be, with the exception of such legacies as I now bequeath. I bequeath to the dame Sophie Dawes, baronne de Feuchères, the sum of two millions. I likewise bequeath to her unconditionally, first, my chateau and park of Saint-Leu;

second, my chateau and estate of Boissy, and all the lands appertaining thereunto; thirdly, my forest of Montmorency and all the lands appertaining thereunto; fourthly, my domain of Morfontaine; fifthly, the pavilion occupied by her and her family in the Palais-Bourbon, as well as the grounds belonging thereunto; sixthly, the furniture contained in that pavilion, together with the horses and carriages kept for the use of the aforesaid dame baronne de Feuchères.

Prophetically, he declared aloud, "There! They've got what they wanted. Now I had better look out for my life."

The last struggle to resist had taken severe toll of his waning powers. He no longer found solace in the hunting field. The doctors shook grave heads and, without much hope of a cure, tried to ease his pain and the inflammation in his legs by forbidding food likely to heat his blood and all but a taste of alcohol. Sophie was more than equal to this. Proclaiming that she would now devote her life to comforting his old age, she sat beside his bed and plied him with rich foods and quantities of wine.

Meanwhile she did not hesitate to remind the d'Orléans family of their promise. The king, wishing to save the Prince de Condé further distress, signified that she should be re-admitted to court without more ado. She was snubbed when she put in her appearance; but in 1830 Charles X fled to exile in England and Louis-Philippe, duc d'Orléans, Sophie Dawes's sponsor and conspirator in the matter of the Condé inheritance, ascended the throne.

Condé declared now that nothing remained for him but to die. He had begun to withdraw more and more to his own chambers, dreading Sophie's approach and fearful of her next outburst. For her part, she realized only too well the danger to her prospects if he should decide to re-write his will. To forestall any such move she instructed her creatures to observe and report on whatever he did or said. She opened all his mail and paid him sudden visits, trying to catch him with legal papers before him.

Condé could stand the reign of terror no longer. He resolved to escape and join the ex-king in exile in England. A large sum in cash was withdrawn secretly from his bank, a carriage and horses prepared at a secret rendezvous. But someone talked. The attempt never took place. Shortly after, the Prince de Condé was seen in the great gallery of the chateau of Chantilly, wearing only his trousers and pointing to a black eye.

"See what she has done to me now!" he cried. "How I wish I were dead!"

On 31 August, 1830, Condé was visited by a former member of the household of Charles X. It may well be that they discussed further plans for securing Condé's escape, for at dinner he seemed to be in high spirits, played a cheerful game of whist afterwards and retired to bed at midnight. His valet—not the one foisted on him by Sophie—helped him to undress and the surgeon treated his swollen legs. He gave instructions that he was to be called at eight the next morning.

At the appointed hour the valet's repeated knocking brought no summons to enter. He tried the door; it was bolted inside. Sophie apparently aroused by the noise, ordered the door to be broken down. It was done. The Prince de Condé was not in his bed: he was hanging from the window frame in a noose made of two handkerchiefs, one of which was marked with his initial and a coronet. A surgeon who immediately examined the body got the opinion that it had been dead since the early hours of the morning.

The surgeon examined the noose. It was so slackly tied that he was able to pass the whole of his hand through it without touching the corpse's neck. From the position of a chair near by he formed the impression that the prince must have stood on it while securing the noose round his neck and then pushed it away with his feet, so strangling himself.

No accurate notes were taken at an early enough stage and the flood of officials who arrived to investigate the death were not all competent. Details became confused and conjecture mistaken for fact. Sophie and her clique took every opportunity to insist that Condé had been out of his mind and had frequently threatened suicide: the valet strongly denied this.

Popular rumour got around that the prince had been strangled in his bed and then hanged to simulate suicide. The medical evidence at the formal inquiry, rather than helping to clarify things, provoked wrangles which were to last for years. What no one sought to explain was how the supposed murderer had managed to bolt the door *on the inside* after leaving the room.

One investigator, though, proved himself a worthy predecessor of Lecocq, Dupin and Sherlock Holmes. Addressing the inquiry, he said: "I asked myself, why should a man intending suicide first trouble to snuff out the candles which had lit him to bed? How *could* he commit suicide by hanging without even disarranging the nightcap on his head?

"It seemed to me to be the blunder of a painstaking assassin, striving to set all in order after a struggle. I therefore turned my attention to that other detail, the 'hanging' itself. How was this effected? By means of two kerchiefs, looped together by secure knots. But monseigneur was old and infirm. He could not even fasten his own cravat. He could not raise his arms above his shoulders—and yet the window-fastening to which the noose was affixed was more than six feet from the floor.

"Still, I reminded myself that most things are possible to one sufficiently determined. I therefore made up a similar noose, attached it to the window-fastening, and, in the presence of witnesses, endeavoured to hang myself. The noose was altogether too slack."

A spectator at the inquiry expressed himself now willing to accept the theory of murder, but for the fact that the door had been found bolted on the inside. The resourceful investigator demonstrated an answer to this. Looping a silk ribbon round the head of the door bolt, he went out of the room, retaining the ends of the ribbon in his hand. He closed the door. A tug on the ribbon from outside and the bolt easily went into its socket. Pulling on one end only the investigator was able to withdraw the ribbon to his own side of the door. "A bootlace or a length of horsehair would have served equally well," he explained.

And so the salons of Paris acquired a new game.

It was widely rumoured that depositions had been deliberately garbled, and that three leading physicians who had expressed belief that the prince had committed suicide had received a million francs for obliging. It was said that the royal family lived in fear of public condemnation of Sophie Dawes, as this would reveal their own connivance in the matter of the Condé inheritance.

When the inquiry ended indecisively a royal prince of a rival line pressed for a fuller hearing. Sophie accepted his challenge with confidence. The examining judge, an old man anxious to retire at a moment when it would most assist the promotion of his son-in-law, a deputy-judge, questioned Sophie searchingly about her treatment of the prince, about whether he had ever threatened suicide, and, most keenly, about Sophie's reported anxiety as to whether any papers had been found in the prince's apartment at his death.

"Were you concerned about the discovery of a will?" the judge asked.

' My chief concern was to find some letter that he might have left for me," Sophie replied. "I could not conceive that he would have left me so cruelly, without writing to me, if he had been in possession of his reason."

The hearing lasted for months. There were more than one hundred and twenty witnesses, and the balance of evidence pointed to murder, with Sophie implicated in some way. In his report the judge found against her; but that report never reached the public. Instead, the judge gratefully accepted an offer that if he would resign immediately his son-in-law would get his judgeship, and withdrew his findings. Two further hearings were forced, but neither found grounds for prosecuting Sophie or her friends.

Although she owed her escape to Louis-Philippe's influence she could no longer rely upon her royal connexions. A coldness had been developing on both sides. For a number of years she lingered in a hostile France, trying to enjoy her wealth. In 1837 she returned to England for good, buying an estate near Christchurch, Hampshire, as well as a fashionable London home.

But she had not long to enjoy them. Her constitution, once as tough as her will-power, began to give way. Dropsy developed. She moved permanently to London, in order to be near the best medical help. Throughout her suffering she gave no sign of remorse, no word or hint of the truth of what really happened at Saint-Leu. She preferred to bid for her place in Heaven with large sums of money, which she gave to charity. "Game to the last!" observed Sir Astley Cooper, her surgeon.

The end came suddenly, and some might say fittingly. She died of suffocation—not by a pair of hands at dead of night, but from *angina pectoris*. The secret of Sophie Dawes died with her.

Tapu

The skull bobbed gently up and down in the waters lapping the shore. Those waters were not always so placid: in their stormier moments they had eroded the low cliffs so that at one point the sketchy track disappeared into a raw new cleft. A few human bones stuck out from what was obviously an old burial ground. Some, like the skull, had dropped or rolled into the sea.

Striding ahead of his sixty native companions, the white man saw the lazily turning whiteness of bone and slithered down the slope towards it. Empty eye-sockets expressed outrage at this rude disturbance of eternal rest. He took a few steps into the ripples. Fishing the skull from the water, he carried it back to solid ground and dug a fresh hole for it with his hands. Then he covered it over and straightened up.

From above came a long wail of despair. Conscious of having done a good deed, he was puzzled by the outcry. He scrambled back up the shallow incline and advanced on his friends.

They backed away.

He laughed, gestured back towards the fresh patch of earth where he had so considerately re-interred the head, and made another move to rejoin them.

Sixty of them, strong men and fearless warriors all, broke in disorder and retreated still further.

He was baffled. "What have I done?"

What had he done, indeed? In broken sentences they explained. He had stumbled across one of their own tribal burying places. The skull was assuredly that of a most venerated chief. But how could they be sure it was that particular chief? Oh, they were quite sure. Not merely had he handled the dead: he had touched a chief, in itself a sin, and doubly terrible when that chief was dead.

The enormity of it dawned on him. He had thought himself well versed in local customs by now, knowing the traditions and etiquette and religious ordinances. He was at home with this people, and knew no other home, no other family. Yet now, by one foolish deed, he had cut himself off from society. With blundering thoughtlessness he had undone the work and comradeship of years.

Frederick Edward Maning had been born in Dublin in 1811. Brought to Hobart by his father, he was not greatly stimulated by the challenges which Tasmania had to offer, and began listening avidly to lurid tales brought back by traders from little-explored coastlines beyond Australia. Out there, it was said, lived a proud race of noble, savage fighters, sometimes friendly and sometimes hostile. Some traders had been allowed to settle and establish their own stores and warehouses. Others had been massacred. Some, it was rumoured, had been eaten. Trade was good but relationships were unpredictable.

At the age of twenty-two, Maning resolved to set out for these fabulous shores. He fell at once under the spell of *Ao-Tea-Rua*, the Land of the Long White Cloud, as Maori settlers from Polynesia called the country which later European invaders were to dub New Zealand.

Maning arrived at the mouth of the Hokianga River, high in the north of the northern island. One of the few European settlements of any size flanked the harbour, a broad inlet running some twenty miles inland between wooded hills, with several tidal tributaries. Then the river narrowed, with another forty miles still to go to its source.

On such rivers, tributaries and inlets along the coast lived the greater number of the Maori. They depended largely on fish for food, so their settlements were generally built on hills near the coast or on easily defended bluffs above winding streams. Shark meat cut into strips and dried was a staple part of their diet, supplemented by the flesh of birds, dogs and rats. They did not know the use of the bow and arrow, but killed animals and birds with thirty-foot spears. Their human prey was usually dispatched in hand-to-hand fighting with long and short clubs, and although cannibalism was not a regular observance they did not object to eating the corpses of dead enemies if other delicacies were scarce.

A resident white man was welcome in most Maori communities. It was useful to have a trader capable of dealing with visiting salesmen in their own language, on their own ground. Muskets and gunpowder were much sought after: the tribe that first amassed a good supply of firearms and ammunition was in a position to settle old grudges and exterminate old foes. A white trader, Maning observed after some experience of the country and its people, was worth about twenty times his own weight in muskets.

The white settler must, however, be scrupulous in his dealings and must demonstrably be a person of good standing. The Maori had a rigid code of honour and a number of clear social distinctions. Would-be cheats and exploiters were doomed to trouble. Vagrants, runaway sailors and travelling swindlers could not rely on the celebrated Maori hospitality; one ne'er-do-well in fact found himself providing a main ingredient of such hospitality, when a warrior used him as the meat course in a meal for some friends.

As a reasonably well-educated young man, and a member of the Church of England—convinced if not by any means conscientious—Maning had reservations about many of the customs of this land; but he came to respect and love its people. Eventually he married into the Ngapuhi tribe, buying from them two hundred acres of land. His wife died a few years after their marriage, but he remained in the community.

He had come as a stranger; became one of the family; and now was worse than a stranger—an outcast, a complete alien.

Standing there above the water, wishing he had never seen that confounded skull and never ventured near it, he heard himself denounced by the men with whom he had been laughing and singing such a short time before. From a respectful distance they told him that he was no longer fit company for human beings. They said it regretfully, lamenting an irreparable loss; but they would not accept him back into their ranks.

It was ludicrous. Just because he had handled a skull, an inanimate relic of some perished barbarian, he was to be rejected? Nonsense, all of it.

They resumed their homeward journey, and he found it was not nonsense. Now the sixty men took the lead and he was forced to trail behind like a wretched pariah dog. He tried to argue, tried to make a joke of it, tried to shame them into seeing the absurdity of it all. In return he got only sorrowing glances. When they camped at nightfall, instead of his going to the fire and talking with them about their ancient heroes and perverse demons, which so enchanted his mind, he had to squat under the shelter of a rock a safe distance away.

The enchantment of those perverse demons became less delightful and more sinister.

It was a bad joke. They couldn't keep it up.

Deep down he knew he was wrong. He was *tapu* . . . and that was no kind of a joke.

An appetizing smell drifted to his nostrils. They were cooking fish caught only a few hours ago, together with some sweet potatoes. He wondered whether he dared to creep nearer; and knew he must not. They had been his friends, but now that the mystical curse had fallen on him there was no telling what they might do.

At last, when the meal was ready, a reasonable helping was carried across and set down ten yards away.

He ought to have stood on his dignity and scorned this offering, but he was ravenous. He collected the food and pulled out his knife. At once there was a howl from the men in the encampment.

"You are not going to touch food with your hands?"

"Indeed I am." Maning sliced a piece from the potato.

"You must not do that! It is the worst of all things. One of us will feed you!"

He was certainly not going to be subjected to a humiliation of that kind. Without more ado he picked up the warm slice of potato and popped it in his mouth. The expression of horror, contempt and pity in their faces convinced him that he had not only offended their deepest susceptibilities, but had also lowered himself yet further in their estimation. Certainly he was a white man, and white men were known to do the oddest things. Often they were excused on grounds of sheer ignorance. But this act was not one which could be easily excused. To conform with the usage of the fearful *tapu* he ought to have crouched over his food with his hands behind his back, bending forward to gnaw the food as best he could. To sit there so brazenly, eating in the usual way was blasphemous.

The Maori began to get to their feet. Maning sat very still. Had he transgressed so abominably that they were going to slay him?

No. Not yet, anyway. They were striking camp. After what he had done, they feared he was capable of strolling into their camp when they were asleep and contaminating them all with his own terrible plague.

They set off to march through the starlit night. Maning defiantly stayed where he was. He would have a good night's sleep and head for home in his own good time. It would all look better in the morning.

But in the morning, with the memory of some disturbing dreams at the back of his mind, he found it looked no better. He knew what he had got himself into and knew that the consequences could be deadly; what he didn't know was whether there was any way out.

Tapu . . .

The Maori envisaged themselves surrounded by conflicting gods and demons. Many spirits of nature had vast resources of evil. The only defence was in ritual observances of great complexity, supervised by priests of different grades. The highest priests were trained in a house of learning and were often chiefs of tribes or the family units within a tribe. There were also lesser sorcerers capable of invoking minor deities and ancestral spirits, and a whole range of specialists religiously gifted with skills in carving, tattooing, building canoes and fashioning weapons. Every function of the community and its individuals was governed by various degrees of *tapu*—the "taboo" which to some was a blessing and to others a curse, consecrating or condemning.

Every chief had a holy *tapu* upon him. This extended to his clothes, weapons, and all personal possessions. To steal such things or molest the chief made the offender liable to a punishing *tapu* in which evil spirits would ravage his body and mind with sickness.

Anyone who handled a dead body or conveyed that body to its grave was under a special *tapu* which could be lifted only after a certain cleansing period. To make a profession of undertaking was to live permanently under this stricture, and so to be cut off from any contact with the living. It was forbidden to enter any house or approach too closely to any normal human being. The hands had become so frightfully unclean as to be useless, and must not touch food.

Maning now found himself in this category.

When he reached the village he tried to swagger cheerfully through it towards his little estate on the far side. Normally there were waves and greetings as he approached. This time, with the news that had been brought by the men who strode ahead, people scuttled for cover, into their thatched houses, behind the outdoor kitchens, into the meeting-house itself. The carved features of the contorted god on the steep roof-end seemed to grimace at Maning.

He would refuse to acknowledge these pagan powers. There was no reason for fear. He could pack up and go. He was a white man, he could return to his own people and turn his back on this mumbo-jumbo.

But would he be allowed to leave? There might be some ruling which decreed that no contaminated person should be permitted to carry his disease into the outer world.

He reached his house. His servants had fled. They would not risk brushing against him, breathing the air he breathed, or soiling their hands on his food and belongings.

Perhaps in due course the villagers would attack him. In addition to this accursed *tapu*, he might be subjected to the violence of the *muru*. In this, when a man suffered disaster his loyal friends descended on him and robbed him of all he possessed in order to ensure that the disaster was complete.

He washed himself. Then, without realizing what he was doing, he washed himself again. Obsessively he scrubbed away. "Out, damned spot!" He had to force himself to stop. He must not succumb to native superstition. He was not unclean. He would not become like those wretches he had seen who allowed the imposition of a *tapu* to derange their minds so that they literally thought themselves to death.

The night went by, and nobody made a move towards Maning's house. When he walked along the beach before the house, they watched from a safe distance. They neither attacked nor helped.

He was excommunicated.

If he behaved with proper humility, would there be a reprieve? He had already transgressed by touching food. In his own house he would eat as he chose; but they probably guessed this, and considered he was sliding even deeper into damnation. Perhaps they would simply leave him to his folly until he perished, if not from starvation then from sheer loneliness.

"But you know me," he wanted to argue. "You know I'm the same man who has lived among you all these years. I haven't changed."

But according to their code he had changed. And they would not let him draw close enough to argue.

There was a raw leg of pork hanging in the house. He was tempted to tear it apart and take lumps of it outside, so they could see him eating it raw. Then he would go berserk and run among them, frightening them as they were trying to frighten him.

For four days he stuck it out. The carving on the meeting-house, rearing above the village palisades, acquired a more and more threatening scowl.

On the third day there had, he observed, been a meeting in there. Had they been settling his fate?

On the fourth day he saw a ragged, hunched creature crouching outside the palisades. It was the burier of the dead. Old and haggard, clad in the most wretched rags, he looked like some twisted red demon—red with a mixture of stinking shark oil and red ochre, the native funeral colour. Twice a day food would be tossed down before him. He, unlike Maning, had the respect to eat it properly, with his hands behind his back. At night he would crawl into a mound of leaves and rubbish, passing the dark hours as well as he could until the even gloomier hours of day came again.

Did he need an apprentice?

"I will run amuck!" vowed Maning. He was talking loudly and aggressively to himself now. "I wonder how many I can kill before they bag me?"

On the morning of the fifth day he was standing dejectedly beside his outdoor kitchen when he saw a canoe edging in towards the beach. There was only one man in it: a stolid old man with only one eye.

Maning recognized him at once. He was a famous wizard, who had lost one eye in the fighting days before he entered the priesthood. Now he paced up the beach, carrying a small basket and mumbling. Maning tensed. This could be the beginning of a final ceremony of banishment; or it could be a spell to liberate him.

The priest came to a standstill, closer than anyone had so far ventured to Maning. He opened the basket and took out a baked yam.

"Here is your food," he said gravely.

Maning held out a cautious hand. The priest dropped the yam into it. Maning took a bite. The priest began a feverish incantation.

Maning bowed his head. At the same time he felt indignation boiling up inside him. That he, a dutiful Christian, should knuckle down like this before the heathen mumbling of a ridiculous old sorcerer . . . !

He was tempted to lash out, give the wizard a black eye, and run for it. But humbly he remained as he was.

The incantation finished. The priest looked past him and said in the singing Maori tongue: "Throw out all your pots and kettles."

Maning stared. The priest stared solemnly back at him. Maning surrendered. He turned to the kitchen, and hurled the pots and kettles one by one on to the beach. When they had clattered to a halt, the priest said: "Fling out all those dishes."

"They'll break."

"I am going to break them all."

The brooding menace of the last four days turned to grotesque farce. Dishes and cups were smashed, knives and forks went tinkling off in all directions.

"And now," intoned the priest, "strip off your clothes."

This was too much. Maning hesitated, then tugged his jacket off. He began to shout in English: "You old thief! How would you prefer being killed?" He took up a boxer's stance, jabbing forward with a left and a right under the impassive gaze of the priest. "Come on—what are you waiting for?"

With no change of tone the priest said, in his own language: "Boy, do not act foolishly. Do not go mad. No one will come near you while you still have those clothes. You will be miserable here by yourself. And what is the use of being angry: what will anger do for you?"

Still resentful, Maning nevertheless took off every stitch. When he was naked, he obeyed a further order to go into the house and seek out every other garment he owned. While he was collecting them up, he heard a smashing and banging outside, and emerged to see the priest battering his last pot to pieces with a large stone.

All the fragments were then piled into a basket together with the clothes and cooking utensils, and deposited in a thicket some way from the house.

The same evening, Maning's servants came flocking back. They beamed at him and fell back at once into their old ways. He had been ill; he was cured.

Yet during all his subsequent years in that country, Maning never felt quite at ease. Some time later, when nobody was about, he went into the thicket to which his belongings had been banished, and retrieved the cutlery. He used his knives and forks and spoons again, and his native servants handled them, with no apparent ill effects. But sometimes, in spite of himself, he wondered whether it would not be wiser to return them to the cache.

He also wondered whether he was really quite clean. People were as affable as they had been in the old days, but they did not seem to come quite as close to him, quite as readily, as they used to. Once or twice he glimpsed the apprehensive turn of a head as he passed.

Perhaps he had not been completely purified from the dread *tapu*. Perhaps he could never hope to be free. He was a white man, so they had decided to let him off lightly; and, of course, they did not want to lose this valuable member of their community. But fond as they might be of him, in their eyes he would always be a man tinged with a terrible infection.

Terror in the Outback

She lay there, watching the moon through the bedroom window. It was quite still outside, the last drunken sounds were over, the breeze had dropped. Jane was at peace with her world.

It was odd, really, how soon she had come to like this world, to be a part of it, this weird outback, this wilderness of a strange and only intermittently believable country where spring was autumn and wild birds and beasts of an extraordinary shape and behaviour fluttered and hopped and shrieked across a landscape like the moon.

Or so she had always imagined the landscape of the moon, back at school in England where its presumed grey emptiness contrasted with a green and moist west country. And if the real thing, the real moon, were not so brightly visible through her bedroom window, she could almost have believed herself upon it.

Jane—Jane Pierce—had been in Australia three weeks, rather more than twenty impression-filled days and nights since her three-masted passenger ship had dropped anchor in the muddy Yarra River near the comically bustling little town of Melbourne, jewel of a proud British colony named after a British queen twelve thousand miles away.

But it was not Jane Pierce who had come to Australia. The nervous girl with heart pounding like a dozen clocks gone berserk, who had walked down the gang-plank, so anxiously scanning unfamiliar faces on the shore, had a different name, Jane-something-else. That day now seemed so far in the past that Jane almost had difficulty remembering that name. Within hours she had become Mrs Pierce, married to the man she loved, a young man who had gone out, a year before, to join the police force of this unruly colony. Frank Pierce had done well in the Victorian police, had managed to discharge his duties while at the same time retaining the affection of most sections of a mixed society, and the admiration of his colleagues. And "colleagues" seemed a comic word for the roughnecks who comprised so large a part of the force; for the Australian police force was not at that time the admirable institution it is today.

But the admiration was mingled with fear. For Frank Pierce was uncorrupted and uncorruptible. He had his pay, he wanted no bribe—from either side. No outlaw could buy his acquiescence, no police officer, anxious for promotion and transfer to a more pleasing part of Her Majesty's Dominions, could get Frank Pierce to trap an innocent man, a scapegoat. No one, in the jargon of a century to come, would be "framed" by Frank Pierce.

Many of the police in the Victoria of 1880 were only too eager to frame a man, and the country abounded with men, in and out of uniform, anxious to bear false witness. The force had a reputation, among honest and corrupt alike, of being more wicked than the wicked it pursued.

It was against such a background that a family of Irish toughs like the Kellys could become folk heroes; and a young murderer like Ned Kelly himself be an Australian Robin Hood. Men like Quinn and Byrne from the Kelly gang would become the Friar Tuck and Little John of Antipodean folk-lore, every bar-room girl a Maid Marion.

Jane Pierce already knew and understood the folk-lore, knew and thought she understood the people of Glenrowan, the hamlet to which her Frank had been posted as lone outpost of law and order. Many of the people she knew and liked were obviously sympathetic to the notorious Ned Kelly and the gang which robbed stage-coaches and banks and murdered policemen. It might have been an awkward position for the young wife of a young policeman, but so goodhearted were these people of outback Victoria that, whatever their views on crime and punishment, they welcomed her as a friend. And it was less than likely that a serious crime would be committed in the immediate neighbourhood. Ned Kelly, Joe Byrne and the rest of them would carry out their escapades in other, distant districts.

Yet, such was their arrogance that the gang might easily come to this very hotel for an evening's drink, vanishing before dawn. "The Glenrowan" was a large, convivial establishment in the middle of nowhere; and "Ann Jones, Prop." with her illegitimate daughter, Helen, made everyone welcome, even a young policeman and his wife. So long as no disorder, no affray and no arrest took place on the premises, the world and his wife were welcome.

So when Frank Pierce was recalled for a fortnight to Melbourne, it had been the natural thing for Jane to move from the isolated shack they were calling their home into the noisy conviviality of Ann's hotel until her husband got back. "Keep you out of trouble, dear," Ann had said with a wink. "Never know what a pretty young thing like you might be getting up to all alone, eh?" Jane was grateful. Life for a woman—any woman—alone in the outback was hazardous, frightening.

And of course, Frank would never have left her without making such an arrangement.

But Jane's stay in the hotel was coming to an end; she would be back home before that moon re-appeared tomorrow, back with Frank in their two-room shack. His Melbourne transfer was ending with the arrival of the train bearing him and a hundred others like him, as well as a handful of black trackers, aborigines—hairless bloodhounds they called them—who could find a man across a thousand miles of desert or Nullabor Plain. Most of the trainload of police would go on to Wangaratta, disembark and fan out in search of the Kelly gang; but to Jane's relief Frank had been ordered back to the job at Glenrowan. He would not be involved, yet, in the business of trying to catch a Kelly.

Jane was sure she had seen one of the Kelly brothers—either Ned or Dan—before she turned in. He was a tall, gaunt, red-haired young man, not unpleasant looking, who had come into the bar where she sat talking with young Helen, her landlady's daughter. He had snapped his fingers and, suddenly, drinks were poured out for everyone. Ten minutes later he was gone. There had been no need for her to ask the identity of the young stranger.

She dozed off and when she awoke, the moon was gone and the sky was a pale dawn blue, with a splash of gold at the top of the window-frame. She lay for a minute watching the light creep down the painted wood as its source crept into the sky. Then, with a contented yawn, she turned her head on the pillow.

The man was standing a yard away.

She saw the pistol pointing down at her breast and her heart beat convulsively, then seemed to stop. She felt the blood drain from her face. "What—what do you want?" she asked. It was a distant, feeble, voice which belonged to somebody else, not her own voice at all.

It was the same man, the silent stranger who had entered the bar a few hours back, and now at last he spoke. "Sorry, Miss. Everyone down to the bar. Everyone's got to be in the bar . . ."

Could he be playing a game, celebrating something? Was he getting everyone into the bar at gun-point—before breakfast—to join him?

"Get *up*," said the man again. He kept the pistol on her for a moment longer, then seemed to realize she was not a woman to tackle gunmen in her bedroom. He straightened up, smiled almost sheepishly, and let his right hand drop below his waist.

She got up in a muddled confusion of fright and feminine modesty and nearly fell as she crossed the bedroom floor to reach a garment to cover her nightdress. Then, in long black cape and pink slippers, Jane Pierce went down the stairs, followed by a man with a gun.

She got to the bar and found the large room filled with men, women and children in various stages of undress. One or two tried to smile, one man guffawed coarsely, but most sat in stricken silence. The sun was up now, the whole orb clear of black and distant hills, a red coal balanced on a heap of black ones.

Ann Jones was behind the bar, smiling a fixed smile in a face that was deathly pale. "Drinks—all round— then . . ."

Some women held up coy little hands in protest, but soon everyone in the room had a glass. Even the kids. Not that they were strangers to it. "The Glenrowan" was different to most other outback inns—women and kids were allowed.

The tall man who had woken her went up to the long polished bar and leant against it. He held up a hand for silence, but there was no point: a match falling on the wooden floor would have echoed in that frightened silence.

"Sorry we got to hold you folk like this, but that's the way it is. Got a bit of business here, in Glenrowan. Got to keep our eyes on everyone. Every single one of you . . ." He looked round, then shrugged his shoulders. "You look pretty all right to me, but . . ."

"Tell them what you're going to do, Ned." Ann Jones looked away from the young man and spoke through half-closed lips.

So this was Ned Kelly. He was just as she had imagined him to be, this Robin Hood of the outback. Bright red hair, youthful defiance. And it was his gang, the Kelly gang, which had decreed what was going to take place.

She felt relieved that Frank was not here. Let him have his bandit-chasing away from her home in Glenrowan. By the time Frank got here—though that was only a few hours distant—whatever devilment the Kelly gang was planning would be over, the gang itself back in the bush.

"It's like this," the man went on. "There's a train full of traps—police, like—and blacktrackers. Coming this way. But youse will know that . . ."

Jane's heart skipped a beat.

"When these traps and blacks get here—well, they just ain't going to get here. The Kelly gang's derailing the train before they get here. They'll be arse over tip, begging your pardon, ladies, at the foot of the embankment." He grinned and showed surprisingly white teeth. "And any of them that's fit to get up and hop away, we shoot 'em. Like kangaroos. Ain't going to be no police, no blacktrackers, left; just an empty train upside down in the scrub. Sorry youse can't see it happen. But the train'll be there, I suppose, for years, so's you can get along and have a look."

She saw Ann Jones and Helen looking at her and there was a world of compassion in their glance. She stared back, then dropped her head in her hands and wept.

There was a long, long silence, broken only by her sobbing and then a man's rough voice. "Fer Gawd's sake—give 'em all a drink, Ann."

A door opened from the hotel kitchen and two more men came in, pushing a tiny, frightened one in front. She looked up through her fingers, saw a man shove the little fellow hard with the end of a rifle and knock him face forward on the floor.

The drinks were beginning to have an effect. Some of those present must have been drinking a long time, perhaps through the night, and Jane primly averted her gaze from a man fumbling to undress a young woman. The girl stood and swayed, an arm on the man's eagerly bent head. A few women in one corner were quarrelling loudly, another little group had begun to sing. A fiddler was playing, excruciatingly.

"Nobody leaves!" She watched in dismay as a little boy stood open-mouthed, then began to make water against the bar. No one seemed to notice.

Another dozen men and women, the plate-layers and their wives who inhabited shacks at the bottom of the hill, stumbled in, shepherded by an armed man. Soon it would be impossible to get more in.

"More drink, fer Gawd's sake," came a voice.

"Not bleeding likely till you pays for it," shouted the lady proprietor. "If you think 'The Glenrowan' is going to keep you lot grogged up till the train comes, you can think again. And you'd better keep your money and your heads till then. Till the shooting. You'll *need* a drink, then . . ."

Young Helen had come up and she gently put a hand on Jane's shoulder. "I'm sorry, Mrs Pierce, really I am. But I just know your Frank will be all right, I *do* . . ."

"How can he be all right? When these cut-throats, these murderers, are going to gun down everyone."

"Shhh. Be careful."

Someone fell and emptied a glass of brandy over her; and at that moment a drunk put his arm round her waist. She swung round, hit him hard on the mouth with the back of her hand, and he capsized backwards. For a moment she was terrified at what she had done, but the man lay there, laughing, his head in a pool of spilled drink.

An old woman vomited and the stuff dirtied the hem of her nightdress. The noise of singing and argument mounted and she sat now in stunned silence, unable to believe what was happening. This was hell, hell on earth, and the real thing could hardly be worse, for the torture of staying in this room, which would grow every minute, could only end, in God only knew how many hours, with the murder of her husband. Death, murder, within half a mile of where she was locked in this den of thieves and drunkards.

A window broke and for a moment there was silence. One of the outlaws—it was Dan Kelly, thicker-set than his older brother—sprang up like a cat and vanished through the door. In a minute he was back.

She saw a stool by itself, raised above the people in the room, most of whom were sitting, lying or struggling on the floor, and she made her way to it. To her right was the little man who had been marched in, a little chap not much over five feet in height, now looking almost defiant as he stared up at the great Ned Kelly. Kelly's lips were twitching in a smile he tried to hide.

She knew now who the little man was: he was Curnow, the school-teacher. A literary figure, too, the local correspondent of the *Wangaratta Times*. She hadn't met him—after all it would be some time before Jane's family would need the services of a school-teacher—but she found herself watching him in admiration.

"Who the devil do you think you are?"

Ned Kelly grinned. "You're game, aren't you, Curnow?"

"Game! That's about the only thing you Kellys recognize as human virtue. But you're murderers, nobody cares whether you're 'game' or not. You will hang, Kelly."

"We'll see."

Jane's attention was distracted by the thud of a couple falling at her feet, almost toppling her stool. The girl's long skirt was up over her waist and she was laughing while the man fumbled and cursed.

"Kelly——"

"Yes, Curnow?"

The violin shrieked.

"Never mind."

The day wore on, the sun disappeared from eastern windows and came in through western, then slipped into the ground. After the first few children had relieved themselves in corners of the room the outlaws had made grudging concession to the call of nature, and embarrassed men and women had gone out for a minute or two at pistol point. But somehow, to Jane, in her shocked horror, her dread of what was going to happen, this room and its hellish inhabitants had ceased to exist. She was alone.

Just as if the conversation had been continuous, she heard Curnow's voice again. "Kelly, I implore you to let me go."

"If I do—do yer give your word yer won't talk?"

She watched the little man as he seemed to ponder this. At last he spoke, very softly. "I do, Kelly. I do."

"Right, then. Your wife and your three kids, you go and get 'em, bring 'em here. I *suppose* it'll be safer for them—"

"Thank you, Kelly."

"And mind you're back in fifteen minutes, or I'll send a bloke after you with a gun. But you're an honest man, Curnow, and I trust you."

The little man almost ran out the door, then straightened up as he went out into the dusk, turned and gave a little bow.

He was gone and the door slammed shut behind him.

With darkness falling—she had been in this hell for almost twelve hours—Jane's dread began to mount. Within an hour the train would reach Glenrowan, that Glenrowan Halt which was destined, they said, to become a real station. The train today would let off three men, one of them her own.

How distant and impossible it seemed, a peaceful, flourishing, Glenrowan, with its own railway station. And its police chief, Frank Pierce. Jane would never see that. She would be back in England, a widow, long before Glenrowan had either of these things.

She realized suddenly that more than fifteen minutes had gone by.

Then the first shots came, a salvo of bullets from all sides, biting through the wood walls of the hotel, screaming as they ricocheted round the bar. Women, screaming louder, flung themselves on the drunk and sick already on the floor. A small child seemed to explode in front of her as a dozen bullets ripped into its face and body, and the blood spurted over her cape. A man screamed—a great roar of sound, starting in the bass register and ending up a pitiful high-pitched wail—and fell head first against her, knocking her stool away, so she fell gasping to the floor.

A bullet shattered the big lamp and the room was in darkness.

The breaking of windows seemed continuous and glass tinkled in a steady stream as it fell inside the room. Surely there weren't that number of windows? But she was numbed by fright, unable to look up.

All round her people were screaming. Dan Kelly himself was hit and pitched forward to lie beside her with blood pouring from a wound in his shoulder.

And now, as she lay there trembling, a new hope mounted within her. Someone—Curnow—must have warned the train, and it had stopped short of the planned derailment. The police had come up under cover of darkness.

The firing stopped.

A distant, faint, voice, called. "Kelly!"

No reply at first, then Ned Kelly got slowly up and went over to a shattered window. Taking cover behind the frame, he called, "Yes. Here I am."

"We will cease fire for five minutes, and you will get those women and children out of the way. Then, if you do not surrender, you will be killed."

There was a roar of defiant laughter from Kelly. Then he spoke. "I'll send them out."

"Well said, man. Give us five minutes to make sure we all understand this. Then, when I fire one single shot, start sending the women and children out. You understand?"

Women and children were shooed from the bar, into the kitchen which led to the back door of the hotel. There was terrified whimpering, the cursing of men.

A single shot and the back door creaked open. A frightened woman rushed out, a child in her arms. Others followed until there was a stream, some weeping, some shouting, "Don't shoot! Oh please don't shoot . . ."

No one quite knew why, but the back door creaked shut again.

Many of the women had not made their escape. As the door closed there was a shot.

The firing began again at far greater intensity, and now to her horror Jane saw flames. The lamp which had been shattered in the first salvo had dropped burning oil on the floor-boards and the room was ablaze. She got to her feet and a bullet grazed her hair.

A strange smell, and she looked down to see the hair of a dead man smouldering. In the light of flames she saw Ned Kelly, badly wounded, stand up and fasten something about him.

It was the armour. She had heard of it, heard from Ann Jones that somewhere in hiding, Ned Kelly had hammered himself a suit of "real knight's armour" from ploughshares. As she backed from the advancing flames, she saw its thick body plates, like the underside of a tortoise, the huge steel helmet, with the horizontal slit. Ned Kelly lurched out into the moonlight.

There was a bedlam of clanging as bullets spattered off the armour. She turned away, began picking a path over bodies to reach the open air: better to be shot than burned to death.

As she reached it all shooting stopped.

She looked up and saw a man. "Pierce—Frank Pierce—is he here? I'm his wife . . ." And she fainted.

When she recovered, he was bending over her. "My darling——" She looked up at her husband and at the same crescent of moon she had watched from her bed the night before. Was she still there? Had Frank come back to the hotel to wake her?

She heard the soft crackle of nearly-burnt timber, and remembered. There was no hotel.

"Is he—is he dead?"

"Who, darling?"

"Ned Kelly."

"No, my darling. Not dead, just badly hurt. He went on shooting till the end, in that armour. He'd have done better without it, the man couldn't see and we just fired at his legs. Almost a game, it was . . ."

She had begun to weep.

"Don't cry, darling. He'll be hanging at the end of a rope before the month's out. *Don't* cry, darling . . ."

The Grease that Caused a Mutiny

Until the year 1856 the standard weapon used by the Indian Army had been the old "Brown Bess" musket, but towards the end of that year the Government decided to replace it by the new and more efficient Enfield rifle. The Enfield used cartridges of a much closer-fitting design, and they were manufactured at an arsenal near Calcutta.

In order to load the new rifle, the soldier had to bite off the greased end-paper of the cartridge, tip the powder into the barrel and ram the cartridge down after it—and it was this apparently unmomentous and innocent routine procedure which was to prove the trigger that fired off the bloody and long-drawn-out Indian Mutiny.

The first hint of imminent trouble was expressed in an official letter to the Government of India in which an officer at the Rifle Instruction Depot at Dum-Dum, near Calcutta, reported that "there appears to be a very unpleasant feeling existing among the native soldiers, who are here for instruction, regarding the grease used in preparing the cartridges, some evil disposed persons having spread a rumour that it consists of a mixture of the fat of pigs and cows". Within a few weeks the rumour had spread hundreds of miles, and sepoys, both Hindu and Muslim, bound by age-old and stringent traditions of religion and caste, were asking themselves the same disturbing question—did the grease used in the new cartridges contain pig or cow fat?

To the Hindu the cow is a sacred animal. If he were to put the fat of a cow to his lips he would become an abomination, lose his caste and be denied his religion—also, his family would be put to shame. To the Muslim the pig is regarded as an unclean animal, and to touch its fat would bring equally undesirable and even disastrous penalties. And so, with these in-built fears and prejudices inflexibly in mind, sepoys of both religions refused to use the new cartridge, despite assurances that the ingredients of the grease were, in fact, mutton-fat and wax, neither of which possessed religious ramifications. When, as a gesture, officialdom agreed that the sepoys would be allowed to make their own grease from a mixture of wax and oil which would be purchased for them from the bazaars, it was already too late—the first stirrings of mutiny and violence were under way.

In that year, 1857, Britain ruled India through the medium of the East India Company and its deputy, Governor-General Lord Canning. Some two hundred and fifty years earlier, a cabal of merchants had been granted a charter from Queen Elizabeth I to trade in India, and thus the East India Company, led by men like Clive, had become so rich and powerful over two centuries that from Cape Cormorin to the Himalayas it had complete control over 838,000 square miles of territory.

By the end of the eighteenth century the British Government, somewhat alarmed at the power which the company by then was wielding, revised its charter. This had the effect of converting the company's officials from traders into tax collectors and landlords; indeed, they governed the country, though held in check to some extent by a Cabinet Minister and Board of Control in the British Government.

The pioneering spirit, so strong a hundred years earlier, was dying a slothful death in these English rulers of India. No longer had they to compete with the French, Dutch and Portuguese. Life had become merely a matter of contending with the climate and amassing as much of a fortune as possible before returning to England to live out a comfortable though possibly dyspeptic life of retirement "at home". Of the civilians in India, few bothered to learn the language of their indigenous subordinates. Life, divided between home, office and club, was more concerned with drinking, gossip and gambling than with the affairs of the restless country in which they were resident foreigners—though few, if any, regarded themselves as such.

The East India Company maintained an army in each of its three centres of government—Madras, Bombay and Calcutta. This last, the only one directly involved in the Mutiny, was known as the Bengal Army, though it operated from the Punjab and Afghanistan in the west to the Ganges Delta in the east. It was composed almost entirely of high-caste Hindus, Brahmins and Rajputs, the majority from Oudh.

At the time of the Mutiny the proportion of Indians to Europeans in the Bengal Army was almost eight to one, i.e., some 300,000 Indians to 40,000 British, and most of the British troops were in action on the troublesome Afghan frontier. In Oudh, the centre of discontent, there were no British troops at all.

The reasons for disaffection were numerous. Since British power had been consolidated the previous Governor-General, Lord Dalhousie, had tried hard to reform Indian society not only politically but also morally, and this merely inflamed the anger of the natives who were then, as now, dedicated to their traditional order and customs.

Dalhousie had planned to cut down the number of feudal states, leaving the larger ones in the hands of puppet rulers under his control. This in itself was a praiseworthy concept, for there were many bad and some tyrannical rulers, and the peasants led miserable lives under these men who had the power of life and death over them.

Thus, despite the fact that the king of Oudh was an ally of the British, his cruel and irresponsible misgovernment persisted despite many warnings, with the result that his territory was finally confiscated and made a part of British India. However well intentioned this move, it was also unfortunate; sepoys returning to their native villages on leave found that they had lost prestige and were no longer protected from local injustice and oppression by the fact that they were Company servants. All in Oudh were now under British rule, and nobody received preferential treatment.

In addition, princes all over India now felt themselves insecure. If loyalty to the British was to be rewarded by dispossession, how long would they themselves remain safe? Landlords also were spreading sedition, for Dalhousie had taken away the land from tens of thousands of owners who held no proper title.

Some of the deepest social convictions of the Indians had been ruthlessly, if justifiably to Western eyes, attacked. The inhuman practice of *suttee*—the obligation of widows to burn on their husbands' funeral pyres—had been banned, and a law had even been passed to permit a widow to remarry (a practice previously unthinkable). The killing of female babies, a commonplace custom, had been suppressed, as had other barbarous traditions.

Such reforms, however desirable and humane they seemed to the British, struck hard at the beliefs of people evolved by and conditioned to a different culture. The British, shocked by certain Indian ritual customs, tended to dismiss the Hindu religion as primitive and disgusting, and many thick-skinned and tactless army officers were misguided enough to try to persuade their sepoys to convert to Christianity.

The Indian Army had been remarkably faithful to its foreign rulers, but mutinies had happened before. They had invariably been put down with brutal severity. The majority of the British officers were blind to the fact that disaffection was rapidly increasing. In 1856 another cherished religious taboo was attacked when all recruits were required to swear that they would cross the sea if ordered to do so. Their refusal in this respect had for a long time inconvenienced the administration; the land journey to Rangoon, for instance, where many Indian regiments were required to serve, was long, expensive and difficult to organize.

This new decree was extremely unpopular, but as it applied only to new recruits the reaction of resentment might have faded out had not the trouble-makers, the religious fanatics and the dispossessed redoubled their efforts to cause a rising. They emphasized, quite rightly, that the sepoys would encounter very little opposition if they attacked the British.

It was at this sensitive moment that the disastrous matter of the new cartridges arose. The grease on the cartridge paper, whether cow, pig or mutton-fat or whatever, acted as a fuel to kindle the embryonic flames of revolt. When it became apparent that the new cartridges would continue to be the focal point of trouble, whatever kind of innocent grease might be employed, Major-General Hearsey, commanding the Presidency Division stationed at Barrackpore, sixteen miles from the seat of Government at Calcutta, ordered a court of inquiry, as a result of which, being a man of considerable experience and insight, he recommended as a matter of urgency that the cartridges should be withdrawn immediately.

His report duly reached General Anson, the Commander-in-Chief of the entire Indian Army, who was stationed with his headquarters staff at Simla—one thousand miles from the Government in Calcutta and the centre of unrest. An elderly man (as indeed were all high-ranking officers, since promotion was determined by seniority), he had seen no military action since the Napoleonic Wars. He flatly refused to withdraw the cartridges, commenting that in his view the reports of unrest were exaggerated and unimportant. The men, he insisted, would learn to obey orders cheerfully.

By this time, whatever action might possibly have been taken, it was far too late for the sepoys to change their attitude. It was no longer even so much a question of the cartridge grease, but a growing conviction that the British step by step were determined to undermine and destroy their own national religions and customs and force them into accepting the alien faith of Christianity.

On 9 February, 1857, General Hearsey, sensing their more fundamental attitude, addressed his regiments. He told the men that far from trying to convert them, no individual would even be permitted to change to the Christian faith without a sincere wish to do so, and there was no intention of offending the religious principles. But although the men listened to him in obedient silence, the invisible harm had already been done.

At Berhampore, a short distance away, the 19th Regiment Native Infantry mutinied. The troops broke into the arsenal and armed themselves. For a while the situation looked ugly, but did not develop into open violence. Their colonel, with guns to back him up, harangued his men until, finding that they were prepared to go quietly back to their lines if the guns were removed, gave the order to take them away. The following morning the men behaved normally and without insubordination.

Colonel Mitchell's action was much criticized at the time —he was blamed for not summarily punishing the mutineers, thereby creating an impression of British weakness. Indeed, whether the next mutinous episode, at Barrackpore, would have followed the course it did had Mitchell acted more severely is debatable. Nevertheless, at the time of the incident Colonel Mitchell had only 200 men against 800 sepoys, and he may have felt he was exercising prudence— though prudence had not so far been responsible for the success of the European minority in India.

When the news of the Berhampore episode reached Barrackpore, the men there became even more restless. Within a few days the first blood was shed. During a parade, a soldier named Mangal Pande, mad with hashish, fired at his sergeant-major, and when a mounted British lieutenant rode over he fired at him also, killing the charger. As soon as Lieutenant Baugh got to his feet he drew his pistol, and he and the wounded sergeant-major prevented Pande from reloading his musket. Pande then attacked both men with his sword, inflicting deep wounds. A blow from another native soldier felled the sergeant-major, and there is little doubt that both men would have been killed had not a gallant Muslim sepoy rushed into the fray and held Pande until the two wounded officers had made their escape.

Throughout the entire incident not another soldier had attempted to intervene—all had gazed sullenly ahead in silence. Meanwhile General Hearsey had been informed. He hurried to the parade-ground and faced the mutineer who by now had reloaded his rifle, demanding his immediate surrender. Pande's nerve broke. He turned the gun on himself and fired, but the wound was not fatal.

Pande was inevitably sentenced to death and hanged, but already he had become a martyr and his name was taken up as a slogan by the trouble-makers. All the time the insurgence was gathering impetus. Though the regiments concerned in many of the mutinies were, after some delay, disbanded, the men merely scattered to spread discontent and subversion.

The Mutiny proper began as a result not of cold-blooded plotting but of panic and humiliation in the most unlikely city in India. Meerut, an important military station, had a higher proportion of British troops than any other, comprising the powerful and prestigious 6th Regiment of Dragoon Guards, the 1st Battalion 60th Rifles, a Light Field Battery, a troop of Horse Artillery and a company of Field Artillery. The native troops were the 3rd Light Cavalry, and the 11th and 20th Native Infantry, none of whom had yet been issued with the new rifles and were armed only with muskets. What happened was the result of short-sighted stupidity in handling a crisis which would never have arisen under more enlightened officers.

On 23 April, Colonel George Smyth, the foolish and arrogant Commander of the 3rd Light Cavalry, returned from leave to be informed that his sepoys would not handle the new cartridges over which there had been so much controversy. Immediately he called a parade, selected ninety of his best native soldiers, and ordered them to step forward and pick up the destested cartridges.

All but five of the men stood still, ashamed and silent, hating to disobey orders but physically unable to touch what they considered to be untouchable. In the end, however, they conceded that they would obey the order if the entire regiment would also do so. Smyth would not accept such a condition—and in the event it is highly unlikely that the regiment as a whole would have complied, anyway.

The eighty-five men who had refused to obey an order were court-martialled on 8 May. Fourteen of the fifteen Indian officers who sat in judgement found them guilty. Now events began to move swiftly, for the Divisional Commander, Major-General William Hewitt, decided on a humiliating and unnecessary course of action—that at the official parade at which the sentences were to be announced the men should be fettered publicly before the station's strength of nearly four thousand officers and men.

At this parade the British troops stood with loaded guns, while those of the Indians were empty. The mutineers were sentenced to a harsh ten years' hard labour. As they heard their sentences they remained stoically silent, but when the fetters were hammered on to their ankles, and their uniforms were ripped from their backs by bayonet points, they cried out to their friends for help, tears of shame streaming down the cheeks of prisoners and sepoys alike.

The folly of this degrading exhibition instigated by the senior officers is difficult to exaggerate. The hour-long humiliation of the native troops, so far innocent of offence, was under the circumstances a match to gunpowder—and the fact that the fettered prisoners were then confined with only a native guard over them was sheer idiocy.

Later that night Lieutenant Gough of the 3rd Light Cavalry was warned by a loyal Indian officer that the men were preparing for trouble. He reported this to his colonel, only to be greeted with scorn. Soon afterwards at the club he talked to Brigadier Archdale Wilson, commanding the station, but the brigadier merely reprimanded him for listening to native gossip. General Hewitt treated the matter as unimportant, and so the other senior officers were unconcerned.

That night a keen ear could have heard the sound of swords being sharpened, and the muttering of voices as the sepoys worked themselves up into a mood of defiance. On the following afternoon, which was a Sunday, many of the men were to be found in the native bazaar, discussing peaceable ways of seeking release for their friends, perhaps by petitioning for a re-trial or requesting a dishonourable discharge in place of the ten-year sentence. As if drawn by a magnet, crowds began to gather and take part in these debates, and among them were the riff-raff of the town who began to taunt and insult the sepoys, calling them cowards who were afraid to rescue their comrades and preferred to lick the boots of the British.

There was a limit to the sepoys' self-control. Injured and humiliated enough already, their restraint broke down. Gathering together they rushed back to the barracks to arm and mount—"To horse, with us brothers, to the gaol", and the cry that was destined to resound in the ears of all throughout the Mutiny, "Din! Din!" (the faith, the faith). The soldiers were followed by the yelling, howling rabble.

The tolling of the church bells for evensong indicated that the British troops would be on their way, unarmed, to the service. Two hundred mounted sepoys rode to the gaol, and at the sight of them the guards fled in terror. In a few moments they had broken down the doors and set free the 85 mutineers, while the hangers-on from the bazaar let loose some 700 civilian prisoners—thieves and murderers—to pillage and kill in the train of the troops.

In the station the 11th Native Infantry, terrified by the

frenetic behaviour of their comrades, pounded at the doors
of the arms store, seeking weapons to defend themselves
against the men of the 20th who were armed and looked
hell-bent on slaughter. Somehow their colonel managed to
keep them partially under control, but time passed and still
no supporting British troops appeared. Then, suddenly,
from the rear ranks of the 20th, a shout of "Din!" rose from
a score of throats. Firearms crackled, and Colonel Finnis
toppled from his horse, riddled with bullets.

This, a mixture of fear and bloodlust, set the seal on the
rebellion. Many of the sepoys, seeing the murder of a British
officer, fled in terror, but the majority became wild with
excitement. With the willing help of the town rabble a
thousand or more bungalows were looted and set on fire.
The soldiers and the mob shouted and danced around the
leaping flames.

Many officers, unable to believe that their men could turn
on them so violently, went bravely to their deaths in trying
to order them back to their lines. But the sabres of the troops
were now red and dripping and they saw nothing but the
hated white faces and wished for nothing more than to see
those same faces bloody beneath their feet.

The terrified women and children could find no place of
safety in the chaos and confusion—on all sides there was
death and mutilation. At one point a driverless carriage was
seen careering down the street, with a screaming European
woman lurching from side to side. Before help could arrive
a native cavalryman rode alongside her and plunged his
sword into her again and again. Two young British officers
galloped up—their swords swept, and the first avenging
blows of the Mutiny toppled the corpse of the Indian
cavalryman into the dust.

Women and children were cut down indiscriminately by
the inflamed troopers, and over the whole scene rose a pall
of smoke from the burning dwellings. Then, as the initial
impetus of the slaughter faded, the sepoys, united by the
cry of "to Delhi, brothers, to Delhi!", assembled together
and galloped from Meerut, leaving the mopping-up operations to the scavenging mob.

By eight o'clock that evening the town was ruled by un-
bridled terror. The rabble, armed with cudgels, knives,
chains and any weapons they could lay hands on, slew and

burned almost unmolested. An officer's wife, heavily pregnant and unable to escape, was delivered by knives as they cut her apart. Lighted brands were flung at children until, burned and exhausted, they fell to the ground and were burned alive by the insane mob. Murder and destruction continued after dark, and the British troops did nothing until it was too late.

Delays had occurred in issuing ammunition, uniforms had had to be changed since it was considered unsoldierly to fight in the white drill worn for church parade, and by the time those fit for action had been summoned to a long roll-call, the massacre was virtually over. When the British at last reached the native lines the marauders had gone and the cantonment was left to the dead and the dying. The rabble had gone back to the anonymity of the native quarters of the town.

Only Captain Charles Rosser of the Dragoons kept his head. He urged that a force should immediately be sent after the fleeing mutineers to cut them down before they could reach Delhi—but Brigadier Wilson and General Hewitt disagreed. This inane decision was to result in the fall of Delhi itself to the mutineers and insurgents and start off a full-scale war that was to drag on for many weary months.

Brigadier Wilson, many months later, tried to explain his conduct. He had felt that the British troops should remain in Meerut for the protection of valuable stores, ammunition, and those women and children who had managed to escape the massacre. And General Hewitt, when he appealed against his removal from the divisional staff of the army as a result of this incredible error of military tactics inexplicably said: "I gave no orders without the Brigadier's permission."

So, as the fires continued to rage among the dead and dying, and as the army bungalows burned themselves into ashes, Wilson and Hewitt merely bivouacked their men on the racecourse. Meanwhile on the dark road to Delhi rode the rebels who were to shed rivers of blood of civilians and soldiers alike, and change the face and future of India.

Terror in the Court of King Thibaw

During the last days of the Second World War, allied troops in northern Burma found an old, old, man living in a teak forest not far from the town of Bhamo. He was a Shan, a member of a peaceful race, perhaps the most peaceful in that hot-tempered country where Burmans, Karens, Chins, Kachins and Shans so often quarrel among themselves.

But "Mister Min", which was the closest that British and American soldiers were able to get to the pronunciation of the old man's name, was no ordinary Shan. His part of southeast Asia, where Chinese Yunnan touches the hill tracts of Burma, is not one of the world's great cultural centres, and men who can read or write are the exception. But Mister Min—who liked that name and discouraged attempts to render the real, polysyllabic, several-toned tongue-twister, which seemed to end on a high-C "mee-*yinn*"—was a different creature. He spoke and wrote, not only many Oriental tongues, but both English and French. He was over eighty, "but modesty, gentlemen, inhibit me from say how much . . ."

Perhaps it was "inhibit" which most impressed his young devotees, for it was a word of which few had heard, in those dim distant, pre-permissive, days of 1945. Some went away and looked it up. Others, believing the old man had simply mispronounced "inhabit", were equally impressed. What a nice way of putting it: "Modesty, gentlemen, inhabits me."

Mister Min must now have departed to join his ancestors, and we can only guess what that tall, thin, parchment-skinned old gentleman thought of the rough young pink-skinned admirers who came to visit him in his bamboo house outside Bhamo. They brought gifts of corned beef, cigarettes and beer, but they were always handsomely entertained in return. Mister Min was well off.

He was, too, the acknowledged leader of his small community, and an epileptic.

The disability made him still more of a personage. It was spread about by the more knowledgeable that Christ and Mohammed had suffered from epilepsy.

Something had happened, years before, to cause it. Mister Min had not been born an epileptic. This much he volunteered after a fit one evening which had distressed his visitors. But they were nothing serious, the fits: he was a very old man—but modesty inhibit—and he was as strong as ever.

But one day Mister Min had the most frightening epileptic fit that anyone, even among his Shan villagers, had seen. At the end he was so weak that he lay speechless through the whole of a day, and anxious bulletins were passed to troops in Bhamo, while little gifts of tinned fruit and dried figs were assembled.

These were duly handed over by an awed delegation. By this time, Mister Min was sitting up, looking very pale. There was little trace of the usual welcoming smile.

"I am sorry to have distress you," he said. "And to have react in such way on receipt of gift was un-unpardonable."

Mister Min so often received gifts that no one was sure what he meant.

"And, most unpardonable of all, I have had gift destroyed. The beautiful red bag . . ."

Someone remembered the bag. It had indeed been a beautiful thing, made of red parachute silk, with a lining of sambhur skin. It could be used either way out. Someone had found it in the market where it must have found its way after being laboriously stitched by some Chinese lady, had bought it and then realized its great size made it a pretty useless possession. A nice thing for an Oriental, perhaps, to carry all his possessions; but a fur-lined red silk bag the size of a hundred-weight sack of coal could have little utility in the western world.

So now, with the offending sack out of sight though much in mind, Mister Min told his story. So fantastic was it, yet so obviously true, that it was hard for his listeners to believe Mister Min had experienced it during the last eighty years. It was a medieval chronicle of horror, something from Genghis Khan. Not from the late nineteenth century.

But it was true, every word of it, and several young men—one of whom would go on to become a respected professor of Oriental history—were to date their real interest in the East from that evening in 1945.

Seeing the eagerness on the faces of his young listeners, Mister Min brightened. He had been resting on the bamboo floor, propped on one elbow, but now he sat up and crossed arms across his narrow chest. "I will begin," he said with a wan smile, "by point out my father was a god. And my brother, too. But not me."

This opening caused some consternation.

"My brother's name was Thibaw." Mister Min's smile had vanished. "He was a wicked god."

And so the tale began.

Min had been born in Mandalay, during the 1860s, the half-brother of Prince Thibaw. Burma was no longer the great state it had been, for the British, goaded to fury by attacks against their Indian possessions, and by the cruelty shown to their small colony of merchants, had been forced to invade it twice and take over large slices of territory. "Burma—Centre of the Universe", as its court still called it, was now a small up-country state, shorn of all coastline, with a glittering and pretentious capital in Mandalay and poverty everywhere else. Its boastful communications to other lands were conveyed east or west across the high mountains which now locked it in. Occasionally an offensive missive to the English was dispatched down the Irrawaddy by river steamer. The general mass of citizens lived in misery, having to support a cruel and extravagant monarchy. Some fifty-two of these citizens had been buried alive outside the gates of the new capital in 1857, when Mandalay was built. This would ensure for the Golden City, with its glittering pagodas, a long life, secure from evil spirits.

King Mindon died on 1 October, 1878, and a younger son, by one of the younger, less important, queens, succeeded to the throne, by a piece of trickery rare even in Burma. We need concern ourselves only with the fact that the Prime Minister, the *Kinwun Mingyi*, wanted a young and pliable man on the throne.

More plotting behind the young man's back gave him one of his numerous half-sisters as chief queen. Supayalat was in fact only a "second queen", because royal custom had forced Thibaw to marry her older sister as well, but she soon got her older sister out of the way.

Many more royal relatives would have to go before Queen Supayalat felt her throne secure. Before the dead King Mindon had been cremated, all the royal princes and princesses were in prison.

There were over eighty of them. And one, a boy in his early teens, was Prince Min.

The young King Thibaw was a weak man, given to drinking, and it was easy for his Supayalat to have her way. She had no trouble pointing out that though the eighty-odd princes and princesses were safe in Mandalay prison, there was no guarantee none might escape. They might prevail upon their guards to perform some dark deed on their behalf. Thibaw's life was not safe as long as a single brother or sister remained alive.

It was true that Thibaw's father, Mindon, had magnanimously spared the life of his own rivals, when he succeeded to the throne. But before Mindon it had been the custom for a king of Burma to make his throne secure by killing off all rivals.

There were minor objections, of course, which the *Kinwun Mingyi*, in a most statesmanlike address, pointed out. One was world opinion, particularly that of the British in the south. But other foreigners in Mandalay had stressed gleefully that the British, as a world power, were declining; they were locked in a war against Afghanistan, and from time to time being defeated by savages in Africa. It might be a pleasing and deliberate insult to English sensibilities to stage a mass execution which they would be powerless to undo or avenge.

Supayalat eagerly made her plans. Thibaw, not so enthusiastic, but in her power, took to drinking more heavily. The young man missed his imprisoned brothers and sisters, for there were now few young people with whom a god could correctly sit and drink: all Burmese kings were gods.

But Thibaw found one or two companions, ex-pupils of the Mandalay school he had attended under the English missionary Dr Marks.

Another pupil from that school, some years younger than his brother Thibaw, had been Prince Min. Min had been a good student, swallowing the English, French and Latin the learned doctor taught. He left the academy at the end of his studies and, like all good Buddhists, donned briefly the saffron robe of a monk before becoming a prince again.

But Prince Min never again lived in the royal palace. He returned from his monastery, his *hponji chaung*, and was rounded up with all his brothers and sisters to be marched off to Mandalay jail.

He had few hard feelings. This was normal royal custom, and the prisoners were well treated. But as the months went by they began to wonder what the future held. Surely, by the enlightened standards of their father Mindon, they should have been released by now?

Prince Min and the rest were not aware as they languished in prison and their brother Thibaw drank incessantly from his golden goblet with the carved devils, that scores of young girls had been set by Queen Supayalat to a certain task: they were stitching red velvet—a rich, red, royal, velvet—into huge, capacious, sacks.

The princes and princesses learnt from their guards, most of whom were friendly, that a tremendous celebration was planned for the middle of February. It was now late in the December of 1878 and some of the younger boys and girls fancied they might be allowed to attend the theatricals, and the concerts, perhaps even the feasting, in honour of the new King Thibaw. None of them wished him harm.

1878 became 1879 and excitement mounted. The prisoners now learnt there would be three whole days of festival, and almost certainly, said the guards, they would be allowed out.

Two stages were being erected within the royal compound. There would be two great shows and loyal subjects could take their choice as to which they attended, could stroll from one to the other, while skilled actors and actresses played parts, and cymbals clashed and choirs sang. From time to time a cannon would roar, in time with the music. Never in history, never in the whole world, had there been anything like it, this tremendous pageantry to mark the reign of a new king in Mandalay.

Some of the older, more thoughtful, princes were haunted by irrational fears. They wondered if, far from being members of an audience, they might be unwilling actors. Was it not true that Queen Supayalat as a young girl had enjoyed trapping small birds and tearing them to pieces in her hands? It was true, and as Supayalat was sister or half-sister to every one of the royal prisoners, many of them had seen it happen. Would she be wanting to repeat the process, on a larger scale?

These dismal forebodings were kept from young Prince Min. Kindness prevented the older prisoners from airing such thoughts in his presence and Min found himself, as February began, eagerly awaiting the celebrations. Perhaps there would be fireworks, too, from China? The prospect appealed, for Min loved fireworks, loved to watch their coloured stars, brighter and more beautiful than real ones.

Outside the prison, excitement ran high, though it was tinged with a certain apprehension, which the king shared. Daily his drinking grew wilder. He had now discovered the gin, whisky and brandy which foreign merchants were only too eager to hand over as a peace offering, and he was able to banish the troublesome world through his waking hours. Supayalat, who thought him a tiresome fool, encouraged it.

In any case, she had enough to do. She had to choose the theatrical piece, lasting three whole days, which would be enacted on one of her two stages, had to choose the actors and actresses and the costumes. She had to decide, with expert musical advice, the number of cannon to be fired, and when. There was the grandstand to erect and decorate, a grandstand big enough to hold hundreds of loyal subjects.

And there was the other, smaller, stage. For this there would be a smaller grandstand and a smaller, hand-picked, audience. And already on the far side of this stage, gangs of non-royal prisoners were digging a trench.

Inside the palace girls were busy stitching their red velvet sacks. Their task was a secret, they were sworn to hold their tongues on pain of losing them, but each one knew the significance of what she was doing. And there was so little time: every so often an older woman in charge would scream, "*Mya mya*— hurry!"

But the tale of the red velvet sacks leaked out, even to the ears of shocked, unbelieving, European residents of Mandalay, who heard it from their servants.

The day dawned.

It was the first of three great days, the 15, 16 and 17 February. The two stages were now complete and decorated, their two grandstands beckoned invitingly with gay paper streamers and tinsel. Musicians, clowns and the singers who were to perform began to file in, their faces carefully whitened.

The audience assembled in the bigger grandstand: ministers, their ladies and lesser mortals. The king and queen took their places amid a hushed and reverent silence, their gold spittoon between them, golden goblets on either side.

The play began.

Hundreds of yards away, the young men and women in the jail heard music strike up. There was a clash of cymbals from the west, near the west gate of the palace where the bigger stage had been erected.

And now, to the delight of Prince Min, the prison gates opened and they were all—or so it seemed to Min—led out to freedom. The sound of cymbals was intoxicating and he almost broke into a run.

Armed guards suddenly blocked the way. To Min's dismay the party was headed off to the east and the sound of celebration faded behind them. They marched on a bit and then, rounding the golden slope of a pagoda, they saw a dais, with well-dressed men and women sitting before it. The men and women turned their heads expectantly as the party approached. Min recognized the Master of the Royal Barges and tried to catch his eye with a friendly smile, but the man ignored him.

On the dais, the stage, were four naked men, each wielding a club. At one side of the stage was a pile of neatly twined silken cords, at the other a neat pile of red velvet sacks. In the distance, the sound of flute, cymbal and drum—but here as Min looked about, no sign of instrumentalist. Perhaps these four naked men were preparing a dance without music.

The cheerful guards who had accompanied them were now suddenly stern and fierce, and as Min considered this development a pair of them came back and seized the prince standing by him. It was Maingtun, an older man than Min, older indeed than their half-brother Thibaw; and now Min, almost unbelieving, heard him let out a shriek of terror. It was taken up as one terrified wail by all the princesses, and at that moment Min's eyes were covered by a pair of hands, and he was turned round, away from the stage.

"You will not look," hissed a voice in his ear. "*Ma kaung bu*—it is bad, and you will not look——"

Trembling, Min nodded his head. There was no need for an older brother to keep him blindfolded like this: he would not turn his head, would not look at the horrifying thing which was taking place.

There was silence, then weeping. Then the dreadful sound of beating and cries of agony, set against the wailing of young girls—his sisters—and the gay laughter of the audience. The cries went on for a minute and then stopped. There was a final convulsive moan, a few seconds' silence and then a dull thud as of a body falling into soft earth.

He stayed with his back towards the dreadful business, fingers pressed hard into his closed eyes. There was a shrill cry and now he knew without looking that it was one of his sisters. The wailing began again, then silence as some dreadful preparation was made.

It was too much and he spun round, shouting "*Ma lok bu*—don't do it, don't do it!" and now a brother tried to cover his eyes with one hand, his mouth with another. Min tore himself free, but someone seized him by the arm before he could rush to the open stage and beat the executioner with his own small fists.

He watched in stunned horror as his half-sister, a girl his own age, was tied with a pair of silken cords. She was forced down into a kneeling position and while one naked executioner pulled back the head by its long, shining, black hair, another began to rain blows on the throat with his cudgel.

And now Min knew what fate held in store for him. This was the traditional method of dealing with unwanted royalty; princesses were battered to death by blows on the throat, princes dispatched by bludgeoning on the back of the neck.

It was soon over. Min watched almost calmly as the still twitching body was tumbled into a red velvet sack and flung into the open trench.

There was worse to come. The executioners had been given orders, permission, to vary their performance and beguile the customers. Pretty ladies clapped small hands in delight: the white-skinned barbarians abroad might have bear-baiting and bull-fights, but there could be nothing in their countries to equal this.

And so, thus early in a performance scheduled to last three days, came a really spectacular trick. The audience watched in delight as an older man, a prince who had recently been Governor of Pegu, was forced to kneel. Two naked men stuffed gunpowder from a golden pot into his nostrils and his mouth. A fuse was jammed between his teeth.

Min turned away and seconds later came the most dreadful sound he had ever heard. When he looked back, peeping between his fingers, the stage was being washed down and something was being loaded into a sack.

He was stunned and he made no resistance when a naked man came up and seized him, propelled him with a hot wet hand in the back of the neck to the centre of the stage. Looking back he saw there were only about two dozen other prisoners and realized that not all his brothers and sisters had been marched out with him. They were being kept for the second and third days of celebration. He stared without emotion at their grief-stained, terrified, faces. Two men tied his wrists and forced him to his knees.

The first blow missed and thudded agonizingly across his shoulders. Already he had made up his mind he would die without a sound. He had hoped the first blow would end it, and now it was all he could do not to scream in frustration.

The second was better aimed and hit him on the neck. To his surprise, he went on living.

A third and terrible blow and he lost consciousness.

When he recovered, he had no idea where he was or what had happened. Slowly he found his wrists were bound and that he was inside a bag and underneath a great weight.

Memory and pain flooded back. He was dead, this was the first stage of after-life. Like other Buddhists, he was being reincarnated—and as something hideous; reptile.

But as he considered this, his teeth were biting at the cord which held his wrists, and before he knew it they were free. He took a piece of cloth in his swollen, painful, fingers and pulled it to his mouth.

At last he had bitten a hole big enough to get both hands into, and he feverishly tore the sack apart. He forced his head out and found himself wedged tight among other, filled, sacks. With the strength of desperation he dragged himself out.

It was dark. In the distance he could still hear music.

Quickly he summed up the situation and thanked the heavens for their help. He could have lain unconscious for an hour or a week, but the small number of red sacks told him this was the end of only the first day. Had it been the final day, all sacks, including his own, would have been earthed over, and the ground would have been rolled flat above them. Tonight, this first night, there was a bright moon above and the trench was only partially full.

He had trouble, after freeing his ankles, in clambering to the top.

He stood gasping at the edge, looking about him, past the deserted, ghostly, stage, to the distant west gate where music still was playing.

The man approached without being noticed and Min, in an agony of terror, felt a hand on his arm. "*Di hma,*" said a voice. "Come——"

Min screamed and began to run, but after two shaky steps he fell down in a faint.

There was a long, long, silence in Mister Min's bamboo house. He sipped daintily from his cracked cup of *PX* instant coffee, looked round him at the open-mouthed young faces in the room, then sipped a little more.

"B-but—what happened, Mister Min?"

"Ah, me, gentlemen. I was fortunate. I had faint—in fact it was first, shall we say, first *episode* of my present disability. But a son of the *Myowun,* the Governor of Mandalay, had found me, and now he pick me up and carry out the east gate. He wait till I recover conscious—till I am conscious again. Then he bid me godspeed. I had strength to get to river bank and make way to a village of Shan people, who make me welcome. My poor mother, you see, she was a Shan."

Mister Min shrugged his shoulders. "My father, of course, was a god."

The First Ascent of the Matterhorn

The Matterhorn is one of the most beautiful mountains in the world. A great pyramid of rock it stands, a solitary peak, across the border between Italy and Switzerland. Seen from the valleys, it is not only beautiful but, literally, awe inspiring. The Swiss peasants would look up at the great peak and in their mind's eyes they would see the summit as a fortress—a home for demons, evil spirits and the souls of the dead. For man to climb to the top of that terrible peak seemed as unlikely as that he should fly to the moon.

But as the second half of the nineteenth century got under way, men began to make their way to the top of the Alpine peaks. One by one, the summits were conquered and Alpine mountaineering was in its golden age. That age was to end when the last of the great peaks fell to man's endeavour, when in July, 1865, men first set foot on the summit of the Matterhorn. It was a moment of triumph that was to turn into tragedy.

There were many men in the year 1865 who wished to be the first to claim the Matterhorn. But there were two special men who could claim pre-eminence in the race. One was a professional mountaineer—a guide. This was Jean-Antoine Carrel, an Italian who lived under the shadow of the great mountain. By the summer of 1865, he had already attempted the Matterhorn from the Italian side, and had been higher up the mountain than almost any other. That year, he was to lead a determined effort to reach the summit, not as the paid employee of one of the talented English amateurs, but in his own right, as an Italian at the head of an Italian party that would claim the achievement for the glory of their country.

Carrel had one rival whom he feared could beat him to the top: the twenty-five-year-old Englishman, Edward Whymper. Whymper had already accumulated an imposing collection of Alpine firsts, but the Matterhorn affected him in a way which no other peak could. It was his obsession. Whymper had already been many times on the mountain and, with Carrel, could claim to know more about the mountain than any other man.

It had always been Whymper's hope that when he climbed the Matterhorn Carrel would be by his side. But Carrel had plans of his own. The summer of 1865 looked like being an infuriating time for Whymper. There he was at the foot of the Matterhorn, and no companion for the climb. He had lost one friend and guide, Michel Croz, with whom he had planned to climb that summer, due to a mix-up over the arrangements for hiring. Now he found that Carrel, far from being eager to climb the Matterhorn with him, was about to set out to climb it without him. He was in an agony of frustration.

It was in this ferocious mood that Whymper met a young Englishman who was accompanied by a man well known to Whymper, one of old Peter Taugwalder's sons. Whymper at once approached the Englishman to ask if he could hire Taugwalder, but the Englishman refused. The two men began to talk. Whymper found his new companion to be Lord Francis Douglas, only eighteen years old but already having one fine first ascent to his credit. As Whymper explained his plans for the Matterhorn, Douglas became interested and the two men agreed to join forces for the ascent. Douglas had seen the Swiss ridge in profile from another peak and believed it to be climbable. At last Whymper had a chance to beat Carrel. They set off for Zermatt at the foot of the Swiss side of the Matterhorn.

In Zermatt, Whymper found to his surprise that the guide Michel Croz was there with a client. Moreover, they were planning to climb the Matterhorn. It must have seemed to Whymper as if everyone was suddenly planning to beat him to his goal. Whymper went to see the client, the Reverend Charles Hudson, and suggested that the two parties join forces. Hudson agreed but stipulated that a young friend, Douglas Hadow, should be a member of the party. Hadow's qualifications? He had "done Mont Blanc in less time than most men". Hadow was a novice, with no experience at all of the type of climbing represented by the rock and ice of the Matterhorn. For Hudson to insist on Hadow joining the party was stupid, for Whymper to agree incredible. But Whymper wanted Croz in the party, and always nagging at his mind was the thought of Carrel and his party on the far side of the mountain. So the party was formed to attempt the Matterhorn by way of the Swiss ridge. The great adventure was under way.

At half past five on a bright cloudless morning on 13 July, 1865, eight men left Zermatt for the Matterhorn—Whymper, Douglas, Hudson, Hadow, Croz, old Peter Taugwalder and his two sons, young Peter and Joseph, who were to act as porters. It was not the ideal party for the task—hastily assembled and almost by chance. It was too large to be manageable, no one was clearly in charge and in young Hadow they had one member who lacked the most elementary knowledge of climbing skills. Yet things seemed to go well. By midday they had climbed the ridge to a height of 11,000 feet. Under a wall of rock on the east face they pitched their tents and waited. The next day would show how the last 4,000 feet would be.

Early the next morning they set off again up the east face, which the guides had reconnoitred the previous day. Young Peter Taugwalder was still with the party, his brother Joseph having been sent back alone with the supplies. Again the going was surprisingly easy. What from the ground had seemed a precipitous wall, turned out on closer inspection to be more like an easily-angled staircase of huge slabs of rock. The party was large, which slowed progress down, but there were no difficulties. Only young Hadow seemed to be having any problems, constantly having to be helped when his feet slid on the holds.

By about ten in the morning they had reached a height of 14,000 feet—less than 800 feet to go. But now the easy work was over. The gentle slope of the east face steepened into a great wall of rock. They were stopped. They would have to leave the face and move back on to the Swiss ridge. But the ridge too was impossible. If they were to reach the summit, then they would have to move further over still—right out on to the north face.

Moving on to the Matterhorn's north face was like moving into a new world—a world where the sun never shone. Michel Croz stepped out into this black, icy world at the head of the party. Before him the rock sloped upwards at a gentle angle. The next few hundred feet would not be difficult climbing, but it was dangerous. Handholds and footholds were jammed with frozen snow, and many of the rocks were coated with a thin, treacherous film of ice. To slip on this glassy slope would be all too easy, and the climber had only to look over his shoulder to see what the results of such a slip would be. A short way below them the gentle summit slope stopped abruptly in the towering cliffs of the north face that fell vertically away down to the Matterhorn glacier, 4,000 feet below.

Slowly Croz moved out across the face. The others, roped together, followed one at a time. It was a desperately slow business. At last Croz began to move upwards again. For sixty feet he climbed, then began to make his way back to the ridge. At the ridge itself, he had to make his way round an awkward outcrop of rock. Whymper and the others followed. At last the way was clear before them. An easy snow slope led upwards in front of them and beyond that was only the blue of the Alpine sky. Whymper, Hudson and Croz untied the rope and raced up the final slope together. At 1.40 p.m. they stood on the summit of the Matterhorn.

Still Whymper could not be quite happy. The summit of the Matterhorn is a 100-yard-long ridge. He was on the Swiss end and the snow here was unmarked. But what of the Italian summit? He hurried along the ridge. There were no marks there either. Whymper peered over. There, below him, he could see the Italian party toiling upwards. The men on the summit began waving and shouting, and Whymper and Croz threw rocks, well clear of the lower party, to attract their attention. The Italians stopped, turned and began to descend. For Whymper it was a sad moment. In his ambition to climb the Matterhorn, he had always hoped that Carrel would be by his side. Instead Carrel had been only a spectator to Whymper's great moment of triumph.

But the sadness was short-lived. The men on the summit were exultant. A flag was improvised out of a tent-pole and an old blue smock, and Whymper broke off the top-most piece of rock from the Matterhorn to take back down the mountain. For an hour they stayed on the summit, taking in the magnificent view, the great panorama of mountains and valleys stretched out all around them. Everything stood out with startling clarity in the thin, pure mountain air. Then, at last, they were ready to begin the descent to Zermatt.

The departure from the summit was an almost casual affair. After all, these men had achieved what they had set out to achieve—they had climbed the Matterhorn. All they had to do now was go back again. There was still that icy roof at the top of the north face, but so long as the party was careful no harm should come to them.

But no one was in charge. Whymper suggested a fixed rope to give extra protection on the north face. Hudson agreed it might help, but no one actually got round to doing it. So the first group set off. Croz went first. On the rope behind him was Hadow, then came Hudson, and finally Douglas. The young novice was safely placed in the middle of the experienced climbers. Whymper stayed behind for a few moments on the summit completing a sketch. Then, with the Taugwalders, he followed the others.

The frozen slope of the top of the north face had been the most dangerous section of the whole ascent. Descending it was doubly dangerous. As every climber knows, coming down is more difficult than climbing up. On the way up, the men had been facing into the rock, their faces turned upwards to the way that they were going. Descending they faced outwards. The glassy slope seemed to curve and curl away from them dragging their eyes towards the great void and the glacier thousands of feet below.

At the top of the slope, old Peter Taugwalder roped on behind Douglas, his employer. The heavy rope that joined the other four was not long enough to take Taugwalder as well, so he took another section and joined on behind. Carefully, they moved off.

It was soon obvious that Hadow was having difficulties. Croz would stop after descending a short way to help the young Englishman, while the others kept the ropes taut as a protection should Hadow slip. It was a slow business as they made their way down. At first, they still moved as two parties, with Whymper and young Taugwalder on a separate rope at the rear. Douglas suggested that they again roped together as one party as they had done on the ascent. The unspoken suggestion was that the extra numbers might help should any one member of the party slip. Everyone's thoughts must have been on young Hadow, whose inexperience was showing more and more as he scrabbled his way down the rocks. Whymper agreed and tied on to old Taugwalder. Now the party was united again.

Moving one at a time, with Croz in the lead, the men began again to descend the Matterhorn.

Suddenly, without warning, there was a cry from below. The rope that old Peter Taugwalder had been carefully paying out to the men below suddenly began to race through his hands, burning and searing deep into his flesh. Hadow had slipped, and in falling had knocked over Croz. Whymper and the two Taugwalders acted instinctively. They threw themselves back against the rock, clutching desperately to the face of the mountain. The shock of the fall below came almost simultaneously on the three men, who were strung out on the face, the rope taut between them. Old Peter Taugwalder was fortunate. He was standing by a large outcrop that formed part of the face, so was able to cling on to it and absorb a good deal of the shock.

The three men could see below them. Their four companions were sliding on their backs, hands and feet clutching and clawing as they tried to find some way to stop the slide that was gaining momentum. As they rushed towards the great cliffs, the rope took the strain between them and the men above. Then with a sharp, terrible crack—the rope broke. Horrified, Whymper watched as the four sped down towards the void where the icy roof ended. One by one they vanished over that edge.

The four bodies fell from precipice to precipice, bouncing from the rocks as though they were straw dummies until they finally came to rest on the great glacier far below. As they fell, they dislodged a small avalanche of little stones that clattered away down the mountain. Then the stones too stopped falling; and as the last echoes of their rattlings died away a terrible silence hung on the face of the mountain.

For a full thirty minutes the three men who remained

on the mountain stayed motionless, paralysed by fear and shock. Standing where they did they had been able to watch the whole progress of the tragedy—to see their comrades slide away from them to bounce in that inhuman way down the cliffs until they were lost from sight. It was a terrifying sight that would have unnerved any man. But, worst of all, they were now themselves stranded at the top of the great mountain, and there was only one way down. They had to go the way their comrades had gone, and they had to pass the spot where one of those men had slipped, fallen and dragged three others to their deaths. In these circumstances, their terror is understandable.

In time old Peter Taugwalder was able to control his shaking limbs. Carefully and slowly he moved his position until he was able to tie his rope around the rock that he had clung to. Now, at last, he was secure—belayed to the mountain. Carefully his son and Edward Whymper climbed down to join him. The first thing Whymper did was to examine the rope that had broken under the strain. He discovered to his horror that it was not, as he had thought, the strong, heavy climbing rope but a piece of thin rope, little better than a clothes-line, that had been brought along merely as a spare. Whymper returned the rope to Taugwalder.

By now it was four o'clock in the afternoon. Whatever they might feel about going on, they knew that they had to move. To stay any longer was impossible—they had a long way to go before nightfall. To stay where they were with night approaching would be suicidal. So the three men set off. They had only a few hundred feet to climb before they could leave that terrible dark northern face. But it was not the difficulty of the climbing that slowed them down; it was the memory of those four falling bodies.

The accounts that have come down to us of that nightmare descent are muddled. The Taugwalders claimed that Whymper was made incapable by fear—Whymper claimed the same for young Peter Taugwalder. Whatever the truth might be, we know that they moved with infinite care over the treacherous slope, attaching ropes to the rocks wherever possible to give extra protection. Somehow, they drove themselves on, but those few hundred feet took them two hours to cover. As at last they stepped off the north face on to a gentle snow slope, it was six o'clock.

On the shoulder where they now rested were the ruck-sacks and provisions they had left there on the way up. There were also the few personal belongings of the dead men. Not surprisingly, the three survivors found that the food stuck in their throats. They prepared to move on again, but were stopped in their tracks by an amazing sight. Away to the south-east, in the direction of Monte Rosa, a great arc had appeared in the sky, vaulting sharp and clear against the heavens. Then, to their astonishment, there appeared two great crosses on either side of the vast arch, almost as though the Alps themselves were paying a last homage to the fallen climbers.

The three men turned away from this strange and moving freak of nature to continue their descent, the taste of fear still bitter in their mouths. Only a few hours of daylight remained, but now, at last, the most difficult part of the climb was behind them. The going was easier, but all mountains are dangerous, and their fear kept them from hurrying, from risking another tragic fall.

Darkness came while they were still high on the Matterhorn and they were forced to spend the night on the cold mountain. The weather remained mercifully good as the three men settled down to find as much comfort as they could in the black night.

At half part three the next morning they were on the move again, after the miseries of a comfortless night in which each man had been alone with his memories of the tragedy. At last they were safely down and, in silence, they made their way back to Zermatt. At the door of the Monte Rosa inn, which they had left so full of hope a short time before, stood the hotel's owner, Alexander Seiler. Word-lessly, Whymper walked past him and climbed the stairs to his room. Seiler followed, and at last asked what had happened. Whymper's reply contained all the bitterness that he had stored up over the long descent.

"The Taugwalders and I have returned."

The first ascent of the Matterhorn was over. There were to be many bitter recriminations, and Whymper and the Taugwalders were to be enemies for the rest of their lives; and Whymper himself became a sad, lonely man. He had achieved the great goal of his life, but had found no content-ment in the achievement.

Today it is difficult to realize the triumph that the first ascent of the Matterhorn represented in 1865. Now fixed ropes guard the difficult sections, and each year hundreds of parties literally queue up to make the climb. But, even now, a man who stands on that northern roof of the mountain and looks out towards the great cliffs that drop dark and sheer down to the glacier can easily feel something of the terror that gripped those three climbers, over a century ago, watching helplessly as their four comrades slid down and away to their deaths.

There is no fortress or city of demons on the summit of the Matterhorn, but the mountain exacted its own terrible price from the men who dared to go and find out for themselves.

The Defence of Rorke's Drift

The story of southern Africa is a text-book example of colonialism, and in particular British colonialism in the nineteenth century. For a long time the Europeans had been gradually infiltrating from the coastal strip into the rich hinterland, engaging in fierce clashes with the native population and eventually dominating the country. For a century and a half the Cape of Good Hope had been a Dutch colony until, during the Napoleonic wars, the British captured it from the once powerful Dutch East India Company and the Boer farmers.

It was to escape from British rule that the Boers, in 1835, started the Great Trek into the interior. Inevitably they came into conflict with the powerful and prosperous Zulu tribe which controlled a vast area stretching from the Limpopo river some two hundred miles north of what today is Johannesburg to the borders of the Cape Colony in the south. Through a succession of bloody and bitter battles the land-greedy Boers fought on, to overcome the hordes of formidable Zulu warriors by superiority of arms and establish their hold on the Zulu lands.

In the area known as Natal, where the town of Durban had first come into being when a group of shipwrecked people landed there, the British settlers were also moving inland from the coastal strip—and in such a positive fashion that Dingaan, the Zulu chief, finally ceded the lands of Natal to the British colonists. Zulu-owned territory shrank to a comparatively small area in the south-east, northwards of Natal.

Dingaan was a cruel and greedy king. In 1840, after he had treacherously slaughtered sixty Boers, he was murdered by his brother Panda, with the support of a Boer commando. Thereafter Panda ruled peacefully for thirty years. When in 1873 he was succeeded by his son, Cetewayo, the Zulus had become a contented and prosperous nation, living quietly in their scattered kraals and occupied mainly by domestic matters.

But the famous army of Zulu warriors, created by the first great king, Shaka, was still maintained and its stringent traditions were preserved. When young men were drafted into impis (or regiments) they were required to live in special military kraals and remain celibate. Their time was spent in looking after the king's cattle—the wealth of the nation—and in drilling for war. They were permitted neither to marry nor to own property until they had proved themselves in war or until the king gave them permission, which was not granted until they had attained the age of forty. Since war was their only means of gaining status, honour and privileges, it is not surprising that the warriors were constantly demanding the opportunity to "wash their spears".

With what the Governor-General of the Cape Colony called "this celibate man-slaying machine" on their doorstep, the colonists lived in uneasy peace—and the knowledge that beyond the Buffalo River which marked the boundary between Natal and Zululand lay thousands of acres of rich land was an added irritation. The situation was unstable, and inevitably it had to explode sooner or later.

In 1879 Sir Bartle Frere, the Governor-General, without provocation and on a flimsy excuse, ordered a British force to cross the Buffalo River and march upon Ulundi, Cetewayo's kraal. Frere's reason was that the Natal frontier had been violated by one of Cetewayo's chiefs who had crossed it to drag back an erring wife and her lover. In fact, it was more in the nature of a "pre-emptive strike", for Frere had an obsession about the Zulu menace and was convinced that Cetewayo intended to wage war on Natal and drive the white man out. With some justification he regarded Cetewayo as a ruthless despot with an army of warriors who thought they could not be defeated, and there were three million natives against a mere 350,000 Europeans, the latter administered by two separate governments in a state of continuing enmity. Frere was determined to force a situation in which Cetewayo would have to accede to certain demands, including the abolition of the Zulu army; but to the Zulu king this was totally unacceptable.

Early on the morning of 12 January, 1879, the final body of British-controlled troops, the Natal Native Contingent, under the command of Colonel Durnford, crossed the river and moved up to join General Lord Chelmsford in command of the invading force. The 24th Regiment of Foot with a number of native units forded the river at Rorke's Drift. Laboriously they made their way into Zululand. The roads had been washed away by continual thunderstorms so that they had to be drained and rebuilt before the wagons, guns and heavy equipment of the advancing army could pass over them. It was not until 21 January that a camp was established—a mere ten miles within Zulu territory.

At Rorke's Drift the morning of 22 January was hot and humid. The thatched roofs of the buildings steamed gently in the sun as they dried out after the rain-storms of the night, and the men went about their tasks with no great sense of urgency or haste. The atmosphere was, if anything, one of anticlimax. The men of B Company, second battalion of the 24th, the King's Own Royal Regiment, had been left behind to guard the base about a quarter of a mile on the Natal side of the river bank. After Colonel Durnford and his men had ridden off to imminent death, Lieutenant John Rouse Merriott Chard of the Royal Engineers, in charge of the garrison, set his men to work.

In the hospital building there were thirty-five sick and injured men to care for. The hospital had formerly been the home of missionary Otto Witt and his family, and was now in the charge of Surgeon Major Reynolds. Supplies had to be checked and stored away in a neighbouring building which had once been a mission chapel. At noon the 87 men of the 24th, a handful of men from other regiments and a detachment of the Natal Native Contingent settled down to a leisurely lunch—quite unaware that at nearby Isandhlwana their comrades-in-arms were engaged in a bloody battle with a 20,000-strong Zulu impi.

Lord Chelmsford had split his force and gone off to establish his next camp. In a ferocious conflict that lasted less
than three hours, the 900 British and 800 native troops left
at Isandhlwana were totally massacred by the Zulus—who
themselves lost 3,000 men. But the soldiers at Rorke's Drift
knew nothing about the fate of their comrades. Lieutenant
Chard was down at the river inspecting the pontoon bridge
when two horsemen, part of the handful who had survived
the massacre, appeared. "They have been butchered to a
man," shouted one of the horsemen, adding the warning
that the Zulu impi was on its way to Rorke's Drift.

Chard and his men promptly galloped back to the mission.
The first decision of the officers was to load the sick men into
wagons and try to make good their escape; but Dalton, the
commissariat officer, persuaded them that with the slow-
moving ox-wagons they would all be caught on the road and
slaughtered—whatever happened they would be on the
defensive and they stood a better chance behind stone walls.
Lieutenants Chard and Bromhead, recognizing the experience and wisdom of an old soldier, for Dalton had been
a sergeant in the British Army, agreed. They immediately
began to barricade as best they could the undefended
buildings.

The only materials available for the construction of barricades were the army provision stores—200-lb. bags of mealies
(sweet corn) and huge square tin boxes of meat and biscuits,
each of which weighed a hundredweight. The two buildings
to be protected stood on a rocky terrace and the surrounding
land fell away to an orchard and a sunken road. Using the
corn bags and the tin boxes the men constructed a four-foot
wall stretching from the perimeter of the hospital, along the
rim of the rocky terrace, to the wall of a stone cattle-pen
beyond the storehouse. A similar wall was erected to link
the rear walls of the buildings, so that there now existed an
unbroken line of defence. Within this outer wall a second
defence line was built from biscuit boxes and mattresses.
Loopholes were made in the mud walls of the buildings, and
the doors were barricaded with more biscuit boxes and
mattresses.

In just over an hour after the garrison had received its
first warning of the Zulu advance there was the sound of
gunfire from the hills where sentries had been posted to give

the alarm. Shortly afterwards a black tide of Zulu warriors swept into view round the ridges of the Oscarberg hill. The sight proved to be too much for the native contingent. As Chard coolly wrote in his subsequent report, employing the characteristic British technique of understatement: "About this time Captain Stephenson's detachment of the Natal Native Contingent left us, as did that officer himself."

There were now only 104 officers and men left at Rorke's Drift to guard a perimeter of some 200 yards and fend off the onslaught of more than 4,000 Zulu warriors—the fresh and untried Undi Corps which had been kept in reserve by Dabulamanzi, the Zulu general who had commanded the Isandhlwana impi, and which he now permitted (despite Cetewayo's order not to invade Natal) to have its opportunity of "washing its spears".

The first black wave of Zulus raced towards the front wall defending the hospital and storehouse and got to within fifty feet of it—but the firing became too hot for the warriors. They paused and took shelter in the scrub and trees below the rocky ledge, while others split off to take up positions around the sides and back of the buildings. Inside the walls a line of defenders fired continually into the mass of black bodies, reloading as fast as they could, encouraged by the regimental chaplain, Smith, who distributed ammunition and exhorted the men with fiery biblical texts. Then, when the assault finally came, wave after wave of screaming Zulus hurled themselves at the wall, climbing it and stabbing at the defenders with their assegais, only to be thrown back in hand-to-hand battles.

In the hospital, the sick men and the handful of defenders stationed there were helplessly pinned down. The interior of this building was divided into a number of small rooms, some of which had doors which led only to the outside. A verandah ran across the front of the house. In the narrow space between the verandah and the corn-bag wall in front of it men desperately loaded guns, tended the wounded and struggled in hand-to-hand bayonet battles with Zulus who leapt onto and over the wall. Inside the hospital the defenders fired their guns continuously through the loopholes, assisted by those patients who were fit enough to load or fire a gun.

In this veritable death-trap, one of the patients, Henry

Hook, a twenty-eight-year-old private in the 24th, reported later: "Large bodies of Zulus kept hurling themselves against our slender breastworks and assaulting the hospital most fiercely." With Hook in the small room was a man named Cole whose nerve eventually deserted him—unable any longer to bear the confined quarters of the trap he went outside and was instantly shot dead. Hook kept on firing from his loophole.

The desperate and single-minded defence of the hospital was successful, and in the course of time it was buttressed by dead Zulus. The worst casualties among the defenders were among those manning the outside wall above the rocky ridge, for they had no protection from the Zulus behind them who were firing from the vantage point of the slopes of the Oscarberg hill beyond the other side of the courtyard.

Although the Zulus were unable to take the hospital by storm, they succeeded in setting fire to its roof which, still damp, burned slowly giving off choking, pungent smoke. It became apparent to Hook that the hospital would have to be abandoned. He left the room he had been defending and joined the patients in the next room; beyond it was one more room in which soldiers were protecting three sick men and its only exit was a door to the outside. The Zulus finally carried this door, dragged out one of the soldiers and assegaied him. Meanwhile, the other soldier, John Williams, smashed a hole in the mud wall leading to Hook's room and dragged his patients through into comparative safety. While Hook guarded the hole, Williams broke through another wall into a further room, and so the process was repeated. The advancing Zulus came upon a succession of empty rooms, with Hook managing to guard without great difficulty the latest broken wall.

It was impossible to get all the patients through in time, and a number of them were inevitably lost to the savagery of the Zulus. The remainder were pushed and pulled in brusque fashion through broken walls to the final room which looked out on that part of the compound between the hospital and the store-room. High in the wall was one small window, and through this escape hatch the sick men had to be lifted and manœuvred, only to run the gauntlet of Zulu fire as they tried to reach the safety of the inner line of defence in front of the store-room. Hook, Williams and two privates named Jones held the "doorway" of the last room against the invading Zulus with their bayonets as they had now run out of ammunition. In the end it proved impossible for them, because of the design of the hospital building and the weak condition of some of the sick men, to bring out all the patients. "We could not save these poor fellows from their terrible fate," Lieutenant Chard reported.

The defenders had now to withdraw to within the lines of their inner redoubt to continue the battle. The improvised fortification consisted of a wall of biscuit boxes and mealie bags to the north and west, the fence of the cattle kraal to the east and rear, and the unbroken wall of the store-room to the south. It was now growing dark, but as the men took up their positions in the new firing line the glare from the burning roof of the hospital lit up the scene for hundreds of yards around.

With faces and hands blackened from powder and smoke, the defenders fired incessantly at the attackers, using bayonets and rifle butts when there was no time to reload. So heavy was the firing that many rifle barrels overheated and became distorted and useless, and broken rifle stocks gave evidence of vicious hand-to-hand fighting. Time and time again the Zulu commander ordered a concerted attack on the store-room, but the warriors were constantly thrown back, leaving their dead behind.

While the battle raged around them, Lieutenant Chard and three of his men set to work to construct a "leep" of an original type. "They succeeded", said the Reverend Smith, "in converting the two large pyramids of sacks of mealies into an oblong and lofty redoubt . . . blocking up the intervening space between the two with sacks from the top of each, leaving a hollow in the centre for the security of the wounded, and giving another admirable and elevated line of fire all round."

"About this time," the Padre continued, "the men were obliged to fall back from the outer to the middle, and then to the inner wall of the kraal." The fighting became more desperate; as the Zulus invaded the cattle kraal the walls that had at first protected the defenders now protected the attackers. The pattern of assault went on until midnight— the Zulus would work themselves into a frenzy with war dances and chants of "Usutu" (which was the name of Cetewayo's faction) and then rushed violently upon the defenders on the "tidal wave" principle of inundation, but always they were forced back by relentless rifle fire and bayonet thrusts.

After midnight the pace slackened and the attacks died down, although sporadic firing continued until dawn. The flames from the burning hospital no longer lit up the battle area, and though a surprise attack in the intense darkness was feasible, the Zulus seemed to be exhausted after eight hours of frantic violence. Behind the barricades the garrison peered wearily and anxiously into the night.

At first daylight, after the longest night the men had ever known, the Zulus had departed—the last of them could be seen disappearing round the shoulder of the Oscarberg hill. Despite a superior strength of about forty to one, the Zulu warriors had decided to opt out of the battle for Rorke's Drift. Even so, taking nothing for granted, Lieutenant Chard sent out a patrol to scout the neighbourhood, while the rest of the men, tired as they were, set to work to repair and strengthen the battered defences. It was time to take toll; seventeen men had been killed and another eight wounded. Three hundred and fifty Zulu dead were found, and eventually buried by the British—the wounded Zulus were carried away by their comrades.

The Zulus had gone, admittedly, but the exhausted garrison at Rorke's Drift waited anxiously for their reappearance. In fact, the Undi Corps had had enough and was only too anxious to retreat quietly across the Buffalo River. When part of Lord Chelmsford's force, having heard of the attack on Rorke's Drift, fearfully approached the column of smoke they could see rising from smouldering buildings, they encountered hundreds of rather contrite Zulus retiring from the scene of battle, and there were no incidents. As they approached the battered buildings of the garrison they saw the figures of men waving flags—the weary but triumphant defenders of Rorke's Drift.

The effect of this improbable but very real victory largely outweighed the terrible disaster at Isandhlwana, and in the annals of British military history it remains a glorious episode. Eleven V.C.s were awarded—the greatest number ever to be awarded for one battle—and those honoured included Lieutenant Chard and Lieutenant Bromhead, Sergeant Dalton and Privates Hook, Williams and Jones.

The Zulu force that attacked Rorke's Drift was a reserve force which had not been involved in the Isandhlwana massacre. After the war, a Zulu officer explained that the intention in crossing over into Natal was simply to steal some cattle; they had no intention of invading Natal, as it would have been contrary to the king's orders.

When Lord Chelmsford's forces encountered the retreating Zulus, a number of British officers asked permission to attack, but Chelmsford refused. Commenting on this afterwards, a Zulu officer said: "We felt that day that the spirits had watched over us. For, had the white force attacked, we could have offered only feeble resistance, having had little or nothing to eat the day before, no sleep during the night; whilst having crossed the swollen Buffalo twice, we were completely exhausted."

The White Death

The Indians called the summer of 1886 the "time of the blue moon". A strange light hung over everything. During the day the sun, shining through a blue haze, hung in the sky like a great ball of steel. At night the eerie colour of the moon filled ranchers and their families with a strange foreboding. "Everybody feels it", wrote one rancher to his friends in Texas, "but nobody can explain it. It's as though something dreadful is about to happen."

The Territories of Montana and Wyoming were only just being settled. Before 1880, because of the hostility of the Indians, most of the land had been virtually uninhabitable. It wasn't until the Sioux had been forced into the reservations and the last buffalo had been slaughtered that this naturally hostile country was finally thrown open to white settlement.

The climate of the Great Plains, especially in the north, is most severe. Temperatures range from more than a hundred degrees in the summer, to more than fifty degrees below zero in the winter. Rain, when it does fall, is heavy. Valleys are flooded almost without warning. Crops and homesteads in low-lying areas and along the water-courses are often swept away.

One specially characteristic element of the Great Plains climate is the constant wind. The level surface and the lack of trees offer the air currents no resistance and the wind howls its way from Canada to Mexico with nothing to stop it but a barbed-wire fence. "Does the wind always blow this way out here?" asked a new settler of an old cowhand. "No," the old-timer replied, "sometimes it turns round and blows the other way."

The winds of the plains fall into four main types. All of them, except one, are capable of bringing death and destruction in their wake. First there is the "hot wind" of summer. Its strength can vary from that of a mere breeze to a gale. It is extremely hot and dry and may be compared to a blast from a furnace. It can totally destroy millions of bushels of corn in one season and burn thousands of acres of grass in a few hours.

The Chinook wind blows only in the north along the eastern slope of the Rocky Mountains. Chinooks are warm winds. During the winter they blow down from the mountain region on to the plain. They raise the temperature and melt the snow, which evaporates so rapidly that the ground on which it has lain is left perfectly dry.

"Norther" is the name given by Texans to the cold wind that blows directly from the Canadian border right down to the warmer plains in the south. It brings dust-storms, heavy rain, hail and snow. During a norther the temperature can drop from twenty-five to fifty degrees in less than an hour. A norther can spell economic disaster to small stockholders or farmers.

Then there is the blizzard, which has to be experienced to be believed. Eastern storms to which the term "blizzard" is applied are but weak, puny, examples of this violent weather phenomenon. It is a combination of wind and snow that no man or beast can face. "The snow and sharp cutting particles of ice find their way through every piece of clothing and every crack and crevice in our cabins", wrote one settler.

Nearly all of this vast area is semi-arid. The only trees to be found are on the river bottoms or in isolated mountain areas such as the Black Hills of the Dakotas. The main form of plant life is grass. On the eastern plains it is "short" grass or "sod"; further west the short grass gives way to "bunch" grass and mesquite. As you might expect, the animals that roam this area are all grass-eaters; in fact only two, the coyote and the wolf, are not.

For a long time the cattle-men of Texas had known of the

vast areas of succulent grass that lay to the north and they often dreamed of driving herds up into the territory and of founding new and profitable ranches. It wasn't until 1880, when the Indians had finally been gathered into the reservations and pacified, that the great feeding grounds were thrown open.

At almost the same time a book was published that caused what can only be described as a "cattle rush". The author was General Brisbin. In his book, entitled *The Beef Bonanza or How to Get Rich on the Plains,* he showed (on paper) how, "if a rancher invested $250,000 in ten ranches and placed 2,000 head of cattle on each ranch he could, by selling beeves as fast as they matured and investing the receipts in new young cattle, at the end of ten years have 45,000 cattle on each range, worth at least $18 per head or $810,000". A cattle company, properly managed, said Brisbin, would pay an annual dividend of twenty-five per cent.

Brisbin's book had phenomenal sales in Britain. Millions of pounds were sent across the Atlantic to be invested in the Great Beef Bonanza. Herds of Longhorn cattle were bought in Texas and driven northwards to Montana or Wyoming Territory to graze and fatten on free-range grass until they were ready to be sold to a beef-hungry world.

Wyoming became the Mecca for wealthy cattle-men. English and Scottish noblemen, French counts and German barons all flocked to Cheyenne to oversee their investments. With them they brought their valets, servants, chefs and butlers. Some, such as the French Marquis de Mores, even built huge country houses, castles or chateaux in which to spend the hot summer. Long before the winter snow began to fall most of these "milords" left to winter in Europe.

By 1880 the Wyoming cattle boom was well under way. Thousands of cattle were driven on to the new ranges until by 1886 they were becoming dangerously overstocked. Millions of dollars and pounds were wrapped up in and dependent upon the survival of those cattle, most of which were quite unsuited to the bitterly cold winters of the north.

The first portent of what was to come struck the plains in the winter of 1880–81, in the shape of a fierce blizzard. It was the first blast of a severe winter that lasted until the following May. In all that time the temperature was seldom higher than twenty degrees below zero. It was often as low as forty, and at one time stayed at that level for three weeks. When, at last, the sun broke through and the warm Chinook blew across the land, thousands of cattle lay dead. "You can walk," said a witness, "from Sheep Creek in the Bolts to the Dearborn in the Rockies and never take your feet off a dead cow."

Many Longhorn cattle escaped destruction because of their natural instinct to drift southwards on to the warmer plains. Whole herds moved more than four hundred miles into Nebraska, eastern Colorado and Kansas. When the winter fury had abated the ranchers sent their cowboys to find the herds and drive them back to the north.

The great cattle companies were determined their herds would not drift south again. All that summer cowhands worked erecting hundreds of miles of "drift" fences from barbed wire. Barbed wire was a new device in the hands of the cattle-men. It had been invented only seven years before, but now thousands of miles of the stuff were strung out across the country.

Two years later came the "starvation winter of the Pikuni". The Pikuni were a tribe of the great Blackfoot nation of Indians who were living on a reservation near the Canadian border. Just after Christmas the Pikuni noticed a glittering mist hanging over the mountains where Glacier Park stands today.

The Pikuni had seen this sign before. They knew what it meant. Almost at once they began to dance and pray to the spirit of the mountain not to persecute his children. The prayers were ineffective.

The temperature suddenly dropped from forty to fifty degrees below zero and stayed there. The Pikuni crawled into their lodges, banked up their fires and waited for the cold to pass. It lasted for weeks. Occasionally a party of hunters left the village and made their way through the snow in search of food. They went on foot for they had long since killed and eaten their horses. They found little. Everything had died or fled from the cold. All they brought home were a few scrapings from the skulls of dead animals, the interior bark from trees and an odd rat.

By February the Blackfeet were dying in their lodges. No help came to them from the Government. More than a quarter of the tribe starved to death. Wolves and coyotes wandered and howled among the rows of tepees. By the beginning of March they were fighting each other for the carcasses *inside* the lodges. By the time the Chinook wind came and sucked up the snow more than six hundred Pikuni had died.

A number of fierce blizzards raged throughout January. At the first signs of the approaching storms the cattle's instinct was to return south. They came up against the barbed-wire fences and halted. Then, panic taking hold of them, they tried to crash their way through the wire, cut themselves to pieces, went down and were trampled to death by equally panic-stricken creatures coming up behind. Those in the rear climbed over the bodies of those in front which were soon stacked higher than the wire.

Hundreds of cattle poured over the top to continue their flight southwards until they reached the next fence where the process was repeated. Thousands died but there were many that got through and no fence nor yipping and yelling cowboys could turn them back. Many cattle "drifted" more than five hundred miles before they finally considered themselves far enough from danger and began leisurely to crop the southern grass and to put back the meat they had lost during their gruelling march.

The following summer more fences were built, stronger and higher, fences that no cattle would break through nor climb over. And all the time dozens of new herds and thousands of head of cattle were being driven up from Texas. The losses of the previous winters did not deter the large cattle companies from adding more and more land and cattle to their feudal-like domains. Profits were not to be expected until five years after the original investment anyway—or so Brisin declared.

It was during the summer of 1886 that the first soft blue haze appeared and changed the colour of the sun. Nobody from the Texas Panhandle to the Canadian border could remember such hot weather.

In October, when the first cool winds usually begin to blow, a long Indian summer kept all cowhands working in their shirt-sleeves. In Cheyenne cattle were being shipped east by the trainload. So were the counts, lords and nobles and their entourages, for in winter most cattle barons were absentee ones. Only the working cowhands and their families remained to look after the precious stock.

There had been no rain for weeks. Hot winds set the grass alight and caused great fires to go galloping across the plains and to burn up everything that stood in their way. But long before the fires destroyed the grass it had already begun to die. By November all but the largest streams and water-holes had dried up. The blue haze, which was the smoke from the fires hanging in the air, drifted over thousands of square miles of territory. Fine ash and cinders began to drop down from the sky, parching the lips, smarting the eyes and covering everything with a fierce white dust, even the floors and furniture in the log cabins. Men ate it with their pork and beans at meal-times. It was impossible to keep clean.

It was in the middle of November that the cowhands began to notice the absence of birds. Those that were sighted were all flying high and heading in the same direction— south. Along the creeks the little muskrats were building their homes taller and thicker and the beavers were working night and day cutting the brush and building their winter quarters. The water coots were already turning white, and even the range cattle seemed to take on heavier, shaggier coats than usual.

Every day the cattle grew more restless. They stood, noses pointing north, sniffing the air and tossing their heads. They would back away, bellow, turn round, begin to head south and then, as though remembering the slaughter at the fences of previous seasons, turn back again. The lack of water and grass had upset their routine and put them all into a state of confusion.

On 16 November the temperature over the Rockies suddenly dropped to below zero and a strong north-west wind began to blow across the prairie. Soon the wind had developed into a howling gale. It began to snow. It seldom snows before Christmas on the northern plains and most ranchers looked upon the sudden cold snap as a freak of nature that would soon pass. But for hours the wind roared, carrying the snow before it. It was a fierce, icy gale, filled with tiny particles of snow or ice like tiny bits of glass or fragments of mica.

The white powder filled the air with white fog. It piled up in great drifts. Cows or horses that stepped into them had their flesh cut to pieces. Within a few hours the whole prairie was completely covered. In the log-built ranchhouses, in spite of the huge fires burning in the potbellied stoves, drifts of snow lay on the floors near the doors and windows; wherever the wind found a crack in the walls. At last a Chinook blew down from the mountains and the unique cold spell passed.

January is known to the Indians as the "moon of the cold exploding trees". This is because, in the forest areas, the intense cold often causes the trees to crack and boughs to break. On a cold night the sharp retorts of cracking bark and splintering branches could be heard by the Indians lying snug in their tepees. During the night of 8 January the exploding trees announced that the temperature had suddenly dropped to twenty-two degrees below zero. In the central mountains it dropped to forty.

By morning the snow was falling. It continued to fall at the rate of one inch an hour for sixteen hours. The whole territory from Canada clear down to Oklahoma lay under a blanket of white more than a foot deep. No Chinook came to drink it up. The cold wind from the north continued to blow and the temperature to fall. By 15 January it had dropped to forty-six degrees below.

Then, on 28 January, the great grandaddy of all blizzards struck from the west. It blew for six days and nights, a howling tornado of knife-sharp cold and white frozen dust. At the height of the storm ranch-house thermometers registered sixty-three degrees below zero.

The storm did not let up until 3 February. When it ended gulches and coulees (stream-beds with steep sloping sides) were filled with snow to a depth of more than a hundred feet. Nearly all landmarks were obliterated and the whole country levelled off by the thick blanket of white. Even ranch-houses had disappeared. It was the worst storm in living memory—even the Indians knew nothing like it. The effect on the new cattle industry so recently established on the wide, open northern plains was catastrophic.

In the land of the Chinook where no warm wind was to materialize for months, the cattle died like flies. When the first snow fell on 16 November the Texas Longhorns tried to head south. When they came up against the drift fences the line-riders, as the cowboys patrolling the fences were called, were waiting to turn them back. Foiled in their attempt to find their way back home the cattle, bawling and utterly bewildered by the unfamiliar snow that covered up the grazing, wandered aimlessly round and round.

The glare from the snow half blinded them. They blundered into the coulees and were buried in the deep drifts. Hunger and thirst led them to the rivers where, in the panic to drink, many of them were trampled to death or drowned in the air-holes in the ice. Others just stood motionless with their backs to the wind and froze to death where they stood. They remained on their feet all winter and did not fall to the ground until the warm weather returned and thawed them out. Others, unable to resist the strong call to return to the south cut themselves to pieces against the drift fences, in spite of all the cowhands could do to stop them. Their frozen bodies lay against the fences for hundreds of miles. Others fell to their deaths over the edges of precipices or into canyons. Every ranch had its quota of dead, frozen cattle lying up against the ranch-house and outhouse walls. Every herd had broken up and scattered.

While men were combing the country trying to gather the cattle and drive them to more sheltered pastures, their wives and children were trying to drive the creatures away from the ranches where they gathered at the doors and windows bawling to be fed.

Hundreds of cattle staggered into the small towns and villages where they collapsed in the streets and died in doorways. Five thousand head invaded the little town of Great Falls, gorged themselves on the town's garbage, tore up the newly-planted trees along the sidewalks and ate them.

And all the time, whether out on the open spaces, round the houses or in the streets, they were hounded by wolves and coyotes who snapped at the hams of the cattle until the sinews were bitten through and the cows collapsed. The wolves and coyotes then pounced on the helpless creatures and ate them alive.

The storm blew itself out on 3 February; but the cold did not abate. Around 5 February a Chinook began to blow across the plains and the snow began to melt and reveal the grass beneath. Suddenly, however, the wind veered to the north, the temperature dropped and froze the newly-melted snow. Whereas before the cattle could paw or nose their way down to feed, they were now as completely cut off from the grass as though a great sheet of thick plate glass had been placed over it. The ice sheet did not melt until the following March.

When the big blow began on 28 January, cowhands were sent out to ride the lines, gather as many cattle as they could find and drive them to the more sheltered parts of the range. The cold was so severe that every rider dressed in at least two sets of long underwear, two pairs of socks, two shorts, two pairs of gloves, overalls and woolly chaps. Overcoats made from blankets and a slicker (waterproof) were worn over all. Instead of Stetsons or sombreros they wore fur caps with mufflers drawn over the ears. As a protection against snow-blindness they blacked their faces with burnt matches.

Thus attired they set out through the snow to find the cattle, pull them from the drifts and drive the starving creatures into the ravines and away from the treacherous rivers. Horses walked shoulder high in snow. The wind-driven frozen particles and the bitterly cold air penetrated deep into the cowhands' lungs and kept them coughing. The tiny particles of ice even found their way through the large coloured neckerchiefs that the men tied round their faces. When a cowhand was forced to dismount he stood in snow almost up to his neck.

Many cowhands never returned. Those unlucky enough to be caught out at night at some distance from the ranch were unlikely to get back. During the blizzard visibility was down to less than fifty feet. At night it was nil. Landmarks had been so completely obliterated that it was virtually impossible to find the way back except by instinct. Even the horses had difficulty. While wandering around looking for some kind of bearing, many a cowboy, caught out at night, froze to death as he sat in his saddle. His horse froze beneath him. Horse and rider stood like an equestrian statue, dead and motionless. Some were found still in the same position when the thaw arrived the following spring.

Stage-coaches did not run for three months. One stage and its occupants were lost and not found in all that time. Newly-laid railroad tracks of the Northern Pacific Railroad snapped and buckled. Trains came to a stop when they ran into deep snow-drifts. Unable to escape from the elements, passengers froze to death in the cars.

The white death also took its toll of people who stayed home. One man left his house to go to his barn for wood for the fire, lost his way in the blizzard and wasn't found again until the thaw. A whole family, completely cut off from the nearest town by the deep snow, ran out of fuel. They sealed all cracks and crannies in the cabin walls to keep the wind out, then, fully clothed, they climbed into one bed and huddled together for warmth. Weeks later, when they were found, they were still in bed—frozen to death.

An Englishman, one of the lordly investors, had decided not to return to Europe that winter but to stay and look after his interests. A neighbouring rancher, not many miles away, invited him to dinner on the night the first blizzard struck. The Englishman, in spite of the deteriorating weather, rode over to the neighbouring ranch dressed in a dinner-suit over which he wore an overcoat. He was soon overcome by the cold. His horse arrived safely but its rider was dead: frozen to death in the saddle.

Dozens of cowhands either died or suffered so severely from frost-bite that they were crippled for life. For weeks, long after the cold remained, all life and movement was suspended. No trains or stage-coaches ran. Whole towns and villages were cut off. Ranchers were frozen to death in their houses. Those who fared best were the ones who, due to their houses being burnt down by the prairie fires the previous autumn, had hastily dug "sod houses" or dug-outs for themselves in the ground. Here, beneath the surface of the earth and with a solidly-built roof to protect them, they were out of reach of the worst of the cold.

The end came at last. Towards the end of March, a month later than it could normally be expected, a Chinook began to waft its warm breath across the land. The first sunshine since the previous December bathed the plains in its welcome light. As the snow melted the terrible destruction the blizzard had wrought was revealed.

Millions of animals, mostly Longhorn cattle, lay dead. Their frozen bodies covered the prairies in every direction. Carcasses of cattle even hung in the trees along the river banks; the cows had climbed the snow mounds to the tree tops to eat the branches and had got caught up in them.

Soon the rivers were in flood. Raging torrents of melted

snow from the mountains roared their way through ravines and coulees, carrying great lumps of ice and bodies of dead cattle with them.

There was hardly a live cow to be seen. Two cattle barons, wintering it out in the Montana capital of Helena wrote to the foreman of their ranch in the Judith Basin to ask how their herd of 5,000 cattle had weathered the storm. Among the cowhands of the Judith was a young cowboy artist, Charles Russell. He replied to his bosses' inquiry. On an ordinary postcard he sketched a miserable-looking steer, knee deep in snow, gaunt, bent-legged and its ribs showing through its hide. Near by he drew a coyote patiently waiting for the steer to die. Beneath this telling scene Russell wrote: "The Last of the 5,000."

Rescue parties with food and other provisions left the towns for the local ranch-houses in the hope that the occupants were still alive. Dead people were placed in barns to await burial; the ground was still too hard for graves to be dug.

At last better days returned and with them the cattle-owners from Europe. As soon as the weather was warm enough they organized a spring or "tally" round-up.

They found hardly anything of their cattle but bones. Thousands of them turned the hills and prairies white— a grim reminder of the cause of the biggest die-up in cattle history. Coulees and wooded areas where the cows had sought shelter from the fierce wind were packed with their remains. Some coulees could not be entered because of the overwhelming stench of rotting beef. But the bones soon disapeared. Bone-pickers from the east collected them in wagons and sold them to fertilizer factories.

It is estimated that more than five million dollars worth of cattle had perished. Losses to some owners was as high as ninety-eight per cent. Hundreds of small-time ranchers and dozens of the great cattle companies went broke. Foreign investors, especially the French and Germans, lost interest in the great American beef bonanza, left the territory and never returned. Banks failed, stockyards closed. A few haggard bovine specimens were all that remained of what had been the finest herds on the American continent.

From the Canadian border clear down to Southern Colorado it was, to say the least, a catastrophe. Ranches were deserted. Thousands of cowboys, many lamed or crippled by frost-bite, lost their forty-dollar-a-month jobs. Many, having perhaps more know-how about the country than the foreign investors, staked claims for homesteads and became farmers or sheep-raisers and, in consequence, the enemies of the very men whose cattle they had protected at the risk of their own life and limbs.

Cattle are still raised on the plains of Wyoming and Montana today. The breeds are mostly Durhams or Scotch Angus. You can trail the territory from one end to the other and you'll not catch sight of a single Longhorn. That creature's fate was sealed for ever in the never-to-be-forgotten winter of the cold exploding trees.

Krakatoa

The greatest volcanic explosion in the last three and a half thousand years happened just before 3 a.m. (G.M.T.) on 27 August, 1883, when Krakatoa, an island in the Sunda Strait between Sumatra and Java, blew up with a violence equal in power to one hundred hydrogen bombs. More than 36,000 people were killed and 165 villages destroyed. The sound wave was heard over a radius of 3,000 miles, rocks were catapulted more than 30 miles into the air and the resulting tidal wave—100 feet high at its point of origin —boosted the water level in the English Channel two days later.

In 1883 Krakatoa was a fertile and luxuriant island with an area of 18 square miles—though uninhabited. It was, in fact, a multiple volcano protruding from the sea at the entrance to the narrowest passage of the Sunda Strait, itself a busy waterway for steamships and sailing ships from all countries of the world making their way from west to east. Although it was known that the island had suffered a violent eruption in prehistoric times, it was now peaceful and its three volcanic cones, Rakata the highest at 2,700 feet, and Danan and Perbowatan at 1,460 and 400 feet respectively, had long been ignored as extinct.

Krakatoa as a volcano was in fact dwarfed by the great peaks on either side—on the coastlines of Sumatra to the north and Java to the south, lying in the most geologically disturbed region of the world. Java itself had fifty active volcanoes which were frequently and apprehensively surveyed by the Dutch rulers of the area. Krakatoa represented only a minor and very dormant threat, but the balance of power was soon to change.

The inward pressure of the earth's crust, reaching some one hundred tons per square inch at a depth of forty miles, retains and controls the heat of the interior. Where it cracks the boiling rocks of the interior, feeling a lessening of pressure, work their way up to the surface. So long as this molten rock can escape in the form of lava, to run down the volcanic mountainsides, there is no danger except to life and vegetation in the immediate vicinity; but when it is bottled up for centuries this pressure becomes infinitely more dangerous.

At Krakatoa the solidified rock in each of the three cones acted as plugs and they prevented the molten rock, or "magma", from escaping. Deep under the earth, two fissures crossing each other in the bedrock released more and more magma until, in August, 1883, the plugs could contain it no longer.

In May of that year many ships passing the island of Krakatoa witnessed fire and steam rising from the Perbowatan peak, which was the smallest of the volcanic cones. When a pleasure-boat carrying eighty-five sightseers visited the island they found it covered with ash and pumice, and two small neighbouring islands, Lang and Verlaten, were also coated in grey. Among the visitors were a photographer and a mining engineer who made a point of inspecting the Perbowatan crater. At that time it was emitting whirling columns of steam to the accompaniment of a deafening noise.

The volcanic activity died down for a while. True, pumice was found floating in the Strait and occasional smoke was seen, but interest waned. On 10 August the island was again visited and found to be completely devastated—ash covered it to a depth of two feet. All three cones were now smoking, and steam was issuing from vents in their sides. Although it was not realized at the time, these eruptions were paving the way for the final catastrophe by letting sea water seep into the magma where it was immediately converted into gas and increased many times in volume and pressure. Finally, on 27 August, the plugs burst open.

With an incredible roar the volcano blew a great cloud of molten debris seventeen miles into the sky and raised the curtain on forty-eight hours of total chaos and destruction. The town of Anjer, in Java, some thirty-one miles from Krakatoa, was the first to be affected. By 2 p.m. local time the town was in inky darkness. Confusion took over—the inhabitants, seizing such possessions as they could, tried to reach boats and put out to sea, but the incessant rain of falling ash made lamps useless, and the sea rose and fell so quickly that it was virtually impossible to launch a boat at all—and as the sea ran higher and higher the boats were smashed, and many more people were injured by falling debris. Eventually, afraid of the rising sea, they ran for higher ground inland, though there was nothing to gain either way.

By now the noise was appalling. The roar of the swelling sea underlined and amplified the continuing volcanic explosions—and it was all just beginning. Many people thought that the hills behind Anjer were the best hope of survival, but in the almost total darkness, with the additional hazards of wild animals and dense jungle, they were well-nigh inaccessible. There was no prospect of aid or relief; the telegraph lines were down and communication with the outside world was cut off. Dawn arrived but never came—it remained dark under the torrential downpour of volcanic ash.

On the opposite side of the Sunda Strait the town of Kalimbang in Sumatra, only twenty-three miles from Krakatoa, was also blacked out. Among the terrified townspeople the Byerinck family with their two young children fled to the hills as a gigantic seismic wave flooded their home and destroyed outhouses. For four hours they groped their way through dense obscure jungle to reach a native village where thousands of groaning and wailing Sumatrans were crying to Allah to protect them from imminent death.

The British barque, *Charles Bal*, had a most miraculous escape. Sailing from Hong Kong to Java Head, she passed within ten miles of the eruption. In the pitch darkness, bombarded by hot stones and pumice, and covered with smouldering ash, she made little headway but nevertheless survived to tell the tale. Surprisingly, ships in the deep water of the Sunda Strait were largely unaffected by the seismic tidal waves, even though they grew greater as the eruption continued.

The *Gouverneur Loudon*, for example, crossed from Anjer to Telok Betong on the Sumatran coast during the afternoon. When Captain Lindemann dropped anchor in Lampong Bay on his arrival he saw boats smashed all along the shore, and a waving harbour-master tried to dissuade him from launching a boat. The jetty had broken away as high seas had flooded the water-front. Nevertheless the *Loudon* stayed at anchor, to be struck by lightning and coated in the detritus of the eruption. Every few minutes Krakatoa was belching out hundreds of tons of magma, and all round the coastline pumice and ash fell constantly.

At about 6.30 a.m. the first of a series of huge seismic waves struck the town of Anjer, driving straight inland for six miles and destroying everything in its path. Those survivors who had reached the comparative safety of the hill were in turn swept away an hour later when the second and even greater wave struck. In the words of an eye-witness at the time: "I saw in the distance an immense enormous black-looking mass of water, appearing at first sight mountain-high, rush on with a fearful roar and lightning-like rapidity. At the next moment the water uplifted and overflowed me with such force that it knocked me over and I performed several tumbles on my head as skilfully as the best acrobat."

But later, having survived the torrent: "A fearful sight met my eyes. Where Anjer stood I saw nothing but a foaming and furiously rushing flood above the surface of which only a couple of trees and the tops of roofs were visible. At a given moment, however, the water fell with great rapidity, and flowed back into the sea . . . What a sight met my half-stupefied gaze. It was a scene of the utmost confusion which no pen can describe. Immense quantities of broken furniture, beams, pieces of wood, trees, broken vessels, human corpses, all these formed a wildly confused mass heaped together in all directions."

In the town of Merak, where many Chinese labourers were employed in quarrying, similar waves struck. Though the Chinese camp had been flooded overnight, many had managed to reach higher ground and had survived the first two great waves, so they imagined they were safe. In the harbour near to the *Loudon* was the gunboat *Berouw*, lying close to the pier. Telok Betong had already been hit by four great waves and only a few houses remained standing. There were no people to be seen apart from a few Europeans on the 122-feet-high Residency Hill. Then at 7.45 a vast killer wave roared in, lifting the gunboat *Berouw* and flinging her into the Chinese quarter of the town—a spot in which she was not to remain for very long. The *Loudon*, still safe but unable to help, decided to put to sea and weighed anchor— but she was destined not to get very far.

At 10 o'clock on the Monday morning Krakatoa finally collapsed. The void left by the discharged magma caused eleven square miles of the island to fall into the abyss beneath it. The sea rushed in—and with a roar that was heard three thousand miles away a mighty wind arose from the dying volcano. The greatest tidal wave in history rushed out from the fallen monster to deal total destruction to the local coastal areas. It reared 100 feet high at the narrowest point of the Strait and then fanned out at the western end, continuing relentlessly on its way until eventually it raised the water level in the English Channel, 11,500 miles away, by two inches.

On the Javanese coast Tjaringin, already devastated by other waves, was completely wiped out. Not a building remained, at least ten thousand people perished and huge chunks of coral were deposited as far as seven miles inland. The plain around Pepper Bay, a little farther south, was sunk without trace, and the town of Penimbang, ten miles from the sea, was totally flooded. The wave was still 30 feet high when it had gone three miles inland. Many villages on this part of the coast, and their inhabitants, disappeared instantly and entirely.

At Merak, those who had taken shelter on a 130-feet hill were swept away and the stone houses at the summit were completely destroyed—but this was the greatest height reached by the wave which had been constricted by the narrowness of the Strait at that point. Out of 2,700 inhabitants, one native and one European survived. Sebessi and Sebukoe, two small islands about ten miles from Krakatoa, were completely submerged. Sebukoe was uninhabited, but 3,000 people lived and suddenly died on Sebessi.

Mrs Byerinck and her family, still in the native village on the mountain slope, sent out messengers to see what had happened to Kalimbang. They returned to say that it had completely disappeared. Although the Byerincks and their companions were above the level of the great seismic wave, they were thrown down by the shock wave and hot ash swept through the huts, burning their hands and faces severely. That night Mrs Byerinck's baby died in her arms.

At Telok Betong there was a moment of relief when light began to filter through the blackness at dawn on the Monday. The people on Residency Hill had escaped the waves which had battered the town during the night and they were getting used to the unending ash and pumice that rained constantly down on them—but at the moment of Krakatoa's final death explosion their terror was renewed. An eyewitness engaged in rescue work near the shore suddenly saw the great wave approaching. In headlong flight he saw a woman giving birth while still staggering towards safety, and another woman collapsing with her child to be engulfed by the advancing wave. It was this wave, reaching a height of 116 feet, which lifted the gunboat *Berouw* from its uneasy berth in the Chinese quarter to sweep it a further mile inland and put it down 30 feet above sea level behind a hill, killing the crew in the process. Meanwhile the *Loudon*, putting out to sea, managed to ride out the wave. Her crew were aghast on looking back to find that the ruins of the town were totally submerged—Telok Betong no longer existed.

The *Loudon* was unable to get clear of Lampong Bay until the Tuesday morning, and then only under conditions which made navigation hazardous and at times virtually impossible. Lumps of floating pumice ten feet thick blocked the waterways, but the vessel eventually forced a way through. Passing close to Krakatoa, the captain observed that there was very little of the island left—the cone of Rakata had split in two, leaving a sheer cliff where formerly there had been gentle and fertile slopes, and Danan and Perbowatan had vanished completely.

In fact, two-thirds of the island had disappeared. Land which had previously risen to some 1,400 feet above sea level now lay beneath 900 feet of water. In all about 13 cubic miles of matter had been spewed up by Krakatoa; while much of it fell within a ten-mile radius of the volcano at least one-third, consisting of dust and finer particles, remained suspended in the earth's atmosphere for several years before slowly settling to the surface. The sound of the explosion was heard 2,968 miles away at Rodriguez Island across the Indian Ocean (the longest recorded distance), and also in Western Australia (1,900 miles away) and Manila (1,800 miles). In Ceylon the noise was loud enough to give rise to anxiety. Not knowing the cause of the explosion searches were made from these countries for ships in distress or any other possible source of the detonations.

The seismic shock wave circled the earth seven or eight times, travelling at almost the speed of sound. It was recorded at Greenwich Observatory for the first time some ten and a half hours after the explosion. Perhaps even more spectacular were the distances achieved by the seismic sea wave. Apart from inflating the level of the English Channel, it produced twelve-inch wave surges in Karachi, claimed a life from someone crossing the harbour at Arugain Bay, Ceylon, and spread abnormal waves as far apart as Cape Town, Cape Horn, the Bay of Biscay, New Zealand and Alaska.

For many months parts of the Indian Ocean were hazardous to ships because of masses of floating pumice in which debris, parts of trees and corpses were frequently embedded. The pumice eventually reached the coast of South Africa where it was first observed in September, 1884. The dust cloud took two months to encircle the earth and was responsible for some remarkable and beautiful sunsets, the colour of the sun ranging from a greenish-blue to intense copper.

The immediate aftermath of the catastrophe followed the general pattern of most natural disasters. Darkness covered the Sunda Strait for three days, and for all it was a period of desperate confusion and misery. The wild seas pounded the shores while inland a thick layer of pungent ash covered everything—land, wells and water-holes, creating problems of starvation and thirst for animals and people alike. Survivors searched for their families, although many of the dead were unidentifiable because of the savage buffeting and partial burial in mud which they had suffered. Although the sea had been the principal killer, thousands also died from burns.

Relief was admirably quick in arriving once daylight had returned. The Dutch, with their estates and plantations destroyed and their labourers dispersed or dead, provided a great deal of money to aid the victims of the disaster. The early reports of the helpers create a picture of unparalleled desolation. The Lloyd's agent at Batavia, making a tour of Bantam, visited what was left of Anjer and wrote:

"It was difficult to realize that the town of Anjer had ever existed. Clothing and bedding were scattered about here and there, but otherwise there was, beyond the graves, nothing to show that a town and a score of kampongs had ever existed." In the European cemetery on rising ground to the south of the town "many of the graves were completely scooped out, and what with the ash-rain and the effects of the volcanic wave there was not a trace of its ever having been a cemetery".

The Resident of Bantam notified the Governor-General on 7 September that 1,517 bodies had been buried at Anjer, while a further 400 awaited burial. As it was "impossible to extricate them from the debris of houses and trees with which they were mixed", he asked for eight thousand cases of petroleum to be supplied so that the bodies could be burned. In addition, to speed the disposal of corpses and so prevent disease and plague, a payment of five guilders was made for each cadaver buried. And, needless to say, looters accompanied the rescue parties, stealing whatever poor salvageable property remained.

The official figures for casualties were subject to serious discrepancies, for many people had been carried off by the retreating wave and were never accounted for. One particular table gave the number of Europeans killed in Sumatra and Java as 37 compared with 36,380 Asiatics. Villages entirely destroyed numbered 165, while another 132 were partly destroyed.

While it seemed that life could no longer exist in these disfigured areas, within a generation Krakatoa itself was again covered in green vegetation and alive with birds, animals and insects. Ironically, volcanic ash is an excellent fertilizer and today, with Anak Krakatoa (child of Krakatoa) already spitting fire and smoke from its new cone on the site of the old, the area bounding the Sunda Strait is once again a thriving community. Scientists who have inspected the new cone are certain that there is little likelihood of another major eruption and collapse within hundreds of years—but the volcano is not extinct and it is still building itself up into a new tall mountain.

San Francisco Shake-up

Ask any American which is the most beautiful city in the United States and he will almost certainly say San Francisco. The city is built on a peninsula of land which curves northwards into the Pacific Ocean to enclose the bright blue waters of a sheltered bay fifty miles wide. Access to this natural harbour is through the mile-wide Golden Gate, so called because of the spectacular colour of the sunsets on the horizon of the Pacific to the west.

The Golden Gate is a narrow gap in the long chain of mountains that runs down the west coast of California. A decade ago it was spanned by what is the longest single-span suspension bridge in the world, its towers soaring 746 feet above the water and its centre span measuring 4,200 feet from pier to pier. Beneath this giant orange-painted bridge and through the entrance to the land-locked harbour sail some of the largest ships in the world.

That the city today is regarded as America's most beautiful is due partly to the dawn catastrophe of Wednesday, 18 April, 1906, when most of San Francisco was destroyed and gutted by fire, and partly to the imagination and foresight of the planners who rebuilt a new and prouder city from the ruins and ashes of the old.

What happened in the early morning of 18 April, 1906, was tersely reported in the San Francisco *Daily News* later that day. The story read:

San Francisco was partially demolished and totally paralyzed by the earthquake which commenced at 5.12 a.m. today and continued with terrific vigour for four minutes.

Great loss of life was caused by the collapse of buildings, and many people met a more cruel death by fire. Flames broke out in all parts of the city.

The progress of San Francisco has received a check from which it will take many years to recover. Thousands of men who went to bed wealthy last night awoke this morning practically bankrupt.

The fury of the tremor was greater than any that has been known in the history of the city. The people are appalled, terror-stricken. Thousands fearful of a recurrence of the dreadful disaster, with results still more dire, are hastening out of the city.

Many heart-rending scenes have been enacted. Families are moving their belongings helter-skelter, and moving aimlessly about, keeping in the open.

The City Hall is a complete wreck. The walls surrounding the grand dome have fallen, leaving only the skeletons of framework and the top of the dome intact. Around all sides of the building the walls have crumbled like so many cards. The receiving hospital was buried.

The surgeons moved to Mechanic's Pavilion which today is a combined receiving hospital and morgue. Dead and dying are brought in by autos, ambulances and even garbage carts.

Insane patients were taken from the emergency hospital to Mechanic's Pavilion. Many of them were hurt. Some broke loose and ran among the dying, adding horror to the scene. At 8.15 a.m. a second sharp quake occurred, accentuating the terror. (*Author's note—minor tremors in fact occurred throughout the day.*)

The fire scenes following the earthquake were and are fearful to behold. Had the earthquake occurred an hour later the entire city would have burst into flames. (*Author's note—presumably because people would by then have been up, cooking and lighting fires.*)

At least forty buildings were aflame within ten minutes after the tremor passed. The sidewalks are literally strewn with wreckage. Many sidewalks have collapsed, falling into the basements.

There are probably not fifty chimneys standing in the city. This means that many more fires are to be expected as flues are cracked everywhere. (*Author's note—a list follows of buildings damaged or destroyed, and dead and injured people.*)

That in journalese remarkably undramatic for an event so traumatic, was roughly what happened to San Francisco. For the reporters of the *Daily News*, themselves stunned by shock and perhaps personal tragedy, it was too soon to evaluate the catastrophe in depth, to obtain figures and statistics, or to recount eye-witness reports. It is doubtful if on that day anyone in San Francisco had either the time or the inclination to read a newspaper at all. But the printed words passed into the archives of history.

In the opening decade of the century San Francisco was a vivid, vital and teeming city. Some sixty years had passed since the famous "forty-niners" had surged westwards in search of gold, and what had originally been a small village of Spanish origin with less that a thousand inhabitants had burgeoned into a thriving metropolis of nearly half a million people. It was a city of contrasts—of riches and poverty, of gaiety and depravity, and it was a principal centre of booming business and international culture.

It was a city of "too much, too soon". It had grown swiftly, in abnormal circumstances. The vast influx of people, mostly men, during the early years of the gold rush had resulted in hasty jerry-building that soon deteriorated into slums, in the notorious "Barbary Coast"—the oddly named red-light area where the heavily outnumbered women entertained the gold-seekers and did a roaring trade—and in Chinatown. This latter district was inhabited by about thirty-thousand unsuccessful Chinese gold-hunters who had been forced to turn to other forms of livelihood. A tourist curiosity, it was also an area of brisk small businesses, many of which acted as a cover for less honourable trades such as drug-peddling, prostitution, gambling and white-slave traffic.

The haste and confusion in which the city expanded was such that the shabbier districts became well established virtually overnight. By the time the original shanty town of the mid-eighties had reached city status they were ineradicable. From time to time attempts were made to clean up the place, but with little success. The colourful—indeed, lurid —reputation of San Francisco persisted, and there was, perhaps, too much corruption and political chicanery in higher circles for anything positive to be achieved.

Even when the gold rush was over, San Francisco continued to thrive. Millionaires lived it up in magnificent houses on Nob Hill and Van Ness Avenue. Theatres, clubs and the Opera House attracted the most famous international stars. Money flowed freely and living was easy and high—though not for all. Nevertheless, San Francisco acquired fame as a city of riches, pleasure and plenty—and vice and corruption.

But this centre of glittering prosperity was built on treacherous foundations. In the first place, since the city was sited on a narrow peninsula and therefore surrounded on three sides by water, expansion to accommodate the ever-increasing population could only be achieved by reclaiming land from the shallow parts of the waterfront. This was just the kind of band-wagon the smart real-estate operators had been waiting to jump on. Every conceivable kind of junk and garbage, suitable or not, was dumped into the offshore waters, to be covered with a layer of sand and earth. On this "reclaimed" ground, and elsewhere throughout the city, badly constructed buildings of inferior materials were being rushed up as fast as the mortar would dry—and they were built higher and higher in order to squeeze the maximum rental from the available space. Some of these buildings, in fact, fell down of their own accord, without the incentive of even a minor earth tremor.

None of this would have mattered very much, perhaps, had it not been for one very important factor—San Francisco's geographical position. The city stands between two geological "faults" in the bedrock; they run parallel, roughly north and south, and are some eighteen miles apart. Of the two, the San Andreas fault is the nearer to San Francisco since it runs under the Pacific Ocean and penetrates the land in the region of the Golden Gate—but it does not lie directly beneath the city. It has, however, frequently been the cause of earthquakes on a minor scale which the local inhabitants had come to take for granted.

Under such conditions, badly built houses on shifting foundations were highly vulnerable to collapse due to earth movements—but whenever this happened they were hastily rebuilt in much the same manner as before. Most earthquakes result in fire, and throughout the latter half of the nineteenth century there is a history of regular conflagrations, fuelled by the wooden buildings and fanned by offshore winds.

The authorities moved slowly. By 1868, however, when a fairly severe earthquake (caused by the more distant Hayward bedrock fault) wrought considerable damage followed by fires, the situation was rapidly brought under control. Perhaps because of this, the people of San Francisco began to feel confident that their city was no longer in any real danger from fire; what they did not appreciate was that on this particular occasion they had been spared because the earth tremor had originated in the remote Hayward fault. Had the San Andreas fault been the culprit, the disaster might have taken on far more catastrophic proportions, for the main water pipelines to the city had been laid close to the nearer fault. The lesson had to be learned in a more terrifying experience some forty years later.

In the big earthquake of 1906 the fire chief was a man of outstanding personality named Danny Sullivan, and he took his job very seriously. As he was only too well aware of the inherent danger in the fact that the water pipelines lay right across the San Andreas fault, he campaigned unceasingly for an inquiry into the possibility of using the salt water from the Pacific Ocean for fire-fighting purposes. The big snag lay in the corrosive nature of salt which meant that the scheme would be costly, and so it was constantly shelved. Sullivan therefore did his best in other directions, paying particular attention to the quality of his men and their training, which included the dynamiting of burning buildings to create a fire-break.

The trouble was that the San Franciscans were too busy enjoying life to heed his Cassandra-like warnings. In mid-April of 1906, with disaster imminent, they were enjoying a special treat with the visit of Caruso and the Metropolitan Opera Company of New York. On the second night of the repertoire Caruso took the leading role in *Carmen*, and crowds of fashionable visitors from out of town poured into San Francisco to hear the famous tenor. Many of them spent the night in the fabulous four-million-dollar Palace Hotel in which Caruso himself was staying. It was the night of 17 April.

In the early hours of the following morning, with no warning whatever, the San Andreas fault "crept". That technical word possesses an ironic quality of understatement—San Francisco trembled and shook with a mighty chaotic roar of noise. At that time most people were still asleep, and few were in the streets to observe what was happening.

A group of journalists from the San Francisco *Examiner* had, however, just finished their night's work. As they left their office building they heard a deep grumbling sound that grew rapidly to a deafening roar such as they had never before heard. The solid ground slipped and lurched under their feet and threw them to the ground. Tall buildings swayed crazily and toppled over, and the building which they had just left changed its position in what they described as "a kind of bound".

The Palace Hotel housing Caruso also shifted so that one end projected into the street, but it did not disintegrate. Elsewhere cornices, chimneys and walls crumbled and crashed to the ground, paved roads undulated as though a great wave was passing beneath them, and vast fissures opened up across the city. Observers reported that "three great shudders ran through the land on which the city stood with a deep-throated roar like that of heavy surf".

Peacefully sleeping people awoke suddenly to find their beds shaking beneath them. William James, the eminent psychologist and brother of the novelist Henry James, was visiting nearby Santa Rosa when the earthquake happened. At the first shock he knelt up in bed, but "I was thrown down on my face as it went fortier, shaking the room exactly as a terrier shakes a rat. Then everything that was on anything else slid off to the floor, and over went the bureaus and chiffonier with a crash as the fortissimo was reached; plaster cracked, an awful roaring noise seemed to fill the outer air, and in an instant all was still again save the soft babble of human voices from far and near that soon began to make itself heard as the inhabitants in costumes and negligees in various degrees sought the greater safety of the street and yielded to the passionate desire for sympathetic communication."

In fact, the "babble of human voices" in the streets rapidly died away as people gazed speechlessly at the fantastic scene before their eyes in the early dawn light. The earth tremors had at last stopped (although each had lasted only some fifteen to twenty seconds they had seemed endless), but buildings continued to topple.

Now the screams of pain and anguish from injured people could be heard among the horrific scene of debris. Falling masonry had crushed people like so many ants, men frantically scrabbled at the ruins which had buried their families, women wept over dead children, and blood-stained corpses lay sprawled around—in all some seven hundred people were killed outright and many thousands were injured. Public utilities broke down: gas and water mains were ruptured, tram-lines and the early electricity cables of the day were ripped apart.

Rudi Schubert, a young man who had recently joined the Fire Force, had just signed off duty when the earthquake shocks began. He returned immediately to the fire-brigade headquarters, to find the building still standing but with a twelve-inch-wide crack in the side walls. Very quickly the rest of the fire-fighting force arrived, for they all knew that fire was bound to follow an earthquake—but the Fire Chief, Danny Sullivan, was dead. He had awoken with the first shock to find that his wife had been killed by a chimney which had fallen from the California Hotel next door. In the darkness he had failed to see the huge hole it had made in the floor, and it was through this hole that he fell to his death three storeys below.

Sullivan's deputy took charge of the fire-fighters. The city's alarm system had been totally disrupted by the earthquake, so he sent his crews out to track down their own fires. At that time it was not too difficult for the fire-fighting appliances to move through the streets. Most of the rubble lay on the pavements, and the main road blockages were due to the collapsed ruins of the City Hall—San Francisco's pride and joy—and the Post Office. But although access to blazing buildings was not greatly obstructed, access to water hardly existed. When hoses were coupled to fire hydrants only a thin trickle of water emerged, and that soon dwindled away.

Danny Sullivan's prediction had come true at last; the water pipes which lay across the San Andreas fault had cracked, and there was no water with which to fight some fifty-two separate outbreaks of fire. Horrified, the firemen could only stare helplessly at each other and at the hungry flames while the onlooking crowd, realizing the truth, was terror-stricken. Compared with the new menace of rapidly spreading fire the recent earthquake seemed almost inconsequential; it appeared that there was nothing to stop the flames, fanned by the brisk Pacific breeze, from destroying the entire city.

Wherever electric wires had short-circuited, or gas-pipes had been broken and chimneys damaged, blazes started.

The many that were successfully extinguished in the early moments merely gave way to others. One housewife on the west side of wealthy Van Ness Avenue started to cook a good breakfast for her family, unaware that she had a fractured gas-pipe, and thus started the famous "ham-and-eggs fire" which destroyed a dozen blocks and caused the only extensive fire damage west of Van Ness.

Rudi and his crews did their best to control the situation, but it proved to be an impossible task, and by mid-day the fire had taken such a hold on the city as to be declared officially "a conflagration". In effect, it was a state of emergency. Local army units now moved in and organized demolition squads on the principle of "if you can't beat it, join it". Army groups evacuated people from pre-determined zones, to be followed by the demolition experts, setting the dynamite charges to create fire-breaks. The roads were full of unfortunate evacuees carrying what few belongings they could from homes that were about to be razed to the ground. There were no objections—the buildings would be razed just as effectively by fire if not by dynamite in the immediate future. Ironically, the broad luxurious stretch of Van Ness Avenue provided a natural perimeter line for a fire-break, and there the palatial houses of San Francisco's millionaires, loaded with priceless treasures, were uncompromisingly blown to pieces.

The great fire took its most relentless grip in the downtown quarter of the city—Chinatown, the Barbary Coast and the docks. The drunk and the drugged, the prostitutes and pimps—all were moved out with frantic haste as the demolition squads closed in. But it was not possible to evacuate everybody. Two unconscious men (presumably doped) in a squalid top-floor room of a dingy apartment block were too heavy to manœuvre down the narrow twisting staircase. Rudi's team men struggled to get the men out while the soldiers were already setting high explosives in the downstairs rooms. "There are two men up here and we've got to get them out," Rudi shouted. "No time," said the demolition officer—and, indeed, there was only time for Rudi and his men to make their own escape before the building exploded. Its two unconscious occupants never knew what happened.

Naturally, the denizens of this lawless quarter of the city

lost no time in grasping opportunities for plunder. Within minutes of the final earth tremor the looters were hard at work raiding the ruined and shattered shops for valuables, food and drink. Even the dead were stripped of their possessions; one man was caught in the act of cutting off a woman's hands to steal her locked bracelets.

The mayor, however, a man named Eugene Scmitz (who had been criticized for his bumbling and even dishonest administration) rose nobly to the occasion. Within a few hours he had issued orders that looters were to be shot, had arranged to commandeer all food stocks, and had set up a Relief Committee to attend to matters of welfare for the homeless. Tented "towns" were erected in parks and open spaces, and long trestle tables were supplied for the free meals which were supplied to all those in need.

Despite ruthless demolition work, the San Francisco fire raged for three days and two nights before it was finally brought under control. It was not until Friday that Rudi Schubert went off duty for the first time since that Wednesday morning of the earthquake. He had no idea what had happened to his wife and he was desperately anxious about her. While walking wearily towards his home street he collapsed from sheer exhaustion and was picked up by a soldier who had him taken to one of the tented camps for the homeless.

There, by chance and good fortune, he met a neighbour —one of the hundreds who had fled from the inferno. She, like most San Franciscans, had by now recovered from the first traumatic shock of the earthquake and was imbued with the spirit of cheerfulness and stubborn optimism which had taken the place of the initial horror and misery.

She told Schubert that his wife had moved out into the country and was safe. "When the fire got to California Street," she said, "we all grabbed what we could and got out. Your wife got dressed, but she had a friend with her who was wearing two night-dresses and nothing else. People were wearing the funniest things. Your wife had your best bowler hat and that new encyclopedia you bought. She'd have done better to have collected some food, but she was mad with worry about you."

There was nothing Schubert could do, for he was unable

to communicate with his wife, and he had to report to work as soon as possible. By Friday evening, however, the telegraph wires were working again; the thousands of private and personal messages had to take their turn in the priority queue, but the relief committee could now ask the outside world for the food and medical services which San Francisco needed so badly.

Help arrived quickly from neighbouring towns—relief workers poured in as swiftly as refugees poured out, using the ferry and the peninsula road (the railway station had been destroyed). The military kept the city under its brusque control and on the Friday organized the burial of the dead who still lay in the streets. And it was the military which, acting as a police force, made sure that the populace obeyed the various edicts of the mayor concerning the use of gas and electricity or naked lights, the cooking of food and the disposal of garbage.

By the Saturday serious attempts were being made to clear the rubble. Citizen volunteers set to work with shovels, for any kind of activity was a relief after days of terror, suspense and waiting. Miraculously, survivors were found buried under the debris. Under the rubble of what had been the main Post Office eight clerks, still alive, were dug out; and other similar rescues proved immensely cheering. And then the fire, which had shown signs of slackening, took on a new lease of life as the wind freshened. Glowing ashes were fanned into active flame once more, and a pall of smoke and soot again covered the city.

The weather, which had been unhappily fine and dry throughout the catastrophe, eventually broke around midnight on the Saturday. Rain came—a steady downpour that signalled the end of the fire threat even though it meant misery for the people camping hobo-like in the streets and the squares of the burned-out city. The rain turned forty-feet-high piles of rubble and ash into soggy masses, and created rivers and lakes in the crevices in the roads.

The rain stopped five days after the earthquake, and the citizens of San Francisco could at last take stock of the damage and turn their attention to rebuilding. The city was a shambles—no less—and the "downtown" quarter in the north-east, the centre of business and administration, was a scene of ash-grey desolation, with here and there the skeleton of a dead skyscraper protruding mournfully from the surrounding ruins.

Altogether an area of nearly five square miles had been totally destroyed by fire, including 28,000 residential houses. Legend has it that the local Italian community fought the flames by emptying their barrels of wine into the streets. Some 400 million dollars worth of loss was caused by the earthquake and the subsequent fire. Only on Telegraph Hill in the centre of the burned-out area remained an island of undamaged houses.

The United States Government contributed generously to the San Francisco relief fund, and so did very many private organizations, companies and individuals. A new San Francisco began to rise, phoenix-like, with incredible rapidity from the ashes. Chinatown and the Barbary Coast had been burned from the city map, although their unsavoury reputation lingered on for another decade.

San Francisco's local authorities did not need to be told that here was a marvellous opportunity to rebuild anew, with vision and imagination. Even before the debris had been cleared a plan had already been drawn up for the replanning of the city, though, because of the necessity for speed, it was not entirely followed in detail. But the result, warts and all, was elegant and beautiful.

Further, a sense of responsibility emerged. Stringent building codes were laid down concerning the foundations, basic structure and height of buildings, and legislation was introduced to enforce the new standards, particularly in the areas of "made" land recovered from the Pacific waterfront.

Perhaps even more important, huge water cisterns were built in all parts of the town to supply the hydrants in the event of another "conflagration". Perhaps there are more earthquakes to come; the bedrock faults are still there. At least San Francisco is now ready to handle such a crisis, and if its claim to be the most beautiful city in America is true then at least it has benefited from its terrifying experience and learned the hard way. Even an ill wind can blow a great deal of good.

Dusseldorf's Reign of Terror

It really began in prison. He discovered how to turn the dark and lonely punishment cells into veritable palaces of erotic and sadistic delight.. Here came the girls he had violated and maltreated, to re-live their sufferings in the dark labyrinth of his mind, and to give him again that fierce and powerful sexual pleasure which was the very mainspring of his life. Here too he re-enjoyed the scenes of blood which had thrilled him so passionately, such as the man whom he saw killed by a street-car, the sight of whose gushing blood gave him an orgasm.

Peter Kurten had been imprisoned for fraud and assault, minor offences compared with the massive crimes and the great terrors which he now planned to inflict upon society because he considered it had treated him so badly. His sexual crimes had not then been discovered.

In the dark and lonely cells he revelled in sadistic fantasies of bloodshed and violence, of stabbings and woundings, and of wilder visions of collapsing bridges and burning buildings in which hundreds of people perished in scenes of awful terror—all caused by him. This was his revenge upon society, a revenge which would be made more perfect by the death in torment of someone entirely innocent.

Prison conditions were harsh in Germany at the turn of the century, as they were everywhere, and Peter Kurten spent much of his time in solitary confinement, often infringing prison rules in order to go there and enjoy these strange erotic fancies which gave him such satisfying sexual pleasure.

In 1912 came release. He lived with a prostitute who was a masochist and encouraged him to beat her and half choke her during intercourse. But though he enjoyed maltreating his mistress, Kurten required the sacrifice of an innocent to gratify the powerful sex urge which he had developed in the erotic incubator of the solitary confinement cell.

On the night of 25 May, 1913, he broke into a house in Koln-Mulheim to rob it. In one of the bedrooms he found the innocent—eight-years-old Christine Klein, whose throat he cut while she slept and whose body he raped while she was dying.

It amused Kurten when the girl's uncle was accused of the murder, though not convicted.

He was thirty. He did not look the monster he was. He was well built, not particularly good-looking, but attractive to women. He was vain, well-dressed, fastidious in his personal habits.

Eight years passed in bitterness, erotic reveries and more plans for bloody revenge upon society. Most of that time was spent in prison for deserting from the Kaiser's Imperial Army in 1914.

After the war he was staying at the house of his sister in Altenburg, posing as a prisoner-of-war returned from Russia, when he met the woman he chose for his wife. Three years his senior, she had not worn well, and had an awful past. She had been a prostitute, and in 1911 had been sent to prison for four years for shooting a lover who jilted her. She was not however a bad woman. She had many sterling qualities and lived under a determination to redeem herself.

It was thought strange that he should be so attracted to her. But to him she was a fellow sufferer whom he could respect, and someone solid and reliable to cling to. Sex for him had little to do with physical attractiveness. But she could not understand his desire to marry her, and she refused him. He then told her bluntly that he would kill her unless she did. Unaware that the threat was a serious one, and flattered at such forthright and determined wooing, she capitulated. She told him everything about her past, and told the story with touching humility.

But he disclosed none of his secrets, rightly believing that she would never understand how he felt. The marriage, however, was not unsuccessful. She was the only human being for whom he felt feelings of normal affection, and the only woman with whom he had ordinary sexual relations. She put the prostitute's skill into more wholesome channels, though he could only respond successfully to her by indulging in fantasies of cruelty with an imaginary partner.

Why did he not grasp her throat and treat her with the "brutality that belongs to love"? Only he knew the answer to this. The simple, repentant prostitute and sinner gave a selfless whole-hearted love and devotion to the sex monster, the vampire, the murderer of little children. Peter Kurten was very sensitive to the love which his wife had for him.

But it made no difference to the secret part of his life. Each night he went out to find a victim for the sadistic love-making which was the only sort which gave him true pleasure. He found many girls who enjoyed being half strangled during intercourse, and a number of them came back for more.

In 1925 he and his wife moved to Dusseldorf. He now had a respectable job as a moulder and was active in trade-union and political circles. On the evening of his arrival in Dusseldorf there was a wild sunset, running blood-red across the sky. Peter Kurten looked at it, aflame with pleasure. To him this was no sunset, but the dawn of the vampire days.

He began quietly enough. Isolated outrages here and there. A vicious attack to gratify his desire for blood. A number of houses and farm buildings set on fire. His criminality ranged wide. He had a theory that if he used a different method every time he would not be caught. It was an intelligent theory, for much police investigation is founded upon the fact that most criminals always use the same method and thus leave their stamp on their crimes.

The long-planned reign of terror did not start at once. He began his baleful activities slowly, working himself up, as his ghoulish appetite grew, with more and more frequent atrocities.

His freedom from detection increased his megalomania. His ego grew as he committed atrocity after atrocity with complete impunity. This one-man war on society was only part of the force which drove him on in his search for victims. His appetite for blood and suffering was his main impulse. He believed himself to be driven on by a force he could not control. He had no sense of guilt, no subconscious desire for punishment, by which so many criminals bring about their own downfall. He considered himself the loneliest man in the world as he walked the streets of Dusseldorf at night in search of fresh victims, his mind tortured with a secret he could not share with another living soul.

By now the city was gripped with terror. Women feared to go out at night. Every policeman sought the monster. Hundreds of arrests were made. The best police brains in Germany were recruited to run the mass murderer to earth, without success.

Kurten avidly read the papers and got tremendous satisfaction out of the terror he had caused. When he read that several unbalanced people had confessed to his atrocious crimes, he laughed. Nut cases who hadn't the guts to do these things, he thought scornfully. Trying to snatch my glory.

He continued his terrible work with renewed vigour and relish. 1929 was his peak year. Late on the night of 3 February he overtook a woman walking home in a lonely suburban road.

"Good evening," he said.

As she turned, he seized her coat and stabbed her rapidly and repeatedly on her head, body and arms. Her screams attracted passers-by and he had to make a run for it. He learned later that her name was Apollonia Kuhn, and she recovered after many months in hospital.

His lust was really on him now. A few days later he came upon a child in a churchyard, stabbed her to death and sexually assaulted her. A week later he stabbed a man to death and drank the blood as it spurted from his wounds. Later he picked up a girl named Maria in a park. She agreed to have sex with him, and during intercourse he strangled her and stabbed her to death. He drank her blood also, then left her under some bushes, returning the following night to bury her body. In similar manner he murdered two other young women, and three little girls, one of whom was five years old.

The Dusseldorf terror had reached its height. Walking through the streets at night, he could sense the fear which had settled on the city, and it gave him an unbelievable pleasure. His wife worked in the kitchen of a restaurant and returned home very late. Like all the other women in Dusseldorf, she was terrified of the Monster who stalked the night, stabbing and slaying. Every evening Peter Kurten escorted her to her place of work, then disappeared into the dark streets of the city in search of victims.

His night's work done, he washed the blood off his hands, and returned to his wife's place of work, his dark mind lingering lovingly over the details of his latest work of horror which gave him a satisfaction incomprehensible to almost every other person in the world.

It was well past midnight when he strode the terror-stricken streets feeling like a dreaming god, the city at his feet and at his mercy. He swept past the poor, frightened denizens with contempt. None of these people knew the god of terror had brushed against them in the street—these people who were too dull to taste the strange and awful pleasures which he alone of men had the capacity to enjoy.

A woman looked over her shoulders with the fear of death in her eyes as his footsteps overtook her in a deserted street. Then her expression turned to one of relief when she saw, instead of the glaring eyes and drooling lips of the vampire-monster, a smart, well-groomed man with gentle eyes who passed her by at a courteous distance.

Frau Kurten was always relieved when her husband arrived to take her home through Dusseldorf's dangerous streets. She herself dreaded the Monster, believing a visitation upon her would be some kind of punishment for her past sins. Peter ridiculed the idea, and told her she had no need to fear, for he would meet her every night. But she was never fully re-assured.

Her past hung over her life like a cloud. She was well aware that her husband did not find her physically attractive, and was unfaithful to her on many occasions. But she was prepared to endure that. He would come back to her in the end, and the truly important thing in her life was security in her old age.

After the hard work in the restaurant kitchen, she was tired when she got to the flat in the Metmannerstrasse. He chatted pleasantly to her, made the cocoa, and then they went to bed. She never slept well, being constantly tormented by her unquiet mind. But he always slept soundly by her side and was never disturbed by evil dreams or conscience. Like the vampire of legend, he sank down in tranquil sleep after sating himself upon the blood of his victims.

One day she came home unexpectedly and found him in bed with a girl. Although prepared to endure his infidelities, it greatly affronted her that her husband should commit adultery in the marriage bed. But she kept her anger in check.

"I don't know who you are," she said quietly to the girl. "But this is my home, so please get dressed and go."

Peter was angry, though there was little he could say in the circumstances, except to assure his wife that there was nothing serious in the relationship. Actually he got a lot of enjoyment out of this girl, whose name was Hildegard. She liked being made love to violently and half strangled during the sex act.

When the terror was at its peak, Kurten's sadistic appetite was in its full flood. The theory of the innocent suffering for the sins of society was overwhelmed by the black pleasures of his tormented mind. And yet he could not himself explain the strange and passionate love he felt afterwards towards some of those whom he had abused and killed.

There was one girl named Maria whom he strangled and stabbed to death during a sexual frenzy. He dug her grave. Then as he lifted her into it he was overwhelmed by tender emotions of a kind which the girl had quite failed to arouse in him when she lived. He caressed the body lovingly before he buried it. This very emotion filled him with terror, for he did not understand it; and the next night he returned to the grave, armed with hammer and nails, intending to crucify the corpse, but the inert body was too heavy for him.

Another night he went to the cemetery and sat upon the grave of one of his child victims. He fingered the soil with tears streaming down his face, thinking strange and tender thoughts about the poor little girl who lay beneath and who had suffered and died so that he, the mighty egotist, might enjoy one single ejaculation. He was conscious that he was evil, but there was no remorse in him. Regret, perhaps. He believed that it was impossible to stop himself doing these things.

Nevertheless, he was aware that the terror had gone too far, and for a while he succeeded in desisting from his activities.

The end came in May, 1930, over the affair of Mara Budleis. She was a girl who had come to Dusseldorf looking for a job. On her arrival, a man picked her up and tried to persuade her to go into a park with him. She had heard the stories about the Monster of Dusseldorf and she refused. As the man was arguing with her Peter Kurten came on the scene, and in his pleasant, soft-voiced manner, asked if he could be of any assistance to her.

Mara turned to her rescuer with gratitude, while the wolf made himself scarce. Kurten offered the girl some refreshment at his home, and she went unhesitatingly to his flat in the Metmannerstrasse. Here Kurten gave her some milk and a ham sandwich, and then offered to take her to a hostel where she could find a bed for the night. She followed him with complete trust and found herself before long alone with him in a park. He started to make passionate love to her, but when he seized her throat she strongly objected.

Kurten then desisted, and asked, significantly, if she could remember where he lived. She said that she could not, and he left her. It was too risky to kill again.

Mara however wrote to a woman friend telling her about her adventure in the park, and this woman, instantly connecting the girl's experience with the Dusseldorf Vampire, went to the police, who in turn interviewed Mara. She did not have much difficulty in taking them to the Metmannerstrasse. Kurten saw the girl with the police and believed it was the end.

Even if the police could not prove he was the Monster, he could be sent to prison for attempting strangulation. All the atrocities would then stop and they would know that he was the man.

Confused, unable to know what to do, he turned to the only person for whom he had a spark of affection, his wife.

"I am the man," he said. "I did it all."

She stared at him uncomprehendingly.

"I have done everything that has happened here in Dusseldorf," he said.

"What do you mean?" she asked.

"The Monster—the Vampire. I am the man."

"I don't believe it," she whispered wretchedly. She had begun to have her suspicions, simply because he had always been out when the atrocities had been committed. But could she believe these ghastly things of him—her husband, the man who slept untroubled at her side during her own hours of guilty wakefulness?

"I did everything—the murders—the attacks."

"Those innocent children too?" She was aghast. She believed him now.

"Yes, even them."

"But why? Why?" There was panic, as well as horror in her voice. Her life was crumbling and crashing around her, the life she had so carefully built up to avoid the horrors of a penniless old age.

He looked into space, his eyes dreaming. He did not seem to care very much. This was the astonishing, the terrifying thing. She thought of those sickening horrors, the things that had been done to those children, those girls, and her whole being was filled with revulsion. Yet to him it did not seem to matter in the least. What kind of man had she married?

"Why?" he said. "I do not know. Perhaps it was that I became another person. Something came over me, and I just had to do these things."

"I cannot believe this of you," she whispered. "This is too awful to be borne."

"Let me tell you about each one," he said.

"No!" she cried, her hands over her ears.

"But I must tell someone. You are the only one I have."

She sat there obediently listening, and life seemed suddenly to become a nightmare as he told her in the most detailed way about each and every one he had killed and savaged. It seemed to her that he was possessed, like a medium being used by some outside power to tell this story of pitiless butchery with its ghoulish horrors of blood drinking and incomprehensible lust.

At last he finished. She sat there, broken and sick, unable to look at him.

"But what is to happen to me?" she whispered.

"There's a big reward for the Dusseldorf murderer," he said rather callously. "You could claim that."

She shook her head. "Blood money? Never."

When she could weep no more, she crept from the house to the police-station, crushed and bewildered, unable to carry alone the weight of this awful secret.

A few days later he was arrested, and at his trial was convicted of nine murders and sentenced to be beheaded.

To Frau Kurten that which she had feared most had come to pass; this was the ultimate punishment for the sins she had committed in her youth. There was not the smallest hope for her now in this world.

As for Peter Kurten, he had long and satisfying psychiatric sessions with Professor Karl Berg, Germany's most famous criminal psychologist. Kurten discussed every crime in detail and revelled in it. Professor Berg found him an intelligent and rewarding subject, and gained a valuable insight into the mind of the greatest sex criminal of his age. Kurten said that the recounting of each atrocious crime gave him nearly as much pleasure as he got when he committed it.

He had not the slightest remorse. "How could I? After all, I had to fulfil my mission. And if I was let loose to-day, I could not guarantee that I would not go and do the same thing again. I can't feel remorse, but only regret for my innocent victims."

He approved of being executed. "But it is doubtful," he said, "if they can wash off with my blood the blood I have shed. When I think about my deeds and in particular about the children, then I loathe myself so much that I am impatient for my execution."

He became morbidly fascinated with his own beheading towards the end, and asked Berg to describe the details of what would happen when his head was chopped off. Would he hear the blood gushing out—for that would be for him the greatest pleasure of all.

Dinner in Valparaiso

Some years ago a journalists' club gave a booby prize for the Least Gripping Headline of the year. It was won by one of the most respected London dailies.

"Small earthquake", ran the *So-and-So*'s headline, "in Chile. Few dead."

And indeed, a busy sub-editor could hardly be blamed for handling such a matter in such a way. Earthquakes are endemic to Chile as probably nowhere else, and the inhabitants accept them as a natural hazard. At Coquimbo observatory, forty earth tremors have been registered, on average, for each one of the past five years.

None of these has equalled a hundredth part of the force which dropped the town of Concepcion into the sea in 1751, or permanently raised the coast near Valparaiso by four feet over an area of 100,000 square miles.

Valparaiso was completely destroyed at that time and completely rebuilt, only to be extensively damaged on a number of other occasions. But in August, 1906, it was again a beautiful Spanish-American town on its semi-circular bay of the South Pacific. Its cheerful population of 180,000 did not care to look back on disaster.

South America has long had its share of Englishmen, or at least men with English names who have become a part of the New World. In 1906, one Englishman whose family had resided there for generations was Ivor Barrett. Like many others, he was completely bilingual, with twin sets of habits and customs and ideas which fitted him as well for life on a Chilean vineyard as for that of gentleman farmer in England. He read and talked a great deal in both Spanish and English—and the newspaper we referred to above was sent him from London in weekly bundles, arriving weeks later to be swallowed with delight and excitement as if the news each bundle held was new and straight from the press. And indeed, in those pre-broadcasting days, most of it was.

Ivor Barrett had frequent occasion to visit Valparaiso. He was a bachelor, and in his own eyes a gay one, but his fairly prosaic ritual was to have dinner in the Grand Hotel, by himself, before going on to the Victoria Theatre or to visit friends and sit up all night gossiping.

On this particular night, 16 August 1906, he was suddenly morose. He had as usual booked a table at the Grand Hotel, and it was only as the head-waiter ushered him to it, pulled out the chair, that Barrett remembered old Captain Lindsay.

With a gasp, he turned to the head-waiter. Ivor Barrett was about to remember a prior engagement, an engagement which would prevent his eating at the Grand that night.

Then with a shrug he sat down, spread napkins over knee and stomach, and accepted the menu. The long list of things to eat was in front of his eyes, but he could not concentrate. In any case, Ivor Barrett knew the list by heart, for its items seldom changed. That was one of the good things about the Grand, for a chap like Ivor: one knew what one was getting, knew it would be not only superb in its way, but familiar.

He pulled himself together and gave his order.

But, damn it—why had he been so foolish as to come back so soon? For it was exactly a fortnight since he had dined, and very nearly at this table, with Captain Lindsay, and now the old sea-dog was dead. Never again would he keep Ivor up until three in the morning with extraordinary tales of adventure around the world. He had died, peacefully and rapidly, they said, of pneumonia. Ivor, back on his vineyard, had not learnt, until it was too late to come and visit the old man on his hospital bed in Valparaiso's Calle de Blanco. He had even missed the funeral, and for this he could not forgive himself. Somehow he should have sensed the captain was unwell, should have kept in touch.

And now, as the first course was put down in front of him, he remembered that today was the 16th. It was already the night of the day Captain Lindsay had warned of.

He took a gold watch from his waistcoat pocket, irritably fumbling with the linen napkin which covered that part of him, and noted that 16 August had four hours to run. He smiled to himself: it had been another of the captain's wild fancies. Some of these came true, some did not—and yet the proportion of winners had been enough to provide Captain Lindsay with a firm reputation in Valparaiso as soothsayer.

What *was* it the old boy had said?

"Don't buy the strip, Ivor. Not until after the 16th."

Ivor had laughed and asked why.

"I'm not really sure I know, my boy. But you can take it from me you mustn't. And if you do, I'll come along and give you a piece of my mind, tell you what a fool you've been."

But Ivor Barrett had gone straight ahead and bought his strip of land. He would have been a fool not to, for he had wanted it for years, to round off the vineyard, and now it was going cheap. Previously his estate workers had been forced into a time-wasting detour on their way to a part cut off from the rest by a ten-acre triangle of weeds and scrub which belonged to someone else. That someone else had now died, the executors were prepared to sell, and Ivor was delighted with the deal. Next year those ten acres would have fledgling vines all over, and a few years later they would have more than repaid their cost.

He looked around him, stared at the handsome, well-bred, well-fed faces of men and women dotted like pale flowers in the semi-darkness of the huge dining-room. There was a peaceful drone of conversation. He thought how relaxing it was to be able to sit alone, and select any one of several conversations to listen to, without straining one's own powers. Half turning his head to listen to the table on his right, he found himself staring at the polished parquet flooring just beyond the shimmering white of his own table-cloth.

He turned back to his meal and as he did, the buzz of

conversation seemed to swell about him like music from the great organ he listened to each Sunday in the Church of Espiritu Santu. The buzz, the music, grew louder and louder.

Suddenly he knew it was not conversation, not human.

He made out just one human sound, a terrifying, spine-chilling sound, as a woman's high voice shrieked "*Terremoto!*"

His bottle of Chilean Cabernet leapt up from the table, moved vertically and quite slowly into the air, as if an invisible wine-waiter had come to pour it. When the bottle came down, the table was gone, and it landed, the right way up, on the parquet floor. It burst, and the red liquid spattered over his evening trousers. But now, suddenly, there was far too much happening for Ivor Barrett to care about trousers.

It was indeed a real, violent *terremoto*, an earthquake. Ivor Barrett had lived through many tremors, little movements of land which made one ask if they were real, but this was quite different. The great dining-room had begun to sway like a ship at sea, a ship in a storm, and the little wooden blocks of the parquet floor he had so admired were popping out like tiddly-winks. Everyone in the room— guests and waiters—seemed to be either screaming or praying. Several women had fainted. He had just time to consider how like a shipwreck it was and how the old sea dog Lindsay would have enjoyed it, before he got to his feet, started moving across a wildly gyrating floor to the door.

The hotel dining-room was on the first floor, with a wide flight of marble steps leading down, but the steps were heaving so crazily that he had to sit on the top one and wait for its movement to slow down sufficiently for him to keep his balance on the way down. A solid mass of men and women was building up behind him and he was almost pushed down the stair by their weight.

A woman making a high-pitched sound of terror the like of which Ivor Barrett had never heard before hurtled over his shoulder and plunged head first down the darkened, swaying, steps.

For it was really dark now: the lights had all gone out. The tremor seemed to be almost over and he lit a match.

Then, very carefully, he started to make his way, with a hundred others, down the marble staircase.

The match went out and at that moment his left foot felt nothing where instinct and a mathematical bent told him there would be a seventh stair. He fumbled for another match, and as he did there was a curse and a man elbowed past him. A moment later he dropped screaming through a gap where the seventh stair should have been.

Ivor jumped the gap and continued, driven by mad panic, to the ground floor, and out into the street.

It was raining heavily and the slowly swaying roadway was deep in mud and slush. The tremor had quickened again, and everywhere people were rushing panic-stricken out of houses. He felt suddenly sick, desperately sick, and as he bent forward a middle-aged woman flung herself at his feet, and lay there with arms about his ankles. "Please, please, señor," she said. "Please come, get my poor children out of the house. They are trapped . . ."

He raised her gently to her feet and followed as she led him down the road. They turned a corner, the woman pointed and suddenly the screams which had been all around them were drowned in the roar of falling masonry. The large building directly in front collapsed like a house of cards. The woman uttered a final piercing shriek and vanished among the debris.

He was alone, but no longer in the dark. All about him fires had broken out, providing a smoky glow as substitute for the street lights, and now Ivor Barrett could see, as in some hideous nightmare, the exact hell into which he had fallen. The shocks were still coming, regularly like labour pains, and with almost each one another building went roaring down in smoke and dust to bury its inmates in a great mound of rubble, and with them a part of the hysterical crowd in the street.

He realized he was almost hemmed in by flames, with only a narrow gap to his left where fires were not raging. Two little girls were standing beside him, weeping, and he picked up one under each arm and plunged through the gap. He put them down, pleasantly surprised at his own strength, and they vanished up the ruined street.

He heard a different type of screaming now, a woman's screaming punctuated by the hoarse grunt of a man's voice, then the sound of blows. Surely in this hell there was no room for a fight between husband and wife? As he approached, a man in a uniform which he recognized as that of a convict from the city jail got up from bending over a prostrate figure and ran away with an axe or a machete in his hand. Barrett reached the figure and knelt down.

Even among all this horror, the shock was so great, so sickening, that he nearly fainted. "Kill me, kill me," said the woman. "Please kill me, señor—"

She was trapped from the waist under tons of masonry, and almost certainly every bone was shattered beyond hope of repair. But it was the bits of her which Ivor Barrett could see which were so horrifying. Both her ears and two fingers from her left hand had been hacked off. And yet the thief, in his haste, had dropped one large ring on the ground.

To his relief the woman fainted—or died—and he stood up. But he went on staring at her in blank horror before he started to run again.

Days later, when Ivor Barrett had somehow survived this and what was to follow, he learnt that the wife of the President-elect had suffered just this fate. She had been dug out from the ruins, been carried on board the warship *O'Higgins*, but either she was dead before she reached it, or she died immediately afterwards. Barrett had never known the lady, but he wondered to his dying day if she had been the woman at his feet.

He staggered on. At last, overcome by exhaustion and horror, he sat down on the doorstep of an otherwise vanished house. There were flames in almost every direction, but he was too tired to care. He dropped his head in his arms.

As if in a dream, another nightmare, he heard the thud of something dropping in the ruined street. It was as if an angry god, not content with causing the earthquake, were hurling missiles from heaven at the survivors left below. He looked up at a particularly loud crash, but saw nothing. There were only the flickering, ugly, flames getting nearer; flames in every direction now, but he was too tired to worry.

It was an odd sound. Rather as if immense packing cases were dropped from a height, off the tops of buildings, to crash in the street and burst with the sound of tearing, splitting, wood.

As he sat there, another three exploded just beyond the circle of flame.

He got up, walked a pace or two, then sat down and closed his eyes. He had begun to realize exactly how a man must feel when he is drowning, when all the events of the past march, skip and gallop behind his closed eyelids. All this was happening to Ivor Barrett, and throughout the pageant of his past there was one face that looked at him, laughed at him, seemed to be providing a running commentary on his own thoughts. It was just as clear as it had been, fourteen nights ago, in the dining-room of the Grand Hotel. Captain Lindsay's old face was smiling, laughing, behind its beard, and the incredibly loud and clear voice was saying, "*Don't*, Ivor. Not until after the 16th. You mark my words, Ivor—the 16th——"

And this was the 16th. How right, tragically right, the old man had been. How he would have enjoyed this moment, this hour of triumphant I-told-you-so. For without doubt, and Ivor knew it, the new strip of land would have suffered in tonight's horror, might even have vanished altogether.

But of course the captain would not be gloating, wherever he was. Even the intrepid Captain Lindsay would be horrified by tonight's tragedy.

He opened his eyes and saw something on the ground a few feet away. It was a man, lying flat on his back, seeming to stare up at the red-tinged cloud of smoke which was blanketing everything. But Ivor could see, by the attitude of the limbs, that the man was dead.

Not knowing why, he got up and walked slowly and painfully to the corpse. It was, as he approached, very much a corpse, and in a state of advanced decay. He fumbled for a handkerchief, held it to his nose.

When he was only a foot or two from it, a large rat scuttled out from under the body. Ivor Barrett, for the first time in his life, screamed out loud. But not at the rat.

There, lying proudly, stiffly, at attention, eyes closed as in sleep but with an unmistakable knowing smile on his thin dead lips, was Captain Lindsay. The uniform was as well-pressed as ever, but the jacket was newly torn and two of the brass buttons were missing, leaving stout black threads behind. The blue uniform Ivor knew so well was grey, almost white, tonight, under its dusting of ash, but the medal ribbons were still in place, still clearly recognizable on the captain's left breast.

"Oh, my God!" screamed Ivor Barrett. "It—it can't be——"

But it was. And when his trembling hand touched the dead face, putrescent flesh came away on his fingertips and a still more sickening smell rose up to drown the reek of smoke.

Ivor Barrett took to his heels and ran—he knew not where—as fast and as far as he could.

A little later—perhaps a lot later, for the weird light in the sky must have been the approaching dawn—he lay down. He had run round the base of a small hill, and on this side of it, east of Valparaiso, there were no flames. And the earthquake was over.

Ivor Barrett survived his earthquake—but only for a few more years. Perhaps it was the shock that shortened his life, for he was only forty-two when the quake came. But he lived long enough to understand his nightmare, to discover how and why he had seen his old friend that night.

In fact, others had seen old friends that night, though most had been bleached and bony and mercifully unrecognizable. For the biggest cemetery of Valparaiso had been, and perhaps remains, on the crest of a rocky hill which overlooks the city. A courting couple who were there that night had been terrified, appalled, by the "dancing gravestones", which shot out of the earth like the wooden blocks from the parquet floor of the Grand Hotel. But the real horror had been reserved for those in the streets below. The local custom in Valparaiso had been to lay many coffins, not in graves dug in the earth, but in niches in the side of the hill. Part of the hill had collapsed during the quake, and hundreds of wooden coffins had been sent hurtling, stick by stick like the bombs of a later era, into the town below. These had exploded on impact, like bombs, and spilt their contents in the streets, on the rooftops, and in one case down a chimney.

Ivor Barrett's soul was scarred, forever. His health was shattered. But he had to admit that Captain Lindsay, of all people, would have enjoyed the joke. Perhaps he had.

The Cellars of Death

In the over-furnished drawing-room of a house beside Petro-grad's Winter Canal four people were indulging in tea and amiable chatter. Two were women—elderly Madame Golovina, widow of a state councillor, and her daughter Maria, more fondly known as Munia, a slight, meek-looking girl with fair hair and pale blue eyes. As Munia sipped her tea, those eyes returned again and again to the elder of the two men there, an incongruous figure for a drawing-room setting, with his peasant's smock and heavy boots, his dirty fingernails and dishevelled long hair and beard. Yet this was clearly the dominant member of that gathering, the focus of attention for both women and for the slim young aristocrat who made up the quartet.

But while the women's gaze spoke frankly of adoration, the young man's seemingly open smile and friendly address to the coarse being hid one vital secret: he was going to kill him.

The name Rasputin has, in the fifty-odd years that have passed since that tea-party, become synonymous with evil. To some extent it is a harsh judgement, based, like most such, on lack of information. There have been many Rasputins in history, some of them out-and-out villains, others men who, given a different background and circumstances, might have been seen as saints. To many people Rasputin was a saint: sage, comforter, healer, practical helper, combined. Hundreds of them queued on his stairs every day seeking an interview, counsel, money. He dispensed all these things, and was impelled to do so by a species of religious fervour backed by instinctive gifts that transcended his humble birth and lack of education.

Unfortunately, his self-confidence in his powers and his virtues had placed him, in his own opinion, above other men; certainly beyond their reproach for whatever he chose to do, whether in the form of the seduction or rape of female admirers, orgies of drink and debauchery involving noblewomen, officers' wives, servant girls and prostitutes, and, more serious in its consequences for Russia herself, his influence over the easy-going Tsar and enraptured Tsarina which enabled him to arrange high appointments for officials shrewd enough to tender him the right sort of gifts in the appropriate quantities.

Rasputin put down his tea cup, leaned across and abruptly kissed Munia on the mouth. It was not a peck of affection, but a harsh smacking, audible kiss. Munia did not resist, nor push his hand away when he placed it on her body. Her mother did not spring up with an outraged protest. To both women, as to hundreds of others of varying social degrees, a kiss and a fondle from the "Little Father" represented a sanctification, rather than an affront.

To Prince Yussupov it appeared differently. Barely able to restrain himself from leaping from his chair and seizing the bigger man by the throat, he managed to smile on unconcernedly, thrusting aside his revulsion by concentrating on the practical question—what would be the best way to commit murder?

It was 1916. Grigori Efimovitch Rasputin was forty-five years old. He had been born in the province of Tobolsk, Siberia, the son of a village carter. As a child he had been a mixture of unruliness, tenderness and serious-mindedness. As a youth he had been dissipated, wenching enthusiastically and drinking himself insensible night after night, even after his marriage to a village girl. One day, while ploughing, he had a heavenly vision: as a child he had been fascinated by the stories and pictures in the family Bible. He wondered whether God had something in mind for him. Then, in his early thirties and working at his father's trade, he chanced to fall into conversation with a theological student whom he was driving to a monastery. The student was amazed by the peasant's grasp of religious essentials and urged him to enter the monastery and develop them. Rasputin took him at his word: he did not drive home that night, but became a monk.

He could not have hit upon a community better suited to his nature than this one. A great many of its members belonged to the heretical creed, Khlysty, which held that salvation could only be gained by repentance for sin; and since one couldn't seek forgiveness for sins one hadn't sinned, it was quite in order to go on sinning merrily in order to acquire ample scope for repentance and build up a formidable claim to salvation. The Khlysty adherents at the monastery were there ostensibly to be disciplined back into Orthodoxy; but their enjoyable creed, offering full scope for the human lusts, had infected many of those who were supposed to be reforming them. It certainly commended itself to a man of Rasputin's tendencies.

It was a Khlysty practice to feign devout Orthodoxy, in order to protect the essential mystery of the faith. Rasputin eagerly set about learning the externals of religious observance which in future he would wear like a suit of clothes. It would be unfair to him to suggest that he adopted the Khlysty practice purely because of the prospect it offered of a life of lust in the name of God. He genuinely believed in the doctrine "Sin in order that you may obtain forgiveness". The fact is, by nature, he was capable of sin on a wholesale basis.

Prince Yussupov, accepting another cup of tea from Madame Golovina's hands, brooded on the unconcealed manifestations of Rasputin's life of divine sinning. Like everyone else in Petrograd, he knew of the luxury of the monk's flat and of the special room reserved there for the initiation of new female disciples. Though many men were amongst the crowds which jammed Rasputin's stairway every day and sometimes thronged the street outside, women predominated. While he would gladly receive men, listen to their troubles and their petitions, accept the banknotes and the hampers of wine they pressed on him, and give them in return his advice, spiritual and worldly, his promise of assistance in the right quarter, or even some of the cash that some wealthier supplicant had given him only minutes before (there was always a balance left over in his favour), it was a woman he really preferred to see coming through the door.

She might be old and repulsive: he dispensed counsel, sometimes gentle, sometimes abusive. Her face might be well familiar—one of his closest band of disciples who gathered daily at the flat to drink tea with him and chatter and make themselves available if he should feel the urge to bring himself a little nearer to salvation. But she might be a newcomer, and pretty: if so, Rasputin indicated the door of his special sanctum . . .

Some women came to the monk from urgent religious need, imbibed his doctrines and gave him their bodies willingly, convinced that they were doing themselves immense spiritual good. The experience genuinely exalted them, and they did not conceal it from their husbands. Not unnaturally, some of the latter objected and there were attempts to confront Rasputin, with violence in mind. They were evaded by the shrewd monk or foiled by the official agents who both kept guard over and spied upon this powerful friend of the royal family. Some men meekly accepted and condoned their wives' quest for salvation through the flesh. Perhaps without realizing it, there were women who rejoiced in this literally Heaven-sent opportunity to obtain sexual satisfaction without the complications and stresses of having a lover. Orthodox religious teaching of the sinfulness of bodily desires was no more gratifying to healthy human beings several decades ago than it is today. With Rasputin, his disciples could satisfy their bodies and improve their souls: almost too good a bargain to be true.

When the monk invited a newcomer into his inner sanctum he would first sit down opposite her, gripping her knees between his strong legs, and talk gently of the need to seek salvation. He would urge her to attend Communion. Sometimes he would dismiss her there and then, telling her to come back in a week and to attend scrupulously to her religious observances meanwhile. But more likely he would begin to talk more urgently of the way salvation would be achieved, of the need to repent, and to sin in order to repent. By now his deep-set blue eyes would be shining with a strange light, his wrinkled face, with its pock-marked nose, somehow no longer ugly, his uncultured voice no longer harsh, but moving, persuasive in its tone as well as in the increasing suggestiveness of the words. The woman, unless she were resistant to what must have been an hypnotic power, would scarcely be aware that his rough, dirty hands were now fondling her, working at her clothing, that he was leaning forward to hiss some obscenity before crushing her mouth with his and ripping her dress.

If, shocked and repelled, the woman held herself back and tried to leave, she might be raped, or nearly, then flung from the room with what clothes she had managed to retain. There was no restraining Rasputin on the road to Glory.

The murder in Prince Yussupov's heart swelled as he thought of these things and tried to forget that pretty, meek Munia, who should have married his late brother, and her mother were amongst Rasputin's most ardent sympathizers. Should he poison him? Or shoot him? Where could he do it, and how could he escape the consequences? For although countless good people were revolted by Rasputin's orgies, his boasting, his influence, and many bad ones wished him ill from jealousy or because he had refused them something they wanted, his following was more than a mere band of supplicants and adoring women: it was headed by the Tsar and Tsarina themselves.

Rasputin had been introduced to Nicholas II—first cousin of George V of England—and Alexandra—formerly a princess of Hesse, and Queen Victoria's granddaughter—at a time of personal anguish at the court of Tsarskoe Selo. Their child Alexei, the Tsarevitch, suffered from the dread disease of haemophilia, in which the slightest injury or bump could cause an external or internal bleeding that nothing could stem. If the bleeding did not halt naturally the child must bleed to death. Though every precaution was taken to safeguard the child, who was frequently denied even ordinary play, he had to hurt himself at times. It was while he was writhing in his bed after some slight injury, in excruciating pain from internal bleeding and likely to die, that the youngest of the royal daughters, Anastasia, mentioned the name of Rasputin to the deeply religious Tsarina. The monk had already created a stir with his devoutness—it was before scandal had begun to rear its head—and was reported to have accomplished many cures of the sick. The Tsarina's own confessor, the Archimandrite Feofan, had been much impressed by him and saw in the inspired peasant an exalted symbol of the worthy Russian people of the soil, the backbone of the country and supposedly trustiest defenders of the monarchy against the flooding tide of revolution.

Desperate for their child, the Tsar and Tsarina agreed that Rasputin should be brought to the palace secretly so as not to inflame the jealousies of court officials at the royal family turning to a peasant for help. Rasputin was accordingly summoned. He arrived as unkempt as ever and immediately seized both the astonished Tsar and Tsarina and kissed them resoundingly. Then he prayed beside the Tsarevitch's bed and began to talk to and caress him, telling him stories about Siberia, and animals, and folk-tales. For the first time for days the child smiled, and then sat up and began to chatter animatedly, and said he no longer felt any pain.

Rasputin was urged to return night after night. Before long the entire royal family had come to regard him as their indispensable counsellor and intimate friend. Aware of the inevitability of revolution, surrounded by traitors and spies, the Tsar and Tsarina cared for little but one another. The mounting discontent in the land was less at what the ruler did than at what he did not do. Neglect of his people was his crime, and a lazy resort to force to quell any objections they ventured to raise. He was a weak man, dominated by the wife he adored, his mind full of forebodings for the future. When Rasputin told him, "If you part from me you will lose your son and crown within six months," the Tsar was only too ready to believe it. Rasputin was openly admitted to the royal circle and many court ladies became his followers. Some were initiated in the usual manner. It has been alleged that the Tsarina herself was among them.

So it was, mused the prince with murder in his heart, that this disgusting being who sprawled opposite him had risen to fortune and notoriety. His influence was tremendous through his intimacy with the royal family, of which he boasted ceaselessly and disgustingly. He behaved scandalously in private and public. The orgies he conducted in the annexe of the restaurant Villa Rode were known to everyone. Every night he took one or more women to his flat, and every night he drank himself unconscious with bottle after bottle of Madeira wine.

Protests to the Tsar had no effect: Nicholas put them down to jealous attacks. Rasputin had taken the precaution of warning him that his enemies were agents of Satan, sent to divide the Holy monk from the Holy Father of all the Russians and destroy them both. Yet he himself had come to be widely termed the Holy Devil.

In June, 1914, a broken-down prostitute named Guseva went up to Rasputin near his home and asked for money. He put his hand in his pocket. She thrust the knife she was holding deep into his stomach, shrieking: "Antichrist is finished!"

Fortunately for Rasputin she continued to rave hysterically, not noticing that he was still on his feet and so not thinking to stab him again. Clutching the wound with his hands, he managed to hold back the gush of blood while he staggered round the corner to his house, where he collapsed. A doctor operated on him on the dining-table and he was removed to hospital, where several times during the next few weeks he nearly died.

The attack had not been a spontaneous one by an aggrieved victim. Guseva, neurotic and suffering from religious mania, had been put up to it by a group of the monk's most devoted enemies. These were growing in number and stature— and now, after the passing of a few more months, they included this handsome, fabulously wealthy, young Prince Yussupov, husband of one of the Tsar's nieces, the beautiful Princess Irina Alexandrovna.

Yussupov seemingly had everything a man could desire— in material terms. But like many Russian aristocrats at that time he was unspeakably bored, lacking any aim in life, grateful for the stimulation of any new activity. His distaste for Rasputin and resentment at the monk's contempt for the aristocracy provided just such a stimulus, and once the prince had decided to murder the man he entered that frame of mind which sees added justification in every report of some new outrageous act or remark. He became convinced that what he intended to do would be from the highest motives and for the greatest good of Russia and its monarchy.

Yussupov mulled over scheme after scheme for disposing of the monk. Some outright form of assassination in the street was out of the question: the thing should be done with style, preferably in some way that would permit Rasputin to realize how he had been tricked and overcome and force him to recognize, even confess, that he was not the all-powerful, invincible demi-God he thought he was, but merely an upstart peasant.

Prince Yussupov had several conspirators, among them a Polish physician, Dr Lasovert, a member of the Duma (House of Representatives), Purishkevitch, a cavalry officer, Lieutenant Suchotin, and Yussupov's own valet. A cunning move was to add to their number a brother officer of the Prince, the Grand Duke Dimitri. As a member of the royal family it seemed highly fitting that he should have a hand in the destruction of this menace to the monarchy; as a lover of decadent literature he would presumably welcome the experience; but, more importantly, as an imperial prince he was not subject to the criminal laws—and it was additionally stipulated that none of the companions-in-crime of any member of the royal family could be prosecuted either. Dimitri was the conspirators' insurance policy: he consented eagerly to join them.

Yussupov began to court the company of Rasputin, hating every moment of it, yet revelling in his intention. Hence the tea-party at the Golovinas', arranged by the unwitting Munia after Yussupov had expressed casual interest in meeting the monk. Rasputin was at the top—or bottom—of his form that day, pawing and kissing Munia, arrogantly shouting his contempt for aristocrats, government ministers and church leaders, talking to Yussupov as if to an inferior, and insisting again and again that he had only to tell the Tsar and Tsarina of anything he wanted done to be obeyed without question. Yussupov fought back his hatred, smiled indulgently, and nodded as if in agreement with every outrageous utterance.

His plan, he saw, must be to gain Rasputin's complete confidence. The monk was no fool. He knew through informants and direct threats that there were men who would kill him at the least opportunity. He was careful not to give them the chance by going about alone where they could reach him, or accepting invitations to places unknown to him. Yussupov must break down this resistance where he himself was concerned; for it had occurred to him that the ideal setting for the murder would be his own grand palace.

Suddenly, a thrill ran through him as he realized that a

short route to his objective lay before him. He had heard
Munia telling Rasputin how talented Yussupov was at singing gipsy songs to his own guitar; and the monk's face had
brightened as he had answered that there was nothing he
liked more than to hear gipsy music. Yussupov agreed to
bring his guitar to their next meeting—and told himself in
his mind that it would be the promise of an evening of gipsy
songs in the Yussupov Palace that would lure Rasputin to
his death.

The conspirators got busy. A disused room in the palace,
partly below ground level, seemed the best place for a
murder: no sound from it would be heard outside. The
prince gave orders for it to be decorated and furnished, and
in a short time the low, vaulted-roofed annexe to the wine
cellars, with its stone floor and walls, took on the appearance
of a gracious little dining-room, luxuriously furnished, that
might always have been used as such.

The method of murder was debated. It was decided to use
poison, which Dr Lasovert would provide. Heavy chains
would be procured, in readiness for weighting Rasputin's
body to sink it to the bottom of the Neva.

Prince Yussupov duly sang and played his guitar for
Rasputin at another of the Golovinas' tea parties. The performance so pleased the monk that he began to address and
treat Yussupov as one of his most valued friends, giving him
the right to enter his flat without ceremony whenever he
chose. These warm gestures might have disarmed many
would-be murderers and made them abandon their plans in
shame. They did not have this effect on Yussupov and his
fellows. The date was set for 16 December and an invitation
sent to Rasputin to come to the Yussupov Palace that evening for some refreshment and music. He accepted.

Yussupov asked Rasputin to arrive very late, because his
parents, who lived in the palace, were regrettably not in
favour of his friendship with the monk and would resent his
being invited there.

The fateful day arrived. Towards evening a friendly fire
was lit in the cellar of death. Yussupov supervised the
servants as they laid places for six people and brought in
wine, tea and cakes, then dismissed them for the night.
When they had gone the other conspirators entered. Lasovert drew a pair of rubber gloves from his pocket, wriggled

his hands into them and then brought out a small box. Carefully lifting the top layer of a large chocolate cake, he sprinkled on the lower half enough potassium cyanide to kill a household. Then he returned the chocolate-coated layer of the cake, which seemed, to the men's eyes, to have grown into something enormous, so dominant an object it had become in that room.

To heighten the effect of casualness they decided to make it appear that they had already taken tea there. A little tea was poured into several cups and allowed to go cold. A few crumbs were scattered on the tablecloth and the items on it disarranged. Chairs were pushed back from the table, as though men had risen from them. Yussupov brought down his guitar and hung it on the wall.

There was some discussion about who should be present in Rasputin's company. He would obviously become suspicious if he entered and found a group of men; but the Grand Duke Dimitri urged Yussupov to let him be there, and if possible, do something positive. The prince stood firm: he alone could receive Rasputin without risk of his taking flight. The others must wait in an upstairs room, where they should play the gramophone to give the monk the impression that the rest of the household was merrily preoccupied in an entirely normal fashion.

With Dr Lasovert in the guise of his chauffeur, Yussupov drove to Rasputin's flat. It was nearly midnight. The streets were dark and empty and bitterly cold, the swept snow lying in great piles along their sides.

Rasputin was ready when the car arrived. He had spent an unremarkable day, resting in the morning from the effects of a more than commonly heavy night's drinking, receiving a few ladies later and taking tea as usual with a gathering of his women disciples. In the evening he had rested more before putting on his best new silk blouse and highly polished black knee-boots.

A late visitor had been an agitated Protopopov, recently appointed Minister of the Interior through Rasputin's influence. He had come to warn his mentor that a new plot was afoot against him and to beg him to take extra care for the next few days. Rasputin smiled and told him he was being over-anxious. God would protect him from any danger.

Rasputin entered Yussupov's car and was driven to the palace, Yussupov trying all the way not to show the fluttering of his nerves and forcing himself not to glance too often through the rear window. They were not followed. They entered the palace by a side door. Dr Lasovert withdrew to join the other conspirators, and Prince Yussupov escorted the unsuspicious monk down to the room that was to be his death-chamber.

Throwing off his fur coat, Rasputin prowled around the room, examining the furniture. Striving to sound casual, Yussupov invited him to take a glass of wine. To his dismay, the monk refused and asked for tea. His knees almost collapsing under him from the nervous strain, the prince drew two glasses of tea from the samovar and handed Rasputin one. Then he pushed towards him a plate of cakes.

This was not the poisoned chocolate cake and the tea had not been doctored, so the prince was able to drink and eat with his victim. Fortuitously, it must have helped to allay any suspicions Rasputin might have had, and steadied Yussupov's twitching nerves. They chatted for a while. Rasputin told Yussupov about Protopopov's warning and boasted how God would never permit the spite and envy of aristocrats to bring him down. If Yussupov was feeling any qualms of conscience about what he was doing, this sneer at his own class probably dispelled them. Without more ado, he passed Rasputin the chocolate cake.

The monk grabbed a large piece and stuffed it in his mouth. He ate and gulped for some moments, then remarked, "It's very sweet"—and reached for some more.

Almost petrified with the drama of the moment, Yussupov just managed not to gape. Lasovert had assured him that the cake contained poison enough to kill several people, and that death would be almost instantaneous; yet, as the prince stared, here was Rasputin licking his lips with satisfaction and stretching out his hand for yet another piece.

Yussupov had to wrench himself out of his amazement. Shakily, he pushed back his chair and went over to the side table where the bottles waited. He poured a glass of the heavily poisoned wine and took it to the monk. Rasputin, munching thickly, nodded and, with a great gulp, washed down the poisoned cake with the poisoned wine.

To Yussupov's horror, Rasputin nodded his satisfaction

and held up his glass for more. It was all the prince could do to pour it. The monk tossed it back and smacked his lips.

"Aren't you going to sing something?" he demanded. "Something gay."

Feeling that he was living a nightmare, the dazed murderer obediently took down his guitar from the wall and commenced to serenade his victim.

The firelight flickered on the walls. The ugly, long-haired monk sat hunched forward in his chair, his elbows on the table, another glass of wine between his hands, his eyes never leaving the prince as Yussupov sang in his attractive voice one of the old gipsy songs Rasputin loved so dearly. The conspirators in the room above were silent now, waiting, wondering why they had not yet received a sign from Yussupov that it was all over.

The prince began another song. Rasputin munched another piece of cake and drank more wine. Out of their hearing the clocks of Petrograd struck half past two. For nearly two hours the monk had been imbibing a poison that should have thrown him into a writhing death agony almost at the first taste.

As Yussupov sang he noticed that the monk's head was drooping somewhat, the lank hair falling on to the tablecloth. He saw him swallow hard, as if with difficulty, and rub his hand across his eyes.

"Are you all right?" the prince asked.

"Just a bitter taste in my mouth." Rasputin heaved himself up and began to pace the room. "Give me some more wine."

The prince poured him some. Rasputin took a deep draught of it. Standing still, his eyes caught and held Yussupov's. Not daring to break the stare, lest it reveal his guilt, Yussupov saw Rasputin's eyes suddenly harden. They seemed to bore hypnotically into the younger man's inmost self. He felt his head beginning to throb, his will subjecting itself to the monk's. If this kept up another few moments he would collapse, or blurt out a confession and beg forgiveness.

Suddenly Rasputin's expression changed. He tossed down the wine, lurched to the side table to help himself to more and drank it off. Yussupov's restraint was shattered. Pointing to a crystal crucifix on a corner cupboard, he shouted, "Father Grigori, you would do well to get on your knees and pray."

Rasputin stood for a moment, seemingly amazed. Then his face once again changed to a look of serene resignation. As he saw this, Yussupov knew that he could delay no longer. He must get it over before all resolution left him.

Whipping out a revolver, he aimed at Rasputin's chest and squeezed the trigger.

In the confined space the explosion seemed tremendous. Rasputin's hands flew to his breast. With a dreadful bellow he crumpled to the richly carpeted floor.

Moments later the door burst open and the other conspirators burst in, wide-eyed. Through the drifting haze of cordite they saw Yussupov standing, revolver in hand. Rasputin lay on his back, eyes shut, face grimacing, fists clenched as if in determination not to succumb. A red stain was spreading over the silk of his blouse.

Dr Lasovert knelt to examine him, and as he did so the agonized features became still. Lasovert's inspection was brief. Nodding to his fellows, he indicated that Rasputin was dead, shot in the heart.

The Grand Duke Dimitri and Minister Purishkevitch heaved the body off the carpet to an area of exposed stone floor before any damning blood could cause a stain. Then the light was switched off and the conspirators left, locking the door behind them, leaving the corpse of the Holy Devil in the dancing firelight.

The tension ended, they could at last chatter and laugh, congratulating themselves on a patriotic deed accomplished. But there was urgent action to be taken. Despite the irregular hours he kept, and his habit of being in several places in the course of a night, Rasputin might already have been missed. And when word reached the Tsar or Tsarina, or any other of his high-placed associates, the search for him would be immediate and vigorous.

"Quickly, Suchotin! You're nearest to his size and build. Put on his coat and hat. Lasovert will drive you and Dimitri in the direction of Rasputin's place. Make sure someone sees you as you go. They'll remember that Rasputin left here safely and made for home. We can't be accountable for what happened to him after that."

"What about the clothes?"

· "They'll be burnt."

Yussupov and Purishkevitch were left alone in the prince's study. An oppressive silence hung between them. They smoked continuously, Yussupov trying to fight back a new urge that was threatening to overcome him . . . to go down and have another look at the body.

He could prevent himself no longer. He opened the study door and listened: there was no sound in the palace. Quietly, the prince went down the steps again and unlocked the cellar door. Bathed in firelight, the body lay there just as he might have expected it to. Yet Yussupov could not quite bring himself to believe that the monster was dead. Any man who could absorb all that poison, it seemed, might even be able to take a shot in the chest and not die. Was he shamming? He was motionless, eyes shut—stone dead . . . And yet . . . Yussupov found himself suddenly shaking the corpse, like one shakes a stopped watch. It had no effect. Rasputin's head lolled and he flopped limply to the floor when his murderer let him go.

Yussupov straightened up . . . and then froze. One of the dead man's eyelids had started to twitch.

It must be a flicker of firelight on the face. The prince bent again. At that instant the eye opened wide.

Now it was really a nightmare, for the other eye had also begun to flicker, and then opened. Like a reincarnated corpse, Rasputin was beginning to stir. Prince Yussupov was helpless to move or cry out. He could only stand and watch the body heaving itself upright, to stand erect and, with an almost sightless stare, blunder towards him, mouth frothing, hands outstretched for his throat.

The next instant Yussupov was in Rasputin's grasp. Perhaps it was the physical contact that broke the spell of horror: but he managed to wrench himself free and stumble to the door. Rasputin stood swaying, muttering the prince's name. Falling with haste, the prince managed to get upstairs to his study, where Purishkevitch raised an astonished face.

"Quick! Your revolver. He's still alive!"

Purishkevitch started to unpack the revolver. It was the Grand Duke Dimitri's, and after using it Yussupov had handed it over to be put back into its case. Purishkevitch's hands were trembling so much that he could scarcely get it out again; and as he struggled they both heard a sound which struck chill terror into them . . . Rasputin was coming up the stairs.

They ran to the head of them and looked down. The monk was crawling painfully up on all fours. Poisoned and shot though he was, it seemed that he possessed more power than they; that if he ever reached them he would find the resources to slay them both. It was with some relief that they saw him reach a small landing, stagger upright again and burst out of a door to the courtyard which Yussupov could have sworn had been locked.

With a desperate tug, Purishkevitch freed the revolver and dashed down the stairs. Hesitating only a moment, Yussupov followed him, seizing a rubber truncheon one of the other conspirators had brought. Before he could catch sight of the other two in the darkness of the snow-covered courtyard he heard two shots, terribly loud in the stillness. Then he saw Rasputin, still walking towards one of the three gateways to the street.

At all costs he had to be stopped. Yussupov started forward with the rubber truncheon, but the crash of two more shots halted him. He saw Rasputin check, stagger, and collapse into the snow. He saw Purishkevitch step forward, gun in hand, and stoop to examine the body, before turning back into the palace. And then, in his shocked state, he became aware of running feet and people's voices. Glancing towards the gate, he saw a policeman entering. So the killing would not go undetected as hoped and planned.

The policeman, recognizing the prince, saluted.

"Shots have been reported, Your Excellency. Has there been some trouble?"

Yussupov heard his own voice answer, "No, no. One of my guests seems to have drunk too much. He started firing a revolver into the air. I'm sorry you've been disturbed."

Yussupov waited for the policeman's next words—but they were not what he expected. The man was saluting again.

"Very good, Your Excellency."

It suddenly dawned on Yussupov that a pile of disturbed snow was hiding Rasputin's body from the policeman's sight. They were going to get away with it, after all. He moved to the gate with the man.

"No need to bother making a report, I imagine?"

"As you wish, Your Excellency."

And the man was gone, ushering the few onlookers away with him.

After some moments, Yussupov went back to where Rasputin lay . . . and again terror struck him. The body was not in the same position. Incredibly, miraculously, the man still lived.

In a dreadful frenzy of frustration, hate and terror, Yussupov raised the rubber truncheon and brought it down again and again on the crumpled figure in the snow, the attack becoming more and more hysterical until the prince finally collapsed in the arms of Purishkevitch and lost consciousness.

When the other conspirators returned and Dr Lasovert saw Prince Yussupov's condition he firmly forbade him to take any active part in what remained to be done. While Yussupov slept deeply on a couch, watched over by Purishkevitch, the others wrapped the corpse in a blanket and drove it through the faint dawn light to one of the bridges across the Neva, at a point where the thick ice on the river had been broken. The chains had been overlooked: instead, they bound the hands and feet with rope, still unable to believe that Rasputin was beyond all ability to escape. Sure that no one was coming, they quickly tipped the heavy body over the railings and let it fall. It went straight into the clear water and was seen to sink at once. Exhausted and nauseated, the men fell into their car and drove away along the silent, snow-piled streets of Petrograd.

But Rasputin's body did not drift away under the all-concealing ice, which would not thaw for several months. It remained where it had been dropped. The policeman did report the shots in the night, and Rasputin was soon reported missing. Some workmen found a blood-stained galosh on the bridge and blood-stains on the rail and on the ice below, and a diver easily recovered the bound body.

It was not long before several strands of circumstantial evidence were quickly woven into a pattern whose logical centre could only be Prince Yussupov and the Grand Duke Dimitri. The Tsarina, who had passed hours in weeping bitterly and praying after hearing the news of the murder, called them furiously to account. The conspirators could not be touched by the ordinary processes of law, but that did not safeguard them from anything the Tsar might order. Nicholas was away at his front-line headquarters, but hurried back. Given her own way, the Tsarina would have had the men summarily executed. In the event, they were merely banished, which, it turned out, saved their lives. For within that same year, in another cellar of death, the royal family with which they were connected were massacred.

Rasputin had prophesied: "If you part from me you will lose your son and crown within six months." Strangely, his own terrible death was reflected in that of the royal family, victims of an equally dreadful revenge for what they represented.

The irony is that the exterminators of the Romanov family bundled them unceremoniously into a cellar, shot and bayoneted them, then burned the bodies with fire and acid in a disused mine-shaft in a forest. The murderer of the peasant Rasputin furnished his cellar of death as a sumptuous room, plied his victim with food and drink—albeit poisoned—and serenaded him to guitar accompaniment. And, after, the empress sent a coffin for the remains, had them buried in royal ground, and prayed over them daily. No one did that for her.

The Killers in the Signal-Box

North of Carlisle, over the River Eden and its marshy meadows, there are only a few miles to go before road and rail reach the Scottish border. For the railway the actual border comes at the crossing of the River Sark north of Gretna Junction, just before the lines diverge, one heading for Dumfries and the other for Lockerbie and the famous climb up Beattock Bank.

Immediately over the border is Gretna Green with all its romantic, if commercialized, connotations. In its heyday the old Caledonian Railway was equally romantic, with its splendid blue-liveried engines and the almost military pride of its drivers. Great expresses from London might be drawn the length of England by Sassenach locomotives; but when they reached Carlisle they had to be handed over to the imperious Caledonian engines for their journey onward into Scotland.

At a quarter to twelve and at midnight on 21 May, 1915, two expresses left Euston for Scotland. They lost time on the way, and by the time they approached Carlisle in the clear light of morning they were running half an hour late. A local passenger-train had been waiting for them to pass, but in view of the delay it was allowed to go ahead so that connexions farther along the line would not be disrupted. This was not an unusual procedure. Less than a mile and a half north of Gretna there were loops on both the up and down lines, into which slow traffic could be diverted when fast trains were hard on their heels.

These loops were situated close to Quintinshill signal-box. The box was just one in a sequence of block posts, controlling blocks or sections of line to ensure that each section was occupied by only one train at a time; but after today's work its name would become famous—or infamous.

As the local entered Gretna, the signal-man's telephone there rang. The caller was Meakin, the duty signal-man at Quintinshill.

"The boy'll get a ride today," he said.

This cryptic observation was perfectly understood by the Gretna man. Meakin was due to hand over at six o'clock but his relief, James Tinsley, often arranged not to come on until half past six. Tinsley lived in the station cottages at Gretna Junction and was in a good position to know when the local was likely to stop at Quintinshill, so that he could cadge a lift on it instead of having to walk the whole distance.

It was quite contrary to regulations that he should ride on the foot-plate. It was contrary to regulations that he should, by private arrangement, report late for duty. There were to be other things in the next hour which would flagrantly contravene regulations. From the moment Tinsley stepped on that foot-plate, the sequence of events had all the hideous inevitability of Greek tragedy.

The local made its way to Quintinshill, only to find the loop off the north-bound line filled by a waiting goods-train. Into the loop on the south-bound side was slowly running a train of Welsh coal empties. Meakin leaned from the signal-box and waved to indicate that he was temporarily switching the local on to the south-bound main line until the north-bound expresses had gone through. There was nothing against this provided due precautions were taken. Nothing to worry about.

When the train had been switched and had come to a standstill, Tinsley and the fireman got down and went to the box.

The brakemen from the two goods-trains decided to join the gathering. This, too, was unauthorized. Rules were explicit. If the guard, brakeman or fireman of any train had cause to communicate information to a signal-box, he should do so as concisely as possible, sign the train register in the box, and go. When a train was shunted on to a wrong line, it was the fireman's duty to report the train's presence to the box, check that the signal-man had placed a safety-collar on the relevant signal-lever, sign the register, and go.

Hutchinson, the fireman from the local, ought to have done just this. But it all seemed a bit pompous. After all, the outgoing signal-man knew the local was on the up main line because he himself had switched it there; and Tinsley, the incoming signal-man, knew it was there because he had just travelled up on its foot-plate.

Tinsley had brought the morning paper with him. Meakin was anxious to skim through the news, but before he could settle down the bell from Gretna asked a "line clear" for the first express. Meakin accepted it. He notified Kirkpatrick, the next block post, which also accepted it. The train entered section, raced through, and roared off safely into the distance.

Meakin now handed over to Tinsley and settled down with the paper. He did not notify anybody that the south-bound main line was occupied by the local; nor did Tinsley think to do so. And Hutchinson did not point out that the safety-collar was not in position.

This collar was essential to safe working. It slipped between the lever and its release catch so that no forgetful operator could move the lever and inadvertently give an all-clear signal on an occupied line. Taken in conjunction with the methodical operation of the block system, it provided an almost foolproof safeguard for the successive sections of track.

Almost foolproof . . .

Having taken over, Tinsley dutifully set danger signals on the north-bound track, and undutifully began to enter up the register. So that the authorities should not discover the half-hour discrepancy, Meakin was in the habit of listing movements after six o'clock on a separate sheet of paper, which Tinsley would then copy into the register in his own handwriting. Meakin concentrated on the newspaper and on gossiping about the war to his companions. Tinsley concentrated on cooking the record-book.

The telephone rang. Tinsley was informed that the

second express, due from Carlisle at 6.5 but now half an hour late, had left and was on its way.

He went on writing, but again was interrupted, this time by the bell from Kirkpatrick asking "line clear" for a south-bound troop-train. Meakin had earlier received and recorded the message that this train would be coming through. That was why he had shunted the slow coal empties to one side.

Tinsley accepted the train.

Hutchinson decided to saunter back to his engine. He signed the book part-way down the page, leaving ample room for Tinsley to complete his entries, then left.

A minute later the bell announced that the troop-train was entering the section. Tinsley sent his own bell signal to Gretna, which agreed to accept the train.

The local which had brought Tinsley himself to this box was standing there below him, in full view. But he was half listening to the conversation of the others and half worrying about getting back to the register before too many things piled up. He reached for the signal-lever controlling the south-bound main line and gave the all-clear for his section.

Another bell snatched at his attention. It announced the second express coming north from Gretna. Tinsley accepted it, and pulled his down signals.

Both the up and the down main lines were now signalled as clear.

At any second during these last few minutes there might have been a chance of averting disaster. One correct action might have cancelled out the mistakes so far made and restored the balance. But the chances were inexorably piling up on one side of the balance only. The victims were racing to meet one another.

The troop-train carried half a battalion of Royal Scots, on their way to Liverpool for embarkation. They all came from families in the Leith area and had been together right through their training. The fifteen passenger-coaches contained fifteen officers and 470 men, and behind them were six vans containing stores and ammunition. The coaches were elderly wooden-framed stock, lit by oil-gas from cylinders slung below the floor-boards, fully charged at high pressure only a short time before.

From north of Quintinshill there was a clear view down

the gently descending three-mile straight which then began to curve slowly under the bridge near the signal-box. The troop-train had been gathering speed down the steep slope from Beattock and the shallower slope approaching the border, and by now was doing a good seventy miles an hour. The signals were clear and visibility was good.

Except for that curve.

The driver and fireman had no cause for alarm. There was an unusual huddle of trains by the signal-box, but obviously they must be standing on the loops. The goods-train in the down siding obscured the main line, but once beyond the bridge there would be a clear view again.

The train raced down the slight gradient and under the bridge. And there, immediately ahead, was the engine of the local train, facing them on their own line.

There was no escape. The two engines met head-on. The impact was heard miles away, like a great explosion. Coaches of the troop-train telescoped and were crushed forward. The local train was driven savagely back some forty yards. The tender of the troop-train wrenched itself round, pulling the splintering coaches with it and heaping wreckage over the parallel north-bound line.

The force of the collision was such that the troop-train's overall length of 213 yards was reduced to less than seventy yards.

In the signal-box, Meakin dropped his paper.

"Whatever have you done, Jimmy?"

"What can be wrong?" Tinsley stared aghast at the instruments and levers. "The signals are all right. What's wrong?"

Smoke, steam and flame gushed up outside the windows of the box. The fire from the troop-train engine had spilled out on to the track, and collapsed on top of it were the shattered wooden carriages. Hot ash thrown from the crumpled local engine added to the blaze.

The equipment vans at the back of the troop-train had broken free and had rolled some way back up the gradient. Before they could start drifting down again, the brakeman of the coal-train dashed up and applied the brakes. At least the fire was saved from the addition of the battalion stores and, above all, the ammunition.

Not that the situation could have been much worse than it already was. There was the sudden puff of an explosion, and then another. The gas cylinders cracked, and the ferocity of the inferno increased.

Tinsley couldn't believe it. He couldn't move.

"Jimmy!" Meakin was shouting hysterically. "Where's the 6.5?"

Tinsley remained frozen where he stood. Meakin made a vain dash towards the levers to set the signals to danger on the north-bound line. He was too late. The second express was already in section.

The driver of the local, panic-stricken as the troop-train bore down on them, had hurled himself under the waiting goods-train. Hutchinson, his fireman, had scrambled under the Welsh coal empties. The guard, thrown off his feet by the impact, was still alert enough when he got to his feet to realize that the signals on the down line were clear and that the express was due. He began to stumble towards Gretna. He didn't have far to go. Not nearly far enough. The express came thundering towards Quintinshill.

It was a crowded train, and with Beattock ahead it had been decided to couple up two Caledonian locomotives at Carlisle. Pistons flashing and wheels racing, they rushed past the guard. The driver saw him waving frantically, and applied the brakes. But no brakes could have worked in that brief stretch between the express's pilot engine and the wreckage.

Its six hundred tons smacked full force into the tender of the troop-train and rammed it further into the tangle of wood, metal, blazing coal and human bodies.

Dazed soldiers had been clambering out of the wreckage. Some tried to haul injured men out, others called despairingly to friends who didn't answer. Many were high up on the mound of debris or tugging vainly at jagged woodwork when the express hit. They were pulped into the existing shambles or tossed murderously aside. When the express jolted to a halt, coal poured from it, burying the driver and fireman of the pilot engine and adding more fuel to the conflagration. More gas-cylinders exploded; the fire grew more ravenous.

In the signal-box Meakin and Tinsley, stricken, saw the results of their slapdash methods spread out before them.

The telephone rang. Neither moved. It rang again. In a stupor, Tinsley answered. The Gretna signal-man wanted to know why he had received no "train out of section" signal for the second down express. And where was the troop-train he had been expecting on the up line?

"We've had a smash up here," whimpered Tinsley.

He put the receiver back, and mechanically sent an "obstruction danger" bell signal to both Gretna and Kirkpatrick.

The telephone rang again. Gretna wanted to know what on earth was happening.

Tinsley cracked. "Send for the plate-layers," he yelled. "Send for the station-master—send for *everybody*."

He was still there, bemused, when the driver of the second express engine staggered in to ask if he had sent for a breakdown crane. Tinsley shook his head.

"Then do it. Now."

Outside, the train crews tried nobly to combat the flames. The driver of the goods-train hauled undamaged trucks away while the rest were blazing, and then tried to use water from his tender to douse the fire. Other drivers found hoses and did their best. A group of soldiers stumbled to some nearby farm buildings and returned with a hand-pump which they used in the ditch beside the line. But all told there was not nearly enough water.

The pall of smoke thickened and rose higher. Men who had been killed in the first or second smash were lucky. Too many were still trapped, and now were burned to death.

Messages began to chatter frantically down the wires. A rescue train set out. Incredibly, nobody thought to send for a fire-engine, and it was three hours later before one arrived from Carlisle.

Doctors fought their way to men ringed by fire. The wreckage flared away throughout the rest of the day and far into the night. Local people brought food, drink and blankets. Ambulances came when they could, from where they could. Carts and trucks were commandeered to remove the charred, unrecognizable corpses.

It was not for a long time that even an approximate reckoning of casualties could be made.

In the express, eight people had been killed and fifty-four injured. Two passengers in the local train had died. The driver and fireman of the troop-train had been killed instantly.

As for the Royal Scots, the roll-call was a dreadful thing. All records had been destroyed in the smash, and it was left to the colonel and one surviving sergeant to round up the few dazed survivors and work things out in conjunction with them.

The survivors were few indeed. Out of fifteen officers and 470 men, 246 had been injured, many of them seriously. There were 227 dead. Their scorched remains did not make a very weighty burden in the funeral procession which eventually marched its slow way through Edinburgh.

The smouldering mass below the signal-box cooled at last. Investigators picked their way over the debris and prepared their formal reports.

And a week after the catastrophe James Tinsley was arrested and taken quietly away to await his trial along with Meakin.

Asked by officials immediately after the disaster how it could possibly have happened, Tinsley had said: "I forgot about the local being on the up line."

"Jimmy forgot about the local," Meakin confirmed.

At the inquest, asked similar questions by the coroner, Tinsley said: "I forgot all about it."

And when at last they stood trial in Edinburgh, the two men's defence counsel quoted Tinsley once more: " 'I simply forgot.' "

He forgot.

He was given a three-year sentence, Meakin eighteen months. It is doubtful whether, after that, awake or asleep, they were ever able to forget.

Desert Flight

The First World War, like any war, saw a great deal of terror. It also had an ingredient of horror that was peculiarly its own: the horror of the trenches of the Western Front, a world of mud and squalor, barbed wire, the drifting clouds of yellow gas, and above all the horror of the millions who died "going over the top" to battle for a few yards of shell-scarred land.

It was a war whose horror and terror could reduce brave men to helplessness. For the men in the trenches, the war in the air far above their heads must have seemed to take place in a different world. There it was a world of clean air and free movement, of plane against plane, man against man. It seemed almost to be a return to an older age of chivalry and individual combat.

But for the pilots, this world too had its terrors. All too often they were sent into combat after a grossly inadequate training, in machines that were dangerously unsafe. And they had no parachutes. High Command had decreed that, while parachutes should be made available to the men in the observation balloons, they were not to be issued to the men in the planes. With their exposed fuel-tanks, there was an ever-present possibility that a machine would be shot down in flames. This gave the crew two alternatives; to go down with their machines and be burned to death, or to jump and be smashed to pieces on the ground.

This is the story of just one of the many incidents when the men of the Royal Flying Corps knew the terror of the new war in the air, and how they reacted to it.

The incident took place in one of the "sideshows" of the war, the Middle East campaign. The British had suffered a major defeat in the war against Turkey at Gallipoli. Now the scene of this war had shifted. Allenby was driving forward into Mesopotamia, on the road to Damascus and Baghdad. The British had successfully defended the Suez Zone from Turkish attacks, during which the brunt of the aerial fighting had been borne by two squadrons, numbers 14 and 17.

In September, 1916, they were joined by No. 67 (Australian) Squadron. On 20 March of the following year, four members of this squadron, Lieutenants Drummond, Ellis and McNamara and Captain Rutherford, set out on a bombing mission against Turkish communications. Their target was a railway line held by the enemy. Four planes were to be used: two Martinsydes and two B.E.2cs. The latter was a two-seater biplane, rather slow and unmanœuvrable, but specially designed for bombing; the former was a single-seater scout aircraft. For this mission, the B.E.s were to carry no observer, so the bombing of the target was entirely the responsibility of the four pilots.

The task was made more difficult, and, as events were to show, more dangerous, by the substitution of four-and-a-half-inch howitzer shells for conventional bombs. This was not unusual: not because the shells were particularly suitable for use with aircraft but simply because bombs were often unavailable. Each aircraft carried six of these shells, which were specially fused so as to give a forty-second delay between their release from the bomb-racks and the explosion. At any rate, this was what was supposed to happen in theory.

The four planes took off, with no expectation of encountering any difficulties on their way to the target. By this stage of the war, the British had achieved complete air superiority, and the flight to the railway over the arid wasteland passed off, as expected, without incident. All arrived safely at the target and circled around waiting until a Turkish train appeared before starting the attack.

As soon as the train was in sight they went in, Lieutenant Ellis leading in one of the Martinsydes. He was followed over the target by Lieutenant McNamara in the second of the scout planes. McNamara dropped the first three of his shells directly on to the train and a fourth on to the railway track. The fifth shell was again intended for the track. He aimed and then pulled the release toggle. The shell was released from its holding but, instead of falling away, exploded directly under the fuselage. The fuse had failed. As the plane rocked and bucketed in the blast, shrapnel ripped through the framework of the fragile machine, leaving gaping holes in the bodywork and the wings, but miraculously missing the engine. McNamara felt a sharp, searing pain. One of the pieces of shrapnel had embedded itself in his right buttock. Blood at once began to flow freely down his leg. He abandoned the attack and turned for home, hoping to make it back to base before the loss of blood became too great.

As he turned, he saw that one of the two B.E.s had crash-landed. The pilot had got out of the plane and appeared to be unharmed. He was busy lighting a distress signal and the dark smoke was spiralling up into the clear sky. From his high vantage point, McNamara could see something else, invisible to the lonely figure on the ground. In the distance was a Turkish cavalry patrol at full gallop, and they were clearly heading straight for the scene of the crash.

Ignoring the wound which had rendered his right leg all but useless, he immediately turned his plane in to land. The ground below looked unpromising, but he managed to come down safely near the B.E. and the stranded airman. He could now see that this was Captain Rutherford, who dashed over to join him. There was no room in the tight little cockpit of the Martinsyde for a passenger, so Rutherford was forced to climb up on to the engine cowling, where he lay, grasping the rigging wire that strengthened the wings to hold himself in position.

There was no time for any nice adjustments by McNamara, for the mounted troops were now clearly in sight. Satisfied that his passenger was as safe as possible in the circumstances, he began manœuvring the Martinsyde into position for take-off.

The attempted take-off was a nightmare of difficulty. As

he had discovered on landing, the ground was waterlogged and uneven. He now faced the task of holding the plane steady into the wind, while trying to keep the movement as smooth as possible to avoid shaking Rutherford from his precarious position. This task would have been difficult enough for any pilot, but for McNamara it was made doubly difficult. To hold a plane on a straight course while taxiing, the pilot used the rudder-bar, operated by the feet, and McNamara's right leg was virtually paralysed. But somehow he managed to get the plane moving forward, gradually gaining speed.

Rutherford clung on to the rigging as the jolting and jarring threatened to throw him off. At each jolt of the wheels McNamara forced his legs to respond to the jerks of the rudder-bar. In this way they moved forward until the plane had almost achieved take-off speed. Just as McNamara was beginning to pull back the stick to lift the plane into the air, the whole craft slewed violently sideways, the nose went down and they crashed to a halt.

The airmen struggled out from the wreckage of the Martinsyde. The plane stood sadly, its nose buried deep into the soft ground, its tail pointing mockingly up to the sky. The whole undercarriage had been torn off in the crash. One of the rules for any airman who had crashed was to destroy his plane if there was any chance of it falling into enemy hands. Although the plane was useless to the two Australians it was certainly not beyond repair, so clearly it had to be destroyed as its capture was a certainty.

The cavalry had by now advanced to within rifle range. They had dismounted and begun to fire on the two pilots, but with no great accuracy. McNamara ignored them completely, and set about destroying his plane. He drew his revolver and fired a shot into the petrol tank. A thin stream of petrol began to flow. He then took his Verey pistol and fired into the stream of fuel. Within seconds the plane was ablaze.

The two men now had to face the threat of the advancing Turkish soldiers. The machine-gun on Rutherford's stranded B.E. still looked as if it might be intact, so McNamara suggested to Rutherford that he should try to get to it and use it to fight off the slowly advancing Turks. It seemed a fairly slim hope to Rutherford, but as their options were decidedly limited he started to run back to his plane. McNamara followed as fast as he could, his injured right leg dragging painfully along the ground. They both reached the B.E. in safety, and Rutherford got ready to use the Lewis-gun on the Turkish troops. But McNamara's Martinsyde had not yet made its last contribution to the contest. With a violent explosion, it blew to pieces. The flames from the burning fuel had reached the last of the howitzer shells.

The explosion halted the Turkish advance. Not knowing how many more unexploded shells there might be to go off, they retreated to a safe distance. This gave McNamara and Rutherford a chance to investigate the damage to the B.E. The landing on the rough ground had torn a tyre from one of the wheels of the under-carriage: the wires that held the central section of the wing firmly in place had snapped; and one of the longerons, the strips that ran down the fuselage to keep it rigid, had cracked. A quick look at the engine suggested that there was nothing much wrong there. However, the impact of landing had jerked loose some of the ammunition drums from the Lewis-gun, and these were now firmly jammed under the rudder-bar.

There was nothing that could be done about the structural damage, but there looked to be a good chance of flying the plane again if the rudder-bar could be freed. Painfully, McNamara scrambled into the cockpit. Working as fast as they could while taking care not to damage the rudder-bar, the two men set to work freeing the jammed ammunition drums. At last they succeeded and the B.E. was as ready as it was likely to be for flight. It seemed that escape was again a possibility.

But they were still faced with the same problem of take-off. For the plane could only be started by swinging the propeller, and this was clearly out of the question for the injured McNamara. So it was left to Rutherford to swing the propeller, and McNamara had again to try to get the plane into the air. At least this time there was the observer's position available for Rutherford, if they could only get the engine started; so McNamara would not have to worry about flying with a man hanging on the outside of the plane. Rutherford climbed down and swung the prop. There was not so much as a cough from the engine. Again he swung, and again there was no response. At last, after repeated efforts, the engine spluttered into life, and Rutherford raced round to jump into the seat behind McNamara.

The Turks had at last realized that there was no more danger from exploding shells; also the noise of the engine brought home to them that there was a chance that their quarry would escape. They had been in no hurry before, believing that both planes were completely useless and knowing that there was nowhere the two Australians could escape to, except the desert. But now as the engine roared, they raced back to their horses and remounted.

As McNamara turned the damaged B.E. into the wind, they started galloping at full speed towards the aircraft. Now McNamara had the plane facing into the wind and began to taxi forward. The pain in his right leg was almost un-bearable as the plane bounced and skidded on the wet, bumpy ground. In spite of his efforts, they had hardly got under way before the wheels stuck in the mud. Furiously, he revved the engine to try to force the machine on again. Rutherford watched, powerless to help, as the Turkish cavalry closed in on them. With a sudden jolt, the plane lurched forward again, and slowly the gap between horses and aircraft grew once more. But again the mud, clawing at the wheels, brought them to a halt; and again only furious revving of the engine by the desperate McNamara drove them forward.

A bizarre race was developing between aeroplane and horses, with the muddy, bumpy earth on the side of the horses. It seemed to be pulling at the battered plane, draw-ing it back, holding it down to itself. For a third time the mud brought the B.E. to a stop. And for the third time, McNamara drove the machine forward again. The Turks had raised their rifles, but the thunderous gallop was frus-trating their efforts to draw a steady bead.

Now the horsemen were only a few yards away. Desper-ately McNamara gunned the engine. The plane stumbled forward, gradually gathering speed as the troops spurred their horses. At last the Australians and their machine were winning. The nose of the plane came up, the wheels finally shook themselves free of the grip of the cloying earth, and the B.E. lifted into the sky. As it rose above them, the cavalry reined in their horses and stood, sweaty steam rising in clouds as they stared after their vanishing prey.

For the two airmen there was a feeling of immense relief. The gods were on their side after all. The situation had seemed impossible: two men stranded in the desert with two useless aircraft, heavily outnumbered by the enemy and with no way of escape. But one of the useless aircraft had flown after all, they had taken her up into the air from a terrain from which it seemed suicidal to attempt a take-off. Now they were back in their own element, the air. The plane, in spite of the damage, was responding to the controls. There seemed nothing now that could stop them flying back to the base and safety. But they had forgotten one vital factor: McNamara was seriously wounded. In all the excitement and frenzied activity he had had no time to concern himself with the shrapnel wound. Even the paralysed right leg had seemed no more than one further obstacle that was trying to prevent them getting away. Now the tension had relaxed, McNamara was aware how much blood he had lost, just how weak he was, how close to collapse. The danger had seemed past. It was not. Another nightmare was beginning.

There can be something peculiarly restful about flying once you have become accustomed to the noise of the engine. The ground slides away under the wings in a perpetual, hypnotic motion as though you were stationary in the air, while the earth were being unrolled beneath you. For McNamara the temptation to let it all drift away, quietly and peacefully, to close his eyes, to blot out the pain, to rest, was well nigh irresistible. He had lost so much blood that he felt almost helpless in his weakness.

And what of Rutherford? In the observer's seat, directly behind McNamara, he sat and watched the pilot's efforts to gather his concentration, to keep the plane flying. And he was powerless to help. He knew that if McNamara once gave in to the weakness seeping through his limbs, then there was nothing he could do to stop the plane from crashing. And if the plane crashed the chances of either of them surviving were negligible. Like the other pilots, Rutherford had no parachute; if McNamara fell, then Rutherford fell with him.

The B.E. had crash-landed some seventy odd miles from the R.F.C. base. To a modern pilot seventy miles is no distance at all, but to the airmen of 1917 it represented the better part of an hour's flying time. McNamara knew this, and he was aware of how slender a hold he had on consciousness, and with consciousness on life. To help keep and hold on to his concentration, he leaned out over the edge of the open cockpit until his face was turned into the full blast of the slipstream. The cool, rushing wind acted like a splash of icy water. He drew back his head and flew on, over the same brown country, the same faceless land.

The B.E.2c was one of the most stable and reliable planes ever built for the Royal Flying Corps, but now this very stability had become another weapon turned against McNamara and Rutherford. If the plane had needed more delicate handling, if there had been more violent reaction to the movement of the controls, then the effort and concentration required from McNamara would have been that much greater. And just as the necessity for action had kept him going on the ground, so too a greater stimulus from the machine was needed to help him retain his consciousness now. Instead, the plane flew on, slowly and making little demand on the pilot. Again and again, the gentle hypnotic movement tempted his weakening body into unconsciousness, and only by repeatedly thrusting his head back into the shock of the slipstream's blast could he save himself from slipping away into the blackness. So he fought on to keep awake, and so Rutherford waited, with no means of knowing how long his pilot could hold out and no means of affecting the issue.

At last the plane came into sight of Kilo 143, the home base of the squadron. Now he had only to make the one final effort. Summoning up his last reserves of strength, he hauled the B.E. round to line up with the runway and came in to land. The plane lurched as the tyreless wheel bit into the ground, but she kept straight on her course. They were down. McNamara and Rutherford were safe again.

McNamara's immense courage throughout the whole of his terrifying ordeal did not go unmarked. The *London Gazette* of 8 June, 1917, carried the announcement that the King had approved the award of the Victoria Cross to Lieutenant Frank Hubert McNamara, No. 67 (Australian) Squadron, Royal Flying Corps.

Invasion From Mars

The radio programme from the New Jersey broadcasting station in New York State started its 8 to 9 p.m. drama slot on 31 October, 1938, in a routine fashion. There were a few unremarkable station announcements, a brief statement that the play to follow—an adaptation of H. G. Wells's science-fiction novel *War of the Worlds*—was strictly fiction, and then music. Autumn was well under way, the nights were rapidly growing darker, television had not yet arrived, and in the New York area, and beyond, countless families were settling down for an evening of relaxation listening to the radio.

The programme faded suddenly. The tense voice of a newscaster said: "We interrupt our programme of dance music to bring you a special news bulletin. Twenty minutes before eight, Professòr Farrell of the Mount Jennings Observatory, Chicago, Illinois, reported several explosions of incandescent gas occurring at regular intervals on the planet Mars."

It was the beginning of the Wellsian fantasy, cleverly presented in a series of terse "news flashes" that kept breaking into a programme of soothing music. The adaptation had been dramatized and enacted by Orson Welles, then only twenty-three years old, but already recognized as a Broadway theatrical prodigy by his portrayal, during the previous season, of a Caesar in modern dress with fascist leanings—the Second World War was still in the future, but not far away.

The stark documentary "newsflash" technique was to become a hallmark of the Orson Welles style, as was so visually evident in films such as *Citizen Kane* and *The Magnificent Ambersons*. But on this last evening of October in 1938 the Wellesian realism applied to Wellsian fantasy provoked a dramatic human reaction which neither Well(e)s could have foreseen. New York panicked and became a terror-stricken city of refugees fleeing the Martian invasion.

According to a New Jersey newspaper on the following day, the simulated news bulletins "had the Martians landing in meteor cars with the shock of an earthquake in the vicinity of Grovers Mills (fictitious locale), New Jersey . . . a 30-second pause for studio music . . . then the octopus-like Martians using the dread 'heat ray', the report of forty persons dead there . . . the Martians eventually succumbed to germs that we worldlings are immune to".

All this was taken as gospel by tens of thousands of radio listeners, despite four cautionary announcements that it was all fiction. The warnings were lost and forgotten in the realism of the portrayal. The "hot news" technique held the radio audience in a grip of mounting hysteria.

Many apartment houses in New York were hurriedly evacuated by terrified occupants flying headlong from the Martians and their poison gas and death-rays. The news spread by second-and third-hand accounts that multiplied the impending peril. Switchboards in newspaper offices and police-stations everywhere were swamped with calls from frantic people. In Newark alone the police received over 3,000 telephone calls, and 15 people were treated for shock in St Michael's hospital.

There were people who reported they could smell the gas and see the flames started by the attackers. In Pittsburgh a woman attempted suicide, saying: "I'd rather die this way than like that."

A world-war veteran, living in Jersey Avenue, became alarmed when he heard the broadcast announcement to "close all windows and tell your neighbours to do the same". Later, laughing about it, he said: "I ran outside to tell my neighbours and found six or seven running over to my house to tell me."

At police headquarters, Lieutenant John Lyons, inundated with calls and inquiries, declared: "I couldn't convince them it was only a radio show." For example, two Highland Park men, their faces white with fear, rushed into police headquarters, and "fairly shook" as they asked questions about the war.

"People are getting killed," they exclaimed. "Tune in on the radio. It's terrible. Why, the gas-masks are being eaten right off people's faces."

"I wouldn't be alarmed," said Lieutenant Lyons. "It's just a play on the radio."

"Oh, no—it's no play," the men insisted, and rushed from the building.

The same pattern was repeated in most areas. It was as if the startled citizens, in the grip of mass hysteria, did not want to believe the truth—that the Martian invasion was simply fiction dressed up as fact. Perhaps many, subconsciously, preferred the excitement of running away from an unimaginable alien invader. It must be remembered that the thirties was the boom period of "pulp magazine" science-fiction in the United States, when many of today's famous science-fiction authors first saw print in lurid publications entitled *Wonder Stories, Amazing Stories, Astounding Stories, Startling Stories,* and so on. Bug-eyed monsters and inter-planetary invasion were already old hat.

In the evening of the radio invasion from Mars, even the authorities were not sure what was going on, though they were more circumspect about it and took the trouble to check. State Trooper John Gentz, for example, was on desk duty when panic calls began coming in to the headquarters on Route 25.

"I told them I didn't know anything about it when the calls first came in," Gentz stated. "Then I got a call from Raritan township local police and another from New Brunswick police, and I thought I'd better find out what it was all about.

"I called the West Trenton headquarters of the state police and they told me 'just another radio show', and then I informed callers that it was just a radio play."

In another police H.Q. a man and a woman hurried in to confront the duty lieutenant. He told them the war was only a radio play.

"Come out here and listen to it yourself," they exclaimed, pointing to their car parked outside the station, with the radio blazing its synthetic tale of horror. The lieutenant obligingly listened to the realistic news bulletin describing how the "men from Mars" were slaughtering thousands of humans.

"I told them it was only a radio show, but they were not convinced," he said. "They seemed to be terribly shocked."

According to another newspaper, all was quiet at the Terrence J. Murphy news-stand on George Street before the invasion play began. James Dooley, of Suydam Street, happened to be tuning in the radio in the rear of the Murphy place when he heard the terrifying news of the destruction near Trenton.

"Hey, listen to this," he called to Murphy. The news-dealer, whose placards in front of his shop were read by a multitude of passers-by, immediately rushed for a piece of black crayon.

Eagerly straining his ears to get the details of the history-making battle near Trenton, Murphy began to post up-to-the-minute bulletins on the placard boards. In no time a crowd began to gather in front of his shop. But Murphy found he could not keep up with the announcer.

The meteor is about 30 yards in diameter . . . Murphy commented: "I thought it was strange that they could measure the meteor. I began to figure I was doing a lot of writing for nothing. Then I knew I was falling for a hoax. I tore up the bulletins. They shouldn't be allowed to put a bulletin like that on the radio."

He added: "I called the local newspaper to find out when they were going to put out an extra edition. People were crowding round my news-stand, but they weren't buying anything, just reading the bulletins. Everybody was just asking questions. It was just like before the World War. It was a heck of a time to pull a stunt like that."

The Lehigh Valley Railroad called Raritan township police headquarters to find out how the roads were in the vicinity of Hightstown and Princeton—the caller wanted to know if it was safe to send trains into the "war area".

And on Route 28, near Penns Neck, a gasoline-station attendant called the state police to report that he had received two "spooky" telephone messages. "One was from

a friend in New York, the other from a friend in Phila-
delphia, and both told me to get out of town," he said. The
Penns Neck station was also asked about traffic conditions
by motorists, and about the identity of the state troopers,
all six of them, who had been "killed" by the Martian
invaders.

In retrospect, the pandemonium seems incredible. Parents
snatched up their children, grabbed a few prized belongings
and fled by car or on foot. Hysterical women ran through
the streets screaming, and frightened men plunged aimlessly into the night. Apartment houses in New York emptied as people fled, their faces covered with towels or handkerchiefs as protection against the "gas attack" of the
Martians. And this was the nation that was destined, little
more than a generation later, to put the first men on the
moon.

The following day, in the wake of the broadcast, there
were angry demands for a full investigation. It was the era
of intensive radio propaganda from Nazi Germany and
Fascist Italy. Nobody took such propaganda seriously, but
here, in the United States itself, was a dramatic demonstration of the immense psychological power of radio broadcasting on the receptive mind—if the right techniques were
used. Orson Welles, in his own way and quite unintention-
ally, made a significant contribution to the science of mind
control on a mass basis. The lessons of the radio version
of *War of the Worlds* were not overlooked.

Frank P. McNinch, then chairman of the Federal Communications Commission, asked the broadcasting company
concerned (Columbia) to furnish the F.C.C. with a record-
ing of the broadcast as well as a copy of the script. "I shall
request prompt consideration of this matter by the commission," he said in Washington.

Jacques Chambrun, literary agent for H. G. Wells, said in
a statement that the famous British author was "deeply
concerned" that the radio dramatization of his book should
have spread so much alarm in the United States. Wells
had cabled Chambrun on the morning after the broadcast,
declaring that: "The Columbia Broadcasting System and
Mr Orson Welles have far overstepped their rights in the
matter . . . and should make a full retraction." Further,
the radio dramatization was made "with a liberty that

amounts to a complete re-writing" and turned the novel into "an entirely different story". It was "a totally unwarranted liberty".

And in Indiana, Senator Clyde L. Herring said that he planned to introduce in Congress a bill "controlling just such abuses as was heard over the radio last night. Radio has no more right to present programmes like that than someone has in knocking on your door and screaming."

What did the genius responsible for the uproar have to say about it? Orson Welles, according to a newspaper report, was "overcome by the unbelievable reaction to his presentation of the Wells thriller-turned-horrifier".

In a statement expressing "deep regret" over the apprehension the broadcast caused among radio listeners, Welles said: "Far from expecting the radio audience to take the programme as fact rather than a fictional presentation, we feared that the classic H. G. Wells story, which has served as an inspiration for so many moving pictures, radio serials and even comic strips, might appear too old fashioned for modern consumption.

"We can only suppose that the special nature of radio, which is often heard in fragments, or in parts disconnected from the whole, has led to this misunderstanding."

The word "misunderstanding" is a generous interpretation of a mass panic reaction without precedent in the history of modern communications. The incident, if it can be dismissed as such, was soon to be followed by a long and arduous world war, engulfing in one way or another practically all nations, and during that war there were many invasions and mass evacuations, but seldom any evidence of widespread hysteria or panic. The mood was rather one of defiance or despair, or both, and the enemy was real.

What then was the real reason behind New York's night of insanity when countless thousands of normally rational citizens found themselves believing that Martian space-ships had landed close to the city and octopus-like monsters were invading the earth? Even allowing for the genius of Orson Welles, and a diabolically plausible script, the phenomenon defies explanation. In a crowded theatre or cinema a shout of "fire" could (and has) cause a stampede for the exits, but this was not a theatre, even though the programme was named "Mercury Theatre of the Air"—it was an audience of radio listeners dispersed in their own homes and cars over a geographical area of many tens of thousands of square miles. But the infection spread rapidly, just the same—despite the fact that the programme was called *War of the Worlds* (a familiar enough title) and that four warnings that it was fiction and not fact were broadcast during the programme.

Could the same thing have happened in Britain, or in Europe generally? Probably not, even with the more excitable—but highly practical—French and Italians. Perhaps in Germany it could, if one can validly interpret the almost universal adulation of Hitler during a regime which in itself held many elements of fantasy as a kind of mass hysteria. The British tend to be stubbornly cynical and not get very excited or enthusiastic about anything; they are apt to dig their heels in and not run away. Indeed, given the news that Martians had landed in Hyde Park, a typical British comment would probably be: "Serves them bloody well right."

The United States is a conglomerate body of mixed races and nations undergoing the growing pains and stresses of long-term integration. It is a young nation and its roots are still short—and this was even more true in the late thirties, when isolationism was the official policy in the interests of security. The U.S. did not much want to become involved in the sinister developments that were taking place in Europe and the Far East. If there was to be a world tornado—and the signs were only too evident—then the U.S. preferred to adopt the rôle of the static eye in the middle.

This could explain the hysterical impact of the radio invasion from Mars. By bending over backwards to avoid involvement in the increasing turbulence of political and military confrontations throughout the world, the United States merely increased its own sense of insecurity—rather like the man sitting in his luxurious home who refuses to lift a finger when the houses on either side of his are on fire. The radio play struck at a vulnerable psychological spot; isolationists are obsessively afraid that their protective barrier might be broken down, and it is fear that gives rise to hysteria when the threat materializes.

By Martians? They were, perhaps, just a symbol of any aggressive force capable of breaking down the protective barrier. Mass hysteria implies mass psychology, and there is no doubt that Orson Welles touched a raw nerve in a basically insecure populace by presenting the invasion of New York in the form of blow-by-blow "live and hot" news bulletins.

One thing is for sure. It could never happen today in the moon-exploring United States of the post-war era. Science-fiction has been overtaken by science, and even Orson Welles couldn't get away with it a second time.

The Day the Germans Hanged Me

"What's all this about?" I asked the jaunty *Oberfeldwebel*, who spoke English with a Cockney twang to it.

"Haven't they told you?" He seemed surprised.

"Told me what?" I said.

The young *Gefreiter* who was assisting him, murmured quietly in German, "If They haven't told him, do you think you ought to, sergeant-major?"

"It would be kinder," the *Oberfeldwebel* said.

"What haven't they told me?" I asked again.

The *Oberfeldwebel* concentrated on the scales on which he had made me stand—already they had measured my height—and began fiddling with the cross-bar.

"Well, it's like this," he said, with a hint of embarrassment in his voice, I thought. "Oh, hell! Look, mate, they're going to hang you tomorrow!"

He gave me a quick glance and put a hand on my arm, as if to steady me.

"You'll be all right," he said. "I promise it won't hurt, and it will be over in seconds."

It had taken me seconds to realize what he had said.

"But they can't hang me yet!" I exclaimed. "I haven't had a trial!"

There was in my voice a note of the indignation which I genuinely felt. In those days and those circumstances I set great store by the right performance of things. To my way of thinking, no matter how foregone a conclusion the outcome might be, a man ought to be put on trial for his life. This had not happened. Since the end of 180 hours of interrogation by the Secret Field Police, no German had been near me until this morning—23 December, 1942.

My protest made the *Oberfeldwebel* smile.

"You're in the front line here," he said. "The general does not have to wait for trials. If he decides a man is to hang, he has to hang. You all right?"

"Yes, I'm all right, thanks," I said. "But I still think I ought to have been court-martialled. That's how we would do things."

Relieved, I think, that my indignation had prevented my having a crisis of nerves, he smiled again, and put his arm about my shoulders.

"You ought to be proud, you know," he told me. "They're going to do it in style, in public in the Baltic Station Square. You are to be an example to all those who have ideas about not co-operating with the Reich."

"You said tomorrow?"

"Yes, tomorrow—Christmas Eve—at ten o'clock in the morning . . . O.K., that's all we want to know. You're not very heavy, are you?"

"How much?"

"Just on 50 kilos."

Two pounds short of eight stone. Two months ago when I had landed, I had weighed twelve stone eight.

The *Oberfeldwebel* told the Estonian warder who had brought me from my cell to the prison office, to take me back.

As I left the room with him, the *Oberfeldwebel* called to me: "Don't worry! I promise you you won't know what's happened."

In March, 1935, I had gone to the Baltic republic of Estonia to teach in a large *gümnasium* and at the newly founded university of Tallinn, the capital. We had stayed there until the outbreak of war in September, 1939.

Since I was, when I arrived, the only Englishman in the country qualified to teach English, I found myself in very great demand. In addition to my two teaching posts, I was also employed by a number of government departments and semi-official institutions to "improve the English conversation" of their staffs. I also had half a dozen distinguished private pupils, and gave an English lesson weekly over Radio Tallinn.

All these activities provided me with a wide circle of acquaintances throughout the country as a whole, which was increased even further when I decided to write a book about Estonia in 1937 and travelled extensively, gathering material. Without wishing to appear immodest, I think I could justifiably claim to be the best-known foreigner in the republic.

The Estonians themselves we found to be a delightful people. They were frank, warm-hearted, generous and hospitable. At the same time they were modest and hard-working, and drew from one a high degree of admiration for their determination to make their little country worthy of its place among the nations of the world.

From October to June we lived in a flat on the outskirts of Tallinn not far from the presidential palace in Kadriorg Park. We were young, and despite the fact that I worked a sixteen-hour day, five days a week, we still had the energy to dine out once or twice a week and to return the hospitality we received.

In the summer, during the long vacation from 31 May to 1 October we moved out of the city. The first year we spent the summer with the American consul and his family at a rented *datcha* (country house) in the middle of the pine forests at Kotka Veski, north-east of Tallinn, and during the last two summers before the war, we were lent a fisherman's cottage in the tiny fishing hamlet of Kiiu Asbla, on the small Kolga peninsula, half-way along the north Estonian coast. There, once we had proved ourselves, we were accepted by the fishermen and their families as one of themselves.

When the Second World War broke out I decided that I must return to England with my young family as soon as possible, and, with very heavy hearts, we said farewell to all our Estonian friends and sailed for home on 5 September. I had no job, of course, but by mid-October I had been invited to join the staff of the B.B.C.'s Digest of Foreign Broadcasts. I remained a sub-editor on the Digest for two or three months, and then became a founder-member of an offshoot of the Digest—the Monitoring Service Intelligence Bureau.

A difference of opinion with the B.B.C. authorities over

my remuneration led to my resignation in March, 1941, when I joined the ranks of the Royal Air Force with a view to taking a commission. This materialized in June, 1941, and as I had had experience in lecturing, I was posted to Bomber Command as a lecturer in intelligence.

Hitler launched his attack on Russia while I was still at the Junior Officers' Training School at Loughborough. It will be recalled that the German panzers drove deep into Russia at high speed, fanning out both north and south, with the central spearhead directed at Moscow.

The rush towards Leningrad in the north, drove the Russians out of the Baltic States. As they retreated the Red Army allegedly destroyed everything in their path that might be useful to the Germans—crops, supplies, power-stations and, so we were told, the complicated machinery at the shale-oil mines in north-eastern Estonia not far from the Russian border.

There were large deposits of oil-shale in this area, which was obtained from open-cast workings. The shale itself, rich in oil and in a number of valuable bituminous by-products, was submitted to a process of distillation. When I had been gathering material for my book I had visited the mines and had the process explained to me.

One day, in the early autumn of 1941, I was told by intelligence that the Germans had been able to repair the distillation plant in the mines and were producing a significant contribution in fuel to the German forces besieging Leningrad. On my return to my station, I worked out a scheme whereby the plant at the mines might be sabotaged. My commanding officer discovered this, and submitted my plan to "higher authority". As a result, I was asked if I would be prepared to carry out the plan myself—I knew the country, the language and the customs, and I had a large number of friends among the population. I said I would, and in January, 1942, I was seconded to Special Operations Executive (S.O.E.).

S.O.E. trained me in all aspects of espionage and sabotage. By October, 1942, I was capable of organizing a resistance movement and an intelligence network, had become a specialist in the sabotage of shale mine plant, an expert in blowing up power-plants, bridges and railways, and was a proficient wireless operator.

On 22 October I was parachuted into Estonia, in the guise of an Estonian merchant seaman.

I had chosen as my dropping point the Kolga peninsula. I had selected it for a number of reasons: I knew the fishermen well and could expect them to help me until I had established myself; there was nothing in the great forests which filled the centre of the eight-mile-long, three-mile-broad tongue of land to attract the Germans; and it was midway between Tallinn, the capital, and my major objective, the shale-oil mines.

Theoretically my drop should have been entirely successful. What we did not know was that since the Germans had overrun Estonia they had established a submarine base on the eastern shore of the peninsula, and that the whole of the peninsula accommodated a considerable concentration of Wehrmacht.

I discovered the presence of German soldiers there at the moment of landing. My parachute was caught up in the branches of a tree and some telephone wires and as I dangled in my harness some six feet above the ground, I found myself surrounded by a party of enemy soldiers in the charge of a sergeant. They had watched me coming down.

By a series of fortunate events, which I have no space here to detail, I managed to evade capture. On the second morning I came to the cottage where we had spent the summers of 1938 and 1939, and where I hoped to find my friend Martin Saarne, who I believed would help me obtain a boat to carry me to Sweden—I had lost my radio and all my equipment, and was, therefore, helpless to do anything effective—from where I hoped to return to England, and begin all over again the following spring.

To my dismay Martin was in Tallinn. From his sister, who did not penetrate my disguise, I learned that he was not due home for some days.

For the next ten days, I moved about the peninsula by night and lay up during the day. I escaped capture by the searching Germans a number of times during this period. Every other night I visited the cottage to see if Martin had returned.

Food was absolutely unobtainable on the peninsula, and for the twelve days until 5 November, I survived on a packet of Rowntrees' clear gums, a slab of Cadbury's chocolate, three-quarters of a pint of whisky and a number of opium and morphine tablets which I had in my pockets. Winter had also come several days too soon. Overnight on 1/2 November the temperature dropped to − 10 deg. C., and a blizzard came down from the North Russian steppes.

I was already beginning to feel the strain, when, on my visit to the cottage in the early hours of 5 November, I found Martin had returned. He recognized me at once, and greeted me with shocked concern.

As the cottage stood only a short way back from the road along which German patrols passed at regular intervals, he suggested we go to his sister's cottage which was on the edge of the forest itself. There I told him of my plan for getting a boat to take me to Sweden.

He was sceptical about my chances of dodging the German naval patrols in the Gulf of Finland, but said he would go and fetch a friend who was more knowledgeable about things than he was. While he was gone, his niece came into the room where I was, and begged me to go away at once, because if the Germans ever discovered I had been there they would shoot all the family. I promised I would go as soon as Martin and I had finished our talk. She went away muttering.

Presently Martin returned with his friends, who had the idea of smuggling me down to one of the islands off the west coast and getting a fisherman to take me over to Sweden. As we were discussing the pros and cons, the niece's little girl came running into the room, crying, "Mummy's coming with the Germans!"

We rushed to the window and saw Martin's niece with two German soldiers half-way up the long garden path.

We scattered. Where the others went I do not know, but I plunged into the forest. But since the snow had come I had got frost-bite in both feet. I was already very lame, and had difficulty in getting along.

I realized that I had no chance against the searchers who would soon be out looking for me in force. Sinking down on a large boulder I knew the moment that I had subconsciously rejected all along had come.

Fumbling with bitter fingers under the lapel of my jacket where my capsule of cyanide of potassium was pinned, to my horror I found it was not there. Somewhere in my travels I must have lost it.

I took from my pocket my Colt ·38, cocked it and put the muzzle to my forehead. But when I squeezed the trigger, it jammed, and nothing I could do would dislodge the bullet wedged in the breach.

I had one last means of dispatching myself left—my fighting-knife, whose finely tempered double-razor-edged steel blade I carried in a special holster. I drew it out and looked at it.

The hesitation was fatal. I just could not bring myself, even after only a couple of seconds, to plunge it into my heart, or to slit my throat with it. Disgusted, I threw it away from me.

How long I sat with my head in my hands cursing my cowardice I do not know, but presently I knew that I had to give myself up. I knew, with equal clarity, that I would be walking to my death, but along the way I would do all I could to confuse and deceive the Germans.

I hid my Colt, my fighting-knife and all my false identity-papers together with the microfilmed details of my transmitting schedule under a boulder, and set off back through the forest.

When I came to the village, the street was deserted. There was not a soul, either Estonian or German, in sight.

Then, suddenly from behind a bush, a small boy stepped, levelling at me from his hip, a rifle as long as he was tall.

"Put up your hands!" he shouted at me with uncertain bravado.

I recognized him and called out his name as I raised my hands.

I saw bewilderment in his eyes.

"Who are you?" he said.

But before I could reply an Estonian fisherman jumped on me from behind and held me fast, muttering, "Bloody Russian! Bloody Russian!"

At that moment Martin came running up.

"It's the Härra Professor!" he shouted.

I had always been addressed in Kiiu Asbla as Härra Professor.

The man holding me loosened his grip.

"Is it true?" he asked.

"Yes," I said.

"I recognize your voice," he admitted. But it was too late Two armed Germans were running towards us, shouting at me to put up my hands.

Later in the day, having been briefly questioned by an imposing array of brass-hats from Tallinn, who had hurried to the Kolga H.Q., I was taken to the city and lodged in the Central Prison, an augean stable bursting at the seams mostly with captured Russian agents, who were executed in batches by machine-gun under my cell window, almost every morning.

My interrogation by the Secret Field Police began next day. For twelve hours a day, with scarcely a pause, for the next sixteen days I was questioned and questioned and questioned. They already had—I do not know from where —a frightening amount of information about the organization and personalities of S.O.E. Every statement I made was checked against this information, and since it rarely tallied I was taken over every point with relentless probing. Fortunately, I have a retentive memory, and was able to adhere to my original statements with an insistence that I know caused them much bewilderment, for there was a great shaking of heads and repeated covering of old ground.

In between my interrogations I was returned to the solitary confinement of the stinking prison. By this time the outside temperature was − 30 deg. C. Inside the prison there was no heating. I had no blanket to cover myself at night, and my daily menu consisted of a mug of hot water at 6.30 a.m. with two ounces of black bread, and a pint of so-called soup at 6 p.m. My feet had now turned black and were extremely painful. The Germans had no medicaments to treat me.

For the next weeks I sat in my refrigerated cell in a plethora of misery, waiting to be brought before a court-martial. I had no soap to wash; it was too cold to take off my clothes at night; I was allowed no exercise; the constant hunger pangs knotted my vitals in painful agony.

Every now and again I would pull myself together firmly. My morale, I knew, was cracking, and that I could not allow, for I was an Englishman, and Englishmen do not crack.

The only break I had from this ghastly place was when I

was taken one day to an office in the government sector of Tallinn, the Toompea. My radio equipment had been found, but to the Germans' amazement there were no oscillating crystals with the transmitter. They asked me what my wave-lengths were to have been. I knew that if I told them, they would make new crystals and use my set to transmit false information to England. I said I could not remember.

In this house I was taken to a large room. I was made to sit in a wooden seat with arms and a tall back. My arms and legs were strapped to the arms and legs of the chair. A broad leather thong was placed across my forehead and my head fixed by it to the back of the chair with such tightness that I could not move it.

Before me was a large mirror. Behind was an arc-lamp whose heat struck the top of my head. The light from the lamp was directed into the mirror so that the reflection shone directly into my eyes.

If I closed my eyes a guard by my side struck me about the face and body.

In the shadow, in a corner of the room, behind a table, sat a man who asked me one question—"What were your wave-length numbers?"

He repeated this question at short intervals. Now and again he was replaced by colleagues, who adopted the same procedure.

As the time passed the heat on the top of my head, the tightness of the thong about my forehead, and the blows I received made me lose consciousness. When I came round I was sodden from head to foot. Still the questioning went on, and the pain and the brief oblivion.

Presently I knew I could stand no more. I must tell them what I knew before they roasted my brain.

I tried to speak, but before the sounds came from my lips, the man at the table came over to me and struck me across the face, and with an oath turned away, telling the guard to take me back to prison.

I could see nothing but the glaring light. I stumbled and almost fell, not from the stiffness in my lately bound limbs, but because I could not see where I was going.

As we had gone into the house a nearby clock had struck nine. When I asked my warder what the time was, he said, "Three o'clock."

"Only six hours," I said. "It seemed a life-time."

"It's three o'clock in the morning," he said. "You've been gone a whole day and half the night."

For the next month or more I could not see. In the prison office, when the *Oberfeldwebel* had weighed and measured me, I could not see clearly. There was a film of light still across my eyes, but it was wearing thinner.

While I had been training we had never spoken of capture and death. It would have been strange, however, had it not passed through our minds now and again. I had rejected it as soon as it had forced its attention upon me. It was the only way, I believed, in which I could go through with it. I cannot remember a time when I have been afraid of the idea of dying; on the other hand, I have found that a family needing one's support is a powerful reason for living.

In 1942 I was a religious man and I was conscious of the many commissions of sin of which I was guilty. Though I could not protect myself against sinning—at least not against the particular sins to which I was prone—the thought had passed through my mind again and again, "What retribution would God exact?"

On one or two occasions when the thought of dying had come to me in moments of depression, I had thought that if ever I knew that I was about to die, I would not be able to prevent myself from falling on my knees and in total abjection implore my Maker to be lenient with me. I had not meant to sin. I had sinned because I was too weak to resist.

When the cell door clanged to behind me, all these thoughts came crowding in on me. I had less than twenty-four hours to live. My immortal soul was in peril. I must go down on my knees and implore the Almighty, entreat Him and show Him abject repentance in the hope that He would, in His overwhelming goodness, decide to treat me not too harshly.

I got down on my knees beside the truckle bed. When it came to the point I did not know how to begin. And presently I knew I need not begin.

In a sudden moment of revelation such as had come on the road to Damascus, I knew that God knew me better than I knew myself; that there was no need for me to plead my cause; that my sins were not only forgiven but understood.

A calmness descended upon me. The inward agitation, which had been on the point of turning my bowels into waters of cowardice, left me.

I got up from my knees and lay down on my bed, my mind a floating disembodied emptiness in which there came now and again thoughts, which stayed for a brief while and passed on, leaving no trace.

The evening soup arrived. I drank it and returned to my bed.

The next thing I knew was the cell door opening and the morning broom thrust into my hands. I swept out my cell, as I had done these past few dozen mornings, and was rewarded with my mug of hot water and my slice of bread.

I washed my face and my hands in cold water and borrowed a comb from the warder to comb my hair and my beard.

Then I sad down to wait.

Time lost its dimensions.

The cell door opened, and the warder, kindly, said, "Come."

At the desk in the central hall a *Feldwebel* greeted me grimly.

"Sign," said the warder at the desk.

The *Feldwebel* signed the document thrust at him.

Outside the main gate of the prison, eight or ten soldiers were waiting, formed up in two ranks.

The *Feldwebel* took me by the arm and propelled me forward until I was in the middle of the waiting soldiers. He gave the command and we started off on the mile-and-a-half walk to the Baltic Station Square.

I remember thinking: "Their fuel position must be bad, otherwise they would have surely sent transport for me."

After a time we were halted. An Estonian with a horse and cart blocked our path. The horse had fallen on the slippery road and could not get to its feet.

On a nearby door was a large red poster which exclaimed: "BEWARE, TYPHUS."

A little dog came running up. He came to me, sniffed and with a yelp and his tail between his legs, loped away and sat down on the kerb of the pavement and began to bay at the death he smelt upon me.

The clock on the Baltic Station said five minutes to ten as we marched into the square.

On the far side from the station, a contraption consisting of a platform, an upright at either end, joined by a cross-bar, had been erected. From the centre of the cross-bar dangled a noosed rope. Two or three dozen soldiers were drawn up around it.

We marched up to it, and halted. It was very cold. I remembered the words of Charles I who had asked for a second under-vest for the walk to the block lest he should shiver and the people would think he was afraid.

I looked at the gallows. It had no significance for me. A strange unreality had enveloped my mind. I knew what it was, but could not connect it with me.

We waited.

The clock showed ten.

Nothing happened.

We waited.

A train ran into the station. Presently a crowd of passengers began to cross the square.

The clock showed five past ten, and I was beginning to become impatient. They had no business to keep me waiting. I stirred uneasily as I looked around for the *Oberfeldwebel*, but could not see him. Looking back, I was still uninvolved in the scene.

Presently a car-horn was heard in the distance, followed by the sound of a motor approaching. It had to be Germans, because only Germans had fuel for motors.

A car drove at speed into the square and came to a jolting stop by the scaffold. A young officer, the *Oberfeldwebel* and the *Gefreiter* jumped out.

The two latter ran towards me and, one on either side, seized me by the arm, propelled me towards the scaffold and bodily lifted me on to the platform. As one strapped my ankles together, the other pinioned my arms behind me.

The *Oberfeldwebel* whispered as he placed the noose over my head, "It won't hurt, I promise!"

Meanwhile the officer was reading in atrocious Estonian to a small crowd that had halted their progress across the square, my crimes against the Reich and the sentence of death. I caught the sounds of several voices shouting, but could not distinguish what they said.

The *Oberfeldwebel* jumped down from the platform, saluted the officer and shouted, "*Alles in ordnung.*"

The officer nodded.

The noise of the crowd filled my ears.

Then suddenly there was a clatter of metal hitting the surface of the square.

The platform on which I was standing gave and I had the impression of falling, followed by a jolt, as the trap fell no further.

The sudden brake threw me off balance. The rope tightened about my throat and I lost consciousness.

The author survived the war. Afterwards it was learned that the scaffold had been erected the afternoon before. During the night some of his former students had screwed a slat of wood across the trap, while others had diverted the attention of the German guards. They could not know that they would save his life. They only knew they must make a gesture.

The Warsaw Ghetto

On 6 September, 1939, the vast steel-clad brute which was the German army bulldozed its way into Poland. Although the Polish Government decided to abandon the capital to the enemy, the people of Warsaw took it upon themselves to defend their city, and their spirit of resistance encouraged the Polish army. But it was a bitter and useless struggle, with an inevitable end. Large areas of Warsaw were reduced to ruins by the German bombardment, and for some 150,000 of its Jewish inhabitants the fall of the capital was their death sentence.

In October, Warsaw was trying to struggle painfully back to life. All utilities had ceased to function, fuel was almost non-existent and food scarce. For the Jews the problems of survival were even more intense. The Germans at once began to pursue their usual policy towards them of terrorization, ill-treatment, cruelty, resettlement, loss of freedom and property, and sometimes death. This treatment the Jews of Europe had come to expect, but they had no idea of the fact that the Nazis were now planning their total extermination.

While the Germans broke into Jewish homes, plundered them on the pretence of searching for weapons, dragged young men off the streets to forced labour, banned Jews from the soup kitchens set up for Aryans and ordered the appointment of a Jewish Council or *Judenrat* to be responsible for Jewish affairs, the people of the Chosen Race remained passive. Their energies were directed towards feeding themselves and avoiding the worst attentions of their oppressors.

As time went on the German treatment of the Jews became more brutal. They were beaten up on the streets, their property was destroyed or confiscated, and those with homes in the better part of the city were forcibly evicted without being allowed to take their belongings with them. Finally the long-threatened decree was carried out and in October, 1940, a ghetto was established, separating the Jewish from the Aryan population once and for all.

The area chosen was a congested slum, already containing a large Jewish population. It was completely inadequate for the 150,000 people from all over the city who were now ordered to move in, in place of the 80,000 Gentiles who moved out. The exchange of dwellings had to be carried out and the move accomplished in two weeks. The Jews were not allowed to take their belongings with them and although the Poles were supposed to leave theirs in exchange they rarely did.

The Speigel family was typical of many. Bernard, a government official, had fled with his wife Hanna and their two children before the advancing German juggernaut and taken shelter with his elder brother Abrasha in Warsaw. After the fall of the city Bernard and Hanna had stayed on, for one of the first things the Germans had done was to expel all Jews from government positions, and Bernard had no job to which to return.

The Speigels counted themselves fortunate, for they managed to avoid the attentions of the Germans and were permitted to remain quietly in their own flat. In the end, however, when they were finally ordered to move to the ghetto they were worse off, for the area was already crowded to overflowing. The fortunate Polish family with whom the Speigels had to exchange found themselves with a pleasant, roomy apartment overlooking one of Warsaw's parks, and expensively furnished. The Speigels gazed with horror upon the four dark and dilapidated tenement rooms which they were now expected to occupy, and which, despite the order that the departing Poles must leave their belongings in exchange, contained nothing but a few essential pieces of furniture. The children, Michel and Sonya, were especially loud in their complaints.

The Speigels were a kindly family and it was not long, therefore, before they were sharing their four small rooms with six other people. Still hundreds of wretched newcomers to the ghetto searched from tenement to crumbling tenement for a place in which they and their sometimes sick or feeble children and old people could find a corner to live.

On 31 October the wall of the ghetto was finished and the gates closed. Its population numbered some half million, and averaged six to a room.

The head of Warsaw's *Judenrat* was Adam Cherniakov, a well-meaning and trusting character who for many months refused to believe the warning of the militant section of the Jews, that deportation to the "work-camps" was in fact deportation to the grave. When, several months later, Cherniakov was finally forced to accept the fact, he killed himself. The *Judenrat* was ordered to establish its own police force, and since being a policeman meant certain privileges there was no difficulty in recruiting two thousand men. Most of these men, and in particular a notorious section known as the "Thirteeners", who were blatantly tools of the *Gestapo*, were despised and hated by their compatriots.

By virtue of his past job and through the influence of his brother Bernard Speigel contrived to be appointed to the *Judenrat*'s administrative staff. This ensured a certain amount of safety for his family and himself. For others the only passport to safety was the work-card which, later on, ensured their immunity from deportation. For starvation wages thousands of Jews worked in the German-run factories which had been established in the ghetto, or in the military shops and railroads outside. The latter were marched out each morning and back each evening, closely guarded, for no Jew could leave the ghetto on pain of death.

In the early months thousands fought among themselves for a crust of bread and a corner in which to sleep. Among those most closely crowded together—the late-comers who had been herded in from country districts—disease soon broke out. Typhus, dysentery and typhoid spread like wild-fire, and by the beginning of 1941 the death-rate from sickness and starvation had reached six to seven thousand a month. From the Speigels' window Sonya, fourteen years old, watched in horror as the daily death wagons came round each morning to collect the naked corpses which had been thrown, divested of their valuable clothes, out into the street.

Bribery, corruption, smuggling, illicit commerce with the "Aryan side" were rife. And while bodies lay in the streets and homeless, parentless children, their bones starkly apparent on their starving bodies, begged for food in the gutter, in some quarters there was plenty. For the few who had managed to bring valuables into the ghetto there were restaurants with well-stocked cellars and larders, and an unlimited supply of smuggled goods. Anything could be bought if you had enough money, for the *Gestapo* were as vulnerable to bribery as anyone else.

For a year or more the struggle for life went on in the ghetto in this fashion. As yet mass deportations had not begun and the only fear was the sudden swoops of police and *Gestapo* upon passers-by in the street, to carry them off to forced labour-camps. Michel, now a strapping eighteen-year-old, was implored by his mother not to go on to the streets. He refused to take any notice: "I might as well be in a labour-camp as live cooped up in these small rooms, and I cannot leave Sonya to take all the risks."

At the mention of Sonya, Hanna Speigel wept with greater despair, for the girl took an active part in the battle for food. To scramble up a wall or to creep through a hole was easier for a child, and with money obtained from the valuables their uncle had managed to smuggle into the ghetto Michel and Sonya, with a small group of adults, would wait at the appointed rendezvous for an Aryan smuggler to hand over the precious food.

Michel was also an active member of the *Bund* youth movement. He had helped to organize the underground movement, deliver handbills and the illegal newspaper, as well as to alleviate the sufferings of the starving and homeless. On the night of 17 April, 1942, the inhabitants of the ghetto were woken by shots, and shouts and gunfire were heard throughout the night. Michel crept to the window and saw two *Gestapo* men dragging from the house opposite a fellow member of the *Bund* youth movement and apprentice printer. Outside the house the young man was ordered to stand against the wall and was promptly shot. Convinced that it was his turn next, Michel fled from the room towards the attic and its skylight.

It was rumoured the following day that the mass executions of the night of 17 April had been aimed at the liquidation of all illegal printing plants and those who operated them. Night after night the executions continued as the *Gestapo* broke into tenements, dragged the people out into the street and shot them. The next morning the Jews had to clear the streets of corpses. Soon afterwards the mass deportations began.

On the evening of 20 July Bernard Speigel came home with horrifying news. The *Judenrat* had been assembled by a group of high-ranking *Gestapo* officials and informed that labour was needed on the Eastern front and that sixty thousand of the ghetto's non-productive inhabitants were to be deported at the rate of ten thousand a day. All who fell within the "non-productive" category, i.e., who did not carry a work-card, were to report at the Umschlagplatz, a square at the ghetto's edge, where the Nazis would select the victims. Michel leapt to his feet. "It has come! Our people will be exterminated, not put to work—the *Bund* has said this all along! We must resist."

"Hush," replied his father. "For us it is all right. As a member of the administration I am immune and so is my family. Besides, you are talking nonsense; these rumours of extermination are melodramatic." With his eyes, Bernard warned his son to silence. Later, while the others excitedly discussed the news, he took him aside.

"My family means you and Sonya and your mother,' he said. "I can do nothing to save your aunt and uncle. Even the false work-cards which the *Bund* have helped to print will hardly help them at their age."

Michel raged angrily off to the *Bund* meeting, but the policy of resistance which the *Bund* recommended was turned down by the *Judenrat*. Among the panic-striken populace the wish to believe that all the Germans intended was indeed deportation to a work-camp was stronger than their ability to face the truth. All the *Bund* could do by illegally distributing leaflets was to persuade the people not to submit voluntarily.

During the next few days even the most optimistic were obliged to face the truth, and panic stalked the ghetto streets. When the Germans, obliged to find their deportees by force, had cleared the prisons and infirmaries and those places where the homeless had crowded in hundreds, they turned their attention to orphanages and childrens' homes, to the beggars and the sick who lay in the streets. No longer could the Jews persuade themselves that work really lay at the end of the journey for such labourers. The Germans' intention was brutally clear.

The *Judenrat* now issued instructions that whole families could be deported together to the labour-camps, that they could take baggage and would be given extra food for the journey. By every means possible the Nazis sought to lull their victims into a sense of security, and to a great extent they succeeded; but while they called for volunteers they still carried out brutal man-hunts through the ghetto.

Abrasha Speigel and his wife were early victims of the German raids. In order to prove their identity and benefit from the protection of Bernard's job, his wife and children were obliged to spend every day sitting beside their father's desk in the administrative building. Such a pastime was not to Michel's liking and he would frequently absent himself, giving his mother hours of anxiety.

In August, at the end of one such tedious day, the family had returned home together. In their tenement building there were sounds of weeping and voices raised in anguish, but this was a common sound in the ghetto. The building however, usually full of life, was strangely empty. A neighbour told them what had happened.

"They surrounded the whole block. They dragged everyone out, beating them with clubs. I hid in a closet and they did not see me, but your brother and his wife were caught. They did not try to run away; they just went, arm in arm, very quietly."

Day after day, week after week, these scenes were reenacted throughout the ghetto. Victims were dragged weeping, hysterical, calm or uncomprehending to the "selection" centre in the Umschlagplatz. There weak or ageing men and women tried pathetically to appear young and virile; they would escape the selection only to be dragged off again a few days later. Women would hide children under their skirts, only to have that child torn from them the next day. Terror and panic spread; the inhabitants lived with death.

By the end of September, 1942, only about 40,000 inhabitants remained out of the original 500,000. The ghetto was reduced to half its size, and all those who lived in the part which was now being lopped off were obliged to find new homes within two days, but this time there was no problem of overcrowding. Shops were open and empty, houses abandoned, unwanted belongings once so sought-after lay scattered about. Where once there was teeming life an occasional figure scurried furtively. Almost everyone who remained in the ghetto was an able-bodied man or woman —the workers.

But at last the resistance workers in the Warsaw ghetto were achieving their aims. The Polish underground movement had finally taken action and had managed to smuggle some arms and ammunition to them. Battle groups were set up under individual leaders, with definite points of defence. Michel spent his days secretly drilling and learning how to make Molotov cocktails and to use a revolver. In the Umschlagplatz the victims sometimes refused to enter the waiting freight cars willingly and the guards were forced to open fire on them. The spirit of resistance was growing and everywhere Jews were digging bunkers, secret tunnels, fortifications and escape routes. It was during one such day of feverish activity that a man came running to the bunker where Michel was working. "They have taken your sister," he cried. "I have seen her, on the way to the Umschlagplatz."

Michel stared, white-faced. "But my father has a workcard, and my family . . ."

"Your sister had gone to try to find food—she was caught . . ."

Michel rushed to his section leader and demanded leave to go, but he was forcibly restrained. "You can do nothing," his friends insisted, "nothing. And you may be taken as well. It has happened to all of us. Do you think we have not lost everyone we love? All that remains is to take our revenge."

Now there could be no doubt that the Germans intended to clear the ghetto of every last inhabitant, nor that the remaining Jews intended to fight to the death. Food became so scarce that the remaining people were on the verge of starvation, fighting for every scrap. Theatres, cafés and stores had disappeared.

Michel's mother and father, no longer protected by the latter's employment, spent their days in a cramped hiding place in the attic of the house in which they lived. Like hundreds of others they tried desperately to preserve their lives to the bitter end, hiding like rats in dark tunnels and bunkers, in holes in the ground and dim crannies in the roofs. In the sewers another, underground, ghetto was established.

For some six months this twilight world continued, while in secret the resistance fighters prepared for the last battle. The combat group was now the power in the ghetto and even the rich Jews were contributing money for arms and food.

The Germans, although aware that resistance was being prepared, under-estimated its strength and so when in January, 1943, they decided to clear the ghetto they used a simple police operation. As the Germans entered the gates they were met by a salvo of shots which drove them back. Much encouraged by this effort the Jews redoubled their resistance arrangements and the Polish underground gave them further help. They were all well aware that it was to be the last battle—that there could be no hope of a successful outcome, but they were prepared to sell their lives dearly.

On 19 April, 1943, the S.S. General, Stroop, launched his final attack upon the ghetto. Two thousand crack troops, tanks and a battery of light artillery rolled in at dawn. Faced with an enemy of a few hundred men, armed with revolvers and home-made bombs, Stroop reckoned that it would take him at the most three days to mop up the ghetto.

Michel and his combat troops had their headquarters close to the wall and from his lookout post at a window Michel saw the first troops moving in. At once he gave warning and his section leader ordered his men to open fire. The Germans were greeted by a heavy fusillade of bullets and one of the tanks was set on fire by a Molotov cocktail. The soldiers promptly attacked, but Michel's group had already prepared lines of retreat, over the roofs of the houses, through cellars and underground passages.

With flame-throwers and artillery the Germans fired on and captured blocks of houses, only to find them already empty. In some places they were even forced to retreat. In the first two days they achieved virtually nothing.

On the second night Michel managed to get away, taking food with him to the hiding-place of his parents. They were still safe, though hungry, and resigned to their fate, aware that it was only at matter of time, aware that Michel's brave talk of escaping through the sewers to the Aryan side and the comparative safety of the country was, for them, meaningless.

Two days later Stroop contrived to round up and deport some five thousand unarmed inhabitants of the ghetto, but Himmler was now becoming impatient and he ordered Stroop to destroy the rest by fire. His forces were soon built up to ten times the original number. Regardless of the protests of the slave-driving factory owners large areas of factories and houses were set on fire. "We noticed that although the fire was much more dangerous, the Jews preferred to go back into it, rather than fall into our hands," noted Stroop. "The best and only way," he added a few weeks later, "to wipe out the Jews is by fire. These creatures understand that they have only two possibilities; to hide for as long as possible or to come out trying to kill or wound the largest possible number of soldiers and *Waffen*-S.S. men."

These tactics were successful up to a point and periodically large groups of unarmed Jews were rounded up and sent to extermination camps; but still the battle raged on.

As the days passed Michel visited his parents whenever he could to take them food. But eventually the inevitable happened: Michel found the house a shattered ruin of crumbling brickwork and gaping holes, and of his parents there was no sign.

Michel's group had now withdrawn and, with its depleted numbers, joined up with the headquarters group under Anielwicz, whose base was a large deep shelter in the centre of the ghetto. On 6 May the Germans attacked the bunker with flame-throwers and artillery. Within the bunker the resistance fighters and a number of women and children who had taken refuge there prepared for the last battle. In the cramped quarters fighting was impossible. Some managed to escape to the sewers (from which they were later driven by gas-bombs), others emerged to fight to the last with the enemy, yet others died in the fire and the bombardment. Michel was among those who ran from the shelter, emptying his revolver, to die face to face with the enemy.

It was virtually the end of the ghetto and by 16 May Stroop could announce that the major operation was over. His troops were withdrawn, but twenty thousand of Germany's best fighting men had been tied up for nearly four weeks and the German war industry had lost, in the ghetto factories, one of its more important supply centres.

Most of the inhabitants died during the battle. A few managed to escape through the sewers to join the partisans in the country. Others survived among the ruins, and for three or four months led an animal-like existence, hunted by German patrols and surviving on hidden stores of food.

For many months the mopping-up operation went on. The ruined buildings were dynamited, a special railway was built to bring salvage out of the ghetto, the last, hunted people were rounded up and deported. By September, 1943, nothing was left of an area which had supported half a million people but a field of rubble, twenty feet deep.

The Final Solution to Oradour

About twenty-two kilometres from Limoges in south-west France, just north of the main road which runs on to Angoulême and thence to Bordeaux and the Biscay coast, lies the small town of Oradour-sur-Glâne. To be more precise, there are two towns of the same name—one living, one dead—and they exist side-by-side. The dead town is enclosed by a high wall, by the main gate of which a large sign urges SILENCE. Beyond the wall lie the remains of a community and township that were massacred and razed by a German *Waffen*-S.S. unit on Saturday, 10 June, 1944—only four days after D-day, when the allied forces made their invasion landing on the Normandy beachheads.

The new Oradour (situated on the north bank of the tiny river Glâne) possesses a neat and well-groomed air which one finds slightly surprising in provincial France where most small towns appear to be faintly (and sometimes alarmingly) decrepit—although there are occasional tiny pockets of smart new development. In itself it holds little for the tourist. Apart from pausing for brief refreshment, most visitors pass through towards the gate marked SILENCE.

Beyond the gate the high street, with its long-rusted tram-track, recedes towards the burned-out shell of the distant church. Grass grows green through the neglected tarmac of the road so that it looks like a long narrow field. The buildings on either side of the road are roofless ruins and rubble; they have not been touched in nearly thirty years. There is, at first, an atmosphere of unreality about the place, as if it were a kind of elaborate film-studio set, but as one walks along the street it all becomes only too real.

The *gendarmerie*, the post-office, the local shops, the private houses—all are destroyed and open to the sky. In some of the houses cooking-pots still lie on ancient rusted stoves. Elsewhere are relics of bicycles, some agricultural machines and burned-out motor-cars of the late-thirties vintage. And the signs: *Ici lieu de supplice—une groupe des hommes fut massacrée et brulée par les Allemandes* (Here is a place of execution—a group of men was massacred and burned by the Germans); not just in one place, but scattered throughout the town in halls, garages and barns where parties of men were taken to be machine-gunned and set fire to by the S.S.

Next to the *boulangerie* another sign announces: *Ici furent retrouvés deux corps calcinés* (Here were found two bodies burned to cinders); and in a hedge bordering a side road: *Ici fut trouvé le corps de Monsieur Poutaraud.*

Beyond the open square in the centre of the town one finally comes upon the church, broken and desolate, with only the tall crucifix outside remaining intact, and behind it a sign which begins: "Here hundreds of women and children were massacred by the Germans. You who pass by, meditate. You who believe, pray for the victims and their families."

The cemetery is signposted *Tombeau des Martyres* (Tomb of the Martyrs—Here sleep the dead. Pilgrims think of them in silence and reflection). It is a vast place with a tall central monument at the foot of which are two glass coffins containing the charred bones of many of the victims of the massacre—the unidentified remains disinterred from behind the church where they had hastily been buried in a trench by the Germans. Elsewhere, in the French fashion, the graves are adorned by small portraits of the dead, and there are mass graves, too. Nearly one thousand people of all ages were murdered in Oradour-sur-Glâne on that warm June day.

*   *   *

It was Saturday in Oradour-sur-Glâne, and the town was

busy with shoppers from the local hamlets of the rural Commune. Around 2 p.m., when most people were engrossed in their mid-day meal (the French always take their eating very seriously, even under conditions of stringent wartime rationing), a convoy of German armoured cars and trucks containing troops wearing the camouflaged denims of the *Waffen*-S.S. drove into the town and stationed themselves in the main square and on the exit roads.

At this stage the reaction of the people was one of curiosity rather than anxiety. Oradour was a quiet town, in no way a centre of underground Maquis activity, and there had been no incidents with the occupying Germans, although the enemy had committed atrocities against innocent civilians in the Limoges area as reprisals for Maquis attacks. The allied invasion forces were surging across the Channel into northern France, and that must surely occupy the attention of the Germans and concentrate their efforts towards the "second front". Oradour itself was in that southern part of France controlled by the Vichy government, so that there was no immediate threat to the Germans deployed there.

On the other hand, the Maquis had been intensifying their operations against German lines of communication and personnel to prevent reserves of troops being rushed north to reinforce their retreating comrades in Normandy. It was therefore to be expected that the Germans would retaliate in their own ruthless fashion wherever a Maquis hotbed was discovered, or even suspected. But on this count Oradour and its surrounding hamlets of Puy-Gaillard and Bregères were in the clear. Basically a rural community, Oradour's population had increased during the war by the arrival of refugees, mainly from Lorraine, and people from nearby Limoges who found country life less harrowing.

The sight of German troops, even the S.S., was no novelty, but never before had they arrived in such large numbers. Few people thought of trying to hide or escape at that time, and in any case the town was now encircled by troops and cut off from its environment.

The next step was a proclamation made by the town-crier ordering every inhabitant—man, woman or child, whether ill, crippled or not—to go at once to the Champ de Foire, which was the square in the centre of the town. Schoolchildren were dealt with in a different way; that afternoon they were due to assemble in various school buildings for a general medical inspection, but the commander of the S.S. detachment issued instructions that they should be taken by their teachers to the church instead, where they would be "safe" if any trouble broke out in the town.

And so to the church went the 191 schoolchildren of Oradour-sur-Glâne, with but one exception—eight-year-old Roger Godfrin, a young refugee from Lorraine who "knew" the Germans from experience and managed to make his escape by crawling through gardens and fields away from the guarded roads. Of the full total of 247 children in Oradour, he was to be the only survivor.

Meanwhile S.S. patrols marched round the small township, forcing their way into each house to make sure that everybody without exception would assemble on the square. And among them, of course, were visitors to the town who did not actually live there—no matter, they had to parade just the same with the rest.

There was still no undue apprehension or panic. This kind of performance was typically Teutonic—probably a check of identity cards, or a pretext to immobilize the populace while S.S. patrols searched houses and buildings for arms or evidence of Maquis activity. In that case there was little to worry about.

The real doubts and fears began when the Germans began methodically to separate the assembled crowd into two sections—the men on one side, and the women and children on the other. The women with their children, which included babes in arms, would be sent to the church to join the schoolchildren who were already assembled there, the commandant explained. That sounded reassuring enough—at least the church was a place of peace and sanctuary—but the women were now afraid for their menfolk—their fathers, husbands, brothers and sons.

After the women and children had been escorted away, the German officer then demanded hostages who would be held as prisoners while the houses of the town were searched. The mayor, Dr Paul Desourteaux, offered himself and his four sons. The officer then demanded that he should name other hostages to make a total of thirty, but this the mayor refused to do. The German officer seemed unconcerned and did not pursue the question of hostages any further. It was all part of the act aimed at demoralizing his now extremely anxious audience.

Meanwhile, beyond the guarded perimeter of Oradour-sur-Glâne, life went on as normal. Visitors were allowed into the town, but not one of them ever left again. They were forced to join the throng in the square and await their fate.

An hour of mounting tension passed uneasily by before the men were again addressed by the German commander. He stated that he had information that somewhere in the town was a secret store of Maquis arms, and that until they were found the men would be divided into groups, taken under escort to enclosed buildings such as barns and garages, and there kept under guard until a thorough search of every building had been completed.

The groups were formed and led away, and the massacre was about to begin. Of all these men only five survived. The firing of the machine-guns could clearly be heard by the women in the church, and they knew the truth—"they are killing our men". But they could not see the true horror of the massacre—the automatic weapons mowing down the men so that they fell one on top of the other in a mass of blood-soaked humanity, not all dead, but many unable to move because of the weight of bodies on top of them. Nor could they see the Germans throwing masses of straw over the bodies, alive or dead, soaking it with petrol, and then setting fire to it.

This was the procedure in all seven of the places selected by the Germans as a *lieu de supplice*, and yet, from these several infernos, as if by a miracle, as many as five men managed to escape. Their names were Borie, Broussaudier, Darthout, Hebras and Roby. The latter, Yvon Roby, was eighteen years old at the time, and his story is recorded in the official dossier of Oradour-sur-Glâne prepared during the subsequent investigation.

Roby and his group were forced inside the barn. Four German soldiers armed with tommy-guns stood at the door to prevent escape. For some five minutes nothing happened and then, acting on a signal fired from the square, the soldiers opened fire. The first to fall were protected from subsequent bursts of fire by the bodies of those who fell on top of them, so that any wounded survivors were pinned helplessly at the bottom of the pile—"some of the wounded were screaming and others calling for their wives and children".

When the firing stopped the soldiers trampled over the heap of bodies, shooting at point-blank range any men who still showed signs of life. Gradually the screams died down and the shots became less frequent until there was a heavy silence disturbed only by the movements and groans of those in their final death throes.

The Germans then covered the mound of bodies with straw, hay, wood and anything that would burn, and then set fire to it. Roby, wounded in the left arm and hampered by the weight of bodies above him, struggled to get free and eventually succeeded. The Germans had gone. In a race against the spreading fire and the suffocating smoke he managed to climb through a small hole in the wall high above the ground and hid in an adjoining loft—where he discovered four friends who had managed to escape before him.

They hid under a pile of straw and dried beans, but even then they were not safe. A German soldier came into the loft and set fire to the straw. Scorched and stifling, Roby and his comrades had to wait until the S.S. man had left before they could attempt a second escape. They managed to get out of the barn and hid in a rabbit-hutch for three hours until that, too, was threatened by the advancing flames.

In the end they were able to reach the cemetery, and from there open country and woodland—and safety at last. Among all the other men there were no survivors.

While all this was happening, some five hundred women and children, locked in the church, waited for two hours wondering what their fate was to be. They had heard the shooting of the tommy-guns and had no illusions left. And yet, when the church door finally opened and two S.S. men came in, hope surged among them—"at last, they are going to set us free!" But it was not to be—only one woman, Madame Rouffanche, was destined to survive the horror that was to come.

The two Germans were carrying between them a large box from which hung what appeared to be cords, but were in fact fuses. They placed the box at the head of the nave near the choir, lit the fuses, then went out again, locking the church door behind them. Almost immediately the box exploded, hurling forth dense black clouds of suffocating smoke.

Panic took over. The women, clutching their babies and children, squeezed themselves into remote parts of the church where they could still breathe. They threw themselves at the solid doors and clawed at the stone walls in a frantic effort to escape. Then, under the sheer weight of human bodies, the vestry door collapsed, and the hundreds of trapped women and children surged towards this new but narrow avenue of hope.

But the Germans had thought of everything. They were waiting in ambush, machine-guns ready to fire through the windows at the terrified people as they struggled desperately to get into the vestry and so out of the church. They were shot down remorselessly in their hundreds, in the church and in the vestry. The bullet marks are in the stone walls to this day.

Madame Rouffanche, the only survivor, said: "My daughter was killed at my side by a shot fired from the outside. I owe my life to having the presence of mind to close my eyes and feign death."

The next step was the ritual of the funeral pyre. Straw, wood and chairs were flung over the bodies lying all over the church floor. Madame Rouffanche, miraculously unwounded despite the carnage, was able to use the pervading obscurity of the stifling smoke to hide behind the high altar. In the wall above her was a high window. With the help of a short ladder used for lighting the church candles she managed to reach the window. The glass was already broken, and she was able to jump through the frame, dropping ten feet to the ground outside.

As she picked herself up to run away she saw another woman at the window, holding out a baby and crying, "Save my child—take her". She dropped the infant to the ground while she herself prepared to leap out of the window to join Madame Rouffanche in a desperate bid to escape through the presbytery gardens. Too late. The screams of the baby had attracted the attention of the Germans.

Shots rang out. In a moment the young mother and her baby were dead, while Madame Rouffanche, wounded by a bullet, managed to reach the comparative shelter of the gardens. And there she lay, motionless, among rows of green peas, until 5 p.m. the following day when at last she was discovered by her own countrymen. No other female of whatever age in Oradour survived.

The final scene in the church, still smoke filled, was the ultimate in horror. Before setting the funeral pyre alight the Germans fired their tommy-guns at random and without respite into the mass of bodies, dead and dying, until there was silence. And then the fire was started. The church of Oradour-sur-Glâne burned for hours.

The Germans spent the night drinking, singing, looting and burning down the town, and then drove away, leaving a smouldering ruin of death behind them. Peace and quiet descended upon the dead who, beneath the ashes that covered them, were sleeping the dreamless sleep of martyrs.

On the day following the massacre it was formally announced in a communiqué by the Germans that "in the course of military operations" Oradour-sur-Glâne had been reduced to "rubble and ashes". No additional comment was made. Two days after the atrocity a unit of German troops returned to the scene of their crime to throw any identifiable human remains into hastily dug trenches behind the church and in other parts of the countryside.

Even so, when the ruins of Oradour were visited a few days later by an official from the Ministry of Health of the Vichy government, charred human debris was found in the church and elsewhere. The remains of the bodies in the church alone were sufficient to fill a large farm wagon.

Why was Oradour-sur-Glâne razed to the ground and all its inhabitants murdered? Too many reasons have been given for any one of them to be individually valid. It has been said that an error was made by the S.S., that Oradour-sur-Glâne was destroyed in mistake for Oradour-sur-Vayres, which was an important Maquis resistance centre. Another story is that weapons had been found in a garage in Oradour by a member of the S.S. who had decided to return with a task force to wipe out the town and its inhabitants.

Or a fight had broken out between a group of rebellious Frenchmen and some German soldiers in which two of the latter were killed—or that two German officers had been killed in an attack on a German "tourist" vehicle visiting the Oradour district—or that a German officer who had been captured by the Maquis and led through the town, his wrists bound with wire, to be shot, had been attacked by some women of the town, but that he had managed to escape and return to Limoges to organize a punitive expedition.

But there has never been any corroboration of these alleged incidents, and although the matter was taken up by the Vichy government with the German High Command in France, no explanation was ever forthcoming. Revenge or reprisal? True, Lidice in Czechoslovakia was also razed to the ground, but that was as a reprisal for the assassination by shooting of no less a person than S.S. *Obergruppenführer* Reinhard Heydrich, one of the Nazi "top brass". No such justification existed in the case of Oradour-sur-Glâne, and one is left with the assumption that the town was murdered to terrorize the population in an area of intense Maquis activity and so discourage co-operation with the underground resistance fighters at a time when the allied forces were already advancing beyond the Normandy beaches into German-occupied continental Europe.

There is one other odd link connecting the massacres and destruction of Oradour-sur-Glâne and Lidice. Both happened on 10 June—Lidice in 1942, and Oradour in 1944. Coincidence?

Hiroshima—Death and Rebirth

Near the south-western tip of Honshu, the largest of the four main islands that make up the boomerang shape of Japan, lies the sizeable industrial city of Hiroshima. Until the closing days of the Second World War comparatively few people in the West had ever heard of the place, and then suddenly, on 6 August, 1945, Hiroshima literally exploded and burned itself immortally into the pages of human history. The world has never been the same since.

At about seven o'clock on that particular morning in the late summer of 1945 the air-raid sirens wailed throughout Hiroshima. Young Yoshio, hurrying on his newspaper delivery round, was unconcerned; nearly every morning American high-flying planes would pass over on reconnaissance missions, but there had been no bombs. The city had been surprisingly free from air attack, even though its harbour, oil refineries, factories, arsenal and garrison of some 150,000 troops made it a legitimate military target.

To Yoshio and many of his fellow citizens the explanation was simple enough. Hiroshima had been spared because so many local inhabitants had emigrated to America before the war and had managed to persuade the U.S. political hierarchy to overlook the city—and it was even rumoured that a distant relative of President Truman was living anonymously in the neighbourhood. On the other hand, ten days earlier an American plane had dropped leaflets on the town warning that it would be among the Japanese cities to be destroyed by air attack unless Japan capitulated immediately. There was no discernible alarm, but then the leaflets had not mentioned that the air attack when it came would consist of one single bomb that had cost £500 million to develop and was destined to change the course of history.

The local authorities were taking the usual precautions. Later in the day, when his job was finished, fifteen-year-old Yoshio would be joining other youths and students in demolishing houses and other property—much of it constructed from wood—to create fire-breaks in the event of bombing. It was all rather fun and somewhat remote from reality.

The population of Hiroshima at that time numbered around 343,000. Although many people and children had been evacuated from the city, there remained about a quarter of a million in the business and residential centre which covered an area of four square miles. It was in that central zone that Yoshio lived in a small house with his parents. In an hour or so, when his work was finished, he would be returning home for a late breakfast with his mother; by then his father would already have left for work in the factory.

As usual, the air-raid alert proved uneventful and the all-clear was sounded soon after seven-thirty. Very few people had bothered to take cover in air-raid shelters. At eight o'clock a radio news bulletin mentioned that two or three American B29 Super-Fortresses had been sighted, but they were flying high at around 30,000 feet and were obviously reconnaissance planes. In fact, as the casual and reassuring news announcement was being made, the bombardier in the B29 Super-Fortress *Enola Gay*, commanded by Colonel Paul W. Tibbets of the U.S. Army Air Force, had already released the first atomic bomb ever to be used in warfare. From a height of five miles it parachuted down with deadly precision to the centre of Hiroshima. At a predetermined altitude of 1,500 feet two slugs of plutonium inside the bomb fused together to form an over-critical mass—the chain reaction of nuclear fission was instant, incandescent and incredibly violent. That one bomb released the destructive impact of 20,000 tons of T.N.T.

All that Yoshio could afterwards remember of that significant moment of history was the blinding white flash in the morning sky and the intolerably searing heat. He was lucky, for he was two miles from the epicentre of the explosion and close to a friend's house. Nevertheless for a few moments he lost consciousness in the heat-flash and blast, and recovered to find himself crumpled against a tottering wall and the air full of flying debris.

Confused and afraid, he dragged himself to his feet and hurried to his friend's house. Only the walls remained standing—the roof, windows and doors had been torn violently away as if by a giant unseen hand. Stumbling into the ruins of the house, Yoshio came almost immediately upon the dead body of his friend, broken among the rubble and skewered by a long shard of glass. He stood for a while, stunned and unable to think, and gradually became aware of his own wounds, but they seemed slight enough—some cuts and abrasions and a painfully bruised shoulder.

His mind still blank and uncomprehending, he went out into the road again. An incredible mass of dark cloud was rising swiftly above the centre of the city and spreading outwards at its summit to form a gigantic mushroom. Beneath it other clouds boiled and unfolded in turbulent motion. Across the city whirlwinds sucked dust and debris into the darkening air. Now there was a new light in the sky—a flickering orange glow from thousands of burning buildings adding their own smoke to the expanding mushroom.

From the wreckage screams and groans came from all directions, but Yoshio had no ears for them. Only one thing mattered at that moment—to return home as quickly as possible and find his parents. He ran desperately, stumbling and gasping in the foul air, making for the city centre where he lived, but soon had to stop in total bewilderment. Before him was a vast wilderness of smouldering ruins. There was no way of finding the street, let alone the house, where he had lived all his life. Almost every building had been razed to the ground, and it was only by the surviving metal ribs of the dome of what had been the Museum of Science and Industry that he was able to gain a sense of direction.

For a long time he wandered around, seeking some recognizable landmarks of his own familiar neighbourhood, but in vain. It was dangerous to stay any longer. The fires were spreading and in places the ground was so hot that it burned his shoes; very soon the centre of the city would be a raging inferno.

Reluctantly he abandoned his quest. Saying a short prayer for his mother and father and silently promising them that he would return, he made his way towards the suburbs, the river and safety. Now he responded to screams and cries from the ruins around him and helped others to dig among the rubble, but the fire spread so quickly that the rescuers were forced to leave the trapped victims to be suffocated or burned alive.

He became aware of horrors around him which he had ignored in the obsessive search for his parents. Men, women and children, their bodies grotesquely burned by the heat-flash of the bomb, dragged themselves painfully away from the fires that threatened to overtake them. Some, whose faces must have been turned towards the flash, no longer had recognizable features, and their unprotected hands were charred claws. Many had found their way to water tanks to immerse their heads and ease the pain—only to die where they lay.

The refugees from the stricken city grew quickly in number. They did not talk nor, outside of family groups, did they help each other. Yoshio found himself one of this strange, stumbling procession of automatons.

Suddenly he heard his name called. He turned and recognized the girl running towards him as his cousin. Her face was scarlet with burns, and her hair and clothes had been severely scorched. He took off his shirt to cover her and observed that the gaily flowered pattern of her kimono had duplicated itself on her body where the heat-flash had penetrated the darker colours and been partly reflected by the lighter ones.

Her story was typical of many. She had been on her way to school when the flash came and the world collapsed around her. For a while she had been totally blinded, but when she could see again the fires had prevented her from trying to return home, so she had simply joined the stream of refugees, too shocked to think for herself. She had no idea what had become of her parents, who were Yoshio's uncle and aunt.

Yoshio decided to get her to hospital for urgent treatment, overlooking the fact that there were thousands of others aiming for the same destination. In fact, so dense was the crowd of injured people surrounding the hospital that it was impossible to push a way through. He did not know that only three of Hiroshima's hospitals were left standing, while most of the doctors and nurses were dead or too seriously wounded to be able to work. Those who remained worked unceasingly day and night with inadequate facilities and supplies until suitable help could be obtained from nearby towns.

Yoshio and his cousin decided to go to a park on the river bank where at least there would be water and shade. Here the grass was still green and relatively unscorched, for it was quite a long way from the epicentre of the explosion. Then came the rain—black and viscous like oil—but it did not last long enough to damp down the flames of the burning city. It was merely precipitation of the hot air from the explosion as it rose and condensed over the city, but it brought down with it the radioactive dust of destruction.

There were thousands in the park, but Yoshio and the girl found a place near to the river where she could lie down to rest. Hunting around the river bank he found a small chipped pot which he filled with water to take back to his cousin. The girl sipped a little with difficulty through her scorched lips and then vomited, but presently she drank some more and seemed easier. He left her in a quiet sleep.

The water incident had not gone unnoticed. All around him, heat-flash victims were asking for water, and for an hour or two Yoshio acted as a water-carrier for those too ill to help themselves. The service ended suddenly when an official knocked the chipped pot from his hand so that it shattered on the ground. Yoshio's angry outburst was silenced when the official explained that water was extremely harmful for people with those kind of injuries.

Early in the afternoon the fire reached the park, but here it was easier to control and a chain of men succeeded in holding the flames at bay—though not before the panic-stricken crowds had pressed towards the comparative safety in such numbers that many of the weaker ones were drowned. Some managed to reach the sandbanks in the middle of the river where they thought they were safe—and so they were, until the tide rose and swept them away. In the park itself the living, the dying and the dead lay side by side. People died quietly, without making a sound.

Towards evening a small naval launch came up the river. On the deck an officer with a megaphone announced that a naval hospital ship was on its way to rescue survivors. The boost in the morale of the people in the park was tremendous; for the first time Yoshio detected signs of optimism and animation. But no hospital ship ever came.

He slept uneasily that night. His cousin had been vomiting again, as had so many of the other heat-flash victims. In the morning when he awoke he found her dead—just one of hundreds who had died overnight.

Weighed down with fatigue and sorrow. Yoshio left the girl's body in the care of a family who had spent the night near by, and decided to make his way back towards the city centre. The fire had now burned itself out. Only twenty-four hours earlier, he reminded himself, Hiroshima had been a busy bustling city starting on a new day, and now it had practically vanished off the face of the earth. At a thousand metres from the epicentre he saw trains that had been hurled like toys many yards from their tracks, trams that had been lifted and dropped on to flattened buildings, and even the bridge by which he entered the city had had its concrete roadway shifted in its entirety.

Near the epicentre what was left of the city was a vast crematorium. Small heaps of ashes indicated where people had been totally consumed where they stood at the moment of the explosion. Perhaps even more macabre were the shadows of people and things etched on to scorched concrete walls by the heat-flash. Thus was immortalized the shadow of a painter, his brush raised, and the shadows of a carter and his horse. Ceramic tiles, with a melting point of 1,300 degrees Centigrade, had dissolved. Marble tombstones had been uprooted and flung as though made of cardboard.

Yoshio, in common with his fellow citizens at that time, had no idea what could have caused this incredible holocaust. It was assumed that many bombs must have been dropped simultaneously in one place, and not for many days was it to be rumoured that a completely new kind of explosive in a single bomb had been used.

After a thorough search of the environs of his former home and the house of his aunt and uncle, Yoshio gave up the hopeless task. He had to reconcile himself to the fact that he was now alone in the world. The most useful thing he could do under the circumstances would be to go to the Red Cross Hospital and offer to help in any way he could.

No relief came to Hiroshima until late in the day, and even then neither doctors nor medical supplies arrived. Police and working crews came in from nearby towns to collect thousands of corpses for cremation and set up food centres to distribute rice balls to those refugees who had not eaten since the previous morning. At the Red Cross Hospital Yoshio's offer of assistance was gratefully accepted. As he knew the city so well he was assigned to search the ruins of other hospitals for any medical supplies that might have escaped total destruction. As a matter of policy the doctors were only treating the slightly wounded for they had already discovered that those who were seriously injured or constantly vomiting would die inevitably, whatever was done for them. Another curious effect was that even small wounds would not heal for a long time, but would remain swollen and painful, and highly vulnerable to infection. This was due to the destruction of the white blood cells by radiation, but this was not realized immediately.

Yoshio was partly successful in his search for medical supplies, discovering quantities of mercurochrome and an analgesic which were more than welcome. Visiting one ruined hospital he came upon a small detachment of soldiers from the garrison who asked him for water. All were dreadfully mutilated, with faces burned away and eye-sockets hollow. He thought they were probably anti-aircraft gunners who had been looking up into the sky at the time of the explosion. He produced a water-bottle but had great difficulty in pouring water into their charred, deformed mouths. Full of pity and horror, he promised to send a doctor to them on his return to the hospital—but, of course, the doctor's reply was as expected: "We have no time to spare for those who are already doomed."

By this time the high mortality rate among those who had suffered no apparent injury was creating apprehension among the survivors. Most doctors thought that blood transfusions were not only useless but possibly harmful, since the patient might continue to bleed once the syringe had been withdrawn. In fact, rest and transfusions were the two main effective treatments for radiation sickness, but only a mere handful of doctors and scientists in the whole of Japan knew anything about it.

Three days after the Hiroshima catastrophe, at 11 a.m. on 9 August, 1945, an American Super-Fortress dropped a second atomic bomb on the industrial city of Nagasaki. As in Hiroshima, every building within a mile radius of the epicentre of the explosion was razed to the ground, apart from a few reinforced concrete structures. The dead in Nagasaki numbered 37,501 and the injured (many of whom died later) 51,580. Hiroshima's toll was higher—78,150 killed and 58,839 injured. Five days after the second A-bomb, Japan surrendered unconditionally

Around this time Yoshio, still working at the hospital, was horrified to find his thick black hair falling out in chunks if he combed it or ran his fingers through it. His fatigue increased, and when his temperature rose and remained high for three days the doctors ordered him to bed. For two weeks he lay there, during which time his white blood cell count fell to such a low level that the doctors despaired of saving him, but as he had worked so willingly and hard for the hospital he was given the most careful and dedicated treatment available, including liver injections and copious quantities of vitamins.

After the Japanese capitulation the American doctors moved in at high speed to Hiroshima and Nagasaki to gain first-hand medical experience about the effects of the A-bomb, about which little was known. They also brought medical supplies and blood plasma, from which Yoshio benefited and slowly made a recovery.

Meanwhile, many of the people who had been terrified to return to Hiroshima had decided to come back and build again in the ruins. It had been rumoured that nothing would ever grow again in Hiroshima and that no one could survive there for at least seven—some believed seventy— years. Nevertheless, there was a steady trickle of returning citizens, though not to the devastated centre of the town. Homes were skilfully constructed from the plentiful wreckage, and in a surprisingly short time Hiroshima, despite the lack of electricity, trams and trains, came back to life. And though the vegetation had been burned, the roots were apparently stimulated by the radiation so that in the season after the bomb weeds grew to rain-forest dimensions all over the city.

A pleasant surprise awaited Yoshio when he was finally well enough to be discharged from hospital. Instead of going back to his former newspaper delivery round, he was offered a job on the staff of the paper itself, the *Choguku Shimbun*, Hiroshima's own "daily". Astonishingly the newspaper was in production again, though the type was being cast in the open air and an air-raid shelter served as a photographic dark-room. For young Yoshio it was the start of a new life and a new career which suited him well.

Reconstruction work in Hiroshima was hampered by nature itself. On 17 September there was a cloudburst, and twenty-four hours later the electricity power-station, which had only been functioning for a few days, broke down. Nearly all the shacks, newly rebuilt and hastily put together, were blown down by hurricanes or washed away by floods.

This latest series of disasters might have been expected to break the spirit of the people, but they rallied and set to work undoing the damage and continuing rebuilding. They were accustomed to flooding, for Hiroshima is built on islands separated by the seven tributaries of the Ohta river, and floods are common enough in the rainy season.

Towards the end of September the American Army of Occupation moved in—an event feared by most of the inhabitants, who no doubt expected brutality and rape. The people of Hiroshima sent away their wives and children, locked their doors and went nervously to work on the day the "foreign devils" arrived. The Americans, for their part, naturally anticipated more hatred and bitterness in Hiroshima (and Nagasaki) than anywhere else in Japan.

The mechanized columns rolled in at mid-day, and it was not long before the G.I.s were breaking the ice by handing out chocolate to the children. The citizens themselves, mainly Buddhists, seemed stoically reconciled to the fate which had dealt them such a terrible blow, and they greeted the Americans with courtesy and even hospitality.

From that point on Hiroshima settled down to a more normal life, and today is a thriving modern city with few signs of the scars of a quarter of a century ago. The American estimate of deaths at the time (78,150) is likely to be too low a figure as people continued to die from the effects of radiation for a long time afterwards. The total death-roll is probably nearer to 100,000.

Many of the survivors of the bomb were known as "keloids" from the thick pink rubbery scars left from the heat-flash burns. Despite the horrors they had suffered, survivors continued to return to Hiroshima, whose population had been reduced to one-third after the bomb. But there were also casualties of a different kind—orphans. Bands of orphan boys turned to the streets to make a good living from black-market deals and even less respectable employment. The guileless Americans were a ready source of supply and demand, and had it not been for them these neglected youngsters would not have found their new way of life so successful. Yoshio himself, with a secure job, felt himself lucky, and spent a great deal of his spare time with these rootless boys, trying to settle them in employment and helping them in other ways.

The spiritual harm to the city of Hiroshima lasted for many years after the dropping of the bomb, the morality of which has exercised the minds of humanists, and indeed all thinking people, since 6 August, 1945. There is perhaps one justification—it has been estimated by military experts that the use of the atomic bomb shortened the war in the Pacific by a year, and saved the lives of a million American troops and a quarter of a million British.

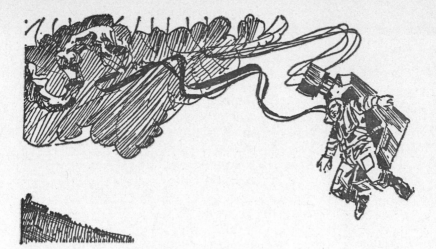

The Test-Parachutist

In the sleepy little village of Higher Denham, in Bucking-hamshire, there stands a factory whose fifteen hundred workers and executives are busily engaged day after day in turning out one of the more remarkable products of the age in which we live. This product, the brainchild of a stocky, eccentric Irishman, Sir James Martin, is a miracle of precision engineering, and to date it has saved almost three thousand lives. It has saved them, moreover, in cir-cumstances when no salvation seemed possible; and salva-tion would not, indeed, have *been* possible but for this strange, complicated invention. The product is the Martin-Baker ejection-seat.

This unconventional, explosive armchair, which is fitted to the high-performance military aircraft of more than forty countries throughout the world, including the United States of America, enables the pilot or crew-member to fire himself to freedom in moments of desperate danger when high speed or low altitude would make unassisted escape a physical impossibility. Its record of life-saving achieve-ment is truly astonishing; from aircraft in flames at eighty thousand feet, from aircraft cart-wheeling out of control along the runway, from aircraft sinking fathoms deep beneath the surface of the sea, the airmen have come shoot-ing out, catapulted to safety by the simple action of pulling hard on a wire-and-rubber firing-handle above their heads.

In the most modern versions of the seat that one action is all that is necessary; the airman, though possibly injured or even unconscious, will automatically be freed from the seat at the zenith of its rocket-propelled climb, his parachute will blossom open without benefit of rip-cord, and, if he should have ejected at high altitude, that opening will be delayed until he has dropped to a level where there is no longer any danger of frostbite or lethal lack of oxygen.

And so today there are nearly three thousand men roaming the world, each with his tale of terror, of having come as close to death as a man can come and still survive to talk about it; but behind all these miraculous escapes, making them possible, there lies another story—the story of the men who have used the ejection-seat not in an emergency but as a necessary experiment; the men who, in cold blood, have fired themselves into the utterly unknown—the test-parachutists. Of this select little band of aviation pioneers, who share between them a vast fund of frightening experiences, a few have achieved fame. There cannot be many modern flyers, military or civilian, who have not heard, for example, of Benny Lynch, Henry Nielson, and Ed Sperry.

So far as ejection is concerned, it was Benny Lynch who set the whole thing moving. For it was he who, on 24 July, 1946, over Chalgrove airfield in Oxfordshire, made the very first test ejection, firing himself out of a Meteor jet-fighter in a neck-or-nothing experiment that was to alter the whole future of aircrew survival. Imagining the silent loneliness of Lynch, cooped up *incommunicado* in the rear cockpit of the Meteor, his only connexion with the outside world a series of flashing lights, facing a critical experience no man had ever faced before, with his life dependent upon another man's calculations, one can only wonder at the mental toughness that enabled him to keep his understandable and inevitable fear under rigid control.

Nielson and Sperry, two of America's finest test-parachutists, provide another example of triumph over terror. One day, fifty thousand feet over the Gulf of Mexico, Nielson was subjected to an agonizing phenomenon hitherto unknown in flying. His high-altitude test ejection was orthodox enough to start with, and he was untroubled as he rapidly gathered pace in the long "free fall" that would plummet him at a hundred and twenty miles an hour through forty thousand feet before his parachute opened automatically at the safe level of ten thousand. Suddenly, however, lying on his back, Nielson began to spin, faster and faster, his legs whipping round and round above his head, a human centrifuge with the blood being dragged from his chest and stomach and forced simultaneously to both his head and his legs.

The pain was almost unbearable, but even worse was the fear, the sense of utter helplessness. For, as has since been discovered by other parachutists, a basic characteristic of the "back-down spin" is that it induces a sense of nausea and enervation so overpowering that the victim finds himself almost incapable of rational action—even such obvious and vital action as pulling the rip-cord and so saving his own life. This Henry Nielson endured throughout a seemingly endless fall of more than thirty-five thousand feet before at last, by an almost superhuman effort of will, he managed to drag the emergency rip-cord from its housing and put an end to his suffering.

He was badly shaken by the experience, but he was every inch of him a professional, and his description of what had happened was both lucid and detailed. The immediate reaction of his senior colleague, Captain Ed Sperry, was exactly what one would expect of such a man. He pondered over Lieutenant Nielson's report, he puzzled as to the probable cause of the spinning phenomenon—and he went up to fifty thousand feet the very next day to duplicate Nielson's test under identical conditions.

He fired himself out of the aircraft, he settled into the steady acceleration of the free fall, and, like Nielson, he began to spin. Unlike Nielson, however, Sperry went into action at once, and to the observers following his flight through the monitoring cameras he looked like a man demented. He was punching and kicking in all directions, performing a Dervish dance with no rhythm or pattern to it—but suddenly he was no longer spinning. His crazed gymnastics had broken up the flow of air over the surface of his body, and the inexorable forces of aero-dynamics were robbed of their chance to assume control. The lesson was learned, the flight reports disseminated throughout air-forces all over the world, and one more step forward had been taken in the march towards aircrew safety. Sperry's ice-cold courage, his total confidence in himself and in the accuracy of his colleague's test-reporting, had won a notable victory over ignorance and fear.

These, then, are examples of the work carried out by men famous in this tiny, esoteric profession of test-parachuting. What follows, however, is the story of a man equally brave, equally dedicated, whose name is scarcely known, even in the specialized world of flying. This is the story of P. J. Page, who briefly shared with Benny Lynch the responsibility of testing the early, prototype versions of the Martin-Baker ejection-seat. Page made the third and the fourth experiments in the seat, after Lynch had made the first two, and his testing career began and ended within the space of seventy-two hours.

After Lynch had opened the era of assisted escape in 1946, there was an interval of just over a year during which the ejection-seat was transformed from an inventor's triumph— a stunt, almost, though a stunt with an important purpose— into a practical life-saving device almost ready for installation in the high-performance aircraft of the time; the Hunters, the Sabres, the several aeroplanes that operated about or beyond the speed of sound. It now became necessary to establish whether the seat would function satisfactorily at such phenomenal speeds and whether, if it did, the man sitting in it would live to tell the tale. In high-speed escape the greatest imponderable was then, and always will be, the limit of human tolerance, the capacity of the body to take punishment. Lynch's first ejections, the proving shots, had taken place at around two hundred miles an hour, Page's first sortie at the same speed; they established nothing more than the feasibility of the project, the basic efficiency of the invention. Now it was time to relate the invention to the circumstances under which it would have to fulfil its promise. James Martin asked P. J. Page whether he would be willing to make an ejection during a high-speed run.

Page, of course, said yes: test-parachutists do not flinch at new assignments. He did not ask his employer at what speed the test would be made, and Martin did not offer the information. He reckoned, one imagines, that a test-man works best with his mind unclouded by apprehension. The step-up was, in fact, immense—one hundred per cent. Page was to be shot out of an aircraft flying at four hundred miles an hour, face-first into the howling blast of the slipstream, subject to an instant deceleration not all that far removed from the braking qualities offered by a concrete wall. Page was about to cross the frontiers of real danger. This is Page's story, and it deserves to be told, if only because he himself has not told it, because he accepted disaster and its appalling aftermath without, characteristically, so much as a whimper.

On 14 August, 1947, he hunched himself into the rear compartment of the Chalgrove Meteor, into a tiny cell with armour-plating all around him and several hundred gallons of aviation paraffin at his back. He was faced with the knowledge, enough to scare any normal man, that the pattern of events to follow would be determined by him and by him alone: the pilot, sure, would bring the aeroplane to the right height, seven thousand feet, and would steer it accurately across the airfield, nose-first into the prevailing wind; the pilot, equally certain, would flash the signal lights to indicate when it was time to leave—but the bit that mattered, the heaving down on the firing-handle, the decision whether or not to go, that depended on one man and one man only—P. J. Page.

Page thought about his task, and shivered. He was a trained parachutist, an ex-soldier of the British airborne forces, but this was something different from dropping out of a slow-moving transport aircraft with a parachute that opened automatically and a watchful air-force instructor at his elbow to ensure that all was well; this was a one-man adventure, a sortie into the dangerous unknown. He was not quite certain, all of a sudden, whether he could handle it.

But now they were at altitude, the Meteor flashing in towards Chalgrove with the needle showing three hundred, three-fifty, four hundred miles an hour, and the time for introspection was over—now there was only one simple snap decision, whether to carry out his voluntary job (Dear God, what had persuaded him to volunteer for it in the first place?), or whether to flash the red signal indicating cancellation and to face up thereafter to a future of intolerable self-knowledge, of the certainty that one was a coward? Page was no coward; when the green light, the executive signal, shone bright on the fascia-board before him, he jerked savagely down on the firing-handle and straightaway embarked upon one of the most hellish parachute descents in history.

The gun fired beneath him, the seat roared up into the air, clear of the aircraft, clear of the tailplane that might have sliced him into segments. For perhaps one-fifth of a second all, it seemed, was going well. Then the slipstream snatched him, and all was going quite unbelievably badly. The straps of his safety-harness failed to hold him securely in the seat, and he was thrust brutally downwards, the rough canvas webbing of the harness cutting into his thighs and the heavy, chunky metal of the "quick-release box", situated normally just above the navel, carving a deep and ugly groove in his chin. Both legs were torn out of the foot-rests and thrown to one side over the edge of the seat; the seat itself slid out from beneath his backside and rode up between his shoulder-blades, where its ninety pounds of solid metal pressed cruelly into his spine. P. J. Page, test-parachutist, was in trouble.

He was aware at once, though, that one factor at least seemed to be acting in his favour; his primary parachute, the one that supported both him and the seat, had opened, and he was floating rather than falling. So much then for his immediate anxieties; he was hurt, certainly, but he knew instinctively that he was not seriously injured—the device he was testing had not worked exactly according to plan, but at least it had worked, and his parachute was drifting him down quite gently towards the earth. He was safe—but was he? He remembered then that only half of the operation was over, that the toughest part, in many ways, was still to come. For in those early days of ejection, the test-man had to make not one cold-blooded action, but two; he had, first, to fire himself out of the aircraft, and then, having survived that little venture into the unpredictable, he had to free himself from the seat and put his trust in his second, his *personal* parachute. He had to unbuckle the straps that held him fast, he had to kick himself clear, in a clumsy somersault, from the seat, and he had then to hold his breath, and his nerve, for something like eight seconds, falling faster and faster, before pulling the rip-cord of his 'chute—he had to be sure that he had dropped away from the danger of entanglement with the seat. This was an effort of will that some of the most experienced test-parachutists confessed to finding harder than the initial experiment; the first move, cold-blooded though it always was, was warmed and eased by a sense of excitement and achievement; the second, cold and clinical, was a simple matter of survival. And this was what P. J. Page was facing now.

He started his preparations coolly and methodically. A test-man, contrary to popular belief, is not a dare-devil who delights in danger but a canny professional who hates the very thought and existence of it; he is a man, experienced in his trade, who not only calculates the risk but strives to minimize it, who checks everything not once but twice at least.

And so Page started sorting out his chances. At best, he could scramble his way back into the seat; he tried it, and he found it impossible. Had it been in front of him, well perhaps—but it was of course behind him, and he could not even reach it, let alone exert any purchase upon it to haul himself upwards. So all right; he could cut himself free, could unfasten the buckles securing himself to the seat and fall away from it into a conventional parachute descent. That, probably, was the answer. The test, after all, was over. As a matter, almost, of subconscious routine, he reached around behind him to check the position of his personal parachute, and as he did so, every emotion drained out of him but pure, chill, undistilled terror. In his groping fingers he found not the safe, solid bulk of the parachute-pack, but only a thin snaking handful of nylon rigging-lines—his parachute, his life-saver, must already be open; yet he, so far as he knew, had done nothing to open it. And if it was opened already, it could not be opened again—it was of no further use to him. Turning, twisting, craning his neck upwards, Page at last located the nylon canopy, and his worst fears were confirmed; it was opened, and it was wrapped haphazard round the crooks and crannies and projections of the ejection-seat. It looked like Mother McGinty's washing in a high wind.

Page was now six thousand feet above the airfield, and on his next decision might depend his life. He was face to face with his Moment of Truth. He could try to drop free, surely, but he had no means of telling whether his parachute would drag itself clear of the seat or whether the

sudden tug of his acceleration down the length of the rigging-lines would knot both parachutes into an inextricable
matrix of cord and fabric with no power to support him.
Then again, if he did fall clear, his parachute might rip
itself to shreds at the moment of parting, and a man falling
helplessly from six thousand feet, fully conscious, takes an
uncommonly long time to die. It was perhaps this thought,
this vision of an endless confrontation with the inevitable,
that spurred P. J. Page to his decision that he would stay
with the seat.

He thought of the bulk of metal sticking into his back,
and he knew that when he hit the ground he must inevitably be injured, no doubt severely—but he could cling to
the hope that he would not be killed or, come the crunch,
that he would be killed cleanly and quickly. He would stick
with his decision and then, one way or another, it would
all be resolved in one blinding second of realization. The
bit that mattered would, above all, be *quick*. No second
thoughts to drive him mad at the last moment; no thoughts
at all—oblivion. Brave men, if they are intelligent, know
their moments of fear.

The thought of staying with the seat, though, was a tough
one, a promise of pain; it would be ridiculous to think that
this was something that one could get away with. There
were several moments on the way down when Page reached
tentatively towards the quick-release box—quick-release,
an ironic term if ever there was one, and there is little doubt
that had he been closer to the ground he would have taken
an all-or-nothing chance on the efficiency of his personal
parachute. But six thousand feet was too high, too long;
the chance he would be taking was simply unthinkable.
Sweating cold, horrified, close to panic but nevertheless
always just in control of his fear, Page tried desperately to
turn his mind from the impact that lay ahead of him, to
console himself with the conviction that what he was engaged in was worthwhile, no matter what the personal cost;
Jesus Christ, he was no longer a fitter from the factory floor,
an anonymous worker amongst millions—he was a pioneer,
an explorer, a man staking his life because that was what
he had decided, cold-bloodedly, to do. He was doing what
his parachuting army buddies had talked about but never,
in peace-time, had done. He was someone.

So P. J. Page decided to come to earth by parachute with an ejection-seat strapped to his back, fated to be smashed by an invention designed to save lives. He knew then and there he was a loser, and there was no hint of self-sympathy, days later, when he talked of his experience from his hospital bed. "I was scared, of course, bloody terrified, but what mattered then was what to *do*. The sodding seat had worked, all right, but it hadn't worked *right*, if you know what I mean. I was okay, on the one hand, but on the other hand, I was dead. It was a bloody awful situation, really, and very frightening."

Page had reason to be frightened. He was falling fast, weighed down by the seat, and he had no absolute knowledge as to whether he would be better with or without his personal parachute. Despite its entanglement it might be giving him some tiny extra lift that might spell the difference between life and death, but on the other hand, if it suddenly came free of the seat it might float up into contact with the other parachute and strangle it. Page gave up kicking and struggling; it would be best, he decided, to stay still and accept what was happening to him as stoically as his screaming nerves would allow. And so, gazing at the ground in horrified fascination, he came sweeping in across the aerodrome. His luck was out to the very last, and the spectators were sickened to see that he was being carried backwards, clear of the grass and on to the tarmacadam of the main runway, the ejection-seat mounted like some grotesque and malevolent hump on his back.

His heels made first contact with the ground, and there came a searing agony as his knee ligaments were torn apart; a split second later came even worse pain as the seat and his shoulders were smashed brutally down on to the unyielding surface of the runway. Worse even than all the physical torture was the old enemy, fear, for what Page remembers most vividly about his terrible experience is the fact that as he lay there broken on the airfield at Chalgrove, he could not breathe. His lungs were full of air, but paralysed by the shock of the landing, he could find no way to expel it and he felt himself drowning on dry land. On the very brink of an unconsciousness that would almost certainly have proved fatal he fought and he fought; his body could make no movement, but his courage and determination were as strong as ever, and at last the constricted muscles of his thorax began to function and the choking air came whistling out of his lungs. When the ground crew lifted Page gently from the shattered wreckage of the seat he was pouring with sweat from the efforts he had made to cling tenaciously to life, and his first coherent description was of the appalling fear that he might have survived such a nightmare only to die with help at hand.

The nightmare, however, was not yet over, for there followed a seven-mile journey over bumpy roads to a hospital in Oxford where the surgeons, almost disbelieving their own diagnosis, announced that the man lying there, cruelly injured but indisputably alive, was the survivor of, of all things, a broken neck. The parachuting career of P. J. Page was over.

His sufferings, however, had not been in vain; in making the high-speed run and in reporting objectively and accurately what had happened to him during those first few frantic seconds in the slipstream Page had fulfilled his function as a test-man. The seat's designer, James Martin, introduced a simple modification, a safety-strap that obviated the risk of a premature development of the parachute, and just two weeks later the Martin-Baker story went marching on. Benny Lynch, resuming the burden of testing, fired himself out of a Meteor at more than a hundred miles an hour faster still, to set a world record for high-speed ejection of 505 m.p.h. For Lynch there was the glory and a long and distinguished test-career stretching out ahead of him. For P. J. Page in his hospital bed there was only the miracle of his survival and the knowledge that he had paved the way.

The Macfarlane Incident

Ask any naval pilot and he will tell you that one of the most nerve-wracking moments in the whole field of flying comes when one is shot from the deck of an aircraft-carrier in a catapult-assisted take-off. Here there is none of the smooth, reassuring surge of acceleration that carries a land-based fighter along more than a mile of runway before it lifts gently into the air, giving the pilot ample time to pull up should things go wrong. Here, instead, there is a demand for total concentration as the aeroplane is whipped from a stationary position to a speed of more than a hundred miles an hour in a matter of seconds; total concentration and a razor-keen sense of perception that will warn one instantly if all is not well.

All *should* be well, for the conscientious pilot, having settled himself comfortably in the cockpit long before the take-off, will have carried out an exhaustive preparatory drill. He will have checked that his seat-harness is securely fastened to prevent his pitching forward in the event of a mishap; he will have checked every single instrument on the complex panel in front of him. He will have checked that his parachute-straps are tightly buckled and will have confirmed that the rubber dinghy-pack that acts as a firm seat-cushion beneath him is fastened by its nylon lanyard to the inflatable Mae West life-jacket he is wearing. He will have switched his oxygen supply on to "normal flow",

and he will have warmed up the engine until it is running
smoothly. He will have checked with the Control Tower
that the flight-deck is clear for take-off before giving the
signal to indicate his readiness. He will have done all these
things and yet, in this as in every other human activity,
accidents will happen.

On 13 October, 1954, Lieutenant B. D. Macfarlane, R.N.,
sat in the cockpit of his Wyvern jet aircraft aboard the
carrier H.M.S. *Albion* preparing for take-off. He was tense,
as always on such occasions, but he was not afraid; he was
an experienced pilot happily unaware that he was about to
suffer one of the most horrific—and most astounding—
experiences in the annals of naval aviation.

He gave the all-clear signal, the aircraft flashed forward,
and Macfarlane's happiness vanished in an instant, for he
knew at once that he was in desperate, terrifying trouble.
He was streaking along the flight-deck, irrevocably committed, but the aeroplane simply would not respond to his
urgent demand for maximum power. He wondered for one
wild moment if the throttle had jammed half-open, but a
swift, horrified glance showed him that the levers were fully
forward and locked in their correct position. His speed was
seventy knots—fast enough for most of us, in all conscience,
but hopelessly inadequate to the task of lifting the heavy
aeroplane into the air with its undercarriage still down and
the flaps, too, still down in the orthodox take-off position.
With no power to fly and with no room to pull up, disaster
was now inevitable, and Macfarlane experienced a crushing
sense of utter helplessness and despair such as he had never
known in a singularly active and self-reliant life. Neither
flying expertise nor the aviation hand-books could provide
any possible answer to *this* emergency.

His mind, however, was crystal-clear as he faced up to the
near-certainty that his life would be over in a matter of
seconds. As if to quench any faint flicker of hope came the
memory that the aircraft he was flying, the Wyvern, was
notorious amongst navy pilots for its unhelpful character-
istics in the event of a "ditching". Some aircraft, if the pilot
has the swift skill to settle them in the water at the correct
angle, will float for many seconds, sometimes even minutes,
giving him some chance of escape. But not the Wyvern,
whose tendency was to sink like a stone. Indeed, Macfarlane

remembered with sickening clarity an incident less than eighteen months before in which he had seen one of his own friends go down in a Wyvern, swiftly, inexorably, and finally, with no hope whatsoever of survival.

But now his crippled aircraft was hurtling helplessly, out of control, over the bows of the carrier, swooping downwards at an angle of thirty degrees, and all coherent thought was bludgeoned from the pilot's mind as it made its stunning collision with the water. True to form, it dived steeply and steadily into the depths of the sea. In the few seconds that followed, in fact, it was not Macfarlane in his dazed unawareness who suffered most, but the crew of a rescue helicopter hovering watchfully but for the moment impotently above him. For as they watched they were chilled and horrified to see the huge iron bows of the *Albion* slice clean through the fuselage of the sinking aircraft, so ending, as it seemed, any faint vestige of hope that the pilot might by some miracle survive. They continued to watch but only, they felt certain, to report the details of a tragedy.

Yet Macfarlane, incredibly, was still alive, and as his mind slowly cleared he began to focus all his will-power, all his strength, all his sheer determination, on the single purpose of remaining so. The water all around him had darkened almost to blackness, and he could scarcely see— but he could *think*. He was injured, he knew, but he did not know exactly where or how badly: he felt generally overwhelmed with pain, and the only part of his body that would respond to his mind's instructions was his left arm. But the repetitive discipline of his service training supplied him with the knowledge of what he must do, and grimly he set out to do it.

In the gathering darkness he thanked God for the foresight of the men who had painted bright yellow the item on the instrument panel he was so desperately seeking—the switch that would automatically jettison the cockpit canopy and so provide at least a chance of escape from his terrible sinking coffin. He peered, he groped, and at last he found it; he flung the switch and felt a swift surge of hope, mingled with terror, as the hood was ripped clear and the cockpit was instantly flooded with churning water. He might yet be about to die, but now there was one chance remaining to him—one chance and one chance only.

This faint hope of survival against all the odds lay in the fact that his aircraft was equipped with a Martin-Baker ejection-seat, an explosive device designed by an Irish engineer of genius, James Martin (now Sir James) to fire a pilot from his cockpit in moments of unavoidable danger. The hope, however, was faint indeed; Macfarlane was in fact only the fifty-third airman to use the seat in an emergency, and not even its inventor had envisaged its use other than in the open air, with nothing to impede the progress of the pilot from his crippled plane. Still, any chance is better than none at all, and with his left hand, even now the only obedient member in his body, he reached up to a wire-and-rubber loop set into the backrest of the seat, above his head—the firing-handle. He heaved down upon it, and hope died within him, giving place to an appalling sense of pure animal fear, as the seat failed to fire.

He was trapped now, he knew, condemned to death as surely as if strapped to the electric-chair, but suddenly the memory of an incident years before flashed vividly across his mind. This hell he was going through was Lieutenant Macfarlane's first attempt to eject from an aircraft—but it was *not* the first time he had used an ejection-seat. Like most other service air-bases, his unit was equipped with another of James Martin's inventions, the training ramp, a terrifying tramway soaring seventy feet into the sky on which pilots could make practice ejections, their climb being arrested by a complicated system of wheels, rails, and ratchets. Macfarlane had once made such a trial run, and on that occasion too the seat had failed to fire. But he also remembered why; he simply had not pulled down hard enough on the handle, and that time he had been using both hands. On the second attempt it had functioned perfectly. Now, when he was acting with only one arm, in an enfeebled condition, might not the same thing happen? God knows, it was worth a try. This time he jerked savagely on the handle, dragging it right down to his chest, and he vaguely heard the muffled roar as the cartridge exploded beneath him. Then he was rushing upwards, semi-conscious as he ploughed like a torpedo through the millions of tons of black water in which he was entombed. He had to make a deliberate effort to force his mind to believe that he really was clear of his shattered, sunken, aeroplane.

By no means, however, was he clear of desperate danger. He was still strapped securely to the ninety pounds of metal that comprised the ejection-seat, and worse than that he was enmeshed like a cocoon in coils of cord and sheets of nylon fabric, for the firing of the seat had automatically opened his parachute, and it was now wrapped round him like—with grisly aptness—a shroud.

He threshed wildly in an agony of claustrophobia, smothering in the cloth of the parachute and drowning in the water seeping through it, but even this situation, grim enough by any man's standards, diminished in its horror in comparison to the fate that he now felt certain lay in store for him. For Lieutenant Macfarlane by now was thinking clearly, all too terribly clearly, and he had become conscious not only of enormous conflicting pressures on his body but of the fact that he was being tossed hither and yon like a barrel tumbling over Niagara. The ice of pure terror seemed to set in his veins as he realized the awful significance of this wild, uncontrollable movement; he had crashed, of course, directly over the bows of the carrier, and now the vast iron bulk of H.M.S. *Albion* was thundering inexorably over his head. He had escaped a quick, clean death to suffer—what? The ancient and unspeakable torture of a keel-hauling, scraped and torn to pieces, his flesh lacerated by the barnacle-encrusted hull of the carrier—or the swifter but scarcely less gruesome mangling and dismembering that would come should his path carry him into the ship's spinning, scything propellers? Mentally Macfarlane shrieked.

The agony of expectation seemed endless before he realized to his bewilderment that the tossing and tumbling had ceased and that for some reason the *Albion* was gone, leaving him unscathed. The reason he could not imagine, not until he had re-orientated himself, had puzzled frantically over the fact that the water was growing not lighter but darker, and that the pressure on his body was actually increasing; it was only then that he could bring himself despairingly to believe that instead of floating, however slowly, towards the surface he was in fact being dragged even further into the depths.

What followed immediately must fascinate any true connoisseur of fear, any speculator upon the nature of death by drowning—or anyone who has ever wondered what it must mean to accept oneself as already dead. For in the midst of his ordeal Macfarlane now experienced a few brief moments of relief. Sheer Hell was to follow, but as he felt himself steadily sinking, fear took a holiday. The vast amount of sea-water he was choking down "no longer tasted unpleasant, but just like a long, long drink of fresh water". He struggled no more but found himself "in a dreamy, relaxed state, comfortable but sad—slowly drifting deeper, and not frightened about it, just sad. In fact, gone." Had he died, in short, Lieutenant Macfarlane, R.N., would, in the last resort, have died easily. But Macfarlane did not die, and the quirk of fate that dragged him back from the brink ˌestored him not to safety but to the return of his terror.

For now, through no conscious action of his own, he was abruptly freed from the snaking, strangling rigging-lines and the huge sodden parachute canopy that were pulling him deeper and deeper, remorselessly, unanswerably to his death. He was no longer ensnared like some modern Laocoon and dimly, almost reluctantly, he brought himself back to the consciousness that he still had a chance to survive. A fool, a pessimist, or an ordinary man would probably have felt that he had fought long enough, rejected the life-chance, and given up there and then. But Macfarlane was none of these. Summoning up every resource of his fogged brain, he began to sort out the situation as coldly and analytically as his senses would allow, and decided that only one thing was still dragging him in the wrong direction —the solid bulk of his dinghy-pack, attached to his life-jacket by its lanyard and drifting beneath him like an anchor. If only he could free himself from its murderous clutch . . .

If only . . . but how, how in God's name, to escape? He was weak now, weak and waterlogged, his mind flashing intermittently like a beacon between bright reason and a weary longing to return to the warm and easy acceptance of death he had experienced only moments before. But, in one of those flashes of clarity there came to him a picture that strangely had not appeared to him before—a picture, clear and lovely, of the wife and baby daughter waiting for him, unsuspectingly, at home. With the picture, and with the thought of all they meant to him, and he to them, the terror returned to him tenfold—and with the terror, the renewed determination to fight to the last breath. And Macfarlane fought, my God how he fought.

Slowly, painfully, he inched his left hand down the length of the lanyard binding him to the heavy, sodden mass of the dinghy-pack wallowing beneath him; each tiny movement was a punishment, each millimetre gained an agonizing mockery of his efforts. Yet he went on, and on, and on, until at last he made contact with the metal release-catch of the dinghy. He pressed it, but his fingers, bloodless and rigid with cold, could make no impression upon it; again he tried to squeeze it, and again there was no response. Taking one final, all-or-nothing risk, he released his hard-won fingerhold, grabbed desperately at the recalcitrant catch with his outstretched hand, and gripped with all his might. A timeless second of doubt, and then came a change in the movement of his body, faint but perceptible; the downward drag had ended, and he was floating on one level or even, perhaps, gently rising. But if he was rising, he was rising far, far too slowly.

He was deep down, fathoms deep; he had been submerged for minutes, swallowing water, and he was swollen like a gourd. He was in a state of shock, which in itself can kill, and he had nothing to sustain him but the thought of his wife and daughter and his own indomitable will to live. He pictured the breaking of the news to his wife; the C.O. there, grave and stumbling for the suitable words; the padre with him to administer spiritual comfort; the Medical Officer hovering in the background, ready to administer the sedatives when such comfort proved unavailing. They had all been through this before; though they hated it, were saddened by it, always, but *she* had not—and, by God, she would not go through it now, not yet.

He bullied, he scolded, he scourged his brain into unwilling resource; there must be some way to avoid this waste and misery. His chest was on fire, his lungs ready to burst, trip-hammers were pounding in his head, and he was dying —yet all he needed was air. Somehow he had to reach the air, and vaguely, if he could only think of it, he knew there was some way in which he could.

He started to swim, kicking upwards like a frantic frog, and realized almost as if it were irrelevant that his legs were functioning—at least, apparently, he had not broken his back. But the action was carrying him nowhere; he was too weak, and his flying-suit, filled with water, was sagging down from his shoulders and hips like leaden ballast, thwarting every scrabbling movement towards the surface, and survival. He was frightened now not only of dying, not only of losing, but of losing within touching-distance of triumph. And mingling with his fear there was anger, for he knew, he *knew* there was something literally vital that he had forgotten. Almost insane with pain and fear and frustration, Macfarlane returned like a child to his earliest teachings: but the teachings in this case were those not of mother or father, but of flying-school, and, almost too late, the answer was suddenly staring him in the face.

The life-jacket—great God, he was drowning in a life-jacket. Feverishly, fumbling, he pawed his way around his chest and belly until finally his fingers closed upon the instant-inflation valve. A frantic tug, an inaudible *whoosh*, and the orange-coloured waistcoat with its head-supporting collar was full of gas: Macfarlane, water spouting from his mouth and nostrils, was rocketed to the surface to lie there helpless, gasping, unbelieving, alive.

Physically he was still in agony, for his body had taken punishment that only the hardiest could even hope to survive, but mentally and emotionally he was experiencing a sense of elation such as few of us will ever know. He gazed upwards at the sunlight, marvelling at the contrast between this and the Stygian blackness of the ocean depths, and he marvelled too at the gift that was his—the chance to die twice.

The little orange-coloured figure bobbing in the waves was spotted at once by the unhappy crew of the helicopter buzzing overhead, but it was spotted with no great sense of excitement. Bodies often do rise quite quickly to the surface, and there is no thrill or excitement in retrieving a cadaver—and Macfarlane, they knew, must be dead. Suddenly, however, they saw that this was a corpse with a difference—this one was waving an arm at them. Incredulously, but swiftly and efficiently none the less, the pilot swooped down to hover over the man returned from the watery grave; a line was lowered, a hook and harness secured, and Lieutenant B. D. Macfarlane, R.N., was hoisted into safety, into warmth, into comfort and unbelieving congratulation.

Within hours he was reunited with a wife and small daughter who learned only later, much later, just how lucky they were—and are—to be members of a whole and happy family, and it is good to know that he had ahead of him just one more bonus—though one of infinitely less importance—to receive as a result of his diabolical experience. It came years later, after he had left the service to run an antique shop in the quiet ambience of the home counties.

Sitting alone in the corner of a pub not far from his home, sipping a reflective pint of bitter, Macfarlane was inadvertent ear-witness to a heated argument between two sedentary citizens palpably unqualified to pontificate upon the subject under discussion. It was possible, one asserted, for a man to fire himself out of an aeroplane by means of some sort of gun attached to his seat. Impossible, said his companion; such ideas belonged to Science Fiction. The first debater, incensed, went on to state that not only was this entirely possible but that some pilot, once, had made such an explosive escape from an aircraft already under the surface of the sea. This was more than could be borne by his companion, who burst into guffaws of derisive laughter; "Come off it Charlie—you've been watching too much Telly."

It was a moment, a wild outstretching of the long arm of coincidence, too rich to be ignored by anyone neither less nor more than human. B. D. Macfarlane is, above all things, human. Downing his pint, edging his way diffidently into the argument, he addressed himself almost apologetically to contestant number two. "I hate to interrupt, sir, but I'm afraid your friend is right."

The Terror at Dead Man's Hill

It began with a tap on the car window. It was dusk on a chilly August evening in 1961. Twenty-three-year-old Valerie Storie sat with Michael Gregsten in the front seats. They had parked in a cornfield at Dorney Reach and were studying a map, planning a car rally for the motor club of the Department of Scientific and Industrial Research, Slough, where they both worked. Michael was thirty-eight, a married man with two children.

The tap on the window was unusual, but at first they were not alarmed, and thought perhaps it was someone from the farm near by wanting to drive a harvesting machine through the gateway.

Michael Gregsten wound down the window. They saw the figure of a man, neatly dressed, standing there silhouetted against the darkening sky. The bottom half of his face was covered with a handkerchief. He poked a revolver through the window.

"This is a hold-up," he said. "I am a desperate man. I've been on the run, so don't do anything silly."

At first Valerie couldn't take it seriously. It was a stupid joke. The gun couldn't be real.

But Michael, closer to the gunman, immediately sensed this was no joke. To him the man looked oddly sinister. He demanded the car keys and ordered him to open the rear off-side door. Michael obeyed and the intruder got in the back seat. He kept the gun pointing at them.

"This is a three-eight. A cowboy's gun. I feel like a cowboy. I haven't had it long." He tapped his pockets. They rattled. "Those are all bullets. I've never shot anyone before," he added ominously.

Valerie was thoroughly scared by now, and had every reason to be. She could tell by the man's attitude that he was extremely dangerous. He didn't look like the real gunman of fiction. He was plainly of low intelligence, and gave the impression of being a psychopath who had got hold of a gun and wanted to imitate a gangster. The frightening thing was that once having succeeded in holding them up, he seemed undecided what to do. In such a state of mind, the gunman might shoot at the slightest provocation.

Pointing the weapon at Michael's head, the intruder made him drive farther into the field away from the road. Then he demanded their watches and money, adding that he was hungry and wanted food.

Michael gave him his wallet containing about three pounds. As Valerie's hand went inside her handbag, the gunman asked her if she had any chocolate. She shook her head. Her hand closed over her wallet and quickly extracted seven pounds she had drawn from the bank that day. As she handed the gunman her bag, she secreted the money inside her bra.

"Why don't you go away and leave us?" asked Michael. "We've got nothing else to give you. You can even have the car if you like."

"You'll get nothing out of us," added Valerie. "You're wasting your time."

"Be quiet, will you? I'm finking," said the gunman, and Valerie particularly noted his uneducated, Cockney way of speaking, and the fact that he was unable to pronounce "th".

He told them that every policeman in England was looking for him, and that he intended to wait till morning, tie them up, take the car and leave. Every now and then he looked at his watch, saying there was plenty of time, but he didn't say what there was plenty of time for.

He repeatedly told them that he hadn't eaten for two days, had been living rough and was soaked with rain. But

Valerie could see from his neat and tidy clothes that this was untrue.

This went on for over an hour. The two in the front of the car got impatient and edgy. Every time they looked round, the gunman raised his gun threateningly and told them not to look at him. He took some trouble to ensure that neither of his victims saw his face, which was not such a difficult thing to do when he was sitting behind them in the darkness.

At 10.30 a light came on in a nearby house and a man came out to put his bicycle away. This made the gunman nervous, and he told them that if the man should come up to the car they must say nothing, or he would shoot the man and them also.

Another nerve-wracking hour passed. Valerie and Michael did everything they knew to persuade him to go away and leave them. But he would not budge. At about 11.30 he grew nervous for some reason.

He put the muzzle of the gun against Michael's neck. "Come on. Start the car. Let's go."

Michael obeyed. "Where to?" His voice sounded agitated, and Valerie knew he was near to breaking-point.

"Take the road to Slough."

Deliberately and without hurry Michael drove towards Slough. Valerie kept touching his hand in an attempt to reassure him. As they went through Slough she noticed that a clock showed a quarter to twelve. The gunman directed them to continue along the A4 towards Heathrow Airport. He was unsure where to go, and that increased their uneasiness. Valerie's attempts to hold hands with Michael were stopped by the gunman irritably threatening them with his weapon.

Fear began to develop into sheer terror. Here they were in a busy suburban main road with other cars passing them all the time, yet they were helplessly at the mercy of this armed maniac.

In an attempt to attract attention Michael had switched the reversing light on and he kept flicking it. The light was operated by a switch under the dashboard and Michael could work it without their captor noticing.

He was busy himself clicking the safety catch on and off, like a child with a new toy. Then he asked how much petrol there was in the tank and Valerie replied that there was only a gallon.

"There's a garage coming up," the gunman said. "Pull up. Get two gallons. Mind you stay in the car. If you try to say anything else than to ask for two gallons, or try to give the man a note, I'll let you have it with the gun."

He gave Michael one pound of the money he had previously taken from him, and Michael did as he was told. The petrol was bought in tense silence. The unsuspecting attendant put two gallons in the tank and then gave Michael 10s. 3d. change.

The gunman took the ten shilling note and passed the threepenny piece to Valerie, saying: "You can have that as a wedding present."

"We're not married," she said icily, a chill running down her spine. He didn't seem to believe her. As if it mattered! She let the coin drop on the floor. Hate was mingled with terror. What could she do? There must be some way out, some means of ridding themselves of this loathsome man in the back seat. She knew that Mike was reaching the end of his tether. Whatever happened, she must keep cool.

The nightmarish ride continued through Hayes and Harrow and across north-west London. In Stanmore they stopped for cigarettes to soothe their ragged nerves. The gunman permitted Michael to get out and buy some from a machine, while he held Valerie as a hostage in the car.

It was a tense few minutes. Valerie wondered if Mike would be able to summon assistance. But there was no one about, and Mike didn't take a chance with the unpredictable gunman holding Valerie at his mercy. Valerie realized that Mike could easily have run away. But the thought of deserting her did not seem to have entered his mind. White-faced, Michael Gregsten returned to the car with the cigarettes and drove on.

Valerie lit two cigarettes, giving one to Michael and handing the other into the back for their captor to take. She noticed he was wearing black gloves. Although the gunman took the cigarette, he said he did not like smoking.

She noticed too that their captor was still in a state of nerves. He kept giving driving instructions from the back seat: "Mind that car," "Mind those traffic lights," "Careful of this corner." His edginess only increased their own fear.

Under the gunman's directions, Michael turned on to the A5 and made for St Albans. He continued switching the reversing light on and off to attract attention, while Valerie constantly looked for a policeman. If she had seen one, she was going to seize the wheel and drive the car straight on to the pavement, and she knew that Mike would not stop her. But throughout the whole of that hideous drive they saw no policeman, nor did Valerie get a proper glimpse of the gunman's face.

Beyond St Albans he made Michael turn on to the A6 and so the drive continued with Michael still trying to attract attention by manipulating his reversing light.

A passing driver turned and pointed. Once more the tension jumped to breaking-point. Valerie held her breath, praying.

Behind her the ragged Cockney voice said: "They must know something is wrong." He made Michael stop. Perhaps the rear light was out. Michael got out at gun-point, followed by the intruder, to examine the lights.

Valerie instantly realized that this was her great chance. She was the only one in the car, was a good driver and could easily have slipped into the driving-seat and made a break for it. The nervous, indecisive gunman would almost certainly have fired at the car, and only a very lucky shot would have hit the driver. Mike, if he had been quick enough, could then have made a successful dive for the gun, and the dreadful story might have had a very different ending.

But Valerie, in the few seconds when she had to make this decision, could not take the risk of the gunman shooting Mike, for up until then he had promised that no harm would come to them if they did exactly what he said. Apart from that she could not bring herself to run away from Mike, any more than he could when he got out of the car to buy cigarettes in Stanmore.

When Michael got back into the car his face was grey. But he continued to try to attract the attention of passing cars by switching the reversing light on and off, and flashing the headlamps from dipped beam to main beam.

Every time they went through a built-up area, Valerie looked desperately for a policeman, but in vain.

They reached St Albans and the gunman told Michael

to take the A6, the road that goes from London to Leicester, Derby, Manchester and Carlisle.

"I'm tired. I want a kip," he said. He told Michael to turn off the road and find a spot where he could sleep. Twice they parked, but found they were on private property.

They finally came to a place known as Dead Man's Hill, where there was a lay-by which was separated from the road by a grass verge on which were some trees. At his instructions Michael parked in the lay-by with the car pointed in the direction of Luton, and turned out the lights.

They were both terrified of their captor's edginess.

"For God's sake don't you use that gun. Don't shoot."

"If I was goin' to shoot you I would've done it before. I want a kip now. But I must tie you up."

He made Michael get out of the car with him to get a piece of cord from the boot. He tied Valerie's hands behind her and fastened them to the door handle, but she managed to keep her wrists apart so that she could easily get them free when she wanted to. Back in the car the gunman looked for something to tie Michael with, and decided to use the cord from a duffel-bag which was in the front of the car and which contained some clean laundry.

Raising his gun, their captor said: "Give us that bag."

Michael picked up the bag with both hands and turned to his left to hand it over to the back seat. Immediately the gunman fired two shots in quick succession at his head, at a range of a few inches. There was a tremendous noise and smell of gunpowder.

Michael fell forward over the steering-wheel; Valerie could hear the blood pouring from his head. She screamed.

"Be quiet!" said the voice behind her.

She turned on him in fury. "You bastard! You shot him, you bastard! Why? Why?"

"He frightened me. He moved too quick. I got frightened."

Her hands were free of the rope, though she kept them together as though they were still tied, terrified he would shoot her too. Michael moved, flopped against the seat. His head fell back. On his face was a look of surprise, even disbelief.

She turned to the murderer. "For God's sake, let me get Mike to a doctor quick. I will do anything you want if you will let me take the car and get Mike to a doctor.' She spoke almost hysterically.

The man replied: "Be quiet. I am finking."

She begged and implored. "Let me take Mike somewhere and get help. I'll drive the car. I'll take you anywhere you want to go. But let me get help for Mike."

From the dimness of the back seat the murderer said: "No, he's dead."

When she continued imploring him to let her get help, he grew irritable and told her to be quiet.

A few moments later he said: "Turn round and face me. I know your hands are free."

Valerie obeyed. She could feel his eyes looking at her in the darkness.

"Kiss me," he said.

She glared at him with terrible hatred.

"What—kiss you?" Her voice was full of loathing.

As they sat staring at each other, a car came from the direction of Luton towards Bedford, and its lights shone on the gunman's face, giving her the first opportunity of seeing what he really looked like. His eyes were very large, pale blue and were fixed in a kind of icy stare. His face was pale. He had brown hair which was combed back with no parting.

"Kiss me," he said again. She still refused.

He pointed the gun at her and said: "If you don't kiss me before I count five, I will shoot you."

He started to count, so she let him kiss her. It was only a brief kiss. She then made a wild grab at the gun, but he was too strong for her.

"That was a silly thing to do! I thought you were sensible. Now I can't trust you."

Her resistance collapsed. Her very flesh began to crawl with fear.

"Don't shoot me," she begged. "Just let me go."

His icy eyes stared at her, revelling in his power over her.

For the first time she now felt real terror. She knew that whatever awful lust possessed this unspeakable creature, he was not satisfied yet. She knew also that she was to be his real victim.

He picked up a cloth from the duffel-bag and covered Michael's face with it. The body was slumped in the driving-seat, the blood flowing down between the seat and the side of the car. Her poor beloved Mike, unconscious and dying, she thought. There was something sinister, obscene, about the way his murderer put that piece of cloth on his face. But now it was her turn. This mad, inhuman creature had not finished yet.

He ordered her to sit in the back seat with him. She refused until he threatened her with the gun. She had no option. It was that or death.

Now he wanted sex. She could not refuse him if she wanted to live. Numbed, she hardly felt it when he started crudely mauling her with his indecent hands. He took off his black gloves, and the strange thing was that she took the opportunity to remove the seven pounds from her bra into her mackintosh pocket. She thought perhaps he would kill her if he found out how she had deceived him over the money.

As for him, he only thought of his lust for this terrified girl, and he raped her at gun-point within a foot or two of the body of her murdered lover, his animal movements a ghastly counterpoint to the rhythmic dripping of Michael's blood.

To her this dreadful experience seemed strangely unimportant. She thought all the time of Mike, huddled there so close to them, bleeding to death, for she could not think of him as dead.

Oh God, she prayed, while the murderer brutally forced his sexual lust upon her, make him go away—now! now! The only thing in her mind was that he should stop so she could go and get help for Mike.

When finally the man had finished with her, he told her to drag Mike's body out of the car, which she did by grasping him under the armpits. She dragged the body round the back of the car to the edge of the concrete strip. He made no attempt to help her and was careful not to get any blood on himself.

She knew then that Mike was dead.

The gunman wiped the steering-wheel, covered up the bloodstained driving-seat, and made her start the engine and show him how the controls worked.

She went and sat by Mike's body, her legs under her, her back to the car. She was past weeping. She just sat there waiting for the monster to go.

Minutes passed. He hung around. She could hear him shuffling in the background, undecided whether to leave her or commit further outrage. He got in the car and then got out again. She sat there overwhelmed with horror and fear.

Then he came up to her and said: "I think I had better hit you on the head, or get something to knock you out, or you will go for help."

"No, I won't. I won't move. Just go away and leave me with Mike. Please . . ." In a sudden impulse she pulled a pound note from her pocket. "Here you are. You can have that if you will go quick."

He seized the pound and walked away. Suddenly his footsteps stopped. Had he changed his mind? Was he angered by that splendid gesture of despairing contempt which the pound note represented?

He started to shoot.

Valerie felt the bullets hitting her with annihilating violence which flung her over on to the concrete. Her body went numb. There was no feeling in her legs. One of the bullets had pierced her neck close to the spinal cord.

More shots came. She lay there in utter terror unable to move. Then the shooting stopped. She heard him walk towards her. As the footsteps came closer, she closed her eyes and tried to stop breathing.

He stood over her, gun in hand. She felt him touching her with his foot. This was the most terrifying moment of that ghastly night—lying there, pretending to be dead, waiting for the final shot which would kill her.

Suddenly he kicked her and walked away. She heard him get into the car and drive off in the direction of Luton.

She lay there paralysed, able only to move her hands. The taste of blood in her mouth made her feel sick. Then she felt a sudden sense of outrage. Curse this man, she thought. May God damn the fiend to hell. She must not die. If she did, no one would know who to look for.

With her right hand, she scrabbled for little stones to make into words—"blue eyes, brown hair' —but there were no stones. She lay there completely helpless, and in utter despair.

It was getting towards dawn, but it was cold and dark in the lay-by at Dead Man's Hill. As vehicles went by on the

A6, she screamed and waved her petticoat which she had managed to pull off. But no one heard or saw.

She then lost consciousness, some six hours after that tap on the car window in the cornfield at Dorney Reach.

Valerie Storie was able to give a remarkably detailed account of her dreadful experience. Her evidence convicted James Hanratty of the murder of Michael Gregsten. Hanratty was hanged on 4 April, 1962. His guilt is disputed in some quarters, though Valerie Storie has always been perfectly certain that he was the man who killed Michael Gregsten and then raped and shot her, as the result of which she is paralysed for life.

Murder Without Motive

At about six o'clock in the morning on 4 August, 1952, a motor-cyclist driving along a winding road near the village of Lurs in the Provence region of southern France was waved down to a halt by a man standing at the side of the road. This was wild open country in a mountainous area, pock-marked with jagged outcrops of granite and scarred by deep ravines. It was off the beaten track of tourists, though travellers would camp in the area from time to time. At this particular moment the place was desolate and deserted in the early-morning sunshine, apart from the man at the side of the road, who was stocky and rugged in appearance and appeared to be a member of the local farming community. He was a youngish man in his early thirties.

The motor-cyclist stopped. The man, in a sullen disinterested fashion, asked him if he would go to the police station at the small town of Forcalquier, about twelve kilometres away, to report that there had been a murder near to a farm called La Grande Terre, near Lurs. He would wait at the roadside until the police arrived.

It was an odd early-morning request, but the motor-cyclist did as he was asked without putting too many questions to his rather bad-tempered informant. Within the hour the police duly arrived to find the squat peasant-like man patiently waiting for them. He introduced himself as

Gustave Dominici, the thirty-three-year-old son of Gaston Dominici, who owned the La Grande Terre farm near by.

Gustave related his story curtly. While asleep at the farm he had been awakened during the night by the sound of gunfire. It had been fairly remote and meaningless, and he had done nothing about it. Later, around five-thirty, he had got up and walked over towards a railway cutting where there had been a landslide. Quite by chance he had come upon the brutally murdered body of a little girl. A little further on was a car, and close to the car he had also found the dead bodies of a man and a woman.

The police took over, sceptical at first, but what Gustave had said was true. Gustave led them away from the road in the direction of the nearby River Durance which flowed through a narrow ravine. About half-way they found the body of a young girl. She could not have been more than eleven years old, and her head had been violently beaten and crushed.

Not far away, on a level area of ground, was a green Hillman estate car with what appeared to be a British registration number. Alongside the car were two folding camp beds with travelling rugs, indicating that the occupants had evidently been camping for the night in the open air. Under one rug the police discovered the dead body of a woman in her late forties. She had been shot five times. Some distance away they came across the dead body of a man, aged about sixty, who had been shot in the back. It was quite obvious that the man, woman and child were a family, almost certainly British, and probably enjoying a camping holiday before violent death had overtaken them during a warm, starlit Provencal night.

The police examined the bodies and the contents of the clothing, and sifted the scene in minute detail. There was no apparent motive for the triple murder. Money and traveller's cheques had not been touched, and no sign that the articles in the pockets of the victims had been tampered with or even looked at. The car had not been interfered with or even opened. There was no obvious indication of sexual assault. The only missing articles, so far as could be ascertained, were watches—but here it was necessary to assume that a touring family would be unlikely not to have at least one wrist-watch between them. But this was a hypothetical point—and would a murderer simply take a watch and not money?

During the course of the long day the police, suitably reinforced, examined every inch of the scene of the crime and the local environment. In due course they found the murder weapon. It was an automatic carbine, a relic of the Second World War, of the type that had been issued to the U.S. Army and had also been used by the French Resistance. The carbine was discovered at the bottom of the Durance river in the ravine. At that time of the year it was little more than a shallow stream, but there were occasional deep pools. The weapon was recovered from one of the deepest of the pools—and this suggested that it had been thrown there by someone with detailed local knowledge, and not just carelessly cast into the ravine by a stranger. Therefore the obvious focus of police suspicion was the Dominici family itself in the La Grande Terre farm near by.

The Dominici family, as subsequent investigation revealed, proved to be more of a tribe—or perhaps a clan. Old Gaston Dominici, aged seventy-six, had nine\grown-up children and sixteen grandchildren, but they did not all live at the farm. The family was of independent peasant stock, inward-turned psychologically and very bloody-minded; during the German occupation they were reputed to have been stubbornly active in the Resistance and the Maquis. They tended to be uncommunicative, and very much united among themselves against the outside world, in a manner characteristic of the southern Latins. The police quickly realized that the Dominicis, as witnesses, would be obstructive rather than co-operative, even though there were no evidence to show that any one of them was involved in the triple murder.

The investigation was taken over by Commissaire Edmond Sebeille, an experienced and thorough officer of the Marseilles Sûreté. It soon became apparent to him that the Dominicis were behaving in a taciturn and secretive fashion, which, even allowing for their natural reticence, suggested that they knew far more than they were prepared to divulge.

Meanwhile, the bodies of the murdered family were removed and identified. They were Sir John Drummond, his wife, Lady Drummond, and their daughter Elizabeth. It was confirmed that they had been on holiday in France, as the guests of Professor Guy Marrian and his wife, who had rented a villa at Villefranche for the month of August.

Sir John Drummond was a biochemist who had received his knighthood during the war for his advisory services to the then Ministry of Food. His first childless marriage had been dissolved, and later he had married his secretary, who had become Lady Drummond. Elizabeth was their daughter. Guy Marrian, their host, was Professor of Medical Chemistry at the University of Edinburgh, and a close colleague of Drummond.

Sebeille's inquiries showed that the first stage of the Drummonds' holiday had passed quietly and uneventfully at the villa. Then the family had decided to visit Digne, some seventy miles away in the mountains, where a local festival involving a mock bull-fight was about to take place. They set off in their estate car, taking camping gear with them as it was to be a leisurely trip involving one or two overnight stops. Although the distance was not great, the road was twisting and difficult, winding through a desolate mountainous region inhabited mainly by dour and clannish peasant families working the land for a meagre living. Speed of travel was not easy to attain, and, in fact, night overtook them before they reached their destination. Being self-contained, they decided to camp until morning—but for them morning never came.

There was plenty of investigation, but no leads. As a result a great deal of speculation arose in general gossip and the press. The case was widely reported. Cloak-and-dagger guesswork hinted at political and even British intelligence involvement. It was rumoured that Drummond had been killed because of wartime activity in the area—that the murders were some kind of obscure reprisal. In support of these rather wild assertions, it was learned that French and American Intelligence were taking an active interest in the police investigation—and public interest increased to a new pitch of intensity when it was discovered that Sir John Drummond had, during his holiday, been making his own private inquiries locally about a certain British officer who had been parachuted into the area during the war with money for the Resistance leaders. The officer was found dead, and the money was never received. It seemed possible, therefore, that the killing of the Drummond family was an assassination rather than a murder, but the theory was not fully supported by hard fact.

There was the curious incident of a diary found in Nottingham which recorded that Drummond had, in fact, been in Lurs in 1947. The diary had belonged to a man who had himself been murdered in the Alpes Maritimes of Southern France. For a reason never properly explained, the diary was destroyed, apparently by the police, at the request of Drummond's relatives.

All in all, a sinister atmosphere of intrigue began to condense justifiably around the Drummond case. It possessed the hall-marks of secret-service machinations, with the truth hinted at but never revealed. The French newspapers openly anticipated sensational disclosures of a political or partisan nature, with a point of origin in wartime Maquis activities and perhaps connected with the spate of "liquidations" which had followed the liberation of France.

Whatever may have been the truth of the matter, and despite imaginative rumour and speculation, nothing sensational emerged from what was regarded as a deliberate conspiracy of silence. If the local people of Lurs knew the identity of the killer, they were keeping it to themselves, and the Dominici family in particular remained arrogantly and even defiantly uncommunicative.

Commissaire Sebeille, patiently pursuing his methodical investigation but getting nowhere, but convinced in his own mind that the Dominicis were the key to the solution of the enigma, decided to apply the full treatment of continuous interrogation to the limits permitted by French law. Only in such a way could variations and discrepancies in statements be detected. The truth remains the same, but lies, being artifacts of invention and memory, tend to vary in points of detail, since it is more difficult to recall the sum total of a contrived lie than it is to remember a true and real experience.

Consequently, on 3 September, a month after the murder, Gustave Dominici was taken to the Forcalquier police station for questioning. He was the key witness; it was he who had found the bodies in the first instance and who had called in the police with the help of the motor-cyclist.

Sebeille decided to go back to square one and cover the ground in more ruthless detail.

For two days Gustave was questioned unceasingly by a team of detectives, and the pattern of questioning was repeated over and over again, and compared with his original statement. This long interrogation produced only two discrepancies: one concerned a minor matter of the precise path which he had taken after finding the dead body of the child (this did not seem particularly significant, since the terrain was wild open country), and the other was an inadvertent admission by Gustave that he had actually noticed Lady Drummond's body under a rug shortly after finding the little girl's body—a fact which he had not mentioned previously. Either his memory was improving or his invention was crumbling—but there was still no evidence that would justify an arrest. Sebeille retired, temporarily defeated but prepared to wait. He knew very well that with the passage of time lies decay more rapidly than the truth.

Another month went by. It was now October, and the tourist season was coming to an end. Sebeille decided on a further bout of intensive interrogation, and once more Gustave was taken to the police station for a two-day session of non-stop questioning. Again he managed to keep accurately to the details of his original statements, but as before, under the stress of interrogation, introduced a new admission which had not been mentioned previously.

This time he confessed that the little girl, Elizabeth Drummond, had actually been still alive when he had first seen her lying on the ground. She had moaned and moved one arm. He had observed this, but nevertheless had done nothing to help her. He had left her to die and had returned to the farm-house.

Now, at last, Sebeille was able to take some action within the framework of the law. He arrested Gustave on a charge, under French law, of failing to aid a person in danger. It was not a major indictment, but it was a step in the right direction, and Sebeille felt that a taste of prison might help to loosen Gustave's tongue. The Commissaire was still taking a long-term view.

In due course Gustave came up for trial. He was convicted and jailed for two months. But during the course of the trial various items of conflicting evidence were presented in court—in particular, questions of time. It seemed strange that Gustave claimed to have found the girl's body around five-thirty a.m., after dawn, when witnesses had heard shots fired at about one-thirty. Yet Gustave had stated previously that he had gone out from the farm-house after hearing the shots. Why the four-hour time lapse? Or, if he had found the body after hearing the shots, why had he gone back to the farm to await dawn before taking any action? Gustav proved to be evasive on this issue, but on the evidence it looked as if he had in fact been callous enough to return to the farm after finding the dying girl, but was now ashamed and reluctant to admit it.

Statements made by Gustave's wife and his brother, Clovis, confirmed that Gustave had said that the girl had not actually been dead when he had found her, but he had been afraid to tell the police the truth in case it caused trouble. But trouble for whom? Sebeille was convinced that Gustave was covering up for somebody else, and that he was prepared to go to jail rather than reveal what he knew. And, of course, to jail he went.

That was the end of the case for a year. Even the newspapers forgot about it. But Commissaire Sebeille did not. There were too many loose threads to satisfy his methodical mind, and so far as he was concerned the imprisonment of Gustave on a minor charge was irrelevant to the main issue. He pursued his inquiries with patient single-mindedness. He called regularly on the Dominici family to ask more and more questions, but always meeting the same sullen barrier of indifference and non-communication. In the long run it was Gustave again, after he had served his sentence and been released from prison, who in his characteristic way added new fragments of information to the ever-changing story.

Questioned by Sebeille on one occasion he said that on the evening before the murders, eleven-year-old Elizabeth had called at the farm to fill a kettle with water. He also admitted in a confused way that at some time during that fatal night he had, after finding the girl's dead body and returning to the farm, made a second visit to the Drummond camp, and had even examined the woman's body to see if she was still alive.

To Sebeille it was clear that Gustave was the weak link in

the Dominici chain, and that sooner or later he would break down under rigorous questioning. So he pursued the interrogation in a stubborn unrelenting way. And in the end his judgement proved to be right. Gustave, unable to stand the strain any longer, and not able clearly to remember what he had said and what he had not said, accused his aged father, Gaston, of the triple murder. It was Gaston, he declared, who had shot the man and the woman, and had clubbed the little girl to death. He, Gustave, and most of the family, were well aware of the truth, and had tried to cover up for the old man—but there had to be a limit. So far as Gustave was concerned, he had already served a jail sentence on behalf of his father and was not prepared to make any further sacrifices.

It was now Sebeille's turn to tighten the screw on Gaston himself. He was a sly, cynical, taciturn old man in his late seventies—a kind of homespun rural philosopher with a cruel aggressive streak which made him a tyrant among his own family, with whom he enjoyed a kind of love-hate relationship.

Sebeille went to the farm-house and talked to Gaston over a bowl of soup. Gustave, he said, had finally told the whole story, and Gaston might just as well speak the truth. Surprisingly, Gaston very quickly confessed; it was as though the betrayal by his son had completely shattered his defiance. The confession, which was later produced at the trial, said:

"It was a crime of love. I watched the woman camper for about twenty minutes. Then I crept close and whispered to her.

"Then the Englishman rose and jumped on me. I picked up the carbine from the floor and I went crazy and shot at him. He ran away and I shot him twice more. The Englishwoman was screaming so I turned round and shot her once.

"Then the girl ran out from the car and I ran after her and gave her a blow on the head with the butt of the gun."

The case again became headline news throughout the world. But Gaston, having made his confession, withdrew it with equal facility and denied everything. At the same time, to make Sebeille's task more difficult, Gustave also withdrew his allegations against Gaston. The rest of the family played safe and said nothing at all.

Nevertheless, Sebeille felt that there was sufficient evidence to proceed with the case. Gaston Dominici was arrested and charged with murder, and brought to trial in November, 1954. As was to be expected, he revoked all confessions, claiming that they had been forced out of him under duress. He proclaimed his innocence very positively, but under examination went so far to admit that: "It was an accident. They attacked me. They took me for a marauder."

The only possible witnesses were members of his own family, but under French law they were not required to give evidence on oath. The testimony of some of them proved to be so conflicting and so full of contradictions and denials that it was of little value. Gaston accused them, and they in turn accused him and each other.

At one point, in a bitter tirade against his relatives, he said he loved his dog "more than all my family".

Sebeille, in court, described the key members of the Dominici family in this way: Gaston, head of the family—hard, severe, without heart, brutal; Marie, Gaston's wife—a good woman, bowing to the authority of her tyrant husband; Gustave—a liar, but he had the key to the mystery; Yvette, Gustave's wife—a dominant woman, with her husband under her thumb.

The most puzzling factor in the case was the lack of an adequate motive. The Drummonds had been murdered for neither robbery nor rape. The elusive hint of some obscure Maquis intrigue was discounted.

Gaston was convicted of murder and sentenced to death. But because of his old age and infirm health he was transferred from the death cell to a prison hospital in Marseilles.

The French Government considered the case so important and controversial that an official inquiry was instigated. The Sûreté Nationale after a long investigation prepared a detailed report of over a quarter of a million words—without reaching a positive conclusion.

The end of the affair was undramatic. After languishing in the prison hospital until the age of eighty-one, Gaston was reprieved, and life imprisonment was substituted for the death penalty. He spent the remaining few years of his life behind bars.

The Moors Murder Horror

It started with a telephone call from a kiosk in Hattersley, a new housing estate near Manchester, to Hyde police station at just before 6.10 a.m. on the morning of Thursday, 7 October, 1965. The caller was David Smith, aged seventeen. He was accompanied by his nineteen-year-old wife, Maureen, and he was carrying a knife and a screwdriver for "self protection". Smith, a shocked and exhausted young man, was reporting a murder. He had been up all night, had witnessed the killing and had been obliged to assist in cleaning up the mess after another young man of his own age, Edward Evans, had received fourteen blows on the head from an axe.

A patrol car arrived at the telephone kiosk within a few minutes, and David Smith and his wife were taken to the police station to tell their story. As a story it was gruesome enough, but it was merely the prelude to an even more horrific story that was to emerge during the course of the subsequent police investigation—a story involving two other child murder victims, and the possibility of even more. But at first the police regarded it as a fairly straightforward single murder inquiry.

What, then, had happened during the pre-dawn hours of that Thursday morning in October, 1965? First it is necessary to look at some of the people involved, and the events leading up to this final act of evil which shocked a country in which capital punishment had only recently been abolished.

David Smith was born in January, 1948, an illegitimate child. At the age of eleven he was charged with wounding with intent; at fourteen, charged with assault causing bodily harm; at fifteen, charged with house-breaking and larceny. He married Maureen Hindley in shotgun-wedding style because she was pregnant. Maureen, two years older than him, was the sister of Myra Hindley.

Esther Myra Hindley, born July, 1942, was an attractive blonde shorthand typist who looked much older than her twenty-three years at the time of the Evans murder. Her father, a former war-time paratrooper, was an invalid after an injury while working on a building site. Her early life and career were unremarkable; she and her family had lived in Gorton, Manchester, all their lives. There was one traumatic experience—at the age of fifteen she befriended, in a motherly fashion, a lively boy of thirteen named Michael Higgins. One hot summer afternoon, when he wanted to go swimming in a local reservoir she declined to join him. He was drowned. She was present when his body was recovered from the slime, and the shock stayed with her for a long time.

In January, 1961, at the age of nineteen, she changed her job and went to work at Millwards Ltd, an old-fashioned chemical company in Gorton, and there she met Ian Stewart Brady, an order-clerk—an odd young man with whom she was to find herself living within a year or two, around about the time of the Great Train Robbery in 1963 and certainly before Kennedy's assassination on 22 November, 1963. It was on the following day, 23 November, that Ian Brady committed his first murder, and one wonders whether the killing of the American President might have triggered a psychopathic mind into imitative action.

Ian Brady, born in January, 1938, was tall and pale, with wiry brown hair. His eyes were large and grey, and invariably cold. He had high cheek bones and pouting lips. He was the illegitimate son of a waitress in Glasgow named Maggie Stewart, but was adopted by a Sloan family in the Glasgow Gorbals slum district.

There is a story which throws some light on subsequent behaviour: at the age of ten he found a starving cat in a bombed house in Glasgow, put it in a carrier-bag and buried it alive in a graveyard. The cat was later released by passing schoolboys. By the age of twelve he had started collecting Nazi souvenirs—knives, a German cap, a photo of Eva Braun and Hitler. When he was fourteen he was bound over for two years for robbing a gas meter, and soon afterwards was bound over again for the theft of 25s. In 1954 he obtained a job with Harland and Wolff for a few months, then left and joined a butcher as an errand boy.

Then, in November of that year, aged sixteen, he was arrested for house-breaking and, by order of the court, returned to the care and control of his real mother. She had changed her name from Maggie to Peggy, had married an Irish labourer, and was living in Moss Side, Manchester. And so Ian Brady travelled to Manchester to resolve his future career.

He went through a number of short-lived jobs, was arrested for theft, was sent to Strangeways prison and then to Borstal at Hatfield, Yorks. After his release in 1957 he took some casual jobs, but was mainly unemployed and on the dole. Around this time the Brady family moved from Moss Side to Longsight in Manchester.

It was there that he finally landed a relatively stable job as a stock-clerk at Millwards Ltd, although his truculence often caused trouble; and it was there, during his seven-year stay, that he met the new company shorthand-typist— the blonde Myra Hindley, with whom he was soon to live in her grandmother's home (Mrs Maybury, aged seventy-seven, regularly taking sleeping tablets and so hearing nothing during the violent nights). And it was during this period that he started collecting his vast library of books on Nazism, war crimes, torture, sex and sadism, including some of the better-known works of the notorious Marquis de Sade.

*　　　*　　　*

From 1963 onwards there were a number of missing children in the Manchester area. The bodies of some were eventually discovered; others have not yet been traced, and may never be. The record runs like this:

12 July, 1963—Pauline Reade, aged sixteen, of Gorton, Manchester. She left home at 7.30 p.m. to join a girl friend

at a "jive session" at a social club half a mile away. She never arrived and has not been seen since.

23 November, 1963—John Kilbride, aged twelve, of Ashton-under-Lyne, near Manchester, the eldest of six children (three brothers and two sisters). Visited a cinema and a market in Manchester. Disappeared on his way to the bus-station to return home.

16 June, 1964—Keith Bennett, aged twelve, of Eston Street, Manchester. Set out in the evening to visit his maternal grandmother half a mile away. He was escorted by his mother across a busy main road. He never arrived at his grandmother's home and was never seen again.

26 December, 1964—Lesley Ann Downey, aged ten, of Ancoats, Manchester. Only daughter, with three brothers. She visited a nearby fair on Boxing Day with her brothers and some small friends, but separated from them at some point and was never seen alive again.

6 October, 1965—Edward Evans, aged seventeen, of Ardwick, Manchester. Family living in condemned house and due to be rehoused in the new year. Went into town for a beer, and then to the Central Station buffet for a bite to eat. Never seen alive again.

In all but the last three "missing persons" cases (since the Edward Evans murder was reported by David Smith soon after it had happened) the police mounted massive searches and investigations. Thousands of people were interviewed, thousands of hand-bills and posters were distributed, canals, rivers and reservoirs were dragged or searched by frogmen. The police chiefs in the area, who included Superintendent Robert Talbot and Detective Chief Inspector Joseph Mounsey—a stubborn, determined man destined to be involved some years later in the Sewell case—pursued their inquiries in a mood of grim single-mindedness, but to no avail. The missing children remained missing.

One remarkable incident happened during the intensive search for John Kilbride. A clairvoyant (Mrs Anne Lansley) was reported to have said that she "saw" the missing boy as out in the open, some way down a slope with the skyline completely barren, with a road on the right and near a stream. In the event, she was almost right, but her clairvoyance did not help the police at that time, and John Kilbride's body was eventually found by methodical police

investigation, while that of Lesley Ann Downey was discovered almost by accident.

* * *

At 11.30 p.m. on 6 October, 1965, Myra Hindley took the
dog for its usual nightly run. She and Ian Brady had driven
by car to the centre of Manchester earlier in the evening,
had visited an off-licence to buy some wine, and then Brady
decided to pick up some beer in the Central Station buffet.
When he arrived he found it closed, and he had also found
young Edward Evans standing by a milk-vending machine.
Evans was dark and slim, wearing a suede jacket, suede shoes
and tight jeans. He looked as if he might be homosexual;
whatever the truth, Evans accepted Brady's invitation to go
back to his home for a drink. He introduced Myra Hindley,
who was driving the car, as his sister.

After Myra had taken the dog out, Brady drank wine
while Evans apparently did not drink anything. That there
was some conspiracy at this stage was evident, for Myra
in fact went to the home of David Smith, ostensibly to make
arrangements for her mother to bleach her hair the following evening. The time was 11.40 p.m. She asked if David
Smith would escort her home as she was "scared in the dark".

So David Smith set off with Myra, reaching the Brady
home around 11.50 p.m. Myra asked Smith if he would like
to come in for some miniature bottles of spirit and liqueurs.
Smith agreed, but Myra insisted on going in first just in case
Brady was "taping a record". Brady was a great tape-recorder
and camera enthusiast, though by no means an expert.

In the event the door was opened by Brady himself, who
took Smith into the kitchen and produced three miniature
bottles. Brady then went back into the sitting-room, leaving
Smith in the kitchen with the door ajar. At that point
Smith had no reason to believe that a visitor, Edward Evans,
was on the premises.

A few moments later there was a terrified scream. Then
Myra shouted: "Dave, help him!" Smith, imagining that
Brady was being attacked by an intruder, rushed into the
sitting-room, grasping a stick which he had brought with
him. To his astonishment Brady seemed to be holding a
flabby dummy by the neck and striking its head with an
axe. The dummy was lying face down on the floor and

Brady was astride it, crouching down and striking the head of the dummy with the side of the axe and not the sharp edge. As he struck, Brady was shouting obscenities. But it wasn't a dummy at all, because Smith could see blood and bone and flesh matted with dark hair flying in all directions.

After fourteen blows to the skull, young Edward Evans died. Brady dragged a cushion cover over the victim's head to contain the flow of blood. Grandmother, in an adjacent room, was awakened by the disturbance and called out, but Myra assured her that it was only the dog. If the neighbours heard any screams, they did not intervene—people seldom do.

The next stage was clearing up and washing up. Smith, who felt sick, was told by Brady that he would have to help, as he was in it "up to the waist". All three cleaned up with hot water and detergents—the walls, the lino, the rugs, furniture and clothing. Brady commented: "That was the messiest yet."

Brady had, in fact, boasted to David Smith on previous occasions that he had murdered a number of people and that one day he would demonstrate to him how it was done. The night of 6 October, 1965, was the night of the grisly demonstration. It was necessary to do something about the body, still lying on the floor. Myra produced a sheet of polythene, a white sheet and a blanket. The polythene was tied round the crushed head with electric flex to hold in the blood, then the body was "jack-knifed" and bundled into the sheet and blanket and tied up in the shape of a large rectangular parcel.

Finally, Smith and Brady dragged the package up some stairs into an unused room where it was dumped under the window, ready for disposal the following morning. During the exertion of getting the corpse up the stairs, Brady quipped: "Eddie's a dead weight, isn't he?"

David Smith finally went home around 3 a.m. and was then physically sick. He woke his wife and told her what had happened. For the first time Maureen realized that her sister was living with a killer who had claimed more than one victim. By dawn they had decided to go out to a telephone kiosk and call the police.

*　　　*　　　*

The arrest of Ian Brady at around 9 a.m. on the morning of 7 October, 1965, was very much a matter of routine. However, because Smith had told the police that Brady had two loaded guns (which he had), two dozen police and six plain-clothes men in half-a-dozen patrol cars were deployed around No. 16 Wardle Brook Avenue. The operation was under the command of Superintendent Robert Talbot, who, unarmed, decided on a subterfuge to gain access to the Brady house. He borrowed the white coat of a local baker's delivery man to cover his uniform and also carried a basket of bread over his arm.

In such a way he gained access to the house when Myra Hindley answered the door to his knock soon after 8.30 a.m. Brady was still in bed, writing a letter to his employer saying that he would be away from work for a day or so as he had hurt his ankle. Searching the rooms of the house, Talbot came upon the blanket-wrapped bundle and felt the stiff outline of its contents. He called in the police photographer and pathologists and forensic scientists.

All that had to do with the murder of Edward Evans. What Talbot and his colleagues did not even begin to imagine at that stage was that in due course the murder by Brady of other children would emerge from the inexorable process of checking and cross-checking.

*   *   *

Some time later, while carrying out a detailed check on Brady's Mini-Countryman car, the police found a wallet containing, among other things, three sheets of paper on which had been written abbreviated tabulated instructions for disposing of a (or perhaps "the") body—instructions such as *Bury head; destroy poly.; inspect car for spots; clean and polish all buttons and clasps; wear glov.; Packamac?* And *for hatch, paper bag*—where "hatch" clearly stood for hatchet, or axe.

At a three-minute hearing on Friday, 8 October, 1965, Ian Brady was formally charged with the murder of Edward Evans. But there was more to come, and Myra was still free.

Meanwhile, checking through papers and note-books in Brady's home, Superintendent Talbot came upon a slim school exercise-book. It contained drawings, doodlings, sums, accountancy exercises and, on one page, a list of names—some film stars, some clearly fictitious, and Ian Brady's own name. Just a random list of about twenty or so names. But among them were the following: *John Sloan, Jim Idiot, Frank Wilson, John Kilbride, Alec Guiness, Jack Polish,* etc.

None of the names seemed relevant to the inquiry, but suddenly one particular name rang a bell in the mind of Superintendent Talbot. *John Kilbride.* A schoolboy aged twelve when first missed on 23 November, 1963, and not seen since. This could be it! Talbot passed a photostat of the page to Detective Chief Inspector Mounsey who was in charge of the Kilbride file.

There were other things as well—albums containing photographs of Myra and friends and Brady himself and bleak shots of the Yorkshire moors, and Myra posing against featureless moorland. David Smith was helpful. Yes, the Brady's used to picnic frequently on the moors, somewhere near Penistone, and sometimes they slept the night there, in the car or outside wrapped in blankets. He had been with them on occasions, and it always seemed to be the same area. But although he went with the police in patrol cars on the moorland Penistone Road travelled by Brady and Hindley he was never able to identify the actual stopping place.

Chief Inspector Mounsey ordered big enlargements of all Brady's out-door moorland photographs in the hope that it might be possible to obtain visual identification of a particular area. Meanwhile, Ian Brady, when questioned about David Smith's suggestion that Brady had killed people and buried them on the moor, denied it, though he tacitly admitted that he had said it—"it was all part of a fiction to impress him".

When a detective put to Brady that Smith had said that he had once been on a grave where Brady and Myra had buried a body, Brady merely said "it was to build up an image". But there was more than an image involved. By 12 October it was decided to start digging operations on the moors. Fifty police were detailed, and assistance was sought from any local inhabitants such as farmers and shepherds who knew the terrain. But the task was virtually impossible in such a vast area of grass and stone. Nevertheless, it gave rise to intriguing newspaper headlines such as "Police in mystery dig on moors" (*Manchester Evening News*). But the dig went on to no avail. The police even dug up the front and back gardens of Brady's house, with no result.

The stalemate was finally resolved during *another* detailed methodical check of the contents of Brady's house (there had been many before). A detective went through all the many books one by one, page by page, shaking them in case there were slips of paper contained therein, folding back the covers and inspecting the hollow cavity of the spine binding. A thankless task, perhaps, but in this case his patience was more than rewarded. Inside the spine of a prayer-book he found a Left Luggage Office ticket, No. 74843, Manchester Central Station, for two suit-cases.

The real horror was now about to unfold.

*　　*　　*

Superintendent Talbot opened the suit-cases on the desk of his office. The contents were more or less as expected: pornographic books, gun ammunition, more photographs and photographic albums, coshes, and magnetic tapes. He placed one tape on a recorder, and listened to snatches of pop music recordings from television, and so on. The other tapes he ignored for the moment.

And then he found a tin box containing a set of photographs—nine of them in all. They were pictures of a terrified little girl in various pornographic poses, gagged with a scarf and naked apart from shoes and socks. He knew immediately that he was looking at photographs of Lesley Ann Downey who disappeared at the age of ten on Boxing Day, 1964. In the final photograph the little girl's hands were raised in an attitude of prayer below the gagged mouth.

Meanwhile on the moors another day of digging had come to its uneventful end. The police and civilian helpers were gathering in the coaches to return home from an area known as Hollin Brown Knoll. A late policeman, coming over a rise in the ground, saw something protruding from the peat—something white, resembling the bone of a small forearm. He called to Chief Inspector Mounsey who was by the coach, waiting to depart: "I think it's Kilbride's body."

The departure of the coaches was delayed. The photographers, pathologists and forensic scientists were again called in to carry out their grim work behind canvas screens in the high wind. Only one point of detail was incorrect. The decomposed body that was carefully recovered from the ground was not that of John Kilbride, but were the human remains of little Lesley Ann Downey. John Kilbride was not far away, but he had not yet been located.

In his office Superintendent Talbot was still working on papers, and now playing the remaining tapes, which he listened to with half an ear as they were mainly music and the kind of rubbish that people record and forget about. And then, suddenly, a new tape presented a different noise. Sounds of movement, bumps, subdued murmuring. And then a scream—the voice of a little girl screaming . . . And the quiet background voice, and another scream and the frantic appeal: *"Don't—please, God help me . . ."*

The tape went on and on for sixteen minutes. Talbot listened to it in a state of virtual petrification, staring at the rotating spool. Less than twenty-four hours after the body of Lesley Ann Downey had been recovered from the grave on the moors, he found himself listening to her defilement, torture and murder. That tape was destined to become one of the most terrifying exhibits in any murder trial, and Mrs Downey, the mother, was to hear it too, in order to identify her deceased daughter's voice—and hear that voice calling for her mother in desperation. The mother had already identified the body, which had lain nearly a year in the ground.

At the end of that tape, after the screams and cries had faded into silence, came Christmas music—*Jolly Old St Nicholas* and *The Little Drummer Boy*. When asked in court during his trial why he had preserved the tape, Brady replied: "Because it was unusual."

*　　*　　*

Hyde Police Station now became a major operations headquarters, with a Press-room that was attended by about fifty journalists from all over the world. Headed by Detective Chief Inspector Joseph Mounsey, the police were making an all-out effort to find the grave of John Kilbride on the moors, for they were convinced that it lay in the areas depicted in the photographs taken by Brady, but so difficult to identify. New professional photographs were taken in the vicinity so that they could be enlarged and compared with the inferior Brady pictures, most of which featured Myra Hindley or himself against an indistinct background. The Brady prints were re-processed to improve definition and compared with the landscape shots taken from known points by official police photographers.

In the end Mounsey's patience was rewarded. He was able to match two of Brady's snapshots with one of the police photographs. The background was the same, and so were the stones in the foreground and the nearby water. The assumption was that Brady and Hindley, in their macabre way, had been standing on or near a grave when the pictures were taken. And so the digging started again, but this time with a geographical centre established by photographs.

On 21 October, 1965, at Hyde Police Court, Ian Brady and Myra Hindley were finally charged with the murder of Edward Evans and of Lesley Ann Downey. At this stage there was no charge relating to John Kilbride as the body had not yet been found. But there was not long to go. That same day, in the early afternoon, police probes finally penetrated the patch of ground that Myra Hindley had appeared to be staring at in one of Brady's photographs. One probe encountered something about two feet below the surface of the ground. The tip, on withdrawal, bore the characteristic smell of putrefaction. John Kilbride's grave had finally been found.

Once more the canvas screens were erected and the pathologists called in, while the police formed a cordon round the site to control the mass of people who were now converging on it. The work of excavation went on as night fell on the moors. Light was provided by naked acetylene flares. Finally the remains were lifted and transferred to a metal stretcher for transport by van to the mortuary.

*   *   *

The trial opened on 19 April, 1966, in the Assize Court at Chester. Ian Brady and Myra Hindley pleaded "not guilty" to charges of murdering Edward Evans. Lesley Ann

Downey and John Kilbride. Hindley was additionally charged with comforting, harbouring and maintaining Brady, knowing that he had murdered John Kilbride.

Brady admitted killing Evans—it was due to a quarrel, he implied. He maintained that Lesley Ann Downey had left the house safely after the photographs had been taken, and he knew nothing at all about John Kilbride.

The all-male jury returned a verdict of guilty on all three .ounts. Brady received three concurrent sentences of life imprisonment, and Hindley two, plus seven years for "receiving, comforting and harbouring". They disappeared to their separate prisons.

As for the other two missing children—Pauline Reade and Keith Bennett—they have never been traced or found, nor is there any evidence to suggest that they met a similar fate and are still buried on the moors. There is only the coincidence of time, place and age-group. All were between ten and sixteen years of age, all lived in the Manchester area, and all vanished suddenly between the years 1963 and 1965 —the year when Brady was arrested for the murder of Evans.

One can't help wondering whether, if David Smith had kept his silence as Brady expected him to, there might by now have been many more missing children in Manchester, perhaps lying in new graves on the bleak moors.

Dance of Death

Club 5–7 was new and trendy and "with-it". It opened at Easter 1970 near the small French town of St Laurent du Pont which itself was some twenty miles from Grenoble in the Alpes Maritimes district of south-east France. As a club it consisted principally of a small dance-hall and restaurant, and was generally patronized by young people. It was destined to be the scene of one of the worst fire disasters in recent history.

The club premises had been designed as a colourful psychedelic grotto with moving rainbow lights playing on plastic-covered walls. A circular interior gallery held boxes for onlookers. The boxes were set quite low so that people in them could lean over the rail and almost touch the dancers on the floor below. Access to the gallery was by means of one single spiral staircase.

On the eve of 1 November, 1970, about one hundred and eighty young people in their late teens and early twenties crowded into the dance-hall and gallery to listen and dance to the lively pop music of the new Parisian group called "Les Storms". Although the group were not well known, they had been working hard and doing fairly well. They had been hired from Paris for the evening, but they were never to go back to Paris alive.

It was in the early hours of the morning that tragedy struck. Club 5–7 suddenly burst into flames. In the resulting confined furnace more than one hundred and forty young people perished.

"They didn't have a chance—the place went up like a match-box," commented one of the firemen summoned to the scene of the disaster. Indeed, it was all over in virtually a few seconds, in one immense sheet of flame. The circular gallery with its cave-like boxes burst into flames first, and many young people were trapped and burned alive there.

In the words of one survivor, Mademoiselle Joelle Dondy, the club cashier: "A huge flame suddenly leapt into the air and then plunged down to the main floor like a whirlwind. I tried to save myself—suddenly I felt my hair burning—everyone was screaming, screaming, and then nothing more except the sound of the firemen arriving. I am sure I was the last person to leave that unimaginable hell alive."

Through dense acrid fumes the young dancers fought their way towards the exits. They piled up at locked doors. The emergency exits had been padlocked to keep gate-crashers out as the Saturday night dance and pop-music session was always popular. The thirty or so people who did escape squeezed their way past a turnstile at the admission entrance, but even so a dozen of them were severely burned because of the resultant delay. It is ironic that the keys of the padlocks on the doors were in the pockets of two of the club managers, both of whom were killed immediately. Many of the dead were suffocated by fumes before the flames reached their bodies.

The shell of the building remained intact, even though the corrugated iron roof had melted in the fierce heat of the flames. Firemen described what they saw when they opened the doors as "horrifying and terrible". Charred bodies were piled on top of each other in a frantic attempt to break down the locked doors—they might have succeeded had they had more time. The few who did escape survived because of presence of mind and fast action after the first shout of "fire" and before the lights failed. "People up in the gallery were enveloped by flames," one young man said. "It all happened so quickly—the whole ceiling seemed to catch alight. Everything was a blazing mass."

Another youth who was in the middle of the hall when the fire broke out said: "As soon as I smelt the fumes and saw the first flames above the bar I shouted and made for the entrance door. I pushed a girl in front of me. She's alive. Then we tried to help the others. A girl was screaming behind one of the emergency doors which was firmly fixed." When the door was finally forced there was behind it "a mass of people with their arms outstretched. If the emergency exits had not been closed very many people would have got out alive."

In the morning a crowd of people, including some of the youngsters who had been in the club earlier that night, stood in stunned whispering groups along the main road as ambulances went to and fro, carrying bodies to the townhall, which had been converted into a temporary mortuary. Parents and relatives, their faces contorted with grief, waited to be called to identify jewellery, rings, keys and charred pieces of clothing which had been placed in carefully numbered envelopes.

As M. Jean Vaudville, Prefect of Isère Department, was talking to newspaper reporters, the door opened. A woman in her early forties, her eyes huge with anxiety, came in. "I am sorry, but I am seeking news of my son." M. Vaudville passed her to a gendarme who led her gently to his colleague who was compiling lists of the missing in the adjoining room. To the reporters M. Vaudville declined to answer questions about the locked emergency exits of the club or the inflammability of the internal decoration. "Everything will be investigated," he said.

When the club had first been opened, construction plans were approved by the local authorities as fulfilling specified safety requirements. The previous building had been regarded as unsafe, but this was a new building, and there was some doubt locally as to whether a formal routine check had been carried out since the opening of the club. It was suggested that the fire was started by an electrical short-circuit, but according to some survivors the cause was more probably a lit cigarette that fell on to a coat. The conflagration was immediate. Although the walls and ceiling of the club were made of expanded polyurethane, which melts rather than burns, there is no doubt that in the sudden intense heat it, too, added to the flames. The club's barman, Christian Rota, commented: "In such a blaze even stones would have burned."

A point worth mentioning is that the pop group, Les

Storms, could have escaped through a door just behind them, but when the blaze started they continued playing to ease the panic. They duly died.

Of the three club managers the only one to survive was M. Gilbert Bas. He was in his office when he saw the signal alarm begin to flash. "I thought that, as sometimes happens in an establishment such as ours, it was simply a fight," he said afterwards. As he headed towards the dance-floor he heard screams and shouts of "fire".

M. Bas was twenty-five years old at the time, and certainly not much older than his customers, but he behaved in a practical fashion. As there was no telephone in the club he raced out of the main door to his car and drove at high speed to the fire-station to seek help. There was nothing he could have done in the club itself.

It is not possible to list the personal tragedies involved in such a catastrophe. The majority of the victims were in the seventeen to twenty age group, and they included some foreign students from Grenoble University. One Swedish girl who managed to escape said she was with a number of Danish students. The victims included seventeen-year-old Sicilian twins, Salvatore and Christiane Morgana—he had taken his sister to her first dance. Another brother and sister, Bernard and Corinne Gillet, aged eighteen and sixteen, perished because they turned back to look for each other before escaping.

On the following day M. Jacques Baumel, Secretary of State for Public Affairs, went to Grenoble to pay respects to the dead on behalf of the French Government. After all, it was the second worst fire tragedy of the century, with a casualty figure only marginally less than the well-known Le Printemps fire of 1921 in which one hundred and fifty people died.

On 2 November, two of the survivors of the Club 5–7 fire died in hospital, bringing the death-toll to one hundred and forty-four, and by 16 November two more had died, so that the final score was one hundred and forty-six. The last to die was a nineteen-year-old French girl.

* * *

The village gymnasium was converted into a mortuary chapel to house the one hundred and forty-two plain

wooden coffins containing the remains of the victims. By
4 November, the day of the funeral, nineteen bodies were
still unidentified—and, indeed, unidentifiable. The name-
less ones were buried in a small private cemetery in St
Laurent du Pont where the families concerned could go
and pray. The other coffins were duly conveyed to the home
towns and villages of the dead.

The small altar which had been erected in the gymnasium was almost hidden by masses of flowers and wreaths
from many countries, and there were wreaths from President Pompidou, M. Chaban Delmas, the Prime Minister,
and other ministers of the Government. For the funeral
service the gymnasium proved to be too small to accommodate the crowd of mourners. It was a harrowing scene of
grief as mothers cried out in despair and beat the coffins
with their fists.

The service was conducted by the Roman Catholic
Bishop of Grenoble, and attended by representatives of the
Catholic, Protestant and Muslim churches. It lasted fifteen
minutes. Ambulances had to carry away some mourners
who collapsed from distress. It is a fact that many of the
parents had not been aware that the tragedy had taken place
until they found an empty bed in the house in the morning
following the fire—and even then they suspected a road
accident.

Catastrophes of this kind always result in an aftermath
of administrative inquiry and statements. The official judi-
cial inquiry into the Club 5–7 fire began on 3 November
—two days after the disaster—and was conducted by an
examining magistrate with a view to investigating the circumstances under which the licence and building permit
had been issued for the club, and whether the fire regulations had been complied with. M. Jean Vaudville told the
press: "Everything will be done to discover the truth and
responsibilities involved. It must not happen again, and it
will be necessary to examine new measures which will make
it possible to prevent such disasters in future."

One factor which emerged was that the plastic lining of
the walls and ceiling, and for that matter the furniture,
was by no means fireproof in intense heat. The blaze was
accelerated by incandescent plastic falling from the ceiling
and walls into the centre of the furnace. Also, the single

winding staircase to the gallery was inadequate to cope with a panic exit of terrified people in the grip of, to use the words of *Paris-Match*, "demense de peur".

M Gilbert Bas, the only surviving manager of the club, said that when he went into the dance-hall "everything caught fire at the same time. This huge sheet of flame burned all of them in a matter of seconds. Even if there had been large doors they would have been burned in the same way. They had already been suffocated. Those who made their way out after the big burst of flame were walking torches."

He added: "The emergency exits were not all locked—that is not true. Three of them were open. They only needed to be pushed from the inside. Occasionally even our dog could push one open. The barman Christian Rota made his way out through one of the emergency exits. He tried to get others to come along with him but they did not follow. I don't know why—it all happened so quickly."

M. Bas was in a badly shaken state, with red-rimmed eyes, and from time to time he contradicted himself. "I do not know—I do not understand," he kept saying. "I know that for many people it would have been better if I too had died. Naturally, I am responsible for everybody. I do not know if I shall be able to look people in the face any more."

Perhaps his feelings of guilt and remorse in a period of bitter stress are understandable, but fire prevention is also the responsibility of local government. The French Cabinet took action by suspending from office the mayor of St Laurent du Pont. The mayor, M. Pierre Perrin, had held office for twelve years and was universally liked and respected. One suspects that the Government made the gesture in haste to demonstrate its determination not to allow the investigation to run into administrative and legal sands, and to appease the growing public demand for sanctions against those responsible for the tragedy—whether directly or indirectly.

M. Raymond Marcellin, Minister of the Interior, said that in his view safety measures prescribed by law and local regulations had not been enforced, and that the mayor had, in fact, played a decisive rôle in initially examining the request for a building permit and authorizing the club. As a result of the Minister's statement, five mayors in the Isère

Department resigned, claiming that Mayor Perrin's suspension was a grave injustice.

As to how the fire started there were various theories, none of which could be conclusively proved. During the inquiry the Public Prosecutor of Grenoble alleged that the fire had been accidentally caused by a young man who threw a lighted match on to a cushion covered with synthetic material. This had immediately burst into flames. He had then attempted to put out the fire by smothering it with his coat, but before he could do so the plastic-covered walls of the gallery box in which he was sitting also caught fire. From that point on the conflagration accelerated with incredible speed. Under the circumstances, however, the true facts must remain a matter for speculation.

Nevertheless, the Minister took the view that the fire would never have occurred if the regulations had been observed, and stated in the National Assembly that the dance-hall had not at any time been inspected by the Fire Department, as required by regulation. Further, he said that the club had been opened to the public without the requisite official authority having been issued by the mayor. "It would be unjust for the mayor to have to bear direct responsibility for the disaster, but the State must check in the minutest detail the extent to which regulations have been enforced and controls carried out."

There is little more to add. Clearly, locked exit doors in a building open to the public can hardly be explained away, gate-crashers or not. The use of synthetic materials for decor and furnishings must obviously be the subject of a big question-mark; they may be cheap and cheerful, but are they safe? And, of course, one can raise the hoary old question of whether smoking should be permitted in public places. Cigarettes and even pipes can be a monumental fire risk, as any insurance company will confirm. Indeed, one wonders why they do not generally charge higher insurance premiums for smokers.

Not that insurance would have softened the tragedy of Club 5–7—but from the evidence available one lighted match, presumably meant to ignite one cigarette, destroyed one hundred and forty-six young lives in a few moments of horror. The awful truth is that it could happen again any time, anywhere.

Frenzy in Bangla Desh

They were tall men, most of them bearded and all of them striking. At first, to the small group of British and West-European journalists and cameramen at the side of the road, they seemed to be actually marching, towering above the squat Bengalis who surrounded them.

Then someone noticed they were not really marching at all. They were hopping, limping, being quite brutally pushed along by the little Bengalis at their rear. These struck them again and again with the butts of ex-British-Army Lee Enfield rifles, struck them in the ribs, over the head, behind the knees, screaming as they did so.

The Punjabis accepted the blows, the screams of rage, in a silence which was perhaps more stunned than dignified.

"*Look*," said the young English engineer who had been hoping for transport this afternoon from the air-strip, an escape from a land which he had learned to love and which now seemed suddenly mad. "*Look*," said the young man again. "*Look at them*. Their hands are tied."

And so they were. Not behind their backs in the usual fashion, but clasped together in front, as if in prayer. Perhaps they really were praying: God knows they had a reason. Perhaps they were praying to Allah for deliverance from the shocking situation in which they found themselves.

The little group moved on past the watchers at the roadside, moved on with feet, mostly bare, kicking up clouds from the red Bengal dust as they went.

It was the hot season and almost unbearably humid, the few long weeks before the monsoon, with heat and tension and the smell of death in the air.

There was desultory firing in the distance. Jessore had been almost quiet for about an hour, but now the racket was starting up again, as if the firing, the shouts of "Jai Bangla!" and the sudden, terrifying crackle of flames were all triggered off by the same mechanism. Many buildings in the town were burning, and not all for an apparent reason. A wooden house would simply burst into flame, and black-and-yellow fire would leap from it. These were often houses where a tracer bullet had lodged minutes earlier.

The little group of Punjabis, a dozen of them, was pummelled down the dusty road to the centre of the town. In a few moments it was out of sight.

There was more random firing and the Englishmen and others took cover as best they could. It was difficult in this city of fifty thousand inhabitants to find out who was firing at whom. There were the local, Bengali, citizens, armed with bamboo staves and spears, with, here and there, a rifle. There were thousands of these civilians, reinforced by the East Pakistan Rifles, a unit of the Pakistan army which had mutinied and was now supporting its fellow Bengalis in a fight against "The Oppressors from the West".

"The Oppressors" took the form of West Pakistani soldiers, Punjabis and Baluchis for the most part, many of them flown in only yesterday to deal with this insurrection. These were well armed, well trained, enormously outnumbered. It would take many, many plane-loads, and ship-loads to the southern port of Chittagong to ensure victory for President Yahya Khan's government against this Bengali uprising.

The Government of India, acting so far as a worried and critical neighbour, was debating its next move. It had already refused permission for Pakistan aircraft to over-fly its territory; and now reinforcements from West Pakistan were only able to enter their eastern province by sea to the port of Chittagong, or by a roundabout and mysterious air-route via staging-posts in China.

It was a few moments past noon on that April day, 1 April

and a Thursday, when the screaming began. There were wails of agony, terrifying screams of agony, mingling with the hoarse shouts of a crowd enjoying itself, men and women inflicting "punishment" with a hideous gusto. There was the sound of blows from bamboo *lathis*, an occasional rifle or revolver shot, the whole mounting to a crescendo.

It stopped abruptly. The party of Europeans looked at each other.

"I suppose," said one of them after a long silence, "I suppose we should be congratulating ourselves, really. The Shaikh's just said the British never taxed his people, and that it's only now, now they've become what he calls a colony and a market for the Herrenvolk of West Pakistan, that they revolt."

There was silence broken by spasmodic firing. Then suddenly there was one hideous, totally isolated, scream which mounted, then slithered into silence.

"Well, they're not doing a bad job of it."

"Of what?"

"Revolting, old man, revolting."

"You can say that again. What I've seen in this town today is the most revolting—well, put it this way, I've never in my life seen anything so dreadful as is going on right now. You heard those screams, I heard those screams, we all heard them. And we damn well know what they mean."

"Oh God!" said someone, and they watched as some forty more of the Punjabi civilians were forcibly marched down the street like the dozen which had preceded. As Punjabis and Urdu-speakers, they were felt to represent the same hated colonialism and exploitation as the Pakistan Army, and in fact to be their spies and fifth-columnists. Somehow they were managing to keep a certain dignity, these tall, contemptuous-seeming Muslims from the western part of the state of Pakistan, who had chosen to live here among voluble, volatile co-religionists in the east. And now these volatile Bengalis wanted to be completely independent, and were demonstrating the fact in a manner which left not a shred of doubt.

The Punjabi civilians moved on down the road, down the road to death. Small men prodded them from behind, shrieked at them, spat at them, kicked them and struck them with *lathis*, while they, hands locked in apparent prayer, held their peace.

The journalists and photographers—not all of them professional—who were present in Jessore on that dreadful 1 April, 1971, wrote thousands of words and took a great many pictures. The words and the pictures which managed to find their way out of Bengal shocked a western world from Bonn to San Francisco. Among them were photographs of the Punjabi civilians being marched to the centre of the town Then, needing no caption at all, were the pictures taken a short time later of the same men--each clearly recognizable.

* * *

It was a situation for which some of the more thoughtful Europeans might feel partly responsible. For this great subcontinent, the one-time "Indian Empire" of an English queen and which once again was exploding, had never been remotely homogeneous. It was British rule which had given it a superficial veneer of unity. When, on the announced departure of the British, a huge segment of the population announced it could no longer go on living with the other, a hasty divorce had been arranged, separating the Muslims from a Hindu majority. The new state of Pakistan had been born, having even less homogeneity than what had preceded it, for it was split into two parts, with hundreds of miles of a new, truncated, India in between.

The petitioner in the divorce had been Mr Jinnah, representing, as he saw it, the Muslim community. But there were many of his co-religionists who thought little of his idea of a separate Muslim state, a "Pakistan", who hoped to go on living where they were, in predominantly Hindu parts of the sub-continent. However, the idea of separation, and the movement of populations which would go with it, to "round off" the edges of the new state, was accepted and backed by the British, now anxious to leave. They saw it both as the price the sub-continent had to pay for independence, and as the only alternative to a far worse confrontation between the communities.

Countless thousands died in the blood-letting that followed.

There were observers then who watched in horror, fearing that the apparent reason for slicing a vast territory into sectors on the basis of religion was a false one The inhabitants of the eastern half of Bengal might be Muslims, but they were as unlike the Urdu-, Pushtu- and Punjabi-speaking Muslims in the west as they were similar to their Hindu, Bengali-speaking neighbours just across the new border.

And the Pathans of the extreme north-west had a strictly limited interest in being part of a new state comprising people they disliked, merely because they shared the religion of Islam. They wanted a further separation, a "Paktoonistan" of their own. If separation had been effected once, it could be done again.

Pakistan came about and under devoted leadership it prospered, but to some outsiders that prosperity seemed to be despite its policy of religious *apartheid*, not because of it. Almost from the beginning the eastern citizens of that state, those in east Bengal, now East Pakistan, began to chafe under the rule, as they saw it, of a government hundreds of miles away. That government seemed to be taking more than it gave, for so much of the wealth of Pakistan, in particular the huge annual crop of jute, came from its eastern wing.

The revolt came, many years after separation, and the atrocities committed in that first half of 1971 were appalling. But before we continue with the fate of the luckless Punjabis who stayed in Bengal we must note the fact that wounds inflicted by Pakistan's army against citizens in the east exceeded almost anything in post-war history. Some estimates put the figure of people killed as high as two millions.

*   *   *

The Punjabis were marched off to death, hands tied in front of them. When some of the Europeans made their way down that same road an hour later, down to where it widened into a large square, they found that each one of the prisoners had been beaten and hacked to death. An hour after the screams, the cheers and the laughter which had seemed so shocking, the prisoners lay in a rough semi-circle. Two or three of them were still just alive, arms and legs threshing feebly for the edification of the crowd.

There had been twelve in this first group, and photographs had recorded the details as they went by. Now, an hour later, those familiar, recognizable, faces, stared sightlessly, eyes open, from among the blood-soaked debris. The photographs taken on that day, before and after the massacre, make a shocking commentary, all by themselves. No need here for words.

But that massacre, though brutal, was motivated: the earlier massacres by the army of Pakistan far exceeded it in size if not in horror. The tension had mounted for months, and in the first weeks of March it grew unbearable. Bengali discontent had risen so that every villager was demanding freedom; the name "Bangla Desh" was on every lip.

Pakistan's President Yahya Khan took a decision to hold the east at all costs. Without it, he reckoned, Pakistan was finished The great old families, the aristocracy, might all live in the west: wealth lay in the east.

The decision was taken to wipe out any potential leadership in East Pakistan.

A few minutes before one on the morning of Friday, 26 March, army tanks roared up to the University of Dacca, the breeding ground, the home, for East Pakistan's intellectual elite.

The tanks lined up carefully. Inside the dormitories of the university, students heard the rumble of their approach. There had been plenty of midnight arrests during the past week, and this would no doubt be another: a few students and faculty members would be unceremoniously led away to a fate no one cared to consider.

Suddenly, in the dormitory of Jangranath Hall, walls and ceilings were lit by the glare of search-lights. Students who had been trying to see from the window fell back, momentarily blinded. There were tanks out there, dozens of them, just outside the compound wall, but no one could imagine what they were about to do.

Orders were shouted in the night air and suddenly a terrific barrage opened up. Within a minute the compound wall had been breached and the tanks were firing on the windows and walls of the dormitories. Windows shattered, walls collapsed. Screaming students fell where they were—many dying in their beds—or managed to escape temporarily to the roofs of their buildings. But by now infantry had swarmed in after the tanks, swarmed in through the windows and open walls of each building in the wrecked university, sprayed every corner of every room with fire from Chinese AK47 automatic rifles.

After half an hour there was hardly a living thing in the university compound. It was a charred shell. And every dormitory had been turned into a charnel-house.

The army withdrew, the tanks rumbled away into the distance. Rescue parties entered the compound, knowing there was little they could do, and took stock of the situation. In one spot the entire large family of a professor had been butchered as they slept. Everywhere children seemed to have been shot in their beds, perhaps because they had cowered there when the search-lights and the shooting began. The bodies of students were scattered from one side of the campus to another. Blood was everywhere.

Elsewhere, on that Friday morning, prominent men had been taken out and butchered in front of their wives and children, mothers had been raped, babies bayoneted, in a sudden and quite deliberate avalanche of terror. To say, as some of the world's press did, that "genocide" was taking place may have been an exaggeration; for certainly the policy of President Yahya Khan was not the wiping out of East Pakistan's population (which after all, grew and processed jute and other things for the west's enrichment) but its terrorization. If a great many potential leaders of revolt could be quickly and publicly eliminated, there would be no more trouble. The dreadful threat of secession would be over and Pakistan could get back to building itself up, a strong and unified nation.

But the scheme overshot itself, became madness.

Unlike the troubles which had accompanied separation and the birth of Pakistan, the underlying cause of the 1971 discontents owed little to religious fanaticism: it was a dispute between one group of Muslims which thought it was being exploited by another. But soon the awful spectre of fanaticism was back, soon there were Hindus butchered in the street, some of them men with uncircumsized penes hacked off in a gesture of hate against non-Muslims. Much of this madness seems to have been straightforward hysteria, but as the fighting went on there grew a tendency, within the Pakistan army, to equate Bengali revolt with Indian encouragement, thus conveniently making the whole affair into a holy war.

Dacca is a city of bamboo, with mud and stone and corrugated iron. One phosphorus grenade or even one incendiary bullet from an AK47 is enough to wipe out acres of housing. The normal population is in the region of two million, but within a few days it was down to a fraction of this, with refugees leaving the charred shell of districts they had lived in all their lives, to head westward to the border and asylum in India. And as these refugees poured over the border and India called for international help in feeding and caring for them—and getting them back again, to a peaceful land of their own—Indian plans became more definite.

The Pakistan army knew that unless it made its control absolute before the monsoon broke in May, it would be unable to fight again until the rains were over. The army's tactics became more ruthless, and the tactics took effect, at least for a time. As one Bengali put it to a group of correspondents: "They want to drag us so far down that we will be reduced to eating grass. They want to make sure no head will ever be raised against them again."

They might have achieved this, were it not for India. Before the Pakistan army was able to complete its suppression of the revolution, Mrs Gandhi moved. Her reasons, as Prime Minister of Pakistan's huge neighbour, were said to be partly an effort to halt the genocide believed to be going on across her border, partly an effort to halt the flood of refugees coming in. And partly to help wipe out the hateful idea of an "East Pakistan", which only a generation before had been a prized and peaceful part of India.

India, with its far greater resources, its control of communications, had little difficulty in putting Pakistan's army on the defensive. There was a strange air of unreality, a sense of theatre, about the whole brief Indo-Pakistan war, which made it an ironic contrast with those days of late March and early April when savageries were perpetrated by bitter, excited men. The partition of India—old "Imperial" India—was so recent that senior officers from the Indian and Pakistan armies had served side by side in the same units; and their friendship, their sudden excitement at finding themselves playing war games together, made some of their actions and most of their utterances mildly, pleasingly, comic. A senior Indian general announced to reporters that he wanted to accept a surrender from his old friend on the other side and then engage him in a round of golf. Others maintained they wanted to get things cleared up, quickly and neatly in order to go out for drinks and a meal with old friends in the opposing army. Local surrenders were pictured in the press, sealed with an embrace.

India won, without too much effort, and these pleasing manifestations of chivalry and comradeship blunted the horror of the months before. It seems unlikely that a future war, anywhere, will have time for them. And it is strange to reflect that a war of such a kind, an old-fashioned, gentleman's war, of a brevity rivalled only by the six-day Arab-Israeli conflict of 1967 and the fourteen days of the Third Anglo-Burmese War in 1885, should have been precipitated by a reign of terror such as the world has seldom seen even in the blood-stained twentieth century.

The war ended and Bangla Desh got its cherished independence. But its troubles were still far from over. A sizeable number of Urdu-speaking Biharis remained within its borders, many of whom had come in as refugees from Hindu India in 1947. These now faced the prospect of persecution as "spies", just as the Punjabis had been persecuted, and perhaps worse, in April, 1971. There were statesmanlike moves to re-settle the Biharis in Pakistan (which had so recently been "West Pakistan" and was now its totality) while moving Bengali settlers in the Punjab back to their ancestral homeland in Bangla Desh.

But after the horrors of those early months in 1971, there was a sincere desire in both India and Pakistan to wipe clean the slate and begin again, in a sub-continent of friends: India, Pakistan and the fledgling Bangla Desh.

If the arrangement, the triumvirate, fails, the failure would not be for want of good intentions. In all three countries there was firm resolve that the clock must not be turned back, that the horrors and the terrors of 1971 must not be repeated.

Notes on Authors

JOHN BURKE saw wartime service with R.A.F., R.E.M.E. and Royal Marines. First novel, *Swift Summer,* won Atlantic Award in literature. Since written eighty books including "book of the film" adaptations. Film and television story editor.

ANTHONY BURTON, once a navigator in jet bombers, is a free-lance author and journalist. His books include *A Programmed Guide to Office Warfare, The Jones Report* and *The Canal Builders.* Fascinated by the phenomenon of fear, he believes it has to be met head on.

CHARLES CHILTON'S expertise in American subjects began to develop in 1938 when he was assistant to Alastair Cooke on his radio programme "I Hear America Singing". Has written and produced many popular radio series; his programme "The Long, Long Trail", a musical documentary on the First World War, was heard by Joan Littlewood, and in collaboration with her developed into the stage show and film *Oh What a Lovely War.*

IAN FELLOWES-GORDON, born in New York, only reached his Scottish homeland at the age of fifteen. Served for nine years in the British regular army. Now works with the B.B.C. World Service in London, and has written ten books. His interest in the weird and occult commenced whilst serving with the spirit-worshipping Kachin irregular levies in the jungles of North-eastern Burma.

MICHAEL and MOLLIE HARDWICK are one of the world's busiest and most versatile husband and wife literary teams. Together and separately they have written some forty books. Subjects on which they have written include lives of Emma, Lady Hamilton and Mrs Disraeli, as well as many books on Dickens and on Sherlock Holmes and his creator Conan Doyle.

DODDY HAY has been teacher and tail-gunner, regular officer and irregular broadcaster, county cricketer and R.A.F. rugger blue, Cresta rider and international sky diver, syndicated journalist and test-parachutist, full-time author and part-time unskilled labourer. Exhausted by the frequent changes, he now lives peacefully in Spain with his wife Jenny and their son Iain.

CHARLES ERIC MAINE, though professionally an industrial journalist and editor, is also the author of twenty-five books, fiction and non-fiction, some of which have been translated into eight languages, including Japanese, Hebrew and Greek. Well known in criminology and science-fiction circles, he believes that writing is a catharsis for many mental pressures, including terror

RONALD SETH was seconded to Special Operations Executive in 1942 and parachuted into Estonia to carry out sabotage and organize resistance. Post-war, he became a full-time writer, specializing in the history, organization and administration of espionage, and in naval and military history for the general reader. Among his forty-odd books for adults are *A Spy Has No Friends, Anatomy of Spying, Stalingrad: Point of Return, The Sleeping Truth*. Having faced the ultimate and by a millions-to-one chance survived, fear and terror have no longer any hold on him.

CLARE SMYTHE is an industrial journalist, a reader for motion picture companies, a feature writer for women's magazines, an expert researcher, and a former editor of children's books. Like most women she is terrified of many things, and also like most women usually outfaces them. She doesn't believe in Women's Lib.

FRANK USHER, author, journalist, criminologist. Under his pseudonym Charles Franklin he has published a number of books of popular history and factual crime, as well as many novels of espionage, mystery and suspense, and radio plays. Says that by writing about fear and terror he has largely exorcized them.

INDEX

A4, 455
Aktari, 42–3, 46
Albigensians, *see* Cathars
Albion, H.M.S., 444–5
Alfred, King, 30, 33
Allenby, 376
American Army of
    Occupation, 431
Anak Krakatoa, 321
Anastasia, 354
Anielwicz, 412
Anjer, Java, 316–17, 321
Anson, General, 268
Arnaud, Brother, 51
Aztecs, 67, 74

Baghdad, 376
Baltic Station Square, 392, 401
Baluchis, 491
"Bangla Desh", 495
Barbados, 180
Barbary Coast, 324, 332
Barcaldine Castle, 132
Barrackpore, India, 268
Barrett, Ivor, 342–9
Bas, Gilbert, 485, 488
Baugh, Lieut., 269
Baumet, M. Jacques, 486
B.E.2c, aircraft, 376
Beane, Sawney, 99–106
Bellamy, Rev. Gervas, 155
Bellamy, Lieut. John, 155
Bengal, 491
Bennett, Keith, 474–82
Berg, Professor Karl, 341
Berhampore, India, 268
Bernstorff, Minister, 161–2
Berouw, gunboat, 317–19

Bhamo, Burma, 274–5
Bombay, 266
Borie, 418
Bourbon, Louis Henri,
    see Condé, Prince de
Brady, Ian Stewart, 472–80
Breadalbone, Earl of, 131
Bregères, France, 416
Briant, Abbé, 240
Brisbin, General, 304
Bromhead, Lieut., 296
Broussaudier, 418
Buckman, negro slave, 170–6
Budleis, Mara, 339
Bund, the, 407
Burdsall, Rev. Richard, 96–7
Burke, William, 226–9, 231–3
Byerinck family, 316, 318–19
Byrne, Joe, 255

Calcutta, 150–9, 264, 266
Caledonian Railway, 367
Calverley, Henry, 91, 93–4
Calverley, Philippa, 89–96
Calverley, Squire, 88–9
Calverley, Walter, 86–98
Cambria, brig, 210–12, 214–15
Campbell, Sarah, 129
Campbell clan, 129–39
Campbell of Ardkinglass, 132
Campbell of Glenlyon, Robert,
    134–8
Canning, Lord, 265
Carey, Mary, 150–2, 155–9
Carey, Peter, 150–1, 155–7
Carlisle, 367
Caroline Matilda, Queen of
    Sweden, 160–8

Carrel, Jean-Antoine, 284–7
Caruso, Enrico, 326–7
Cathars, 49–55
Cetewayo, Zulu chief, 294–5, 297, 299–300
Chalgrove airfield, Oxon., 434, 437
Chambrun, Jacques, 387
Chao Kao, 12–19
Chard, Lieut. John Rouse Merriot, 295–7, 299–300
Charles I, King, 402
Charles IX, King of France, 75–76, 78–9, 84–5
Charles X, King of France, 238, 241
Charles Bal, barque, 316
Charringworth, 108–11, 115, 118
Chelmsford, General Lord, 295–296, 300–1
Cherniakov, Adam, 406
Chester, 481
Cheyenne, 304, 306
Chinook wind, 303, 305–6, 308, 309, 311
Ch'in Shih Huang Ti, 11, 13–14
Chipping Campden, 107–18
Chittagong, 491
Choguku Shimbun, 431
Christchurch, Hampshire, 244
Christian VII of Denmark, King, 160–8
Citizen Kane, film, 384
Claude, Duchess of Lorraine, 79–80, 83–4
Clive, Sir Robert, 158, 265
Cobb, Captain, 207–11, 213–14
Cobham, Lord, 89–90, 92
Coligny, Admiral, 77–9, 81, 83, 84
Concepcion, Chile, 342
Condé, Prince de, 235–44
Cook, Captain, 211, 214
Cooper, Sir Astley, 244
Copenhagen, 161, 162, 163
Coquimbo Observatory, 343
Corey, Giles, 141–8
Corey, Martha, 141–2, 144–8
Cortes, Hernando, 66–74

Croz, Michael, 285–90
Curnow, schoolteacher, 260–2

Dabulamanzi, Zulu general, 297
Dacca, University of, 495
Dalhousie, Lord, 266
Dalton, Sergeant, 296, 300
Damascus, 376
Damballah, snake-god, 171, 172
Darthout, 418
Daw, "Dicky", 236
Dawes, James, 240
Dawes, Sylvie, 235–44
Dead Man's Hill, 457
De Feuchères, Victor Adrien, 237–8
De' Medici, Catherine, 75, 77–80, 84
De Mirepoix, Pierre Roger, 53
De Nançay, Captain, 82–4
De Perella, Corba, 47–8, 53–5
De Perella, Raymond, 51–5
De Rully, Madame, 238
Desourteaux, Dr Paul, 417
De Valois, Marguerite, 75–85
Digne, France, 465
Dimitri, Grand Duke, 359
Dingaan, Zulu chief, 293–4
Dominici, Clovis, 468
Dominici, Gaston, 463, 469
Dominici, Gustave, 463
Dondy, Joelle, 484
Dooky, James, 386
Dorney Reach, 452, 461
Douglas, Catherine, 61–4
Douglas, Elizabeth, 64
Douglas, Lord Francis, 285–90
Downey, Lesley Ann, 474, 479
Downey, Mrs, 480
Drummond, Elizabeth, 464
Drummond, Sir John and Lady, 464
Dubois, Abbé, 196
Dum-Dum, Calcutta, 264
Durance, River, 463, 464
Durnford, Colonel, 295
Dusseldorf, 335–41

East India Company, 151, 152, 156, 158, 265–6

East Pakistan Rifles, 491
Edinburgh, 225–33
Eleazar ben Yair, 24–7
Elizabeth I, Queen, 86–7, 265
Elizabeth II, Queen, 168
Ellis, Lieut., 374
Enola Gay, Super-Fortress, 424
Estonia, 392–3
Evans, Edward, 471, 474–5
Eyre, Jane, 29

Falmouth, 214
Fearon, Colonel, 211
Feofan, the Archimandrite, 354
Finnis, Colonel, 272
Fleming, Malcolm, 58
Forcalquier, France, 462, 466
Fort William, Calcutta, 152
Fort William, Glencoe, 130, 132, 138
Frere, Sir Bartle, 294–5
Fu Su, 12, 18

Gallipoli, 376
Gandhi, Mrs, 497
Genghis Khan, 39–46
Gentz, John, State Trooper, 385
George III, King, 160
German High Command, 422
Gestapo, 406–7
Gillett, Bernard and Corinne, 486
Glencoe, 128–39
Glenrowan, Australia, 255–63
Goathland, 28–37
Godfrin, Roger, 417
Golovina, Maria, 350–1, 354
Good, Sarah, 141–3, 145
Gough, Lieut., 271
Gouverneur Loudon, S.S., 317–19
Graham, Sir Robert, 58, 61, 63–5
Greenwich Observatory, 320
Gregsten, Michael, 452–4, 461
Gretna, 367, 368
Guise, Duke of, 76–8, 83
Gurth of the Mill, 32
Guseva, Russian prostitute, 356
Gytha of the Mill, 31–7
Gytrash of Goathland, the, 28–9, 36–7

Hadow, Douglas, 286–90
Haiti, 169–77
Hall, Sir John, 64
Hall, Sir Thomas, 64
Halstead, Admiral Sir Lawrence, 221, 224
Hamilton, the Duke of, 139
Hamilton, James, 134, 136, 139
Hanratty, James, 461
Hare, William, 226–9, 231–3
Harland & Wolff, 473
Harrison, Edward, 108–9
Harrison, William, 108–18
Harrow, Middlesex, 454
Hattersley, near Manchester, 471
Havana, 224
Hawkins, Sir John, 178
Hayes, Middlesex, 454
Hayward fault, 325
Hearsey, Major-General, 268–9
Heathrow Airport, 455
Hebras, 418
Helena, Montana U.S.A., 312
Henry V, King, 59
Henry of Navarre, King, 75–7, 81–4
Herring, Senator Clyde L., 388
Hewitt, Major-General William, 270–1, 273
Heydrich, Reinhard, 422
Hicks, Baptist, Viscount Campden, 108
Higgins, Michael, 472
Higher Denham, Bucks, 433
Hill, John, 130, 132–4, 136
Himmler, *Reichsführer* S.S., 412
Hindley, Esther Myra, 472, 475, 480
Hindley, Maureen, 472
Hiroshima, Japan, 423
Hobart, Tasmania, 246
Hobbs, Mother, 146
Hokianga River, N.Z., 246
Hollin Brown Knoll, 479
Holwell, Governor of Bengal, 150–9
Honshu, Japan, 423
Hook, Private Henry, 298–300
Hudson, Rev. Charles, 286–90
Huguenots, the, 82–5

Hu Hai, 12–16
Huitzilopochtli, 70, 72

India, 491, 497
Indira, 197–205
Inquisition, the, 50–5
Irina Alexandrovna, Princess, 356
Isandhlwana, Zululand, 295, 297, 300–1

Jameela, 197–205
James, Henry, 327
James, William, 327
James I, King of England, 91, 99, 104
James I, King of Scotland, 56–65
James II, Stuart king, 130, 131
Jews of Europe, 404
Joan, Queen of Scotland, 57–65
Jones, Ann, 256–9
Jones, Helen, 256, 258–9
Jones, Private, 299–300
Josephus, 27
Judenrat (Jewish Council), 404, 406
Judith Basin, Montana U.S.A., 312
Juliane Marie, Queen, 161–7
Julian of Goathland, 29–35

Kadriorg Park, Tallinn, 393
Kali, goddess, 187–8, 194–5
Kalimbang, Sumatra, 316
Kelly, Dan, 256–60
Kelly, Ned, 255–63
Kent, East Indiaman, 206–15
Kerr, James, 183–6
Khlysty, religious sect, 352
Kiiu Asbla, Estonia, 393
Kilbride, John, 474
Klein, Christine, 334
Knox, Dr Robert, 225–8
Kotka Veski, Estonia, 393
Krakatoa, 314–21
Kronborg, Elsinore, 165, 168
Kuhn, Apollonia, 336
Kurten, Frau, 334–5, 337–41
Kurten, Peter, 333–41

La Grande Terre, farm, 462–3

Lal, Dhunraj, 189–93
Lal, Dhurum, 189–93
Lambot, aide-de-camp, 240
Lang Island, 315
Lansley, Mrs Anne, 474
Lasovert, Dr, 357
Lecomte, hairdresser, 240
Leech, Mr, 157
Lehigh Valley Railroad, 386
Lehzen, Pastor, 166–8
Le Printemps, 1921, fire, 486
"Les Storms", Pop group, 483, 486
Levenside, Loch, 129
Lidice, Czechoslovakia, 422
Limoges, France, 414
Lindemann, Captain, 317
Lindsay, Captain, 343–4, 348–9
Lisle, David, 181–6
Li Ssu, 11–18
Livingstone, Colonel, 133–4
Louis XVIII, King of France, 237, 238
Louis-Philippe, Duc d'Orléans, 239, 240–1, 244
Louise Augusta, Princess, 168
Lyons, John, Police Lieut., 385
Lurs, Provence, 462
Lushington, Mr, 151–2
Lynch, Benny, 434

MacDonald, Alasdair Og, the Younger, 131, 136–9
MacDonald clan, 128–39
MacDonald, Iain, 138
MacDonald, John, 134–9
Macfarlane, Lieut. B. D., R.N., 444–51
MacGregor, Lt.-Gen. Sir Duncan, K.C.B., 209, 212
MacIain, Alasdair, 129–36
Maclean, ship's mate, 218, 221–4
McNamara, Lieut., 376
McNinch, Frank, 387
Madras, 266
Magnificent Ambersons, The, 384
Magpie, S.S., 216, 218
Maingtun, 281
Mandalay, 276–83

Maning, Frederick Edward, 246–253
Maori, the, 246–53
Maquis, the, 416, 417, 418, 422, 464, 466
Marcellin, M. Raymond, Minister of the Interior, 488
Marina, Doña, 67–74
Marks, Dr, 278
Marrian, Professor Guy, 465
Martin, James, 433, 436, 446
Martinsyde aircraft, 374, 375
Marty, Bishop Bertrand, 51–5
Masada, 20–7
Matterhorn, the, 284–92
Maurevert, 77–8
Meakin, duty signal-man, 368–7, 374
Meerut, India, 269–73
Melbourne, Australia, 254, 256
Meldrum, John, 216–24
Merak, Java, 317–18
Mesopotamia, 374
Meteor, jet-fighter, 434
Mexico, 67
Millwards Ltd, 473
"Min, Mister", 274–83
Mindon, King, 276, 277, 278
Mitchell, Colonel, 269
Molotov cocktails, 410
Moltke, Marshal, 161
Mongols, the, 38–46
Monitoring Service Intelligence Bureau, 393
Montana, 302, 304, 312, 313
Montezuma, 67–73
Morgan, Henry, 119–27
Morgana, Salvatore and Christiana, 486
Mounsey, Det. Chief Inspector, 474, 478, 480
Muslims, 493

Nagasaki, Japan, 430
Nazi souvenirs, 473
Neva, River, 358
New Jersey Broadcasting Station, 383
Ngapuhi tribe, 247
Nicholas II, Tsar, 354

Nielson, Henry, 434, 435
Nizapur, India, 188–9, 191
Nurse, Francis, 144–5
Nurse, Rebecca, 144

Ohtu, River, 431
Oradour-sur-Glâne, 414, 415, 421
Oradour-sur-Vayres, 421
Ortega, Anselmo, 119–27
Osborne, Mrs, 142–3
Oudh, India, 266

Page, P. J., parachutist, 436
Pakistan, 493
Panama, 120–1, 123–4, 127
Panda, Zulu chief, 294
Pandatu, 197, 198, 200, 203, 205
Pande, Mangal, 269
Parris, Rev. Samuel, 140–1
Pearce, John, 109, 112
Penimbang, Java, 318
Perrin, M. Pierre, 488
Perry, Joan, 112–15, 118
Perry, John, 108–18
Perry, Richard, 113–15
Petrograd, 350, 352
Pierce, Frank, 255–6, 259, 261, 263
Pierce, Jane, 254–63
Pikuni, American Indian tribe, 305–6
Pinner, Middlesex, 159
Plaisterer, Edward, 110
Protopopov, Russian minister, 359
Pudupettah, Bengal, 196–205
Punjabis, 491
Purishkevitch, 357, 362
Putnam, Ann, 143, 146
Puy-Gaillard, French village, 416

Quetzalcoatl, 70
Quinn, outlaw, 255
Quintinshill signal-box, 368

R.A.F. Bomber Command, 394
Rantzau-Ascheberg, Count, 164–165, 167
Raritan Township, U.S.A., 386

Rasputin, Grigori Efimovitch, 350–66
Reade, Pauline, 473, 482
Reed, William, 109, 112
Red Cross Hospital, Hiroshima, 429
Resistance, French, 464
Reventlow, Councillor, 161
Reynolds, Surgeon Major, 295
Rio Chagres, 119–20
Robey, Yvon, survivor of massacre, 418
Rodriguez Island, 320
Rorke's Drift, 293–301
Roshun, 191–4
Rosser, Captain Charles, 273
Rota, Christian, 485, 488
Rouffauche, Madame, 419
Royal Flying Corps, 374
Royd, Alice, 88–9
Rukt Bij-dana, 187
Russell, Charles, 312
Rutherford, Captain, 374

Saarne, Martin, 395
Sade, Marquis de, 373
Saint-Domingue, Haiti, 169–77
St Laurent du Pont, 483, 487
Salem, Massachusetts, 140–9
San Andreas fault, 325–6
San Francisco, 322–32
San Lorenzo, 119–20
Santa Rosa, California, 327
Schubert, Rudi, 328–31
Sebeille, Police Commissaire Edmond, 464–5, 467
Sebessi Island, 318
Sebukoe Island, 318
Seiler, Alexander, 291
Shaka, Zulu king, 294
Shakespeare, William, 87, 91, 98
Sharp, Granville, 182, 184–6
Sharp, William, 182
Siberia, 355
Silva, Flavius, 21–4
Simla, India, 268
Simpson, Abigail, 229–33
Slough, Bucks, 455
Smith, David, 471–2, 475
Smith, Lieut., 216–21

Smith, Regimental Chaplain, 297, 299
Smyth, Colonel George, 270
Special Operations Executive, 394
Speigel family in Warsaw Ghetto, 405–10
Sperry, Ed, 434–5
Stanmore, Middlesex, 454
Stephenson, Captain, 297
Stewart, Maggie (Peggy), 472
Stewart, Sir Robert, 60
Stewart, Sir Walter, 58–60
Storie, Valerie, 452–61
Strong, Jonathan, 179–86
Stroop, S.S. General, 411–12
Struensee, Dr Johann Friedrich, 162–8
Stuart, Arabella, 91
Suchotin, Lieut., 357
Sullivan, Danny, 326, 328
Supalayat, Queen, 277–9
Suraj-ud-Daula, 151–2, 158
Sûreté, in Marseilles, 464
Surval, Baron de, 240
Suttee, 196

Talbot, Robert, Police Superintendent, 474, 477, 480
Tallinn, Estonia, 392
Taugwalder, Joseph, 286
Taugwalder, Peter, 285–92
Taugwalder, Peter, jnr., 286–92
Telok Betong, Sumatra, 317–19
Temuchin, see Genghis Khan
Tenochtitlan, see Mexico
Thibaw, King, 276–8
"Thirteeners", the, 406
Thugs, 188–95
Tibbets, Col. Paul W., B.29 pilot, 424
Tinsley, James, 368
Tituba, 141–2
Tjaringin, Java, 318
Tobolsk, Siberia, 351
Tombeau des Martyres, 415
Toompea, 399
Toulouse, 49–55
Trenton, New Jersey, 386
Troubadours, 50

Truman, President, 423
Tsar and Russian Royal Family, 351, 354, 365, 366
Tsarskoe Selo, 354
Turpin Plantation, St-Domingue, 173-6

Udfeldt, Leonora Christine, 163, 167
Ulfeldt, Corfits, 163, 167
Ulundi, Zululand, 294

Valparaiso, 243-9
Vaudville, M. Jean, Prefect, 485, 487
Venta Cruces, 119-122, 124
Vera Cruz, 211
Verlaten Island, 315
Victoria, Queen, 168
Villa Rode, restaurant, 355
Villefranche, 465
Voodoo, 170-7

Waffen S.S., 412, 414, 416
Wangaratta, Australia, 256
War of the Worlds, The, 383

Warsaw, 404
Welles, Orson, 383
Whymper, Edward, 285-92
William III, King, 130, 131, 133, 139
Williams, Abigail, 143
Williams, Private John, 298-300
Wilson, Brigadier Archdale, 271, 273
Wilson, sailor, 221-2
Witt, Otto, 295
Wyoming, 302, 304, 313
Wyvern, jet aircraft, 444

Yahya Khan, 491, 495
Yarra River, Australia, 254
Yesugei, 39
Yisugen, 40-6
Yisui, 40-6
Yoshio, boy of Hiroshima, 423-5
Yussupov, Prince, 351-2, 258-60

Zealots, the, 20-7
Zermatt, Switzerland, 285-6, 288, 291
Zombies, 170, 172, 174